DISASTER
MENTAL HEALTH SERVICES

DISASTER
MENTAL HEALTH SERVICES

A Primer for Practitioners

Diane Myers, R.N., M.S.N., C.T.S.
David F. Wee, M.S.S.W.

Routledge
Taylor & Francis Group
New York   London

Routledge
Taylor & Francis Group
270 Madison Avenue
New York, NY 10016

Routledge
Taylor & Francis Group
2 Park Square
Milton Park, Abingdon
Oxon OX14 4RN

© 2005 by Diane Myers and David F. Wee
Routledge is an imprint of Taylor & Francis Group, an Informa business

Printed in the United States of America on acid-free paper
15 14 13 12 11 10 9 8 7 6 5 4
International Standard Book Number-13: 978-1-58391-064-1 (Softcover)

Cover design by Elise Weinger
Middle Image Cover Photo: © Najiah Feanny/CORBIS SABA

Library of Congress Cataloging-in-Publication Data

Myers, Diane Garaventa.
   Disaster mental health services : a primer for practitioners / Diane Myers, David F. Wee.
      p. cm.— (Routledge psychosocial stress series)
   Includes bibliographical references and index.
   ISBN 1-58391-063-8 (hbk.—ISBN 1-58391-064-6 (pbk.)
   1. Disaster victims—Mental health. 2. Disaster victims—Mental health services. 3. Disasters—
  Psychological aspects. 4. Disaster relief. I. Wee, David F. II. Title. III. Series.
  RC451.4.D57M947   2004
  616.85'21—dc22

                              2004001188

Visit the Taylor & Francis Web site at
http://www.taylorandfrancis.com

and the Routledge Web site at
http://www.routledge.com

CONTENTS

III New Issues and Challenges

"Don't you remember me?" asked a young woman enrolled in my class at Purdue in 1982. After she helped me to remember, I realized that she was a freshman in high school when I came to her home in 1975 to interview her family who lived 40 minutes from Indianapolis, Indiana. I was co-investigator on a federal grant to collect data about their experiences the previous year when they survived a direct hit by a tornado that destroyed their home, barn, and other buildings. I recall that only her father—let us call him Mr. Pendleton—had no discernable postdisaster stress symptoms. She said that after everything was rebuilt and new sod in the front yard was in place, he broke out in hives and experienced 6 months of panic attacks. Mr. Pendleton apparently experienced a "delayed" reaction, although I would guess that with better methods we could have found that his reactions were not delayed but were reactions that were part of a continuum of normal reactions people often experience after an abnormal event such as a tornado. The challenge of disaster mental health services is to be able to know what someone like Mr. Pendleton needs and offer it, and, at the same time, sense what he does not need and avoid offering it.

This book is the latest in the Brunner–Routledge Psychosocial Stress Series. *Disaster Mental Health Services: A Primer for Practitioners*, as the title suggests, is designed for traumatologists who have the skills for helping traumatized people in crisis but not the special skills, knowledge, perspective, and procedures that are required for helping survivors much like Mr. Pendleton in the chaotic aftermath of disaster.

Could there ever be a greater need for a book that assists practitioners to prepare for helping their community recover from a major traumatic event? If only this book had been available in New York City in September, 2001. The difference that would have made is illustrated by one of the Green Cross Projects. The Green Cross Projects had been asked for assistance by a major international union with a headquarters blocks from ground zero and an 800-member staff, but with nearly 2,000 union members right at ground zero. It was clear from the very beginning which Green Cross volunteer practitioners had disaster work experience and which did not. The Green Cross Projects volunteers who practiced the concepts in this book and understood disaster mental health work were more able to provide the needed and appropriate assistance. In contrast to therapy work, disaster work departs from the practice of psychotherapy and all the niceties of "building a therapeutic alliance," creating a safe environment, and applying only empirically grounded treatment methods. Disaster work is crisis intervention in the field (or whereever you need to be to make contact with the traumatized), long hours, chaotic scenarios, intense emotions, situations that cannot immediately be "fixed," and sometimes working as a neighbor rather than a mental health practitioner. Like Mr. Pendleton and those in New York, the traumatized often have little experience with psychotherapists and even less patience with psychotherapy formalities. The practitioner who has the special skills, knowledge, perspective, and procedures, and provides services that are timely, relevant, and appropriate is more effective.

The authors of this book together have several decades of experience studying and helping the traumatized. They talk about their experiences throughout the book. For example, they both have extensive experience training practitioners to provide disaster mental health services, and managing crisis intervention programs and disaster mental health programs since the early 1980s. They have conducted a number of field-based evaluations of such programs since 1990 and have widely published their experiences and findings.

This book is written for managers who guide organizations in responding to disasters, to provide disaster mental health services as well as for practitioners who provide the services. The authors worked on this book for more than 5 years, including a complete rewriting after the September 2001 terrorist attacks. They organized this book as a practical guide to assist mental health clinicians, traumatologists, and paraprofessionals to draw effectively upon the authors' unique knowledge and skills to help the traumatized in a wide variety of situations: those that are unique, complex, chaotic, and highly political. They wrote the book also for managers and professionals in public and private agencies, nonprofit organizations, medical centers, and universities, and for private practitioners who are interested in providing services in disaster. Such people may be pressed into action when disasters affect their community. This book will provide a vital source of direction and orientation because clinical skills and expertise are essential but not sufficient for functioning effectively in disasters.

Wisely, the authors divide their seven chapters among three parts, which make it highly readable and quickly accessible to the reader. Part I, "Disaster Concepts and Roles," includes chapter 1: "Disasters and Their Impact" and chapter 2: "Special Populations in Disaster." After part I covers the central conceptual issues and knowledge foundation of disaster mental health, part II, "Services, Programs, and Workers," reviews basic disaster mental health services for citizens and stress management for disaster mental health workers in chapter 3: "CODE-C: A Model for Disaster Mental Health Service Delivery"; chapter 4: "Stress Management and Prevention of Compassion Fatigue for Psychotraumatologists"; chapter 5: "Critical Incident Stress

Management in Large-Scale Disasters"; and chapter 6: "Support Groups in Disaster Mental Health Programs." Last, part III covers some of the newest issues and challenges facing disaster mental health workers and traumatologists in chapter 7: "Weapons of Mass Destruction and Terrorism: Mental Health Issues and Interventions." Together they provide a comprehensive yet readable and concrete orientation to helping the traumatized during and following a wide variety of traumatic events.

Unfortunately, this book was not available either in New York in 2001 or in Oklahoma City in 1995. It would have served as a critical orientation to the well-meaning and clinically experienced mental health practitioners who assisted without any prior training or expertise in disaster response. It should now be on the bookshelf or (better yet) in the "get go" bag (items packed and ready for deployment to a disaster) of everyone who may work following a disaster in the future.

Charles R. Figley, Ph.D.
Series Editor

INTRODUCTION

MENTAL HEALTH PROFESSIONALS FREQUENTLY FACE NATURAL AND HUMAN-caused disasters in their communities and may be called upon to assist the community and its residents following disasters. Recent disasters provide vivid examples of the impact disasters can have on entire communities. The Los Angeles civil disturbance of April 1992 was called the "the worst urban riot in contemporary U.S. history." It followed the acquittal of four Los Angeles Police Department officers tried for using unreasonable force to subdue a citizen, Rodney King. The civil disturbance provided challenging opportunities and dilemmas for mental health professionals providing disaster mental health services in the aftermath of violence. The Loma Prieta earthquake on October 17, 1989, and the Northridge earthquake on January 17, 1994, both caused frightening destruction of physical structures and affected many lives. Recent air disasters have brought attention to the psychological needs of survivors' loved ones as well as the needs of personnel involved in aviation disaster operations, and resulted in legislation requiring more attention, focus, and services for those impacted. The Oklahoma City bombing on April 19, 1995, killed 168 and injured over 700 people in the Alfred P. Murrah Federal Building and the downtown area of Oklahoma City. Prior to September 11, 2001, the bombing was considered the worst terrorist act in the United States. The terrorist attacks of September 11 were a disaster of unprecedented magnitude and horror for the United States, and placed unique challenges and demands upon disaster responders and mental health professionals.

Although each of these disasters had unique characteristics and dynamics, they all had in common the psychological trauma of the victims and disaster responders. This book is written to assist mental health clinicians, traumatologists, and paraprofessionals in utilizing their knowledge and skills effectively in the unique, complex, chaotic, and highly political field of disaster. It is intended for professionals in public and private agencies, nonprofit organizations, medical centers, universities, or private practice that are interested in providing services in major crises. Clinical skill and expertise are essential but not sufficient for functioning effectively under these circumstances, especially in the initial waves of intervention. This book will help clinicians to "make the bridge" between their existing knowledge and skills and the unique environment that is our focus. This book combines information from a vast reservoir of prior research and literature with the authors' practical experience in providing disaster mental health services in a wide variety of situations.

The manuscript for *Disaster Mental Health Services* was almost finished when the events of September 11, 2001, shocked the world. In light of the nature and scope of the events and the challenges they presented to disaster mental health professionals, the manuscript was revisited and revised. We have included as much information and "lessons learned" from the terrorist events and their aftermath as possible. The new material includes the concluding chapter of the book, "Weapons of Mass Destruction and Terrorism: Mental Health Issues and Implications."

Disaster Mental Health Services is based on the knowledge, experience, successes, and challenges of the authors working in collaboration with hundreds of emergency service workers, disaster workers, and disaster mental health workers during local, state, national, and international disasters. Because disaster mental health work is a team-based, collaborative, and integrated approach to service delivery, there is always a rich exchange of ideas, information, and knowledge. We have made every effort to credit the original work of others. Still, in all likelihood, professionals in the worldwide disaster mental health network will see ideas and approaches they have contributed to the field without ever having been recognized. To all of our colleagues who have collaborated with us in this most heart-wrenching and rewarding of work, and who have contributed to the development of contemporary disaster mental health concepts and practices, we give our most sincere thanks and acknowledgment. To our families, who sent us on our travels into danger with their blessings and prayers, who tolerated our absences, and who shared us with our computers and our editor as we wrote this book, we give our deepest thanks, appreciation, and love.

Disaster Mental Health Services is divided into three parts to assist the practitioner gain an organized and efficient understanding of disaster mental health services. Part I, "Disaster Concepts and Roles," includes chapter 1: "Disasters and Their Impact" and chapter 2: "Special Populations in Disaster." While part I covers the central conceptual issues and knowledge foundation of disaster mental health, part II, "Services, Programs, and Workers," covers basic disaster mental health services for citizens and stress management for disaster mental health workers. Chapters include chapter 3: "CODE-C: A Model for Disaster Mental Health Service Delivery"; chapter 4: "Stress Management and Prevention of Compassion Fatigue for Psychotraumatologists"; chapter 5: "Critical Incident Stress Management in Large-Scale Disasters"; and chapter 6: "Support Groups in Disaster Mental Health Programs." Last of all, part III covers some of the newest issues and challenges facing disaster mental health workers and traumatologists in chapter 7: "Weapons of Mass Destruction and Terrorism: Mental Health Issues and Interventions."

Chapter 1, "Disasters and Their Impact," provides an overview of disasters and their various impacting factors. Definitions and types of disasters, human stress response, and the concept of "normal people having normal reactions to abnormal events" are explored. Risk factors as well as the types of trauma caused by disaster are important for disaster mental heath workers to understand in order to plan services most effectively. Kai Erikson's conceptualization of individual trauma and collective, or community, trauma is presented as a basis for understanding types of appropriate intervention. The immediate, intermediate, and long-term phases of disasters are discussed. The various phases have common psychological reactions and social behaviors, and understanding the phases of disaster will provide the foundation for the phase-appropriate roles of mental health professionals.

Chapter 2, "Special Populations in Disaster," provides a conceptual understanding of the impact of disasters in relation to age, gender, culture, and socioeconomic factors. Disaster affects individuals in unique ways related to patterns of beliefs, behaviors, and resources. The common reactions of various populations such as children and adolescents, adults, and older adults are presented. In addition, cultural groups, socioeconomic factors that influence how disaster affects individuals and families, and issues concerning assisting people with serious and persistent mental illness are discussed. Mental health workers must understand the important issues these groups face in order to appropriately provide effective disaster mental health services. Guidelines are also provided for referral of disaster survivors for psychological or medical evaluation and treatment.

Chapter 3, "CODE-C: A Model for Disaster Mental Health Service Delivery," discusses how disaster mental health service delivery necessarily differs from traditional mental health service delivery in nondisaster times. A disaster mental health model of action must include goals and objectives, key concepts that guide the disaster mental health program, and appropriate services, phasing and duration of services, and linkage with other providers of service. The CODE-C model for disaster mental health programs was developed by the authors and colleagues during Hurricane Andrew in November 1992. The CODE-C model for disaster mental health programs has been used extensively by the authors to develop and implement disaster mental health programs and services since that time, during consultations following both natural and human-caused disasters, including terrorism, and in training of disaster responders and emergency management professionals. The CODE-C model for disaster mental health programs is a model of five service components. The acronym CODE-C identifies the major core components. First, there is an assessment of community mental health needs following disaster, taking into consideration the factors discussed in chapters 1 and 2. Next come the five core components, *consultation, outreach, debriefing and defusing, education*, and *crisis counseling*. Needs assessment is the systematic gathering of information about the physical and emotional impact of the event and about the mental health needs of the population, and the identification of possible service delivery strategies. Consultation is the provision of mental health services, collaboration, advice, education, training, and assessment services to decision makers, managers, supervisors, and line workers. Consultation is directed at supporting decision makers in solving problems involving policy, organization functioning, and service provision. Outreach is important in order to reach as many people as possible. Outreach is provided to victims, survivors, disaster workers, and members of the community in their natural environments. Debriefings and defusings are psychoeducational groups that address stress reactions by providing participants, whether citizens or disaster workers, with opportunities to receive information on normal stress reactions and to obtain information on coping strategies and recovery resources. Education services provide information and training on topics specific to disaster psychology and mental health in order to support individual, family, and community recovery. Educational services may include workshops, presentations, conferences, and intensive use of the media. Crisis counseling involves brief interviews with people impacted by disasters in order to provide psychological crisis intervention. The objective of crisis counseling is to assess needs, identify disaster-related distress, and provide support. Interventions include crisis intervention, problem solving, encouragement of expression, and development of individual, family, and community support. For individuals needing more intensive psychological evaluation or treatment, referral to a higher level of care is always indicated.

Chapter 4, "Stress Management and Prevention of Compassion Fatigue for Psychotraumatologists," is an important issue in disaster mental health. Studies of disaster mental health workers have identified that these professionals can have stress reactions to the disaster itself as well as to doing disaster mental health work, resulting in patterns of mental and physical distress. The traumatologist's ability to be present and to empathize with the experience of victims of disasters and violence in the community can help them to be truly effective in their work with victims. While such first-hand experience and empathy can aid the disaster mental health worker in helping others heal, the mental health worker can also be affected by the pain and suffering disaster survivors share.

The Alfred P. Murrah Federal Building bombing is presented as a case example to illustrate how disaster mental health workers are affected as a result of their work in providing mental health services to victims of the bombing. After the bombing, a Presidential Disaster Declaration authorized funding by the Federal Emergency Management Agency through the Center for Mental Health Services to the Oklahoma Department of Mental Health and Substance Abuse Services. The funding supported Project Heartland, a crisis counseling program providing mental health services to victims and responders affected by the bombing. The crisis counselors were surveyed 9 months after the bombing about their experiences with the disaster, about their work with victims of the bombing, and their psychological reactions to providing disaster mental health services. The results indicate the crisis counselors were strongly impacted psychologically by their work, with many of the crisis counselors exhibiting some degree of severity for posttraumatic stress disorder and substantial risk for compassion fatigue and burnout.

Chapter 4 presents stress management strategies to support disaster mental health workers during their disaster work. Strategies include predisaster briefings, supervision, consultations, continuing education, and psychotherapy. Prevention of compassion fatigue also includes making provision for organizational support and workplace strategies, defusing, and debriefing. Working as a team, professional development strategies and personal strategies are equally important. The stress that can accompany the closure of disaster mental health programs includes planning for the end of services, program closure activities, critique of services, debriefing of staff, recognition of staff, and follow-up of staff some months later. Preserving the physical, mental, social, and spiritual health of traumatologists during disaster response and recovery is important both to the worker and the quality of services.

Chapter 5, "Critical Incident Stress Management in Large-Scale Disasters," provides a detailed description of how critical incident stress management (CISM) has been successfully applied to large-scale disasters to mitigate the impact of disaster stress and accelerate the recovery of persons impacted by disaster. The group crisis intervention known as critical incident stress debriefing (CISD) is reviewed along with other CISM interventions, and a variety of debriefing models useful in disaster. Strategies to use CISM services in large-scale disasters, along with some of the challenges and limitations, are covered.

The authors have extensive experience managing crisis intervention programs and disaster mental health programs that utilized critical incident stress management since the early 1980s. They have conducted a number of field-based evaluations of CISD since 1990. Both are trained trainers since 1995 in the Basic Group Crisis Intervention Course and since 1999 in the Advanced Group Crisis Intervention Course, both courses based on curriculum approved by the International Critical Incident Stress Foundation.

The ongoing debate concerning the effectiveness of CISD and CISM within the field of crisis intervention is important to expanding the body of knowledge about the mental health needs of persons exposed to traumatic events and what approaches are effective in providing psychological first aid. The debate and research will continue. The authors support the use of critical incident stress management as a multicomponent, comprehensive system of crisis intervention following traumatic events and disasters. The chapter presents a thorough review of the research literature and examines the empirical evidence that challenges the efficacy of CISD and CISM and the empirical evidence that supports the efficacy of CISD and CISM.

Chapter 6, "Support Groups in Disaster Mental Health Programs," suggests that support groups are a mainstay in disaster mental health programs. Support groups are effective because they provide normalization, universalization, education, and sharing of resources, and they help members to feel understood and to optimize and reinforce accomplishments, coping, and recovery. Practitioners are guided through support group typologies, development of support groups, designing groups, group format, promotion of groups, and facilitation of support groups. Support groups are described for providing services during the immediate response period, as well as the transition to group formats that are consistent with the psychological and social needs that emerge during long-term recovery. Support group tasks, interventions, and transformations found in participants are key issues. Termination strategies that must be developed for ending support groups are presented.

Chapter 7, "Weapons of Mass Destruction and Terrorism: Mental Health Issues and Interventions," includes much information and "lessons learned" from the Oklahoma City bombing of 1995 and the September 11, 2001, terrorist events and their aftermath. Terrorism intends as its primary goal to instill terror and to accomplish a political or social goal through a violent act by the intentional creation of fear and disequilibrium, and perceived personal, community, or governmental vulnerability. Types of terrorism, including chemical, biological, radiological, nuclear, explosive or incendiary devices, and cyberterrorism, are described, along with their psychological effects. While psychological trauma is a frequent side effect of other types of disaster, with terrorism, the infliction of psychological pain is the very purpose of the behavior (Flynn, 1998). Terrorism incidents require that disaster mental health professionals think differently than they do with other disasters about how, when, and where psychological sequelae will present themselves. It is essential that mental health services be seamlessly integrated into other disaster health preparedness, response, and recovery efforts (Flynn, 1998). The "CODE-C" model of mental health response to disaster, discussed at length in chapter 3, can be used as a model for the range of services that will be needed following terrorist incidents in the future. The behavioral health and psychological consequences of a terrorist event may well be the most widespread, long-lasting, and expensive consequences (Warwick, 2001). Comprehensive planning for terrorist events must include the psychological impacts of these events on the survivors and on the responders, or planning efforts will not be complete and will not recognize the most fundamental of damages inflicted by terrorism. The information in this book will hopefully be used by practitioners to plan, respond to, and evaluate recovery activities following terrorist events that have significant impacts on the well-being of entire communities.

I
DISASTER CONCEPTS
AND ROLES

DISASTERS AND THEIR IMPACT

DEFINITION OF DISASTER

DEFINITIONS OF DISASTER ABOUND: DIFFERENT PEOPLE OF PARTICULAR VIEWPOINTS define disasters in various ways. The Federal Emergency Management Agency (FEMA) offers 48 definitions of disaster in its course "Hazards, Disasters, and the U.S. Emergency Management System" (FEMA, 2001). There is no consensus either in the United States or abroad on the definition of disaster. Views range from a more traditional approach that focuses on the physical hazard as the disaster event to a more human-oriented approach wherein ". . . behavioral aspects of disasters can only be understood by looking at them subjectively, particularly from the viewpoint of victims" (Quarantelli, 1998).

Quarantelli (1986) attempted to pull together what social and behavioral scientists assume when they use the term *disaster* and states that disasters have been equated with seven various concepts:

1. Physical agents: earthquake, floods, fires, and explosions.
2. Physical impact: a noticeable physical impact on some part of the environment, such as land and water movement in an earthquake.
3. Assessment of physical impacts: There must be a benchmark or threshold of damages beyond which the event can be called a disaster.
4. Social disruption: Magnitude of the impact is high enough to result in disruption of social life.
5. Social constructions of reality: perceptions of the seriousness and meaning of the impact.
6. Political definitions: official disaster declarations that affect subsequent actions and assistance.

7. Imbalance between demand and capability in a crisis: Disaster exists when the demands for action exceed the capabilities for response in a crisis.

In the field of emergency management, a distinction is drawn between emergencies and disasters. Emergencies are "routine" adverse events that do not have the vast impact of disaster. Likewise, emergencies do not usually require extraordinary use of resources or procedures to bring conditions back to normal. Local, routine community resources and procedures are used to manage the emergency (FEMA, 2001), although some emergency organizations may need to expand their activities (Quarantelli, 1987). For example, an automobile accident, a house fire, a broken water main, or a heart attack, while in all likelihood constituting a disaster for individual victims, would be considered an emergency within the scope of standard operating procedures in most local fire, police, and emergency medical service jurisdictions (Drabek & Hoetmer, 1991).

Disasters are traumatic events. Such events are dangerous, overwhelming, and usually sudden (Figley, 1985). The American Psychiatric Association (1994) defines a traumatic event as a psychologically distressing event, outside the range of usual human experience that would be markedly distressing to almost anyone. A traumatic event, under this definition, contains two elements: It involves actual or threatened death or serious physical injury to the individual or to others, and it involves intense fear, horror, and helplessness.

While a traumatic event may impact a single individual, a disaster is a traumatic event that affects an entire community or a large part of a community. Unlike traumatic events affecting individuals or small groups, disasters can overwhelm the available community resources and further threaten individuals' and the community's ability to cope (Ursano, McCaughey, & Fullerton, 1994). Sociologist Charles Fritz (1961) formulated the classic definition of disaster in this way:

> An event, concentrated in time and space, in which a society, or a relatively self-sufficient subdivision of a society, undergoes severe danger and incurs such losses to its members and physical appurtenances that the social structure is disrupted and the fulfillment of all or some of the essential functions of the society is prevented.

In the United States, the Robert T. Stafford Disaster Relief and Emergency Assistance Act provides authority for the federal government to respond to disasters and emergencies in order to provide assistance to save lives and protect public health, safety, and property. The Stafford Act defines a major disaster as, "… any natural catastrophe (including any hurricane, tornado, storm, high water, winddriven water, tidal wave, tsunami, earthquake, volcanic eruption, landslide, mudslide, snowstorm, or drought), or, regardless of cause, any fire, flood, or explosion, in any part of the United States, which in the determination of the President causes damage of sufficient severity and magnitude to warrant major disaster assistance under this chapter to supplement the efforts and available resources of States, local governments, and disaster relief organizations in alleviating the damage, loss, hardship, or suffering caused thereby."

PLANNING ASSUMPTIONS

The Federal Response Plan, which spells out the federal role in disaster, operates on the following assumptions:

1. A major disaster or emergency will cause numerous fatalities and injuries, property loss, and disruption of normal life-support systems, and will have an impact on the regional economic, physical, and social infrastructures.
2. The extent of casualties and damage will reflect factors such as the time of occurrence, severity of impact, weather conditions, population density, building construction, and the possible triggering of secondary events such as fires and floods.
3. The large number of casualties, heavy damage to buildings and basic infrastructure, and disruption of essential public services will overwhelm the capabilities of the state and its local governments to meet the needs of the situation, and the President will declare a major disaster or emergency.
4. Federal agencies will need to respond on short notice to provide timely and effective assistance.
5. The degree of federal involvement will be related to the severity and magnitude of the event as well as the state and local need for external support. The most devastating disasters may require the full range of federal response and recovery assistance. Less damaging disasters may require only partial federal response and recovery assistance. Some disasters may require only federal recovery assistance (FEMA, 2000a).

This section has outlined the vast differences in the definitions of the concept of disaster. The term disaster has been used in the literature to describe an extensive array of dissimilar events, for example, earthquakes, fires, floods, air raids, atomic attacks, tornadoes, train and plane crashes, the sinking of ships, explosions, accidents at nuclear power plants, exposure to toxic waste, interment at concentration camps (Warheit, 1988), terrorism, and weapons of mass destruction (WMD). These phenomena differ from one another in many important ways: source, onset, warning time, duration, magnitude, frequency of occurrence, social context (Warheit, 1988), political context, consequences, and meaning attributed to the event. It is not surprising, therefore, that there is no consistency in the literature regarding the specific mental health impacts of disasters.

FREQUENCY OF DISASTERS

On average, a disaster occurs somewhere in the world each day (Norris et al., 2002). In the 1990s, FEMA declared 460 major disasters due to severe weather events and natural phenomenon, double the 237 disasters declared in the 1980s and more than any other decade on record. In the United States, about $1 billion is spent every week on disasters. Worldwide, about $5 billion is spent each week (Goss, 2000b).

According to the International Strategy for Disaster Reduction, a group created by the United Nations to carry on the work of the International Decade for Natural Disaster Reduction, which ended in 1999, the 53 greatest natural disasters that occurred between 1990 and 1999 alone resulted in $479.3 billion in economic losses (Goss, 2000b). The 10 costliest disasters in the United States all occurred in the 1990s. Of the 24 largest weather-related catastrophes, 21 struck in the 1990s.

Disasters exact a heavy human toll. On average, about 510 people lose their lives in disasters in the United States each year. In the year 2001, over 3,000 people lost their lives in the terrorist attacks of 9/11. Globally, 128,000 lives are lost annually in disasters.

Since the late 1980s, we have experienced unprecedented devastation from major disasters of all types. There are no clear answers to why disasters are worse now and seem to be more frequent. There are, however, several factors that come into play: Current climate cycles of increased weather extremes are resulting in more natural disasters. The increase in population and urbanization with more people living in high-risk areas is another factor. Economic growth and technological advances have created new disaster challenges (Goss, 2000a). Likewise, increasing numbers and types of terrorist threats and the September 11, 2001, terrorist attacks on the United States have prompted efforts to deter and respond to terrorism by strengthening capabilities to prevent, detect, defeat, and manage the consequences of terrorist use of weapons of mass destruction (FEMA, 2000b).

TYPES OF DISASTERS

As we have seen in the section on definition of disaster, even the most basic term disaster has not been adequately defined (Smith, North, & Price, 1988). While attempts have repeatedly been made to categorize disaster by types and characteristics, the field still lacks a single agreed-upon comprehensive typology of disaster characteristics and consequences (Drabek, 1986). As a result, when making conclusions about the social and psychological impacts of a disaster, one needs to look at both the generic and situationally specific features of the event (Bolin, 1988). Nonetheless, in this section we will address the most salient characteristics of three types of disaster: natural disaster, technological disaster, and terrorism.

A distinction frequently drawn is between "natural" disasters and "technological" disasters. Natural disasters are often euphemistically described as "acts of God," a term that automatically eliminates human cause and responsibility from consideration. Natural disasters are frequently described as uncontrollable, although many are predictable and avoidable (Bolin, 1988). Natural disasters include such events as fires, floods, mudslides, earthquakes, tsunamis (seismic sea waves), hurricanes, tornadoes, droughts, or blizzards.

Technological disasters include events such as large transportation accidents, structural collapse, hazardous materials events, explosions, toxic pollution, and nuclear accidents. There is a lack of consensus in the literature about what constitutes a technological disaster. Such diverse events as nuclear accidents, toxic chemical spills, shipwrecks, plane crashes, explosions, structural failures, fires, dam breaks, kidnapping, and war-related incidents have been included in the general category of technological disasters. The heterogeneity of events within this category makes it difficult to draw general conclusions about the psychological effects of technological disasters (Smith et al., 1988). In addition, It does not require intense scrutiny to see that disasters are not clearly divided between natural and technological. Naturally occurring events can provoke additional environmental and structural impacts that are obviously not "acts of God," such as the 1906 earthquake igniting massive urban fires while destroying the infrastructure necessary to fight those fires (Haas, Kates, & Bowden, 1977). Likewise, the collapse of the I-880 Cypress Structure freeway in Oakland, California, during the 1989 Loma Prieta earthquake was a result of a naturally occurring event impacting a human-built structure not designed to withstand that event. If people did not build homes in flood plains, floods would be floods and not disasters (Bolin, 1988). Reisner (1986) points out that the "Dust Bowl" of the 1930s, one of the most significant natural disasters in U.S. history, would not have been a disaster if farmers had not destroyed groundcover trying to farm the semi-arid land, thus producing massive erosion of topsoil. There is often not a clear division between natural disasters and those in which human practices, intentionally or from ignorance or neglect, play a role.

It is also important to point out that in Western countries an "act of God" usually means the power of the elements. In other parts of the world, divine intervention may be seen as the cause of both natural and technological disasters. Islamic fatalism, for example, explained the stampede and crushing deaths of more than 1,400 people in a tunnel during the Haj (pilgrimage) in Mecca in 1990, as God's will (Weisaeth, 1994).

Despite the difficulties of categorizing disasters as natural or technological, God-made or man-made, and despite the wide variety of subtypes within each category, some attempts have been made to differentiate psychological consequences based on perceived differences between natural or technological disasters.

Technological disasters may involve human negligence, fallibility, or intentionality. Baum, Fleming, and Davidson (1983a) define technological catastrophes as "events that are human-made in that they are accidents, failures, or mishaps involving the technology and manipulation of the natural environment that we have created to enhance our standard of living." In keeping with this definition, intentional (purposeful) disasters such as acts of terrorism and war-related events are considered in a separate category.

Technological disasters invariably cause resentment and blame among victims (Baum et al., 1983a; Bolin, 1988; Sorensen, Soderstrom, Coperhaver, Carnes, & Bolin, 1987). Smith et al. (1988) found in a study of a flood with subsequent dioxin contamination that 92% of victims of contamination blamed others, including businesses for improper disposal of waste products and the government for inadequate regulation of disposal activities and poor flood control. The dynamics of blame frequently involve investigation of culpability and subsequent litigation, prolonging the recovery process and keeping emotional wounds raw until matters are settled legally.

An obvious characteristic of natural disasters is the unambiguous physical impact, resulting in property damage, injury, and death of victims. They often have a clearly identifiable "low point" at which, from the victim's point of view, the "worst is over" and restoration and recovery can proceed (Bolin, 1988; Baum et al., 1983a). Baum and his colleagues suggested four characteristics that separate technological disasters from natural disasters: duration of impact, unexpectedness, perceptions of control, and absence of an identifiable low point (Baum et al., 1983a; Baum, Fleming, & Singer,

1983b; Baum & Davidson, 1986). For example, technological disasters such as toxic or nuclear contamination and environmental pollution may have no visible, tangible physical impacts and no identifiable low point after which things can begin to get better (Levine, 1982; Sorenson et al., 1987). The aftermath is often fraught with fear regarding health consequences that may occur at a nonspecific point in time. There may be dissatisfaction with medical advice and confusion about the real health effects (Weisaeth, 1994). However, similar effects can result from a natural disaster such as drought, long-term malnutrition, or epidemic. Likewise, unexpectedness and loss of control would occur in both an earthquake and a plane crash. Baum and colleagues point out, however, that people usually view technology as something which *should* be under control, whereas in natural disasters, people perceive a lack of control over something that *never was* under control (1983b). After technological disasters, confidence in future controllability of technology is likely to be eroded (Baum et al., 1983a).

Some studies and authors claim that the more human causation behind a disaster, the more pathogenic it seems to be in terms of psychiatric morbidity (Baum, 1986). Smith et al. (1988) report that rates of psychiatric disturbance following technological disaster vary as greatly as the number of disasters studied. For example, studies of the 1972 Buffalo Creek, West Virginia, dam collapse and flood suggest that virtually everyone was affected (Lifton & Olson, 1976), with 90% of the survivors symptomatic after 2 years and over one third still suffering from disabling psychiatric symptoms 5 years later (Gleser, Green, & Winget, 1981). Most of the symptoms fell into the categories of generalized anxiety disorder (GAD) and major depression disorder (MDD). Many years later, these data were reanalyzed for probable posttraumatic stress disorder (PTSD) which had not been a diagnosis at the time of the original study (Green et al., 1990, 1991). They found a rate of PTSD at 2 years was 44% among adults and 32% among children. Rates of PTSD remained high 14 years after this disaster (Norris et al., 2002).

In contrast, Bromet and Dunn (1981) and Bromet, Parkinson, Schulberg, and Gondek (1982) studied a high-risk population of mothers with young children living near Three Mile Island and found that only 14% received a psychiatric diagnosis during the year after the accident. Green (1985) cautions, however, that these differences between studies in findings of disaster impact may be attributable to how, when, and on whom the data were collected.

Smith et al. (1988) provide a thorough discussion of technological disasters and various factors that may influence their effects on human beings. In attempting to illuminate differences between natural and technological

disasters, they cite Solomon (1989) in summarizing that "previously proposed differences in mental health effects of the two different kinds of
disaster might be explained on the basis of the bias in various contributors
to the overall severity of the disaster agent rather than on the intrinsic basis
of a possibly arbitrary division between technological vs. natural disasters
themselves." They conclude that, while it is clear that psychological effects are
to be expected among significant numbers of affected populations, "it is not
clear whether the consequences of technological accidents differ from those
associated with natural hazards."

Norris et al. (2002) found that samples of disaster victims who experienced
technological disasters were not significantly more distressed, on average, than
samples who experienced natural disasters, although the trend was in that
direction. They found that, in the United States and other developed countries, the mean aggregated severity rating for 35 natural disasters was 2.1 (on
a scale of 1 to 4, 4 being most severe). Mean aggregated severity rating for
39 technological disasters was 2.5. This difference was statistically significant,
$t(72) = 2.26$, $p.05$, and the effect size (0.5) was moderate.

Studies of the Exxon Valdez oil spill disaster in Alaska in 1989 showed
that even when technological disasters do not injure or kill human beings,
they may have quite serious mental health consequences (Norris et al.,
2002). Palinkas, Russel, Downs, and Petterson (1992) found that 43% of
people highly exposed to the environmental damage had one or more
psychological disorders, compared to 23% of those not exposed. Severity of
exposure also predicted declines in social relations and increased conflicts with
family members. Arata, Picou, Johnson, and McNally (2000), in a study that
began 6 years after the spill, found that psychological consequences of the
disaster were long lasting.

A third type of disaster must be examined in addition to natural and
technological events. This type encompasses human-caused disasters that are
acts of *commission* as opposed to *omission*. These intentional acts include
violence, war, and terrorism. Numerous researchers and authors have documented the psychosocial effects of violence (Davis & Friedman, 1985;
Ochberg, 1988; Spungen, 1998; Young, 1989) and war (Gelsomino &
Mackey, 1988; Hogencamp & Figley, 1983; Laufer, 1988; Rosenheck &
Fontana, 1994; Stretch, 1986; Ursano & McCarroll, 1994). Norris et al.
(2002), in a review of 160 samples of disaster victims (60,000 individual
victims) from 1981 to 2001, found that people were more likely to be
impaired if they experienced mass violence (e.g., terrorism, shooting sprees)
rather than natural or technological disasters. Of the samples of victims who
experienced mass violence, 67% were severely or very severely psychologically impaired, compared to 39% of the samples assessed after technological

disasters and 34% of samples assessed after natural disasters. None of the incidents of violence in the Norris study was found to have minimal or fleeting effects among survivors. In the aftermath of the September 11, 2001, terrorist attacks on the United States, a thorough discussion of terrorism, its psychological impacts, and mental health implications is both timely and important. Chapter 7 of this book will discuss these topics in detail.

FACTORS AFFECTING THE MENTAL HEALTH IMPACTS OF DISASTER

Identifying the mental health effects of disasters is a complicated task. Each disaster constitutes a complex set of existential features that those affected experience in highly variable ways. Thus, not only the stressors of the disaster itself but also the appraisal of the disaster (each individual's event-related perceptions) have a role in the outcome (Baum & Davidson, 1986; Weaver, 1995). Each disaster also initiates a complex set of social processes and intensifies preexisting social and economic situations in impacted communities (Bolin, 1988). Various researchers and practitioners have set forth paradigms attempting to illustrate the myriad stressors and impacts associated with disaster events. A summary of some of these paradigms that make a disaster stressful is presented here.

Barton (1969) describes four characteristics of disaster that are important: scope of impact, speed of onset, duration of impact, and social preparedness. In 1980, Berren and associates proposed a five-factor typology which examines disasters in terms of type of disaster agent, duration of disaster, degree of personal impact, potential for recurrence, and control over future impact (in Smith et al., 1988).

Quarantelli (1986) suggested eight aspects that were important in understanding the stress of disaster: preparation of the involved population, social centrality of the affected population, length of involvement of the affected population in the crisis, rapidity of involvement by the population in crisis, predictability of involvement in a crisis, unfamiliarity of the crisis, depth of involvement of the population in the disaster, and recurrency of involvement.

Bolin (1986) lists several *impact characteristics* that will affect the level of trauma potential: *terror and horror* involved in experiencing or witnessing the event; *duration of impact; unexpectedness* of the event (i.e., those events without warning having the maximum psychological impact); *threat,* as determined by preimpact interpretation of risk; *impact ratio,* or proportion of the community directly affected or suffering loss; *sociocultural changes* such as activities of daily living, control over events, social support networks in the postdisaster environment; *symbolism* of events (the meaning of the event to an individual, particularly the differentiation between "acts of God" and human-caused technological or terrorism events); and *interactive and cumulative effects* of these and other pre- and postdisaster issues upon victims and helpers, who vary greatly in personality types, predisaster emotional state, and ability to manage stress (Bolin, 1986; Weaver, 1995).

In their review of research covering 20 years of disasters, Norris et al. (2002) found that specific stressors have been found to affect mental health. Those include bereavement, injury to self or family member, life threat, fear, panic during the disaster, peritraumatic responses, horror, separation from family, property damage or financial loss, and relocation. Most studies found injury and threat to life to have stronger or longer lasting consequences for mental health.

Norris et al. (2002) found that location of the disaster also influenced the severity of its effects. Severe or very severe psychological impairment was observed in 25% of the U.S. samples, 48% of the samples from other developed countries, and 78% of the samples from developing countries. High risk in developing countries is not an unexpected finding, in part because of the greater severity of many of their events and in part because they must recover in a context of fewer resources (Norris et al., 2002). However, the finding that samples from developed countries other than the United States experienced more adverse consequences compared to U.S. samples was not expected. The researchers point out, however, that the events experienced by the most impaired samples in developed countries outside the United States were severely traumatic, including the bomb-induced Pan American air crash in Lockerbie, Scotland (Brooks & McKinlay, 1992; Livingston, Livingston, & Fell, 1994) and the sinking of the Jupiter cruise ship filled with adolescents from the United Kingdom (Yule, Bolton, Udwin, O'Ryan, & Nurrish, 2000).

In addition to impact characteristics of the disaster, Bolin (1986) also describes the importance of victim characteristics in disaster vulnerability. He identifies individuals as *primary victims* (those directly experiencing physical, material, and personal losses) and *secondary victims* (those who witness the disaster but do not experience the actual impact). While both levels of victims may have comparable levels of psychological distress, he points out that secondary victims are less likely to seek professional mental health help, perhaps because they do not feel "entitled" to such help (Bolin, 1982). Bolin (1986) also emphasizes the importance of demographic characteristics, citing the numerous studies indicating the vulnerability of children in disaster, as well as studies indicating that certain demographic groups seem less vulnerable in disaster. These groups include those with higher educational levels and incomes (Bolin, 1982), those with extensive social support networks, and the elderly, who were previously thought to be at risk (Lucas, 1969; Bell, 1978; Huerta and Horton, 1978; Kilijanek & Drabek, 1979; Bolin, 1983).

Another factor related to the individual disaster victim is predisaster functioning. Norris et al. (2002) found 26 research articles reporting predisaster functioning on postdisaster outcomes. Whether they were assessed retrospectively or before the disaster, predisaster psychological symptoms were almost always among the best predictors of postdisaster symptoms. North et al. (1999) found that victims of the Oklahoma City bombing with predisaster disorder were more likely to experience PTSD specifically related to the bombing, with a rate of 46%, than victims with no prior disorder, for whom the rate of bombing-related PTSD was 26%. Shore, Tatum, & Vollmer (1986) found a variation on the same theme, that is, prior clinical cases exposed to disaster are more likely to have a relapse than cases not exposed to disaster.

There has long been the belief that factors-related coping styles, methods, and strengths influence psychological outcomes for better or worse. This belief has survived despite little supporting evidence (Norris et al., 2002). In fact, of the studies reviewed, far fewer showed an inverse relationship (more coping, less distress) than a positive relationship (more coping, more distress). Norris et al. conclude that research indicates that coping should be conceptualized as a response to distress or even as an indicator of it. In short, distress leads to increased coping, not the opposite (coping leads to reduced stress). The research did consistently suggest that avoidance coping is problematic, as is the assignment of blame. One recent study (North, Spitznagel, & Smith, 2001) did find that three types of coping (active outreach, informed pragmatism, and reconciliation) to be associated with decreased risk for psychiatric disorders over time. Norris et al. found that the disaster research findings were very consistent regarding the benefits of one's beliefs about one's own ability to cope. That is, what matters is not how individuals actually cope, but rather how they perceive their abilities to cope and control outcomes, as reflected in such constructs as self-efficacy, mastery, perceived control, self-esteem, optimism, future temporal orientation, and hope. The perception that one can cope is strongly predictive of good psychological outcomes (Benight, Ironson, et al., 1999; Benight, Swift, Sanger, Smith, & Zeppelin, 1999).

Myers (1985) discusses various stress-producing factors affecting *disaster workers* as a disaster-affected subpopulation. She presents a typology that divides stressors into four categories:

1. *Factors related to the individual worker* (health, preexisting stresses, previous traumatic experiences, coping skills, prior disaster experience, self-expectations, and perception and interpretation of the event)
2. *Interpersonal factors* (strength of social support system, preexisting stresses in relationships, expectations and needs of others, and status of family members in disaster)
3. *Community factors* (size of the community, previous degree of social solidarity, prior disaster experience, amount of social disruption due to the disaster)
4. *Factors related to the disaster* (warning, contrast of scene, type of disaster, nature of the destructive agent, degree of uncertainty, time of occurrence, duration of the disaster or continued threat, scope of the disaster, and location of the disaster)

Stressors predicting psychological impact for disaster workers include the intensity and duration of interactions with families of deceased victims, identification with the victims, and role conflict (Bartone, Ursano, Wright, & Ingraham, 1989; Hodgkinson & Shepherd, 1994). Duration of exposure is a risk factor for workers who must handle bodies (Jones, 1985) or identify victims (McCarroll, Fullerton, Ursano, & Hermson, 1996). Epstein, Fullerton, & Ursano (1998) found working with child victims to be a risk factor.

Baum and Davidson (1986) describe duration of the disaster, nature and extent of the impact, predictability and expectance, and control as the four important factors that contribute to trauma in disaster.

DeWolfe (2000) describes a dose-response relationship between community devastation and psychological impact. When entire communities are destroyed, everything familiar is gone. Survivors become disoriented at the most basic levels. Researchers have found higher levels of anxiety, depression, posttraumatic stress, somatic symptoms, and generalized distress associated with widespread community destruction (Solomon & Green, 1992). When some fabric of community life is left intact (e.g., schools, churches, commercial areas), there is a foundation from which recovery can occur. Social support occurs more readily when community gathering places remain. Survivors are then more able to continue some of their familiar routines. Family roles of provider, homemaker, or student are more able to be fulfilled when structures and institutions remain.

DeWolfe (2000) also lists probability of recurrence as a factor that will affect human response to disaster. When the disaster has a seasonal pattern, such as hurricanes or tornadoes, survivors are concerned they will be hit again before the season ends. During the low-risk portion of the year, communities rebuild. Vegetation grows back and visual reminders of the disaster diminish. At the one-year anniversary, the reminder that the area is potentially at risk again causes disaster stress and hypervigilance to resurface. In some types of disasters, such as earthquakes and floods, the probability of immediate recurrence is high. The aftershocks following an earthquake, or the increased risk of flooding due to ground saturation and damaged flood control structures following major floods, keep many survivors anxious and preoccupied.

Warheit (1986) developed a comprehensive classification of factors influencing disaster stress. Patterning his scheme along a stress paradigm, he divided potential risk factors into those related to the event, to the community, and to the individual (Smith et al., 1988). Factors related to the event include suddenness of impact, salient response required, unavoidability of the event, high risk to life and property, persistence over time, fluctuations of intensity, and pervasiveness of impact. He listed community-related factors as lack of prior experience with the event, lack or loss of relevant community resources, community dissensus or conflict, ambiguous or conflicting definitions, and long-term disruption. Individual characteristics included preexisting predisposing factors, loss of interpersonal support networks, cultural–structural integration, lack of prior experience with similar situations, lack of relevant resources, and loss of coping resources.

In addition to the above-described impact characteristics, Weisaeth (1994) lists additional risk factors for psychological trauma. Among them are the type and severity of the disaster, the amount of geographical displacement, the degree of threat to life, and the degree of loss and community disruption caused by the disaster. He describes the major psychological aspects of trauma to which disaster victims are subjected to include: (1) the overwhelming threat to one's own life, (2) the often severe and mutilating injuries, (3) the experience of losing loved ones, and perhaps helplessly witnessing their deaths, and (4) facing impossible choices such as helping others at great risk to one's own survival.

Norris et al. (2002) found that when natural disasters cause extreme destruction and disruption, as was the case with Hurricane Andrew in 1992, their psychological effects become quite severe. As of 2001, Hurricane Andrew was the most thoroughly researched disaster in U.S. history (Norris et al., 2002). Ironson et al. (1997) found that 33% of Andrew's victims met the criteria for PTSD, and they also found several physiological measures indicative of lower immune functioning. Perilla, Norris, and Lavizzo (2002) sampled highly exposed residents of the area and found that 25% met the criteria for PTSD, with symptom levels varying strongly with severity of exposure. Most studies of Hurricane Andrew pointed to a high prevalence of psychological disturbance, especially in the neighborhoods with the most losses and where the danger had been the most severe (Norris et al., 2002).

Norris and Uhl (1993), in a survey of 1,000 adults following Hurricane Hugo, found that disaster-related acute stressors (including personal loss, financial loss, and especially injury and life threat) predicted elevations in seven domains of chronic stress (marital stress, parental stress, filial stress, financial stress, occupational stress, ecological stress, and physical stress), as well as symptoms of depression, anxiety, and somatization. Norris and Kaniasty (1996) found that many adverse mental health effects from Hurricane Hugo were related to deterioration in perceived social support.

Studies of the Three Mile Island nuclear accident found that proximity to the source of toxicity increased levels of psycho-physiological symptoms (Cleary & Houts, 1984; Baum, Gatchel, & Schaeffer, 1983; Fleming, Baum, Gisriel, & Gatchel, 1982; Davidson, Fleming, & Baum, 1985; Bromet et al., 1982; Dew & Bromet, 1993; Dew, Bromet, & Schulberg, 1987).

The lack of certain factors can also increase the likelihood that the disaster will have serious traumatic effects. These include lack of familiarity with the hazard; lack of anticipation, warning, and control; lack of predictability; and lack of leadership (Weisaeth, 1994). Raphael (1986) points out that damage to, or destruction of, home, property, or things of value are of secondary importance, as shown by low psychiatric morbidity in disasters with less severe threats to life. This is not to imply that the loss of a home is insignificant. Fried (1963, 1982a, 1982b, 1984) poignantly describes the powerful effects of home loss on individuals, families, and neighborhoods. He makes it clear that "home" means much more than the physical or social environment. It is integral to the sense of self, and when it is lost, a reorganization of the self becomes necessary. Without a home, self-identity, family identity, and hope for the future are threatened.

A particular, unique stressor in disaster is exposure to dead bodies, especially when the condition of the bodies reflects the violence of the disaster. Bolin (1986) uses the term *horror* to describe the witnessing of death in disasters, including the accidental discovery of bodies, the unsightly physical condition of corpses, and the nature of the cause of death. He concludes that horror is a significant generator of mental health problems and cites the exposure of survivors to the horror of death in the Buffalo Creek flood and dam collapse (Lifton & Olson, 1976). Ursano and McCarroll (1994) provide an in-depth discussion of exposure to traumatic death for workers involved in body recovery, identification, transport, and burial in the Gander, Newfoundland, military air disaster of December 1985 and in the Persian Gulf War. Factors involved in the traumatic impact of dealing with bodies included the stress of anticipation of the experience; inexperience with handling the dead; nature of the stress of exposure to traumatic death; sensory stimuli; novelty, surprise, and shock; identification and emotional involvement with the deceased; unique combat stresses; and coping strategies before, during, and after exposure to the dead.

As discussed in the section on types of disaster, there are varying opinions on whether type of disaster (e.g., natural vs. technological) influences the traumatic effects on the survivors. Some researchers have suggested that whether a disaster has natural versus human-made causation is an important factor in determining the extent of its psychological consequences (Smith et al., 1988; Berren, Beigel, & Ghetner, 1980; Baum et al., 1983a; Logue, Melick, & Hansen, 1981; Gleser et al., 1981; Beigel & Berren, 1985; Frederick, 1980). Some researchers indicate that technological disasters produce distinct psychological sequelae (Berren et al.; Logue et al.; Gleser et al.; Lindy, 1985). Baum et al. suggest that technological disasters result in more long-term psychological impairment and require more long-term treatment. It has also been suggested that technological disasters, due to their unique characteristics, may require different mental health interventions and treatment techniques than do natural disasters (Baum et al.; Gleser et al.). Quarantelli (1986), on the other hand, has rejected the idea that the psychological effects of disaster are agent-specific and calls the distinction between natural and technological disasters "unrewarding" (Smith et al., 1988).

In addition to factors contributing to the traumatic impact of disaster, there are factors that seem to mediate the traumatic impact. These include the individual's biological makeup, developmental history, and repertoire of coping skills; previous experience and disaster preparedness; social supports; appraisal of what can be done to manage the situation; and mastery of necessary recovery tasks (Solomon, 1986a, 1986b; Solomon, Smith, Robins, & Fischbach, 1987; Ursano, McCaughey, & Fullerton, 1994; Weiseath, 1994).

PHASES OF DISASTER

Numerous sources have described the pattern of individual and community activities and reactions in the aftermath of disaster (DeWolfe, 2000; Farberow & Frederick, 1978; Kafrissen, Heffron, & Zusman, 1975; Myers, 1985, 1989b, 1994a, 1994b; Myers, O'Callahan, & Peuler, 1984; Myers, Spofford, & Young, 1996; Stein & Myers, 1999; Weaver, 1995; Young et al., 1998; Zunin & Myers, 1990). The phases of disaster, depicted in Figure 1.1, are relatively predictable, but there is individual variation in the

Phases of Disaster

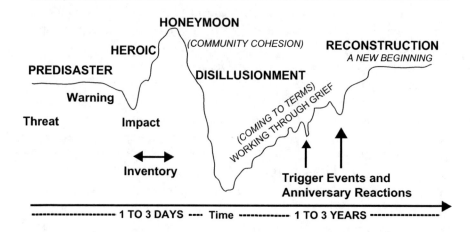

PHASES OF DISASTER
Diane Myers and Leonard Zunin
Previously published by DeWolfe, 2000, in public domain

reaction of survivors and variation in the duration of each phase. The phases may overlap and movement along the timeline is not strictly linear: The mood of an individual or the collective mood of the community can move "backwards" on the chart with intervening events, reminders, or recurrence of disaster impacts (e.g., aftershocks of an earthquake). Nonetheless, it is useful for disaster mental health practitioners to be familiar with and able to recognize the phases, as mental health interventions appropriate in one phase may not be appropriate or helpful in another.

PHASES OF DISASTER
Diane Myers and Leonard Zunin
Previously published by DeWolfe, 2000, in public domain

THREAT

The threat phase is the time before impact during which a hazard or a number of hazards exist that could potentially strike the community. For example, major threats to California include earthquake, fires, and floods; the Midwest faces the threat of seasonal tornadoes and blizzards; hurricanes and severe storms threaten the East coast. Reactions during the threat phase vary. While some citizens engage in disaster preparedness activities appropriate to the local threat, many people chose a head-in-the-sand approach, believing either that disaster will not strike or that it is futile to prepare for the unthinkable. The challenge for emergency management professionals during this phase is to elevate collective anxiety sufficiently to move people to prepare, while not frightening them into inaction.

WARNING

The warning phase occurs when it is a known fact that a disaster is highly likely to occur. In tornado country, for example, a "tornado watch" constitutes a threat: weather conditions exist that are ripe for the formation of a tornado. A "tornado warning," on the other hand, means that a tornado has actually been spotted and people are warned to take cover.

A warning provides people with the opportunity to prepare both physically and psychologically for the impact. Those disasters that occur without warning have great psychological impact because people are denied the opportunity to prepare themselves and have little control over their surroundings or their situation when the impact hits.

People often respond to warning with initial disbelief and reluctance to act. This is particularly common when past warnings have failed to materialize, as in the case of hurricanes which, despite the most advanced meteorological technologies, often fail to follow a predicted path or direction. People may not heed warnings because they are reluctant to evacuate and feel that if they stay in their homes, they can "protect" their homes and themselves from the impact. People may "normalize" or psychologically downgrade the importance of warning information and obvious threatening conditions, consciously or unconsciously reframing or redefining the situation into one of less danger. A frequently cited example in disaster lore is of citizens hearing the roar of an approaching tornado and thinking they were hearing a freight train—in a community without train tracks. When people do not heed warnings and suffer losses as a result, they may experience guilt and self blame. Even if they may have specific plans for how they might protect themselves in the future, they can be left with a sense of guilt or responsibility for what has occurred (Dewolfe, 2000). Warnings need to be given by credible and respected public officials, with clear instructions about actions to be taken and leaving no loopholes for denial or disbelief on the part of citizens.

The challenge for emergency officials is to give warnings in such a way that they will be believed and heeded by the community. Most people, even those who ignore warnings, will seek safe haven and take protective action when impact is imminent, albeit often too late.

IMPACT

This is the period of time during which the disaster strikes. It may last for seconds, minutes, hours, days, or much longer as in the case of disasters such as drought, famine, or war. In disasters of discreet and rather sudden impact, people may experience intense fear but rarely panic (Kafrissen et al., 1975; Quarantelli, 1954, 1957; Quarantelli & Dynes, 1972; Weaver, 1995). Many people experience the physical symptoms of stress and fear during impact, including increased pulse, rapid shallow breathing, tremor, and sweating or chills. Most people behave adaptively, taking action to protect themselves and their loved ones. Many people report time distortion, a majority reporting that "time slowed down" during the impact. Immediately after impact, most people experience stunning, confusion, and disbelief at what has happened. Most typically, people focus on the survival and physical well-being of themselves and their loved ones. When families are separated from their loved ones during the impact of a disaster (e.g., children at school, adults at work), they typically experience considerable anxiety until they are reunited (DeWolfe, 2000).

Secondary impacts (as in the case of earthquake aftershocks) often produce more profound symptoms of fear than the original impact. This is perhaps due to the cumulative effect of stress, coupled with the undeniable knowledge of what damages have already been wrought by the disaster. One elderly California resident jokingly quipped after the 7.6 Richter scale Landers/Big Bear earthquake of 1992 that he could accurately calculate the Richter reading of a Q-tip hitting the floor, he was so nervous from all the aftershocks (*Seniors Cope*, 1993). Some people, on the other hand, handle secondary impacts reasonably well, perhaps having gained confidence and survival skills from the initial impact.

HEROIC

The heroic phase, sometimes called the "rescue" phase, occurs immediately after impact. People rapidly recover from stunned disbelief and move into action, victims helping other victims as well as helping rescue workers to save lives and property. Both individuals and the community as a whole direct inordinate amounts of activity into the necessary tasks of helping, sheltering, emergency repair, and cleanup (Young et al., 1998). Heroism and altruism are predominant. Neighbors often report meeting their neighbors for the first time in years, helping each other to turn off utilities and shore up damaged homes. Contrary to myth, antisocial behavior such as looting is uncommon in natural disasters, although it is widespread in civil disorders (Bush, 1982; Quarantelli & Dynes, 1970, 1972). People are grateful to be alive, and often report a feeling of euphoria and sense of personal invulnerability. While people are shocked and horrified by damages and losses, morale is typically high for people directing their energy into concrete, necessary, and meaningful tasks. Physiological arousal results in a high level of activity but cognitive impairment (confusion, difficulty comprehending, problem solving, and setting priorities) often contributes to a low level of efficiency and effectiveness. People rushing to help others are often inattentive to safety, and injuries frequently occur in this phase.

INVENTORY

The inventory phase may overlap the impact and heroic phases. It is the time period in which people try to orient themselves to what has happened and to assess the scope and extent of the impact. Even while stunned, disoriented, confused, and in disbelief, people engage in information-seeking behaviors. Their greatest concern is finding information about the whereabouts and condition of loved ones from whom they are separated. Predisaster planning within the family can ease this task considerably, for example, by establishing reunification locations or setting up an out-of-town phone contact who can become the family switchboard for messages when local phone lines are inoperative but long-distance lines are still working. Cellular phone circuits quickly become overloaded and email becomes undependable with electricity and phone lines down.

People also seek information about the condition of their homes and neighborhoods, and become distraught and angry with public officials when not allowed to return to their neighborhood or home to assess the damage and collect belongings. Public officials are advised to provide frequent press conferences and meetings with the public to keep citizens apprised of conditions and to give information about when they can return to their homes. Mental health personnel can assist victims in obtaining news about what has happened by providing such things as television and radio, newspapers, bulletin boards, and maps (detailing damages, road conditions, and resource sites) in shelters or other sites where people congregate (Myers, 1989a).

HONEYMOON

Literature indicates that the honeymoon phase may extend between 1 week and 3 months postdisaster (Farberow & Frederick, 1978). Among seasoned disaster mental health workers, however, the opinion is that this honeymoon phase is much shorter than reported by Farberow and Frederick. It usually begins immediately after the valiant efforts of the heroic phase and lasts in most cases for a maximum of several weeks.

During this phase, also known as the "remedy" phase, optimism and expectations for a swift, complete recovery are generally high. Media attention keeps the impacted community in the news, resulting in an outpouring of support and donations from around the nation and sometimes the world. The community pulls together in a spirit of survival, supporting community leaders and recognizing community heroes. There is a strong sense of having shared with others a dangerous, catastrophic experience and having lived through it (Farberow & Frederick, 1978). There is a sense of relief that the worst is over.

Large-scale relief efforts are underway, bringing massive amounts of resources (financial, material, and human) to the impacted area. Preexisting and emergent community groups rally to the cause. Visits from prominent politicians and leaders, with promises of a seemingly endless wealth of resources, buoy hopes and anticipation. People expect that insurance policies and government programs will completely and efficiently rebuild what was damaged or lost, not realizing that there are serious limitations on both the amount and duration of available aid. As survivors begin to try to collect damages from their insurance companies and to apply for assistance from government and nonprofit agencies, they are confronted with reality of endless regulations, complicated forms, and complex procedures. As outside resources begin to diminish, the media coverage lessens, and VIPs are no longer visiting, the complexity of rebuilding and restoration becomes increasingly apparent (Young et al., 1998). Energy begins to wane as people struggle to cope with bureaucratic complexities, financial strain, and temporary housing. Fatigue and eroded expectations set the stage for the next phase.

DISILLUSIONMENT

The disillusionment phase begins from several days to several weeks after impact. It lasts for many months to several years, and the mood of disillusionment often overlays the entire process of reconstruction and recovery.

Disillusionment begins for some when they encounter the rules, regulations, redtape, hassles, delays, and disappointments of government and insurance programs. Promised aid does not materialize or falls short of expectations (Weaver, 1995). Survivors discover that significant financial benefits are in the form of loans, not grants; that home insurance is not what they understood it to be; that politics, rather than need, shape many decisions; that a neighbor with a damaged chimney received greater benefits than a neighbor whose roof collapsed (Young et al., 1998). Zoning laws change, and fire victims learn they cannot rebuild homes on their lots because of landslide dangers in the absence of destroyed vegetation. However, they will have to continue to make mortgage payments on the destroyed home until the loan is paid off. Insurance companies go bankrupt or inadequately reimburse clients for their losses. Unscrupulous contractors gouge prices or simply disappear with down payments for jobs.

For some, disillusionment begins physiologically, as adrenaline runs down and numbness and shock wear off and fatigue sets in. Living in temporary housing becomes increasingly stressful and individuals become irritable. Family stresses can lead to disruption of intimacy and support, and domestic violence may occur. There may be fear, anxiety, and a sense of vulnerability related to potential recurrence of the disaster or related to concern for the future. Health problems may occur as a result of public health problems such as contaminated water, bad food, and crowded living conditions. Stress-induced symptoms may include high blood pressure, cardiac symptoms, exacerbation of existing health conditions, immune system decline, and allergies. Sleep problems, related to living conditions or related to stress, contribute to fatigue, cognitive impairment, and irritability. Symptoms related to posttraumatic stress may increase (Young et al., 1998), and depression may occur.

In the community, cohesion and collaboration begin to decline as old and new conflicts arise among groups and agencies over allocation of blame, allocation of resources, and disparate priorities for action. Outside groups and agencies phase out and go home, leaving victims with feelings of disappointment, betrayal, and abandonment. Grassroots organizations often collapse for lack of funds, lack of volunteers, or the inability to adapt to changing needs of the community. The feeling of "shared community" diminishes as individuals concentrate on rebuilding their own lives and solving their individual problems (Farberow & Frederick, 1978). It becomes obvious to survivors that their world has been permanently changed, and that they will need to take personal responsibility for solving the problems of rebuilding their homes, their businesses, their beliefs, and their lives.

RECONSTRUCTION

In the reconstruction phase, individuals and communities work to reestablish normal, predisaster functioning (Weaver, 1995).

Reconstruction involves rebuilding physically, financially, emotionally, and spiritually. Community reconstruction entails rebuilding of architecture, infrastructure, programs and, in some cases, relationships among community groups. Disaster survivors have no idea, in the beginning, how long it takes for that rebuilding. At a minimum, it takes several years.

As survivors move forward, the groundwork already done through their efforts begins to produce observable changes. Applications have been approved or denied, loans have been worked out or not, but somehow reconstruction begins to take place. Over these years, there will be disappointments, delays, and events that retrigger memories and stress reactions. There will also be the overcoming of obstacles and many small and large successes. Anniversaries of the disaster will rekindle memories and inspire commemorative and sometimes celebratory events (for a full discussion of disaster anniversaries and anniversary reactions, see Myers, 1994a). The physical and social rebuilding of the community reaffirms the survivors' belief in that community and in their own capabilities and abilities (Farberow & Frederick, 1978). With the passage of time and the healing of physical and emotional wounds wrought by the disaster, most survivors are able to reflect on their recovery journey with appreciation and perspective. They are able to *look back* and to recognize how far they have come, the challenges they have overcome, and the lessons they have learned. They are able to *look inward* and to recognize and appreciate the courage, stamina, endurance, and resourcefulness of themselves and their loved ones throughout the process of recovery. They are able to *look around them* and appreciate the loved ones and friends who have helped with the rebuilding and the healing. Finally, they are able to *look forward* to a renewed sense of life and purpose, and to see themselves not as disaster victims but as disaster survivors (Myers, 1992).

KEY CONCEPTS OF DISASTER MENTAL HEALTH

Having reviewed thus far the characteristics and phases of disaster that affect the mental health of survivors, we turn now to the basic concepts of providing mental health assistance in the disaster environment. The following guiding principles, originally published by Myers (1994a), form the basis for disaster mental health intervention programs. Not only do these principles describe some departures and deviations from traditional mental health work, they also orient administrators and service providers to priority issues. The truth and wisdom reflected in these principles have been shown over and over again, from disaster to disaster (DeWolfe, 2000).

NO ONE WHO SEES A DISASTER IS UNTOUCHED BY IT

In any given disaster, loss and trauma will directly affect many people. In addition, there are many other individuals who are emotionally impacted simply by being a part of the affected community. Myers (Hartsough & Myers, 1985) addresses the extensive kind of personal and community upheaval that disaster can cause:

> A disaster is an awesome event. Simply seeing massive destruction and terrible sights evokes deep feelings. Often, residents of disaster-stricken communities report disturbing feelings of grief, sadness, anxiety, and anger, even when they are not themselves victims. . . . Such strong reactions confuse them when, after all, they were spared any personal loss. These individuals find comfort and reassurance when told that their reactions are normal in every way; everyone who *sees* a disaster is, in some sense, a victim.

Even individuals who experience a disaster "second hand" through exposure to extensive media coverage can be affected. This includes children whose parents may not be aware of how much disaster material their children are seeing and hearing on television. The nonstop coverage of the terrorist attacks of September 11, 2001, affected virtually everyone in the United States. In the aftermath, the Department of Veterans' Affairs (Hamblen, 2001) stated that those who watch more media coverage are at higher risk for PTSD and associated problems. Mental health workers have, in essence, a whole population to educate about common disaster stress reactions, ways to cope with stressors, and available resources (Myers, 1991). Therefore, mental health education about the effects of disaster, self-help interventions, and where to call for additional help must be provided to the *community at large.*

THERE ARE TWO TYPES OF DISASTER TRAUMA

In his classic study of the Buffalo Creek, West Virginia, flood of 1972, sociologist Kai Erikson (1976) described two types of trauma that occur jointly and continuously in most disasters. Disaster mental health services must take both types of trauma into consideration to address all of the needs of the community.

Individual trauma is defined as "a blow to the psyche that breaks through one's defenses so suddenly and with such brutal force that one cannot react to it effectively."

Collective trauma is "a blow to the basic tissues of social life that damages the bonds attaching people together and impairs the prevailing sense of communality."

Individual trauma manifests itself in the stress and grief reactions which individual survivors experience. Bolin and Bolton (1986) emphasize that collective trauma can sever the social ties of survivors with each other and with the locale. These may be ties that could provide important psychological support in times of stress. Disaster disrupts nearly all activities of daily living and the connections they entail. People may relocate to temporary housing away from their neighbors and other social supports such as church, clinics, childcare, or recreation programs. Work may be disrupted or lost due to business failure, lack of transportation, loss of tools, or a worker's inability to concentrate due to disaster stress. For children, there may be a loss of friends and school relationships due to relocation. Fatigue and irritability can increase family conflict and undermine family relationships and ties.

Collective trauma is often less "visible" to mental health clinicians trained to work with individuals. However, it is essential to identify and address collective trauma in disaster mental health programs. People will find it difficult, if not impossible, to heal from the effects of individual trauma while the community around them remains in shreds and a supportive community setting does not exist (Erikson, 1976). Thus, mental health interventions such as outreach, support groups, community organization, and advocacy, which seek to reestablish linkages between individuals and groups, are essential.

MOST PEOPLE PULL TOGETHER AND FUNCTION DURING AND AFTER A DISASTER, BUT THEIR EFFECTIVENESS IS DIMINISHED

There are multitudes of stressors affecting disaster survivors. In the early "heroic" and "honeymoon" phases there is much energy, optimism, and altruism. However, there is often a high level of activity with a low level of efficiency. As the implications and meaning of losses become more real, grief reactions intensify. As fatigue sets in and frustrations and disillusionment accumulate, more stress symptoms may appear. Diminished cognitive functioning (short-term memory loss, confusion, difficulty setting priorities and making decisions, etc.) may occur because of stress and fatigue. This can impair survivors' ability to make sound decisions and take necessary steps toward recovery and reconstruction.

MANY DISASTER STRESS REACTIONS ARE NORMAL RESPONSES TO AN ABNORMAL SITUATION

Most disaster survivors are normal persons who function reasonably well under the responsibilities and stresses of everyday life. However, with the added stress of disaster, most individuals will usually show signs of emotional and psychological strain (Farberow & Frederick, 1978), including posttraumatic stress and grief responses. These reactions are *normal* reactions to an extraordinary and abnormal situation and are to be expected under the circumstances. Survivors, residents of the community, and disaster workers alike may experience them.

Green, Wilson, and Lindy (1985) emphasize that the posttraumatic stress process is a dynamic one in which the survivor attempts to integrate a traumatic event into his or her self-structure. The process is natural and adaptive. It should not be labeled pathological (i.e., a "disorder") unless it is prolonged, blocked, exceeds a tolerable quality, or interferes with regular functioning to a significant extent.

Myers, Zunin, and Zunin (1990) point out that, in addition to stress and anxiety, grief reactions are a normal part of recovery from disaster. Not only may individuals lose loved ones, homes, and treasured possessions, but hopes, dreams, goals, optimism, and assumptions about life and its meaning may be shattered. Zunin and Zunin (1991) emphasize that the grief responses to such losses are common and are not pathological (warranting therapy or counseling) unless the grief is an intensification, a prolongation, or an inhibition of normal grief.

Relief from stress, the ability to talk about the experience, and the passage of time usually lead to the reestablishment of equilibrium. Public information about normal reactions, education about ways to handle them, and early attention to symptoms that are problematic can speed recovery and prevent long-term problems (Hartsough & Myers, 1985).

PSYCHOLOGICAL REACTIONS TO DISASTER MAY CAUSE SERIOUS PSYCHOLOGICAL IMPAIRMENT

While many stress reactions fall into the category of "normal reactions of normal people to an abnormal event," serious psychological impairment, requiring referral and treatment, can occur. Norris et al. (2002), in their study of overall severity of impairment of 60,000 disaster victims studied between 1981 and 2001, found that 11% of the samples studied had minimal impairment, indicative of transient stress; 51% had moderate impairment, indicative of prolonged stress; 21% had severe impairment, indicative of significant psychopathology or distress; and 18% had very severe impairment.

Specific psychological problems found in the research studies reviewed by Norris et al. (2002) included symptoms of depression, anxiety, posttraumatic stress, dissociative responses, and other psychiatric problems. Criterion-based conditions of PTSD, major depression disorder (MDD), generalized anxiety disorder (GAD), and panic disorder (PD) were found. PTSD was assessed and observed in 68% of samples. Depression was the second most commonly observed psychiatric problem, identified in 36% of samples, with related symptoms such as suicidality and remorse increasing with severity of exposure (Norris, Perilla, Ibanez, & Murphy, 2001; Warheit, Zimmerman, Khoury, Vega, & Gil, 1996). Anxiety was found in 20% of samples. While not as prevalent as PTSD or MDD, GAD has been diagnosed in disaster-stricken populations using structured diagnostic measures. In addition, death anxiety, phobias, and panic disorder have been observed, though only occasionally (Norris et al., 2002). Nonspecific distress, or the elevation of various stress-related psychological and psychosomatic symptoms, was identified in 39% of the samples studied by Norris et al. (2002).

These findings have significant implications, particularly for disaster mental health programs such as the American Red Cross (ARC) Disaster Mental Health (DMH) Services and the FEMA and Center for Mental Health Services (CMHS) Disaster Crisis Counseling Program. Both of these programs provide screening, crisis intervention, education, and support services for disaster victims. They do not, however, provide ongoing treatment for psychological problems caused by disaster. Norris et al. (2002) found that 62% of the samples studied had only minimal to moderate impairment, indicating transient to prolonged stress, which could well be categorized as "normal reactions of normal people to abnormal situations," and which could probably be well addressed by both the Red Cross DMH services and the FEMA Crisis Counseling Program. However, with Norris and colleagues finding that 39% of samples of disaster victims had severe to very severe impairment, resources for psychological treatment are imperative. Both the ARC and FEMA disaster mental health programs refer people needing treatment to community treatment resources (public and private). However, an important part of community needs assessment following disaster is to determine if adequate treatment resources for providing appropriate treatment modalities at fees affordable to impacted disaster victims exist in the community. If they do not, such resources will need to be developed or long-term mutual aid will need to be provided from resources in a nearby geographic area.

MANY EMOTIONAL REACTIONS OF DISASTER SURVIVORS STEM FROM PROBLEMS OF LIVING CAUSED BY THE DISASTER

Because disaster disrupts so many aspects of daily life, many problems for disaster survivors are immediate and practical in nature (Farberow & Frederick, 1978). Norris et al. (2002) found *chronic problems in living* to be infrequently assessed but commonly observed following disasters. They concluded that in the months following a disaster, victims are more likely than nonvictims to experience hassles or life events that serve as stressors in their own right. They found that secondary stressors often revolved around troubled interpersonal relationships and new family strains and conflicts. In addition, they documented work-related stressors, such as occupational and financial stress, and other strains that emerged from transactions between persons and their physical environment, such as environmental worry, ecological stress, and continued disruption during rebuilding. People may need help locating missing loved ones; finding temporary housing, clothing, and food; obtaining transportation; applying for financial assistance, unemployment insurance, building permits, and income tax assistance; getting medical care, replacement of eyeglasses or medication; obtaining help with demolition, digging out, and cleanup; and obtaining financial and physical assistance in relocating or rebuilding (Myers, 1994a, 1994b).

DISASTER RELIEF PROCEDURES HAVE BEEN CALLED "THE SECOND DISASTER"

The process of obtaining temporary housing, replacing belongings, getting permits to rebuild, applying for government assistance, seeking insurance reimbursement, and acquiring help from private or voluntary agencies is often fraught with rules, red tape, hassles, delays, and disappointment.

People must often establish ties to bureaucracies to get aid they can get nowhere else. However, the organizational style of the aid-giving bureaucracies is often too impersonal for victims in the emotion-charged aftermath of the disaster (Bolin, 1982). Munnichs (1977) has noted that "bureaucracy means impersonality in social relations, routinization of tasks, centralization of authority, rigid rules and procedures. . . ." To complicate the matter, disasters and their special circumstances often foul up the bureaucratic procedures even of organizations established to handle disaster (Bolin, 1982). Families are forced to deal with organizations that seem or are impersonal, inefficient, and inept.

Many individuals are unable to obtain the benefits for which they are eligible in a timely manner from the agencies involved. Individuals who felt competent and effective before the disaster may suddenly experience serious erosion of self-esteem and confidence. Feelings of helplessness and anger are common (Farberow & Frederick, 1978). In response, mental health staff may assist individuals by reassuring them that this "second disaster" is a common phenomenon. The staff can reassure them that most people have difficulty wending their way through the bureaucracy. Simply hearing the phase the "second disaster" often brings a wave of relief to survivors, often with some welcome laughter.

Mental health personnel may need to help individuals to find constructive channels for their anger and frustration. This may involve helping them not to misdirect it (toward family, for example), nor to sabotage their own efforts by "blowing up" at the agencies trying to help them (Project COPE, 1983). Mental health staff may also help individuals by providing information about how specific agencies work. Survivor support groups are often very helpful in this regard, with individuals offering each other concrete advice and suggestions about how to deal with bureaucratic problems.

In addition, mental health personnel may provide consultation or training to disaster relief agencies. The goal of such consultation is to influence programs toward maximum responsiveness to needs of disaster survivors. Mental health staff may also intervene directly with agencies on behalf of disaster survivors. Such advocacy may be case centered, seeking to benefit an individual client, or may be issue-centered, seeking to benefit a group of clients or the general population by encouraging positive system change (Myers, 1989b).

MOST PEOPLE DO NOT SEE THEMSELVES AS NEEDING MENTAL HEALTH SERVICES FOLLOWING DISASTER AND WILL NOT SEEK OUT SERVICES

Many people equate "mental health" services with being "crazy." To offer mental health assistance to a disaster survivor may seem to add insult to injury—"First I have lost everything and now you think I'm mentally unstable." In addition, most disaster survivors are overwhelmed with the time-consuming activities of putting the concrete aspects of their lives back together. Counseling or support groups may seem esoteric in the face of such pragmatic pressures. Very effective mental health assistance can be provided while the worker is helping survivors with concrete tasks. For example, a mental health worker can help a survivor in sorting out demands and setting priorities by using skilled but unobtrusive interviewing techniques while they are sifting through rubble together, or by talking with survivors while they are standing in line for food or for services.

DISASTER SURVIVORS MAY REJECT DISASTER ASSISTANCE OF ALL TYPES

People may be too busy with cleaning up and other concrete demands to seek out services and programs that might help them. Initially, people are relieved to be alive and well. They often underestimate the financial impact and implication of their losses and overestimate their available financial resources. The bottom-line impact of losses is often not evident for many months or, occasionally, for years.

The heroism, altruism, and optimism of the early phases of disaster may make it seem that "others are so much worse off than I am." For most people, there is a strong need to feel self-reliant and in control. Some people equate government relief programs as "welfare." For others, especially recent immigrants who have fled their countries of origin because of war or oppression, government is not to be trusted. Pride may be an issue for some people; they may feel ashamed that help is needed, or may not want help from "outsiders" (Farberow & Frederick, 1978). Tact and sensitivity to these issues are important.

DISASTER MENTAL HEALTH ASSISTANCE IS OFTEN MORE "PRACTICAL" THAN PSYCHOLOGICAL IN NATURE

Most disaster survivors are people who are temporarily disrupted by a severe stress but who can function capably under normal circumstances. Much of the mental health work at first will be to give concrete types of help (Farberow & Frederick, 1978).

Mental health personnel may assist survivors with problem-solving and decision-making. They can help them to identify specific concerns, set priorities, explore alternatives, seek out resources, and choose a plan of action. Mental health staff must inform themselves about resources available to survivors, including local organizations and agencies in addition to specialized disaster relief resources. Mental health workers may help directly with some problems, such as providing information, filling out forms, helping with cleanup, locating healthcare or childcare, and finding transportation. They may also make referrals to specific resources, such as assistance with loans, housing, employment, and permits.

In less frequent cases, individuals may experience more serious psychological responses such as severe depression, disorientation, immobilization, or an exacerbation of prior mental disturbance. These situations will likely require referral for more intensive psychological counseling. The role of the disaster mental health worker is not to provide treatment for severely disturbed individuals directly but to recognize their needs and help link them with an appropriate treatment resource (Farberow & Frederick, 1978).

DISASTER MENTAL HEALTH SERVICES MUST BE UNIQUELY TAILORED TO THE COMMUNITIES THEY SERVE

The demographics and characteristics of the communities affected by disaster must be considered when designing a mental health program (Myers, 1991). Urban, suburban, and rural areas have different needs, resources, traditions, and values about giving and receiving help. It is essential that programs consider the ethnic and cultural groups in the community and provide services that are culturally relevant and in the languages of the people. Disaster recovery services are best accepted and utilized if they are integrated into existing, trusted community agencies and resources. In addition, programs are most effective if workers indigenous to the community and to its various ethnic and cultural groups are integrally involved in service delivery.

MENTAL HEALTH STAFF NEED TO SET ASIDE TRADITIONAL METHODS, AVOID THE USE OF MENTAL HEALTH LABELS, AND USE AN ACTIVE OUTREACH APPROACH TO INTERVENTION

The traditional, office-based approach is of little use in the field following disaster. Only very few people will come to an office or approach a desk labeled "mental health" in a disaster shelter or service center. Most often, the aim will be to provide *human services* for problems that are accompanied by emotional strain. It is preferable not to use words that signify psychopathology, such as psychotherapy, psychiatric, psychological, neurotic, or psychotic (Farberow & Frederick, 1978). While the stigma of mental illness has decreased in recent years, many people are still wary of mental health services. Mental health staff usually identify themselves as crisis counselors or use other terminology that does not imply that their focus is on pathology. Workers seem less threatening when they refer to their services as "assistance," "support," or "talking" rather than labeling themselves as "mental health counselors" (DeWolfe, 1992).

Mental health staff need to use an active outreach approach. They must go out to community sites where survivors are involved in the activities of their daily lives. Such places include impacted neighborhoods, schools, disaster shelters, service centers, family assistance centers, respite centers for workers, meal sites, hospitals, churches, community centers, and memorial services.

SURVIVORS RESPOND TO ACTIVE INTEREST AND CONCERN

They will usually be eager to talk about what happened to them when approached with warmth and genuine interest. Mental health outreach workers should not hold back from initiating conversation with survivors out of fear of "intruding" or invading their privacy.

INTERVENTIONS MUST BE APPROPRIATE TO
THE PHASE OF DISASTER

It is important that disaster mental health workers recognize the different phases of disaster and the varying psychological and emotional reactions of each phase. For example, it will be counterproductive to probe for feelings when shock and denial are shielding the survivor from intense emotions. Once individuals have mobilized internal and external coping resources, they are better able to deal with their feelings about the situation. During the "heroic" and "honeymoon" phases, people who have not lost loved ones may be feeling euphoric, altruistic, and optimistic rather than bereaved. During the "inventory" phase, people are seeking and discussing the facts about the disaster, trying to piece reality together and understand what has happened. They may be more invested in discussing their thoughts than talking about feelings. In the "disillusionment" phase, people will likely be expressing feelings of frustration and anger. It is not usually a good time to ask if they can find something "good" that has happened to them through their experience.

Most people are willing and even eager to talk about their experiences in a disaster. However, it is important to respect the times when an individual may *not* want to talk about how things are going. Talking with a person in crisis does not mean always talking *about* the crisis (Zunin & Zunin, 1991). People usually "titrate their dosage" when dealing with pain and sorrow, and periods of normalcy and respite are also important. Talking about ordinary events and laughing at humorous points is also healing. If in doubt, *ask* the person whether they are in the mood to talk.

SUPPORT SYSTEMS ARE CRUCIAL TO RECOVERY

The most important support group for individuals is the family. Workers should attempt to keep the family together (in shelters and temporary housing, for example). Family members should be involved as much as possible in each other's recovery.

Disaster relocation and the intense activity involved in disaster recovery can disrupt people's interactions with their support systems. Encouraging people to make time for family and friends is important. Emphasizing the importance of "rebuilding relationships" in addition to rebuilding structures can be a helpful analogy.

For people with limited support systems, disaster support groups can be helpful. Scanlon-Schlipp and Levesque (1981) point out that support groups help to counter isolation. People who have been through the same kind of situation feel they can truly understand one another; they find reassurance that they are not alone or "weird" in their reactions. Groups help to counter the myths of uniqueness and pathology. They not only provide emotional support, but survivors can share concrete information and recovery tips and benefit from the guidance of other experienced survivors. Besides the catharsis of sharing experiences, they can identify with others who *are* recovering and can begin to feel hope for their own situation. Mental health staff may involve themselves in setting up self-help support groups for survivors or may facilitate support groups.

In addition, mental health workers may involve themselves in community organization activities. Community organization brings community members together to deal with concrete issues of concern to them. Such issues may include social policy in disaster reconstruction or disaster preparedness at the neighborhood level. The process can assist survivors with disaster recovery by not only helping with concrete problems but by reestablishing feelings of control, competence, self-confidence, and effectiveness. Perhaps most important, it can help to reestablish social bonds and support networks that have been fractured by the disaster.

SUMMARY

This chapter has discussed disaster definitions and frequency. Various types of disaster have been described, with information about the effects of each type of disaster on human reactions. Factors affecting the human impact of disasters and phases of disaster have been presented. Key concepts of disaster mental health have been discussed. In the following chapter, the psychological, emotional, physical, and behavioral reactions of people to disasters will be presented.

REFERENCES

American Psychiatric Association. (1994). *Diagnostic and statistical manual of mental disorders* (4th ed.). Washington, DC: Author.

Arata, C., Picou, J., Johnson, G., & McNally, T. (2000). Coping with technological disaster: An application of the conservation of resources model to the Exxon Valdez oil spill. *Journal of Traumatic Stress, 13,* 23–39.

Barton, A. H. (1969). *Communities in disaster: A sociological analysis of collective stress situations.* Garden City, NY: Doubleday.

Bartone, P., Ursano, R., Wright, K., & Ingraham, L. (1989). The impact of a military air disaster on the health of assistance workers: A prospective study. *Journal of Nervous and Mental Disease, 177,* 317–328.

Baum, A. (1986). Toxins, technology, and disasters. In G. R. Vanden Bos & B. K. Bryant (Eds.), *Cataclysms, crisis, and catastrophes: Psychology in action.* Washington, DC: American Psychological Association.

Baum, A., & Davidson, L. (1986). A suggested framework for studying factors that contribute to trauma in disaster. In B. J. Sowder & M. Lystad (Eds.), *Disasters and mental health: Contemporary perspectives and innovations in services to disaster victims.* Washington, DC: American Psychiatric Press.

Baum, A., Fleming, R., & Davidson, L. (1983a). Natural disaster and technological catastrophe. *Environment and Behavior, 15,* 333–354.

Baum, A., Fleming, R., & Singer, J. E. (1983b). Coping with victimization by technological disaster. *Journal of Social Issues, 39*(2), 117–138.

Baum, A., Gatchel, R., & Schaeffer, M. (1983). Emotional, behavioral, and physiological effects of chronic stress at Three Mile Island. *Journal of Consulting and Clinical Psychology, 51,* 565–572.

Beigel, A., & Berren, M. R. (1985). Human-induced disasters. *Psychiatric Annals, 15*(3), 143–150.

Bell, W. D. (1978). Disaster impact and response: Overcoming the thousand natural shocks. *The Gerontologist, 18,* 531–540.

Benight, C., Ironson, G., Klebe, K., Carver, C., Wynings, C., Burnett, K., et al. (1999). Conservation of resources and coping self-efficacy predicting distress following a natural disaster: A causal model analysis where the environment meets the mind. *Anxiety, Stress, and Coping, 12,* 107–126.

Benight, C., Swift, E., Sanger, J., Smith, A., & Zeppelin, D. (1999). Coping self-efficacy as a mediator of distress following a natural disaster. *Journal of Applied Social Psychology, 29,* 2443–2464.

Berren, M. R., Beigel, A., & Ghetner, S. (1980). A typology for the classification of disasters. *Community Mental Health Journal, 16,* 103–111.

Bolin, R. (1982). *Long-term family recovery from disaster.* Boulder: University of Colorado, Institute of Behavioral Science.

Bolin, R. (1983). *Social support and psychosocial stress in disaster.* Paper presented at the meeting of the Western Social Science Association, Albuquerque, NM.

Bolin, R. (1986). Disaster characteristics and psychosocial impacts. In B. J. Sowder and M. Lystad (Eds.), *Disasters and mental health: Contemporary perspectives and innovations in services to disaster victims.* Washington, DC: American Psychiatric Press.

Bolin, R. (1988). Response to natural disasters. In M. Lystad (Ed.), *Mental health response to mass emergencies: Theory and practice.* New York: Brunner/Mazel.

Bolin, R., & Bolton, P. (1986). *Race, religion, and ethnicity in disaster recovery* (Monograph No. 42). Program on Environment and Behavior. Boulder: University of Colorado.

Bromet, E. J., & Dunn, L. D. (1981). Mental health of mothers nine months after the Three Mile Island accident. *The Urban and Social Change Review, 14,* 12–15.

Bromet, E. J., Parkinson, D. K., Schulberg, H. C., & Gondek, P. (1982). Mental health of residents near the Three Mile Island reactor: A comparative study of selected groups. *Journal of Preventive Psychiatry, 1,* 225–276.

Brooks, N., & McKinlay, W. (1992). Mental health consequences of the Lockerbie disaster. *Journal of Traumatic Stress, 5,* 527–543.

Bush, S. (1982, Winter). Disaster myths. *Response, 13.*

Cleary, P., & Houts, P. (1984). The psychological impact of the Three Mile Island incident. *Journal of Human Stress, 10,* 28–34.

Davidson, L., Fleming, I., & Baum, A. (1985). Post-traumatic stress as a function of chronic stress and toxic exposure. In C. R. Figley (Ed.), *Trauma and its wake* (pp. 57–77). New York: Brunner/Mazel.

Davis, R. C., & Friedman, L. N. (1985). The emotional aftermath of crime and violence. In C. R. Figley (Ed.), *Trauma and its wake: Vol. 1. The study and treatment of post-traumatic stress disorder.* New York: Brunner/Mazel.

Dew, M., & Bromet, E. (1993).Predictors of temporal patterns of psychiatric distress during 10 years following the nuclear accident at Three Mile Island. *Social Psychiatry and Psychiatric Epidemiology, 28,* 49–55.

Dew, M., Bromet, E., & Schulberg, H. (1987). A comparative analysis of two community stressors' long-term mental health effects. *American Journal of Community Psychology, 15,* 167–184.

DeWolfe, D. (1992). A guide to door-to-door outreach. *Final report: Regular services grant, western Washington floods.* State of Washington: Mental Health Division.

DeWolfe, D. (2000). *Training manual for mental health and human service workers in major disasters* (2nd ed.). (DHHS Publication No. ADM 90-538). Retrieved March 14, 2001, from http://www.mentalhealth.org/publications/allpubs/ADM90-538/index.htm

Drabek, T. (1986). *Human system responses to disaster.* New York: Springer.

Drabek, T. E., & Hoetmer, G. J. (Eds.). (1991). *Emergency management: Principles and practice for local government.* Washington, DC: International City Management Association.

Epstein, R., Fullerton, C., & Ursano, R. (1998). Posttraumatic stress disorder following an air disaster: A prospective study. *American Journal of Psychiatry, 155,* 934–938.

Erikson, K. T. (1976). *Everything in its path: Destruction of community in the Buffalo Creek flood.* New York: Simon & Schuster.

Farberow, N. L., & Frederick, C. J. (1978). *Training manual for human service workers in major disasters.* Rockville, MD: National Institute of Mental Health.

Federal Emergency Management Agency. (2000a, April 25). *Federal response plan.* Washington, DC: Federal Emergency Management Agency. Retrieved February 14, 2001, from http://www.fema.gov/r-n-r/frp/html

Federal Emergency Management Agency. (2000b, April 25). *Federal response plan: Terrorism incident annex.* Washington, DC: Federal Emergency Management Agency. Retrieved February 15, 2001, from http://www.fema.gov/r-n-r/frp/frpterr/html

Federal Emergency Management Agency. (2001, January 4). *Hazards, disasters, and the U.S. emergency management system: An introduction (working draft)*. Emmitsburg, MD: Emergency Management Institute. Retrieved February 15, 2001, from http://www.fema.gov/emi/edu/ hazdisusems.html.

Figley, C. R. (Ed.). (1985). *Trauma and its wake: Vol. 2. Traumatic stress theory, research, and intervention*. New York: Brunner/Mazel.

Fleming, R., Baum, A., Gisriel, M., & Gatchel, R. (1982). Mediating influences of social support on stress at Three Mile Island. *Journal of Pediatric Psychology, 13*, 14–22.

Frederick, C. J. (1980). Effects of natural vs. human-induced violence upon victims. *Evaluation and Change,* Special Issue, 71–75.

Fried, M. (1963). Grieving for a lost home. In L. J. Duhl (Ed.), *The urban condition: People and policy in the metropolis*. New York: Basic Books.

Fried, M. (1982a). Endemic stress: The psychology of resignation and the politics of scarcity. *American Journal of Orthopsychiatry, 52*, 419.

Fried, M. (1982b). Residential attachment: Sources of residential and community satisfaction. *Journal of Social Issues, 38*(3), 107–119.

Fried, M. (1984). The structure and significance of community satisfaction. *Population and Environment, 7*(2), 61–86.

Fritz, C. E. (1961). Disasters. In R. K. Merton & R. A. Nisbet (Eds.), *Contemporary social problems* (pp. 651–694). New York: Harcourt.

Gelsomino, J., & Mackey, D. W. (1988). In M. Lystad (Ed.), *Mental health response to mass emergencies: Theory and practice*. New York: Brunner/Mazel.

Gist, R., & Lubin, B. (Eds.). (1989). *Psychosocial aspects of disaster*. New York: Wiley.

Gleser, G., Green, B., & Winget, C. (1981). *Prolonged psychosocial effects of disaster: A study of Buffalo Creek*. New York: Academic Press.

Goss, K. C. (2000a, February 15). Remarks at the Dedication of the J. W. Morris Emergency Management Training Center. Searcy, AR. Retrieved February 14, 2001, from http://www.fema.gov/pte/gosspch86.html

Goss, K. C. (2000b, June 13). Remarks at the 5th Annual "Technology Partnerships for Emergency Management" Workshop and Exhibition. Colorado Springs, CO. Retrieved February 14, 2001, from http://fema.gov/pte/gosspch100.html

Green, B. L. (1985) Conceptual and methodological issues in assessing the psychological impact of disaster. In B. J. Sowder (Ed.), *Disasters and mental health: Selected contemporary perspective* (DHHS Publication No. ADM 85–1421). Washington, DC: U.S. Government Printing Office.

Green, B., Korol, M., Grace, M., Vary, M., Leonard, A., Gleser, G., et al. (1991). Children and disaster: Age, gender, and parental effects on PTSD symptoms. *Journal of the American Academy of Child and Adolescent Psychiatry, 30*, 945–951.

Green, B., Lindy, J., Grace, M., Gleser, G., Leonard, A., Korol, M., et al. (1990). Buffalo Creek survivors in the second decade: Stability of stress symptoms. *American Journal of Orthopsychiatry, 60*, 43–54.

Green, B. L., Wilson, J. P., & Lindy, J. D. (1985). Conceptualizing post-traumatic stress disorder: A psychosocial framework. In C. R. Figley (Ed.), *Trauma and its wake: Vol. 1. The study and treatment of post-traumatic stress disorder*. New York: Brunner/Mazel.

Haas, J., Kates, R., & Bowden, M. (1977). *Reconstruction following disaster*. Cambridge, MA: MIT Press.

Hamblen, J. (2001, September). *What are the traumatic stress effects of terrorism?* National Center for PTSD Fact Sheet. Retrieved October 16, 2001, from http://www.ncptsd.org/facts/disasters/fs_terrorism.html

Hartsough, D., & Myers, D. (1985). *Disaster work and mental health: Prevention and control of stress among workers*. (DHHS Publication No. ADM 87–1422). Washington, DC: U.S. Government Printing Office.

Hodgkinson, P., & Shepherd, M. (1994). The impact of disaster support work. *Journal of Traumatic Stress, 7,* 587–600.

Hogencamp, V. E., & Figley, C. R. (1983). War: Bringing the battle home. In C. R. Figley & H. I. McCubbin (Eds.), *Stress and the family: Vol. 2. Coping with catastrophe.* New York: Brunner/Mazel.

Huerta, F., & Horton, R. (1978). Coping behavior of elderly flood victims. *The Gerontologist, 18,* 541–546.

Ironson, G., Wynings, C., Schneiderman, N., Baum, A., Rodriguez, M., Greenwood, D., et al. (1997). Posttraumatic stress symptoms, intrusive thoughts, loss, and immune function after Hurricane Andrew. *Psychosomatic Medicine, 59,* 128–141.

Janoff-Bulman, R. (1985). The aftermath of victimization: Rebuilding shattered assumptions. In C. R. Figley (Ed.), *Trauma and its wake: Vol. I. The study and treatment of post-traumatic stress disorder.* New York: Brunner/Mazel.

Jones, D. (1985). Secondary disaster victims: The emotional effects of recovering and identifying human remains. *American Journal of Psychiatry, 142,* 303–307.

Kafrissen, S. R., Heffron, E. F., & Zusman, J. (1975). Mental health problems in environmental disasters. In H. L. P. Resnik, H. L. Ruben, & D. D. Rubens (Eds.), *Emergency psychiatric care: The management of mental health crises.* Bowie, MD: Charles Press.

Kilijanek, T. S., & Drabek, T. E. (1979). Assessing long-term impacts of a natural disaster: A focus on the elderly. *The Gerontologist, 19,* 555–566.

Laufer, R. S. (1988). Human response to war and war-related events in the contemporary world. In M. Lystad (Ed.), *Mental health response to mass emergencies: Theory and practice.* New York: Brunner/Mazel.

Levine, A. (1982). *Love Canal: Science, politics, and people.* Toronto: Lexington Books.

Lifton, R. J., & Olson, E. (1976). The human meaning of total disaster: The Buffalo Creek Experience. *Psychiatry, 39,* 1–18.

Lindy, J. D. (1985). The trauma membrane and other clinical concepts derived from psychotherapeutic work with survivors of natural disasters. *Psychiatric Annals, 15,* 153–160.

Livingston, H., Livingston, M., & Fell, S. (1994). The Lockerbie disaster: A 3-year follow-up of elderly victims. *International Journal of Geriatric Psychiatry, 9,* 989–994.

Logue, J. N., Melick, M. E., & Hansen, H. (1981). Research issues and directions in the epidemiology of health effects of disasters. *Epidemiologic Reviews, 3,* 140–162.

Lucas, R. A. (1969). *Men in crisis: A study of a mine disaster.* New York: Basic Books.

McCarroll, J., Fullerton, C., Ursano, R., & Hermsen, J. (1996). Posttraumatic stress symptoms following forensic dental identification: Mt Carmel, Waco, Texas. *American Journal of Psychiatry, 153,* 778–782.

Munnichs, J. (1977). Linkages of old people with their families and bureaucracy in a welfare state, the Netherlands. In E. Shanas & M. Sussman (Eds.), *Family, bureaucracy, and the elderly.* Durham, NC: Duke University Press.

Myers, D. (1985). Helping the helpers: A training manual. In D. M. Hartsough & D. G. Myers (Eds.), *Disaster work and mental health: Prevention and control of stress among workers* (DHHS Publication No. ADM 87-1422). Washington, DC: U.S. Government Printing Office.

Myers, D. (1989a). Mental health and disaster: Preventive approaches to intervention. In R. Gist & B. Lubin (Eds.), *Psychosocial aspects of disaster.* New York: Wiley.

Myers, D. (1989b). *Training manual: Disaster mental health.* Unpublished manuscript. Sacramento, CA: California Department of Mental Health.

Myers, D. (1991). Emotional recovery from the Loma Prieta earthquake. *Networks: Earthquake Preparedness News, 6*(1), 6–7.

Myers, D. (1992). *Patterns of psychological response to disaster: Loma Prieta earthquake, Los Angeles riots, and East Bay fire.* Paper presented at the symposium conducted by Alta Bates Medical Center and City of Berkeley Mental Health Services October, Berkeley, CA.

Myers, D. (1994a). *Disaster response and recovery: A handbook for mental health professionals* (DHHS Publication No. SMA 94-3010). Washington, DC: U.S. Government Printing Office.

Myers, D. (1994b). Psychological recovery from disaster: Some key concepts for delivery of mental health services. *National Center for Post-Traumatic Stress Disorder Clinical Quarterly, 4*(2), 1–5.

Myers, D., O'Callahan, W., & Peuler, J. (1984). *Human response to disaster: Training human service workers* [Videotape]. California Department of Mental Health, National Institute of Mental Health, and Federal Emergency Management Agency.

Myers, D., Spofford, P., & Young, B. (1996). *Responding to traumatic events: A training manual.* Pacific Grove, CA: National Disaster Mental Health Consultants.

Myers, D., & Zunin, L. M. (1990). *Disaster mental health.* Unpublished training manual.

Myers, D., Zunin, H. S., & Zunin, L. M. (1990). Grief: The art of coping with tragedy. *Today's Supervisor, 6*(11), 14–15.

Norris, F. J., Friedman, M. J., Watson, P. J., Byrne, C. M., Diaz, E., & Kaniasty, K. (2002). 60,000 disaster victims speak: Part I. An empirical review of the empirical literature, 1981–2001. *Psychiatry, 65,* 207–239.

Norris, F., & Kaniasty, K. (1996). Received and perceived social support in times of stress: A test of the social support deterioration deterrence model. *Journal of Personality and Social Psychology, 71,* 498–511.

Norris, F., Perilla, J., Ibanez, G., & Murphy, A. (2001). Sex differences in symptoms of post-traumatic stress: Does culture play a role? *Journal of Traumatic Stress, 14,* 7–28.

Norris, F., & Uhl, G. (1993). Chronic stress as a mediator of acute stress: The case of Hurricane Hugo. *Journal of Applied Social Psychology, 23,* 1263–1284.

North, C., Nixon, S., Shariat, S., Mallonee, S., McMillen, J., Spitznagel, E., et al. (1999). Psychiatric disorders among survivors of the Oklahoma City bombing. *Journal of the American Medical Association, 282,* 755–762.

North, C., Spitznagel, E., & Smith, E. (2001). A prospective study of coping after exposure to a mass murder episode. *Annals of Clinical Psychiatry, 13,* 81–81 .

Ochberg, F. M. (Ed.). (1988). *Post-traumatic therapy and victims of violence.* New York: Brunner/Mazel.

Palinkas, L., Russel, J., Downs, M., & Petterson, J. (1992). Ethnic differneces in stress, coping, and depressive symptoms after the Exxon Valdez oil spill. *Journal of Nervous and Mental Disorders, 180,* 287–295.

Perilla, J., Norris, F., & Lavizzo, E. (2002). Ethnicity, culture, and disaster response: Identifying and explaining ethnic differences in PTSD six months after Hurricane Andrew. *Journal of Social and Clinical Psychology, 21,* 20–45.

Project COPE. (1983). *A community-based mental health response to disaster.* Final Report: FEMA Crisis Counseling Project. Santa Cruz, CA: County of Santa Cruz Community Mental Health Services.

Quarantelli, E. L. (1954). The nature and conditions of panic. *American Journal of Sociology, 60,* 267–275.

Quarantelli, E. L. (1957). The behavior of panic participants. *Sociology and Social Research, 41,* 187–194.

Quarantelli, E. L. (1986). What is disaster? The need for clarification in definition and conceptualization in research. In B. J. Sowder & M. Lystad (Eds.), *Disasters and mental health: Contemporary perspectives and innovations in services to disaster victims.* Washington, DC: American Psychiatric Press.

Quarantelli, E. L. (1987). What should we study? Questions and suggestions for researchers about the concept of disasters. *International Journal of Mass Emergencies and Disasters, 5*(1), 7–32.

Quarantelli, E. L. (Ed.). (1998). *What is a disaster? Perspectives on the question.* London: Routledge.

Quarantelli, E. L., & Dynes, R. R. (1970). Property norms and looting: Their patterns in community crises. *Phylon, 31,* 168–182.

Quarantelli, E. L., & Dynes, R. R. (1972). When disaster strikes. *Psychology Today, 5,* 67–70.

Raphael, B. (1986). *When disaster strikes: How individuals and communities cope with catastrophe.* New York: Basic Books.

Reisner, M. (1986). *Cadillac desert.* New York: Viking.

Rosenheck, R., & Fontana, A. (1994). Long-term sequelae of combat in World War II, Korea, and Vietnam: A comparative study. In R. J. Ursano, B. G. McCaughey, & C. S. Fullerton (Eds.), *Individual and community responses to trauma and disaster.* Cambridge, UK: Cambridge University Press.

Scanlon-Schlipp, A. M., & Levesque, J. (1981). Helping the patient cope with the sequelae of trauma through the self-help group approach. *The Journal of Trauma, 21,* 135–139.

Seniors cope with disaster [Videotape]. (1993). San Bernardino County, CA: Department of Mental Health.

Shore, J., Tatum, E., & Vollmer, W. (1986). Psychiatric reactions to disaster: The Mount St. Helens experience. *American Journal of Psychiatry, 143,* 590–595.

Smith, E. M., North, C. S., & Price, P. C. (1988). Response to technological accidents. In M. Lystad (Ed.), *Mental health response to mass emergencies: Theory and practice.* New York: Brunner/Mazel.

Solomon, S. D. (1986a). Enhancing social support for disaster victims. In B. J. Sowder & M. Lystad (Eds.), *Disasters and mental health: Contemporary perspectives and innovations in services to disaster victims.* Washington, DC: American Psychiatric Press.

Solomon, S. D. (1986b). Mobilizing social support networks in times of disaster. In C. R. Figley (Ed.), *Trauma and its wake: Vol. 2. Traumatic stress theory, research, and intervention.* New York: Brunner/Mazel.

Solomon, S. D. (1989). Evaluation and research issues in assessing disaster's effects. In R. Gist & B. Lubin (Eds.), *Psychosocial aspects of disaster.* New York: Wiley.

Solomon, S. D., & Green, B. L. (1992). Mental health effects of natural and human-made disasters. *PTSD Research Quarterly, 3*(1), 1–8.

Solomon S. D., Smith, E. M., Robins, L. N., & Fischbach, R. L. (1987). Social involvement as a mediator of disaster-induced stress. *Journal of Applied Social Psychology, 17,* 1092–1112.

Sorensen, J., Soderstrom, J., Coperhaver, E., Carnes, S., & Bolin, R. (1987). *The impacts of hazardous technology: The psychosocial effects of restarting TMI-1.* Albany, NY: SUNY Press.

Spungen, D. (1998). *Homicide: The hidden victims.* Thousand Oaks, CA: Sage.

Stein, B., & Myers, D. (1999). Emotional intervention after trauma: A guide for primary care physicians. *Journal of the American Medical Women's Association, 54,* 60–64.

Stretch, R. H. (1986). Post-traumatic stress disorder among Vietnam and Vietnam-era veterans. In C. R. Figley (Ed.), *Trauma and its wake: Vol. 2. Traumatic stress theory, research, and intervention.* New York: Brunner/Mazel.

Ursano, R. J., & McCarroll, J. E. (1994). Exposure to traumatic death: The nature of the stressor. In R. J. Ursano, B. G. McCaughey, & C. S. Fullerton (Eds), *Individual and community responses to trauma and disaster.* Cambridge, UK: Cambridge University Press.

Ursano, R. J., McCaughey, B. G., & Fullerton, C. S. (Eds.). (1994). *Individual and community responses to trauma and disaster.* Cambridge, UK: Cambridge University Press.

Warheit, G. J. (1986). A propositional paradigm for estimating the impact of disasters on mental health. In B. J. Sowder & M. Lystad (Eds.), *Disasters and mental health: Contemporary perspectives and innovations in services to disaster victims.* Washington, DC: American Psychiatric Press.

Warheit, G. J. (1988). Disasters and their mental health consequences: Issues, findings, and future trends. In M. Lystad (Ed.), *Mental health response to mass emergencies: Theory and practice.* New York: Brunner/Mazel.

Warheit, G., Zimmerman, R., Khoury, E., Vega, W., & Gil, A. (1996). Disaster related stresses, depressive signs and symptoms, and suicidal ideation among a multi-racial/ethnic sample of adolescents: A longitudinal analysis. *Journal of Child Psychology and Psychiatric and Allied Disciplines, 37,* 435–444.

Weaver, J. D. (1995). *Disasters: Mental health interventions.* Sarasota, FL: Professional Resource Press.

Weisaeth, L. (1994). Psychosocial and psychiatric aspects of technological disasters. In R. J. Ursano, B. G. McCaughey, & C. S. Fullerton (Eds.), *Individual and community responses to trauma and disaster.* Cambridge, UK: Cambridge University Press.

Young, M. A. (1989). Crime, violence, and terrorism. In R. Gist & B. L. Lubin (Eds.), *Psychosocial aspects of disaster.* New York: Wiley.

Young, B. H., Ford, J. D., Ruzek, J. I., Friedman, M. J., & Gusman, F. D. (1998). *Disaster mental health services: A guidebook for clinicians.* Menlo Park, CA and White River Junction, VT: Department of Veterans Affairs.

Yule, W., Bolton, D., Udwin, O., O'Ryan, D., & Nurrish, J. (2000). The long-term psychological effects of a disaster experienced in adolescence: I. The incidence and course of PTSD. *Journal of Child Psychology and Psychiatry and Allied Disciplines, 41,* 503–511.

Zunin, L. M., & Myers, D. (1990). *Phases of disaster.* Unpublished training materials.

Zunin, L. M., & Zunin, H. S. (1991). *The art of condolence: What to write, what to say, what to do at a time of loss.* New York: HarperCollins.

2

SPECIAL POPULATIONS IN DISASTER

INDIVIDUALS EXPERIENCE DISASTER IN THEIR OWN, UNIQUE WAY. WHAT happens to people during the impact and aftermath of a disaster varies from person to person and is influenced by what they saw, heard, felt, thought, feared; what they lost (loved ones, friends, property, job, health); and the demands the postdisaster environment places on them.

In addition, individuals bring their own unique pattern of beliefs, behaviors, and resources to the disaster experience. Understanding and assessing their stress reactions to disaster must take into consideration a number of important areas about each survivor's unique background (modified from Young, Ford, Ruzek, Friedman, & Guzman, 1998):

- Individual biopsychosocial resources and vulnerabilities
- Individual sociovocational resources and limitations
- Family heritage and dynamics
- Ethnocultural and spiritual beliefs, values, and traditions
- Community practices, norms, and resources
- Prior experience with trauma
- Specific experiences during and since the disaster

Chapter 1 lists numerous factors that can cause the disaster to be traumatic for individuals. In simplified format, the following "risk factors" should be considered in assessing the potential for traumatic stress reactions in survivors:

- Death or serious injury of a loved one
- Severe personal injury
- Fear of own or a loved one's death

- Destruction or major damage to dwelling
- Substantial property loss
- Loss of job
- Exposure to traumatic stimuli (sensory exposure to distressing sights, sounds, odors, events)
- Familiarity or identification with victims
- Worry about safety of significant others
- Stress reactions of significant others
- Preexisting stress
- Major trauma or loss, especially within the past year
- Lack of social support
- Lack of material supports
- Poor coping skills based on past experiences

Although the reactions of individuals to disaster will vary, most fall into a common group of posttraumatic symptoms that have been called by experienced disaster mental health practitioners as the "normal reactions of normal people to an abnormal event." This phrase reassures most disaster survivors that, though they are stressed by the situation and distressed by their stress symptoms, their reactions are common, normal under the circumstances, and usually not a reason for alarm. Researchers point out that most people fully recover from moderate stress reactions within 6 to 16 months (Baum & Fleming, 1993 ; Bravo, Rubio-Stipec, Canino, Woodbury, & Ribera, 1990; Dohrenwend et al., 1981; Green & Lindy, 1994; La Greca, Silverman, Vernberg, & Prinstein, 1996; Steinglass & Gerrity, 1990; Vernberg, LaGreca, Silverman, & Prinstein, 1996). Most disaster victims can be assisted with a range of mental health services of a crisis intervention nature. However, Norris et al. (2002a) found that 39% of samples of disaster victims had severe to very severe impairment, so in addition to crisis intervention services, resources for psychological treatment are also imperative in a disaster-impacted community.

DeWolfe (2000) provides a list of thoughts, feelings, and behaviors that are common to all who experience a disaster:

- Concern for basic survival
- Grief over loss of loved ones and loss of valued and meaningful possessions
- Fear and anxiety about personal safety and the physical safety of loved ones
- Sleep disturbances, often including nightmares and imagery from the disaster

- Concerns about relocation and related isolation or crowded living conditions
- Need to talk about events and feelings associated with the disaster
- Need to feel one is a part of the community and its disaster recovery efforts

Each disaster-impacted community has its own demographic composition, cultural representation, and prior history of disasters or other traumatic events. When disaster program planners review the groups impacted by a disaster in their community, consideration should be given to special groups unique to the locale (DeWolfe, 2000). This chapter will discuss the impact of disaster under the following classifications:

- Age groups
- Gender
- Cultural groups
- Socioeconomic groups
- People with serious and persistent mental illness

AGE GROUPS

CHILDREN AND ADOLESCENTS

For a number of reasons, children are considered at risk for psychological problems following a disaster. First, their cognitive skills are less developed than adults and may limit the ways in which children understand and process events. Their experience coping with adversity may likewise be limited, and they may lack adult coping skills and defense mechanisms for managing stress. Their limited verbal skills may impede their processing of events and expression of reactions. They are limited in their ability to act independently, and are dependent on the adults in their lives for material resources and psychological support. Most importantly, their development is at risk if they remain preoccupied with the trauma of the disaster and are unable to proceed with the normal activities and developmental tasks of childhood.

Norris et al. (2002a), in reviewing 20 years of research on the psychological impacts of disaster, found that sample groups composed of youth were more likely to fall into the severe range of impairment than samples composed of adults. Almost 52% of the school-age samples experienced severe or very severe effects compared to 42% of the adult survivor samples. The research review indicated that preschool children may not be highly affected. The four preschool samples showed children to be affected very little, aside from some short-term behavioral problems (Bromet et al., 2000; Cornely & Bromet, 1986; Durkin, Khan, Davidson, Zaman, & Stein, 1993;

Saylor, Swenson, & Powell, 1992). Green et al. (1991) found children younger than 8 to be less affected by the Buffalo Creek dam disaster than youth aged 8–15. However, other researchers found that Hurricane Hugo most affected youths from the ages of 9–12, with less effects in the 13–16 age range (Lonigan, Shannon, Taylor, Finch, & Sallee, 1994; Shannon, Lonigan, Finch, & Taylor, 1994).

Review of the disaster literature shows that parents have a strong influence on children's psychological response to disaster (Norris et al., 2002a; Wasserstein & La Greca, 1998). After the Buffalo Creek dam collapse, psychopathology in parents was predictive of negative outcomes for children, and parents who were less irritable and more supportive had healthier children (Gleser, Green, & Winget, 1981). A summary of the research finds that parental distress is a strong, and sometimes the strongest, predictor of children's distress (Norris et al., 2002a).

The common responses of children and adolescents fall into the following categories:

1. *Change in behavior*: Any significant change in a child's behavior, occurring at or after the time of the disaster, may be an indication that the child is emotionally affected. A normally extroverted child may become quiet or may withdraw; a normally well-behaved child may become aggressive or defiant. A child may suddenly become very well behaved in an effort to avoid placing additional demands or burden on an already stressed family.
2. *Fear and anxiety*: Children may be fearful of a recurrence of the disaster, of the place they were in when the disaster occurred, and of separation from parents, or may become more fearful and worried in general. Specific fears may relate to injury, death, separation, and loss.
3. *Reexperiencing the disaster*: They may experience intrusive thoughts and memories of the event, dreams of the disaster or other scary dreams, or may engage in repetitive play about the disaster and their feelings.
4. *Confusion*: Children may not understand the cause of the disaster and their own or others' response to the event, and may be confused and concerned about their future and what will happen next.
5. *Regression*: Most children and adolescents experience some regression to an earlier phase of development. Young children may return to thumb-sucking, bed-wetting, or fighting with siblings, and may show a decline in previously responsible behavior. Teens may alternate between responsible adult-like behavior and regression to more dependent roles.

6. *School problems*: Children may try to avoid school, possibly out of fear of separation from the family or the family's fear of separation from the child. Children may fall behind in their assignments due to absence, fatigue, or mental preoccupation with the disaster, and may experience a decline in grades. Behavior changes may result in disciplinary measures and further stress for the child.

7. *Sleep problems*: Sleep disturbance is one of the most common reactions to disaster for children and adolescents (Farberow & Gordon, 1981). Behaviors may include resistance to bedtime, not wanting to sleep alone, desire to sleep with the light on, wakefulness, early rising, and nightmares.

8. *Physical complaints*: Children and teens may suffer from a wide range of physical complaints. Headaches and stomachaches are among the most common. Frequently, the school nurse or other school personnel may identify a pattern of physical symptoms in a child and may recognize it as a symptom of disaster-related stress.

DeWolfe (2000), Farberow and Gordon (1981), Lystad (1985), Myers (1989), Norris et al. (2002a), Pynoos and Nader (1993), and Young et al. (1998) list some of the typical reactions of various age groups, along with appropriate interventions:

PRESCHOOL (1–5)

Behavioral

- Resumption of bed-wetting, thumb-sucking
- Clinginess
- Separation anxiety
- Fears of the dark, animals, or weather
- Avoidance of sleeping alone
- Increased crying
- Regression
- Incontinence
- Dependency
- Helplessness and passivity
- Hyperactivity
- Lack of verbalization
- Withdrawal
- Aggressive behavior

Physical

- Loss of appetite
- Stomachaches

- Nausea
- Sleep problems, nightmares, refusing to sleep alone
- Speech difficulties
- Tics
- Loss of bladder or bowel control

Emotional and cognitive
- Fears
- Anxiety and insecurity
- Powerlessness
- Irritability
- Angry outbursts, temper tantrums
- Sadness
- Confusion
- Difficulty identifying feelings

Interventions
- Give verbal assurance, support, rest, and physical comfort
- Provide frequent attention
- Arrange for consistent caretaking
- Provide comforting bedtime routines
- Avoid unnecessary separations
- Allow time-limited regression
- Permit child to sleep in parents' room temporarily
- Encourage expression regarding losses (i.e., deaths, pets, toys)
- Give names to feelings
- Offer repeated clarifications when child is confused
- Provide explanations of death, if necessary
- Monitor media exposure to disaster trauma
- Encourage expression through play activities

CHILDHOOD (6–11)
Behavioral
- Decline in school performance
- School avoidance
- Aggressive behavior at home or school
- Disobedience
- Hyperactive or silly behavior
- Whining, clinging, acting like a younger child
- Fighting with siblings or friends
- Increased competition with younger siblings for parents' attention
- Decline in previously responsible behavior (chores, etc.)

- Inability to enjoy previously pleasurable activities
- Withdrawal
- Traumatic play and retelling

Physical
- Change in appetite
- Headaches
- Stomachaches, nausea
- Sleep disturbances, nightmares
- Hearing or visual problems

Emotional and cognitive
- Trouble concentrating, distractibility
- Irrational fears
- Fear of darkness
- Irritability
- Depression
- Angry outbursts
- Obsessive preoccupation with disaster or safety
- Responsibility and guilt for the trauma
- Monitoring parents' anxieties
- Separation anxiety
- Excessive concern for others

Interventions
- Give additional attention and consideration
- Patience and tolerance
- Relax expectations of performance at home and at school temporarily
- Set gentle but firm limits for acting out behavior
- Provide structured but undemanding home chores and rehabilitation activities
- Encourage verbal and play expression of thoughts and feelings
- Listen with understanding to the child's repeated retelling of disaster event
- Provide realistic, age-appropriate information about what happened and will happen next
- Identify and discuss "triggers" and reminders that bring up memories and feelings
- Involve the child in preparation of family emergency kit, home drills
- Rehearse safety measures for future disasters

- Develop school disaster program for peer support, expressive activities, education on disasters, preparedness planning, identifying at-risk children

PRE-ADOLESCENCE AND ADOLESCENCE (12–18)

Behavioral
- Decline in academic performance
- Rebellion at home or school
- Resistance to authority
- Decline in previous responsible behavior
- Agitation or decrease in energy level, apathy
- Aggressive behavior
- Antisocial behavior
- Social withdrawal
- Substance abuse
- Life-threatening acting out (suicide, reckless driving, unsafe sex)
- Premature adult behaviors and attitudes ("too old, too soon")
- Lack of involvement in community recovery activities

Physical
- Appetite changes
- Headaches
- Gastrointestinal problems
- Skin eruptions
- Complaints of vague aches and pains
- Sleep problems
- Menstrual irregularity

Emotional and cognitive
- Loss of interest in peer social activities, hobbies, recreation
- Sadness or depression
- Feelings of inadequacy and helplessness
- Shame and guilt
- Self-consciousness, preoccupation with self
- Confusion

Interventions
- Give additional attention and consideration
- Relax expectations of performance at home and school (temporarily)
- Encourage discussion of disaster experiences with peers and significant adults
- Avoid insistence on discussion of feelings with parents

- Encourage physical activities
- Rehearse family safety measures for future disasters
- Support resumption of social activities, athletics, clubs, and so on
- Urge participation in community rehabilitation and reclamation work
- Address suicidal ideation and reckless behavior
- Develop school programs for peer support and debriefing, preparedness planning, volunteer community recovery, identifying at-risk teens

ADULTS

Adult responsibilities include attention to family, home, career, financial stability, social relationships, and community activities. Some family units include adults, children, and also extended family and elderly parents. Predisaster life often involves maintaining a precarious balance between competing demands. Following a disaster, this balance can be lost with the introduction of the enormous time, financial, physical, emotional, and spiritual demands of recovery (DeWolfe, 2000). Thompson, Norris, and Hanacek (1993) found an increased risk for psychological problems among middle-aged adults after Hurricane Hugo to be explained by greater chronic stress and burdens. What was found to be important was the balance of support received and support given. Both younger adult and older adult groups maintained a good balance between the amount of support received and the amount provided to others. Middle-aged people received more support, but they provided even more (Norris et al., 2002a).

In Norris and others' review of 20 years of disaster research (2002), they examined the reactions of 17 samples of adult disaster victims. In 88% of the samples, the psychological impact of disaster declined with age. In every American sample in which middle-aged adults were differentiated from younger and older adults, the middle-aged adults were most severely and adversely affected. The stresses following disaster can result in a wide variety of behavioral, physical, emotional, and cognitive symptoms.

CULTURAL FACTORS AND AGE

Cultural, spiritual, and gender-based factors may affect how individuals express their emotions, seek support, utilize resources, and react psychologically. For example, Norris, Kaniasty, Conrad, Inman, & Murphy (2002b) found that culture affected age-related psychological effects. In their cross-cultural postdisaster study of American, Mexican, and Polish adults, they found that middle-aged Americans were most affected, whereas among Mexicans and Poles, the most affected were the youth and older adults, respectively.

Anthropological research shows differences in family life cycles among these cultures that undoubtedly account for the variances. Thus, it is important to recognize that worldwide, there is no one consistent affect of age; rather, it is dependent upon the social, economic, cultural, historical, and other factors in the impacted community.

FAMILY FACTORS AMONG ADULTS

In reviewing 19 articles regarding family factors in the aftermath of disaster, Norris et al. (2002a) found some data suggesting that married status is actually a risk (Brooks & McKinlay, 1992), especially for women (Gleser et al., 1981; Solomon, 2002). For men, the reverse is sometimes true (Fullerton, Ursano, Tzu-Cheg, & Bhartiya, 1999; Ursano, Fullerton, Kao, & Bhartiy, 1995). After the Buffalo Creek dam collapse in 1972, married women had more overall symptom severity than unmarried women, although men's symptoms did not differ related to marital status (Gleser et al., 1981). An interesting finding in this study is that, with effects of severity of exposure and other demographics controlled, husbands' symptom severity predicted their wives' symptom severity, and vice versa. However, the husbands affecting the wives' symptom severity was stronger than the wives predicting the husbands' symptom severity (Norris et al., 2002a). In any case, it has been found that marital stress increases after disasters (Norris & Uhl, 1993).

Parenthood is also associated with postdisaster stress, as found by Gleser et al. (1981), who determined that the presence of children was positively correlated with symptomatology in all but unmarried women. In the St. Louis flood/dioxin contamination disaster, Solomon et al. found adults with children more impacted with anxiety and other symptoms than those without children (Solomon, Bravo, Rubio-Stipec, & Canino, 1993). When there is fear of future health threats for their children, mothers become extremely concerned about their children's health (Norris et al., 2002a). After the Three Mile Island nuclear accident, mothers with young children were particularly at risk, due to concerns about long-term health effects of exposure (Bromet, Parkinson, Schulberg, & Gondek, 1982). Likewise, after Chernobyl, only women with children under the age of 18 showed residual psychological effects after 6 years (Havenaar et al., 1997).

DeWolfe (2000), Myers (1989), Norris et al. (2002a), and Young et al. (1998) have described the following reactions among adults:

Behavioral
- Crying
- Anger and aggression
- Hyperactivity and restlessness

- "Robot-like" behavior
- Increased level of activity in response to disaster-related demands
- Decreased efficiency and effectiveness of activities
- Decline in job or academic performance
- Absences from work
- Increased irritability, conflict, and estrangement within family
- Domestic violence
- Hypervigilance for danger
- Excessive disaster planning and preparedness activities
- Isolation and withdrawal
- Change in eating patterns
- Substance abuse
- Avoidance of reminders of the disaster
- "Trigger" and anniversary reactions

Physical
- Fatigue, exhaustion
- Sleep problems (insomnia, nightmares, early wakening)
- Arousal and increased startle response
- Appetite changes, weight gain or loss
- Headache, bodyaches and pains
- Muscle tension
- Gastrointestinal distress
- Impaired immune response
- Increase in allergies
- Worsening of chronic health conditions
- Increase in blood pressure
- Change in libido
- Menstrual irregularities

Emotional and cognitive
- Shock, disbelief, numbness
- Need for information
- Intrusive thoughts, memories, or flashbacks
- Sadness and depression
- Grief about loss of loved ones, home, health, lifestyle, community
- Lost sense of control over life
- Irritability, anger
- Mood swings
- Frustration with relief efforts
- Anxiety
- Fear, worries, insecurity

- Concern about the future
- Despair, hopelessness, helplessness
- Changes in religious faith (strengthening or weakening of beliefs)
- Decreased self-esteem
- Loss of pleasure from regular activities
- Suicidal ideation
- Guilt, self-doubt, self-blame
- Memory problems
- Disorientation and confusion
- Dissociation (e.g., perceptual experience seems "dreamlike," "spacey," or "on automatic pilot")
- Depersonalization, derealization
- Decline in cognitive abilities (problem solving, setting priorities, decision making)
- Impaired concentration and attention
- Time distortion

Interventions

- Provide supportive listening and opportunity to talk in detail about disaster experience
- Give opportunities for grieving over losses
- Assist with prioritizing and problem solving
- Offer information on disaster stress, coping, children's reactions, and impact of disaster on the family
- Facilitate communication among family members
- Encourage use of social supports
- Urge practical steps to resume ordinary day-to-day routines
- Facilitate resumption of normal family, community, school, and work roles
- Assist survivors in taking practical steps to resolve pressing immediate problems caused by the disaster
- Teach relaxation techniques
- Address physical health problems or exacerbation of prior conditions
- Assess and refer when indicated
- Provide information on referral resources

Self-help and coping suggestions for adult survivors include the following (Mitchell & Everly, 2001; Myers, 1995; Myers & Zunin, 1992):

- Be patient and expect change with the passage of time and opportunity to talk about the experience.

- Remember, you are normal and having normal reactions.
- Be willing to talk about what happened and express your thoughts and feelings. This will help you to feel better and to heal more rapidly.
- Talk truthfully with family members about your expectations and needs. Be honest and be flexible.
- Try to maintain as normal a schedule as possible. This includes building in "down time" with family and friends who comfort and support you.
- Be gentle with yourself—there are always things that could have been done differently. "If only" is a temporary way the mind reflects back and tries to make sense of the experience.
- Draw on supports that nurture you. Make time for friends, reading, recreation, religion, meditation, and exercise.
- Play with your children.
- Take care of yourself physically—good diet, adequate sleep, rest, and exercise—even if you do not feel like it.
- If needed, give yourself permission to spend some time alone, but do not totally withdraw from social interaction.
- Reach out—people do care.
- Remember the healing aspects of touch, such as a hug, a pat on the back, a brief neck or back rub.
- Try different forms of self-expression, such as writing, music, dance, art.
- Laugh as much as possible. Cry as much as needed.
- Say goodbye to what is gone.
- Be aware of numbing the pain with overuse of drugs or alcohol.
- Do not neglect health and grooming.
- Avoid becoming distracted, reckless, or accident-prone.
- Stop from time-to-time and take four or five deep, cleansing breaths.
- Attend debriefing groups, support groups, and stress education programs that may be offered.
- Develop and practice disaster plans for home, workplace, and school.
- Remember that healing has three elements—time, talk, and tears.

OLDER ADULTS

It is often assumed that the elderly are at particularly high risk following disaster. Research findings on this assumption, however, present contradictory results. Research by Norris, Phifer, and Kaniasty (1994) found that middle-aged victims (55–64) had the most difficulty coping, a finding previously reported by Gleser et al. (1981). This may be related to the fact that middle-aged adults are most likely to be responsible for both children and parents. In addition, they are approaching retirement, and financial and material losses may threaten their dreams for their retirement years. Norris et al. (2002a) found that adults aged 65–74 were affected relatively little by disaster. Very old adults (75+) were affected more than those aged 65–74 (perhaps due to poorer health), but still affected less than middle-aged victims (Norris et al., 2002a). In the review of the 20 years of research on psychological impacts of disaster conducted by Norris et al. (2002), only 2 out of 17 samples of adults found older persons at greater risk than other adults. These studies were a sample of adults impacted by the Newcastle earthquake in Australia (Ticehurst, Webster, Carr, & Lewin, 1996) and a sample of adults effected by the Polish floods of 1997 (Norris et al., 2002b).

Eysenck (1983) proposed that exposure to stress increases resistance to subsequent stress and ultimately can protect individuals from harm. Age has particular relevance to this theory of "stress inoculation" in that, relative to younger adults, older persons bring a rich history of experience to bear on any crisis. Norris and Murrell (1988) suggest that older adults may in fact be a particularly hardy subpopulation, in that their prior experience with handling life's adversities may have prepared them better than most for coping with the losses and disruption caused by disaster. Bell, Kara, and Batterson (1978) proposed that it was experience with crisis that accounted for the resilience of older adults in a study of tornado victims. In corroboration, other studies have also found that older persons either are not seriously affected by disasters (Cohen & Poulshock, 1977; Kilijanek & Drabek, 1979; Melnick & Logue, 1985–1986) or are affected less than are younger victims (Bolin & Klenow, 1982–1983; Huerta & Horton, 1978; Ollendick & Hoffman, 1982). Taken together, these findings challenge the earlier assumption that older persons are at high risk following disasters (Norris & Murrell, 1988).

Norris et al. (1994) did find that the floods they studied influenced the mental and physical health of older victims. Those who suffered losses or damages commonly felt down in the dumps, worried, anxious, fearful, and more easily upset. However, they did not develop psychiatric illnesses. Likewise, they experienced physical symptoms of fatigue (feeling worn out, having trouble sleeping, and having more aches and pains), but did not develop major physical illnesses. They found, however, that older adults' reactions to disaster lasted much longer than their reactions to other life trauma and losses. Whereas the emotional reactions of older adults to other traumatic life events were generally limited to about 6 months, their reactions to the floods persisted for up to 2 years. In their work, Norris and Murrell (1990) found that the only other event to engender such enduring effects was the death of one's spouse.

Although in general older adults are not particularly at high risk for emotional problems following disaster, their individual situation must be reviewed, including their predisaster health and income, degree of independence, and coping skills at the time of evaluation. In addition, the impact of the disaster, including losses and trauma exposure, must be considered.

We also know from disaster experience and research that older adults with financial limitations tend to live in lower-cost dwellings that are susceptible to disaster damages due to the site and age of the buildings. Their limited income may make it difficult to make repairs or to afford an increase in rent after landlords have made repairs (Myers, 1990). They may continue to live in damaged or unsanitary conditions because they do not have the money, physical strength, stamina, or cognitive abilities to undertake cleanup and restoration (DeWolfe, 2000). Problems of vision, hearing, or mobility may cause difficulties in obtaining resources and starting over (Myers, 1990), and may present challenges to continued independent living.

Physical injury and exacerbation of preexisting illnesses may also hinder recovery for older adults. Research indicates that they are less likely to heed warnings, to perceive situations as being hazardous, and to evacuate, which can lead to injuries and traumatic rescues. Older persons may not have the ability to use automobiles or have access to private or public transportation, which may limit their opportunity to shop, obtain water or medications, or relocate (Young et al., 1998).

A major concern of the elderly is loss of independence or institutionalization. When injuries, health problems, financial problems, or other disaster-related needs arise, they tend to underreport them, to conceal the full extent of the problems, and to postpone seeking medical attention. They also tend to underutilize disaster assistance compared to other age groups (Myers, 1990), reflecting a generational emphasis on independence and "carrying one's own weight" and the stigma of "public welfare" if they accept disaster assistance from the government or an agency (Norris et al., 1994). They do not react to situations as quickly as younger adults, and may not seek agency assistance until deadlines for applications are past (Myers, 1990). Mobility impairment or lack of transportation may make it impossible for them to go to disaster assistance centers. They may not have prior experience working through a bureaucratic system. This is often true for older women whose spouse assumed responsibility for bureaucratic or financial matters. They may have cognitive or vision problems that present difficulties in completing applications or understanding regulations or directions (Young et al., 1998). Because of older adults' reluctance to report problems and seek assistance and their difficulties in physically obtaining assistance, disaster agencies and disaster mental health staff must take a proactive, outreach approach to this population. They may also need to encourage elders to view government assistance as a form of "insurance" that they have purchased through years of paying taxes and to realize that using such resources will not deprive other victims of their fair share of assistance.

Medical and mental health staff must thoroughly assess the impact of the disaster upon the older adults and their health and well-being. Home visits, conducted jointly by a mental health worker and public health nurse, are especially effective. An older person's sense of smell, touch, vision and hearing may be less acute than that of the general population. A hearing loss may cause older adults not to hear what is said in a noisy environment, whereas a diminished sense of smell may mean that they are more apt to eat spoiled food. These diminished faculties can affect their welfare in a disaster services setting and at home alone. They may be more susceptible to the effects of heat or cold, which can be critical if heating or air conditioning is affected by the disaster (Young et al., 1998). Health conditions such as blood pressure and diabetes may be affected by stress, and medication dosages may need to be adjusted. Confusion and memory problems may be exacerbated by disaster stress, and health and medication regimens may be adversely affected. Repeated health and mental health assessments may be necessary to ensure that the health of the elderly person is not declining rapidly over time due to the disaster. Often, concrete practical assistance with housing, finances, replacement of lost possessions, and transportation are necessary (Myers, 1990). Assisting older adults to accept appropriate resources for recovery and stabilization may allow them to continue living independently (DeWolfe, 2000).

Social support is equally important. Encouraging elders to reestablish family and social contacts, to use peer support and support groups, and to find ways to be involved in community recovery efforts is important. Older adults may experience intense grief over the loss of irreplaceable mementos, photographs (some of them passed down through generations), pets, and plants and gardens that were the result of years of effort and care, and were indeed a part of their identity. Mental health workers need to explore the meaning of these losses, encourage grieving, and provide reminders, such as it is never too late to plant a new garden. Older adults working as peer counselors or outreach workers to the elderly community are especially effective in these roles.

Older adults need a sense of control and predictability. Reestablishing routines and having a permanent, clean, and safe place to live can help to increase a sense of security, stability, and control. Feelings of confidence and self-worth can be enhanced by talking about past successes and by setting manageable goals. Because so much has been lost, older individuals also need to restore feelings of connectedness. Many have little left besides memories. Simply helping them to remember and talk about their life can be a starting point that helps them reconnect with their unique perspective as a part of the history of mankind (U.S. Administration on Aging & Kansas Department on Aging, 1995; Young et al., 1998).

Farberow and Frederick (1978), Myers (1990), and DeWolfe (2000) list the disaster stress reactions common among older adults along with appropriate interventions:

Behavioral
- Withdrawal and isolation
- Reluctance to leave home
- Reluctance to report full extent of losses, injuries, or health problems
- Postponement of seeking medical care
- Avoidance of government resources ("welfare")
- Underutilization of insurance
- Mobility impairment
- Difficulty adjusting to relocation

Physical
- Worsening of chronic conditions
- Increased somatic symptoms
- Depression of immune system leading to increased susceptibility to communicable disease
- Accelerated physical decline
- Susceptible to hypo- and hyperthermia
- Physical and sensory limitations (especially sight and hearing) may lead to injuries or interfere with recovery

Emotional and cognitive
- Depression
- Grief
- Suspicion
- Confusion, disorientation
- Memory problems
- Irritability, agitation, anger

- Apathy
- Fears of institutionalization
- Anxiety with unfamiliar surroundings
- Embarrassment about receiving assistance or "handouts"

Interventions
- Do thorough assessment of disaster impact (e.g., repeat observations, geriatric screening questions, home visits, and discussion with family), as problems may be underreported
- Provide strong and frequent verbal reassurance
- Arrange for orienting information
- Assist in resuming routine activities of daily living and socialization as soon as possible
- Give special attention to suitable residential relocation
- Help to reestablish family and social contacts
- Try to reestablish familiar surroundings and acquaintances
- Assist in maintaining or reorganizing medical regimen and medications
- Support in obtaining housing, health, and financial assistance
- Facilitate overcoming physical and psychological barriers to utilization of disaster assistance resources
- Aid with recovery of possessions
- Engage providers of transportation, chore services, meal programs, home health, home visit, and companion services as needed
- Encourage peer support and a buddy system among survivors in disaster recovery activities
- Urge discussion of disaster experiences and expression of emotions
- Encourage involvement in community recovery efforts
- Inspire "starting over" (e.g., planting a new garden, replacing lost possessions, or "giving shelter" to another)
- Encourage disaster preparedness activities in home and neighborhood

GENDER

In their review of 160 samples of disaster victims over 20 years, Norris et al. (2002a) found 49 articles describing a statistically significant gender difference in postdisaster stress, distress, or disorder. Of these, 46 (94%) found that females were more adversely impacted, irrespective of whether they were children, adolescents, or adults, or whether the event was a natural disaster, technological disaster, or incident of mass violence. Women and girls were especially vulnerable to developing PTSD, and numerous disaster studies found them at least twice as vulnerable as men and boys (De la Fuente, 1990; Green et al., 1990; North et al., 1999; Steinglass & Gerrity, 1990). The only exception was that men were more likely than women to abuse alcohol (Dooley & Gunn, 1995; Gleser et al., 1981; North, Smith, & Sptiznagel, 1994).

CULTURAL GROUPS: ISSUES AND CONSIDERATIONS

Culture is defined as the totality of socially transmitted behavior patterns, arts, beliefs, institutions, and all other products of human work and thought, as well as the predominating attitudes and behavior that characterize the functioning of a group or organization (*American heritage dictionary*, 2000). An individual's understanding of the meaning of disaster and their behavioral response to disaster will be governed by cultural beliefs and practices. It is essential that disaster mental health programs and practitioners understand the cultures of a disaster-impacted community and respond specifically and sensitively to the various cultural groups affected (DeWolfe, 2000).

A variety of factors needs to be considered. Specific racial groups may share patterns of belief and behavior that constitute specific cultures, based upon history and life experience. The country of origin will dictate many cultural beliefs and practices, especially for recent immigrants. It is important to understand the nature and quality of life in the country of origin, and the factors leading to immigration (Myers, 1998). In countries where war, oppression, or other trauma forced people to flee, one can expect a preexisting level of posttraumatic stress in some of the population. Disaster scenarios such as mass care shelters or feeding tents, National Guard units, and helicopters may remind people of prior traumatic experiences or of refugee camps, reactivating their trauma. Disasters in the country of origin may also affect behavior. In the 1989 Loma Prieta earthquake in Northern California, many Mexican-American families whose homes were damaged refused to seek refuge in mass care shelters in schools and auditoriums, preferring instead to erect tents and lean-tos in city parks, despite drenching rainstorms after the quake. Many refused to return to their prior homes even after the buildings were evaluated by structural engineers as being safe. The same phenomenon occurred following the 1994 Northridge earthquake in Los Angeles. For these families, the memory of the devastating 1985 Mexico City earthquake was still vivid, whether they had been in Mexico City at the time or had loved ones living there. In that 8.1 magnitude earthquake, followed by a 7.5 quake 36 hr later, the Mexican government issued 5,400 death certificates. However, international relief agencies estimated that over 10,000 people died. Over 100,000 housing units were destroyed and thousands of buildings totally collapsed (Mexico City earthquake, 2000). After the Northridge earthquake, bilingual, bicultural "reassurance teams" of social workers visited families living in tents to assure them of the seismic safety of engineer-inspected buildings, and to encourage them to move out of the tents into more permanent lodging (B. Baird, California Specialized Training Institute, personal communication, June 8, 2001). This example illustrates the importance of understanding the links between events in the country of origin and behavior in a current disaster.

Individuals' immigration status or fear and suspicion of government agencies may negatively influence their willingness to seek disaster assistance (Myers, 1998). Likewise, groups that take pride in their self-reliance may be reluctant to seek or accept help, especially from mental health workers (DeWolfe, 2000). Bolin and Bolton (1986) found that following Hurricane Iwa on the Hawaiian island of Kauai in 1982, only 20% of disaster-affected Japanese families applied for assistance as compared to 50% of affected families from other cultural groups who used aid.

Language barriers may exist, and during times of stress and intense emotion, many people are more comfortable communicating in their native language. Mental health programs must make every effort to provide services by bilingual, preferably bicultural staff. Working through a translator is less than ideal, but a trained translator is always preferable to using a family member, especially children, to translate, because of privacy concerns regarding sensitive issues and the importance of preserving family roles (DeWolfe, 2000).

Literacy is a factor to consider, regardless of language spoken. For individuals with limited literacy, written materials need to be at an appropriate reading level. In addition, alternative forms of communication should be considered, such as radio and television announcements, word of mouth, and brochures and fliers in cartoons, pictures, or symbols.

Styles of verbal and nonverbal communication are also important. Body language, eye contact, and physical proximity or contact during conversation must be understood and respected. In some cultures, verbal expression of emotion is not seen as desirable; rather, stoicism is the respected response to adversity. Finding acceptable and effective mental health approaches requires a thorough understanding of the cultural beliefs about suffering, healing, health, mental health, and asking for or receiving help. Likewise, culture will shape the definition of those who are valued and trusted as helpers, whether physician, priest, shaman, or mental health worker.

Culture influences the definition of a family. Who is included in the family and who makes decisions varies (DeWolfe, 2000). In some cultures, single nuclear groups are the norm, with extended family taking a peripheral (if any) role in activities and decision making. In other cultures, extended families may live together or apart, but are valued, relied on, provide significant social support, assist with child rearing, and participate in decision making. Roles of father, mother, children (in some cases, in order of birth or according to gender), and elders vary from culture to culture. Gender roles, responsibilities, and expectations are also culturally defined (Myers, 1998).

Likewise, specific religions constitute a community of people with a common culture, beliefs, and behaviors. Tradition, rituals and ceremonies, spiritual practices, and symbolism are shared within religions, as well as specific beliefs about good and evil, life, loss, and death. When deaths have occurred in a disaster, religious beliefs may dictate the care and final disposition of a body, the timeframe for burial or cremation, and the rituals with which a body is handled. Sometimes, a disaster precludes the return of a body to loved ones for disposition. In the crash of Alaska Airlines Flight 261 in January 2000, human remains were not identified for everyone who died on the flight. The same situation occurred in the February 2001 collision of the USS Greenville and the fishing vessel Ehime Maru. In these situations, spiritual care leaders of the family's religion can help them to understand and cope with the absence of a body and the inability to lay their loved one to rest within the requirements and traditions of their faith.

Religion and personal philosophy may also influence a person's beliefs about the cause and meaning of disaster. Whereas some see disaster as an act of nature or of man, others see it as "God's will," as a form of punishment, or simply as fate. In some cases, belief about the cause and meaning of the disaster will influence an individual's behavior in the aftermath. Following the 1989 Loma Prieta earthquake, mental health outreach workers encouraged citizens to develop personal disaster preparedness plans in their homes, preparedness being the antidote for anxiety about aftershocks or another earthquake. In the Hispanic community, outreach workers used churches as a place to make preparedness presentations to people, addressing congregations and suggesting supplies to have on hand, and so on. At one church service, a woman raised her hand during the presentation and said, "The earthquake was God's will. If he wants to send another one, and it's my time to go, buying flashlights and storing water isn't going to save me. Why should I bother?" The outreach worker making the presentation answered, "Well, God sent a big flood once, but he told Noah to get ready and build an ark." Only someone with knowledge of scripture (and a quick wit) could have answered the woman's question within the context of her religious belief.

In summary, it is essential that disaster mental health workers become familiar with the cultural norms, traditions, local history, and community politics from leaders and human service workers indigenous to the groups they are serving. Workers are most effective when they are bilingual and bicultural. Cultural sensitivity is conveyed when disaster information and application procedures and forms are translated into primary spoken languages and available in nonwritten forms. When developing disaster mental health programs, establishing working relationships with trusted organizations, service providers, religious and community leaders is helpful. Being respectful, nonjudgmental, well-informed, and following through on stated plans dependably is especially important for disaster mental health workers seeking to establish the trust of a particular cultural group (Farberow & Frederick, 1978; DeWolfe, 2000).

SOCIOECONOMIC GROUPS

Many affluent, middle- to upper-middle class people live with a sense of security and see themselves as invulnerable to the devastation and tragedy associated with disasters. Because of their financial resources and life situations, they may have been protected from financial crises in the past, and most have purchased insurance for protection in the future. For these families, shock, disbelief, self-blame, and anger can predominate after a major disaster, as the reality of losses and the hard work of recovery begins to sink in (DeWolfe, 2000).

Families with healthy incomes may never have had to accept assistance from social service agencies before. In the immediate aftermath of the disaster, they may find themselves staying in a mass-care shelter, and they may need to accept clothing, food, money, and personal care items from disaster relief agencies. This can be very difficult and sometimes humiliating for them. However, many have insurance, financial, social, and family resources that can be engaged relatively quickly and that can help to buffer the disaster's impact (DeWolfe, 2000).

Middle- and higher-income families often utilize professionals for support and assistance. Disaster mental health programs can educate local healthcare professionals and religious leaders about disaster stress so that disaster issues can be addressed in their care to survivors (DeWolfe, 2000). Stein and Myers (1999) and the Center for Mental Health Services (1995) are helpful resources for these professionals.

Poor families and large families have the most trouble recovering from disaster (Bolin & Bolton, 1986). Norris et al. (2002a) found that in 13 out of 14 groups studied in the disaster literature (93%), lower socioeconomic status was consistently associated with greater postdisaster distress. Large families may have more financially nonproductive dependents. Low-income groups may be disadvantaged in disaster because they live in housing that is more vulnerable to damages: older buildings vulnerable to fire; dwellings in low-lying areas prone to flooding; mobile homes subject to wind, storm, and earthquake damage. In the Coalinga, California, earthquake in 1983, Hispanics were twice as likely to have suffered a high level of structural damage as Caucasians (Bolin & Bolton, 1986).

In addition, low-income families or individuals have fewer financial and material resources and often do not have insurance coverage or savings. If low-income disaster survivors have been renters, they may be faced with unaffordable rent increases after landlords have invested money to repair their rental units (DeWolfe, 2000). Although kinship reliance is an important part of emotional recovery, low-income families often are not a source of economic aid (Bolin & Bolton, 1986). Thus, low-income survivors may have the social support of extended family, but kin may not have the space or financial ability to provide housing or other needed resources postdisaster. Finding affordable postdisaster housing may be a long and arduous process. Usually, survivors with the fewest resources are those who stay in mass care shelters the longest because housing is not available. They may be dislocated to temporary disaster housing that is undesirable and may be removed in distance from their original neighborhood and family and friends.

Often, low-income families move multiple times after disaster, attempting to find housing that is suitable, affordable, safe, and in a familiar neighborhood. Bolin and Bolton (1986) reported that low-income Hispanic families were more likely than Caucasians to have been displaced more than twice after the Coalinga earthquake. Relocation may make transportation and getting to appointments more difficult (DeWolfe, 2000), and children may suffer by being moved to a new school away from familiar teachers and friends.

Government disaster programs provide only for serious and urgent needs, and do not replace all losses. Because of limited income, it is more difficult for those of lower socioeconomic class to qualify for some government programs, such as homeowner loans for rebuilding (Bolin & Bolton, 1986). Uninsured, poor families often have unmet needs and should be referred to nonprofit disaster relief organizations and "unmet needs" committees when government resources have been exhausted (DeWolfe, 2000).

Bolin and Bolton (1986) found that African Americans and Hispanics were more likely than Caucasians to evaluate government aid as inadequate and to recover economically more slowly. He studied a 1982 tornado in Paris, Texas, in which half of the affected population was African American and half was Caucasian. Nearly 20% more African Americans reported a drop in postdisaster standard of living, and 20% reported more family disruption, strain on relationships, disruption of routine, and experienced neighborhood disruption or relocation as an impediment to recovery. The average government loan to Caucasians was twice the amount of the average loan to African Americans (based on eligibility protocols that those who had more predisaster lost more and qualified for more aid). African Americans also used significantly more *nongovernmental* aid sources (including churches and nonprofit groups) than Caucasians. At 8 months postdisaster, significantly more Caucasians that African American families reported financial and emotional recovery, and twice as many Caucasians reported having received adequate financial aid. Bolin and Bolton concluded in their study on race, religion, and ethnicity in disaster recovery that the formal aid system has been proven to be a key element in disaster recovery, but policies and standards that exclude minorities and the poor must be reexamined unless disasters are to create increasingly large social inequities.

Faced with these many challenges and assistance that falls far short of solving the problems and meeting the needs facing them, low-income survivors can feel overwhelmed and depressed. Disaster mental health workers must be able to provide concrete problem-solving assistance that facilitates addressing priority needs. Workers must be knowledgeable about the full range of community resources available to people of limited economic means and actively engage this resource network with those in need (DeWolfe, 2000).

PEOPLE WITH SERIOUS AND PERSISTENT MENTAL ILLNESS

Clinical field experience has shown that disaster survivors with mental illness function fairly well following disaster, if essential services are not interrupted. These individuals often "rise to the occasion" and perform as well as the general population during the immediate aftermath of the disaster (DeWolfe, 2000). Some perform heroically, volunteering to assist neighbors and sometimes assisting disaster relief agencies. Many are well able to handle the stress of the disaster environment without exacerbation of symptoms, provided their medication regimens are uninterrupted. Unfortunately, in the confusion of the disaster environment, individuals often forget to take their medication or medication supplies are destroyed or lost. In such situations, survivors with mental illness may experience an exacerbation of symptoms and will need to be reevaluated and helped to reestablish a regular medication regimen.

For some survivors with mental illness, the added stress of disaster disrupts their homeostasis and coping, and additional mental health support services, medications, or hospitalization may be necessary to gain stability. For individuals diagnosed with Posttraumatic Stress Disorder (PTSD), disaster stimuli (e.g., sirens and helicopters) may trigger an exacerbation due to associations with prior traumatic events (DeWolfe, 2000).

Many people with mental illness are vulnerable to sudden environmental changes and an upset of routine. Dealing with new resources and agencies for disaster relief assistance can be confusing and stressful for them. Disaster mental health workers can support the mentally ill survivor in problem solving and utilizing new resources, and can advocate on their behalf and build bridges that facilitate access and referrals where necessary. Disaster mental health services designed for the general population are equally beneficial for those with mental illness, as disaster stress affects all groups. When case managers and community mental health counselors have a solid understanding of disaster mental health issues, they are better able to provide services to the mentally ill population following a disaster (DeWolfe, 2000).

WHEN TO MAKE REFERRALS

The sections above outline the "normal reactions of normal people to an abnormal event" and discuss how cultural and socioeconomic factors can affect postdisaster recovery. Although most people cope reasonably well in the aftermath of disaster, there will be times when physical or psychological symptoms require a careful assessment and may require medical or psychological treatment. Disaster mental health and outreach workers whose roles may be very time-limited with any given disaster survivor or disaster workers should not hesitate to make a referral for evaluation and treatment, and should be knowledgeable about the resources for such services.

Any disaster survivor or disaster worker who has a potentially life-threatening condition, such as high blood pressure, heart problems, diabetes, or symptoms related to substance abuse and is not under the care of a health professional should be referred for evaluation and possible treatment (American Red Cross, 1995). Individuals who are receiving care for such conditions must be aware that stress, exertion, and changes in eating and sleeping patterns postdisaster can exacerbate health problems, requiring changes in their treatment or their medication, and a visit to their health-care professional is recommended. Any individual experiencing chest pain; collapse; cardiac arrhythmia (rapid or irregular heartbeat); sudden weakness and numbness of face, arm, or leg; difficulty speaking or understanding speech; sudden severe headache; heat stroke; excessive vomiting or vomiting blood; blood in stool or urine; or loss of consciousness should be referred for immediate medical evaluation.

Any survivor or disaster worker with preexisting mental health problems that are exacerbated by the disaster or its aftermath may need a referral for evaluation, treatment, or reevaluation, adjustment, or change in medication (American Red Cross, 1995).

Referrals should be made for mental health evaluation and possible treatment when an individual appears to be experiencing more severe or persistent symptoms than those commonly seen. Hospitalization may be necessary when a person is judged to be a danger to self or others. The following list covers a variety of circumstances in which a disaster mental health worker should refer a survivor or another worker to local mental health professionals for specialized evaluation and care (American Red Cross, 1995; Myers, 1989; Young et al., 1998):

- Significant disturbance of memory
- Disorientation to person or place
- Inability to perform necessary everyday functions
- Inability to care for one's personal needs
- Loss of simple decision-making skills
- Inability to recognize familiar people
- Preoccupation with a single thought
- Repetition of ritualistic acts
- Extreme hyperactivity or immobility (inability to be aroused to action)
- Abuse (rather than misuse) of alcohol or drugs
- Talk that "overflows"—shows extreme pressure in speech
- Excessively "flat" emotional expression
- Serious withdrawal
- Suicidal or homicidal talk or actions
- Reckless behavior that may be life-threatening (driving under the influence of drugs or alcohol, unsafe sex, etc.)
- Psychotic symptoms
- Frequent and disturbing occurrence of flashbacks, excessive nightmares, and excessive crying
- Persistent "inappropriate" emotion such as laughter or uncontrolled anger

- Serious regression
- Inappropriate anger or abuse of others
- Episodes of dissociation
- Inappropriate reaction to triggering events

SUMMARY

This chapter has presented the common reactions of various populations to disaster, including children, adults, and older adults. It has discussed cultural and socioeconomic factors that influence how disaster affects individuals and families, and issues pertaining to individuals with mental illness. Last, it has presented guidelines for referral of disaster survivors for psychological or medical evaluation and treatment.

REFERENCES

American heritage dictionary of the English language (4th ed.). (2000). Retrieved June 6, 2001 from http://www.bartleby.com/61/11/C0801100.html

American Red Cross. (1995). *Disaster mental health services: Part 1. Participant's workbook* (ARC 3077–1A).

Baum, A., & Fleming, I. (1993). Implications of psychological research on stress and technological accidents. *American Psychologist, 48,* 665–672.

Bell, B. D., Kara, G., & Batterson, C. (1978). Service utilization and adjustment patterns of elderly tornado victims in an American disaster. *Mass emergencies, 3,* 71–81.

Bolin, R., & Bolton, P. (1986). *Race, religion, and ethnicity in disaster recovery.* (Monograph No. 42). Boulder: University of Colorado Press.

Bolin, R., & Klenow, D. (1982–1983). Response of the elderly to disaster: An age-stratified analysis. *International Journal of Aging and Human Development, 16,* 283–296.

Bravo M., Rubio-Stipec, M. C., Canino, G. J., Woodbury, M. A., & Ribera, J. C. (1990). The psychological sequelae of disaster stress prospectively and retrospectively evaluated. *American Journal of Community Psychology, 18,* 661–680.

Bromet, E., Goldgaber, D., Carlson, G., Panina, N., Golovakha, E., Gluzmanr, S., et al. (2000). Children's well-being 11 years after the Chernobyl catastrophe. *Archives of General Psychiatry, 57,* 563–571.

Bromet, E., Parkinson, D., Schulberg, H., & Gondek, P. (1982). Mental health of residents near the Three Mile Island reactor: A comparative study of selected groups. *Journal of Preventive Psychiatry, 1,* 225–276.

Brooks, N., & McKinlay, W. (1992). Mental health consequences of the Lockerbie disaster. *Journal of Traumatic Stress, 5,* 527–543.

Center for Mental Health Services. (1995). *Psychosocial issues for children and families in disaster: A guide for the primary care physician* (DHHS Publication No. SMA 95-3022). Washington, DC: U.S. Government Printing Office.

Cohen, E., & Poulshock, S. (1977). Societal response to mass relocation of the elderly. *The Gerontologist, 17,* 262–268.

Corneley, P., & Bromet, E. (1986). Prevalence of behavior problems in the three-year-old children living near Three Mile Island: A comparative analysis. *Journal of Child Psychology and Psychiatry and Allied Disciplines, 27,* 489–498.

De la Fuente, R. (1990). The mental health consequences of the 1985 earthquakes in Mexico. *International Journal of Mental Health, 19,* 21–29.

DeWolfe, D. (2000). *Training manual for mental health and human service workers in major disasters* (2nd ed.). (DHHS Publication No. ADM 90-538). Retrieved March 14, 2001, from http://www.mentalhealth.org/publications/allpubs/ADM90-538/index.htm

Dohrenwend, B. P., Dohrenwend, B. S., Warheit, G. J., Bartlett, G. S., Goldsteen, R. L., Goldsteen, K., et al. (1981). Stress in the community: A report to the President's commission on the accident at Three Mile Island. *Annals of the New York Academy of Sciences, 365,* 159–174.

Dooley, E., & Gunn, J. (1995). The psychological effects of disaster at sea. *British Journal of Psychiatry, 167,* 233–237.

Durkin, M. S., Khan, N., Davidson, L., Zaman, S., & Stein, Z. (1993). The effects of a natural disaster on child behavior: Evidence for posttraumatic stress. *American Journal of Public Health, 83,* 1549–1553.

Eysenck, H. J. (1983). Stress, disease, and personality: The inoculation effect. In C. L. Cooper (Ed.), *Stress research.* New York: Wiley.

Farberow, N. L., & Frederick, C. J. (1978). *Training manual for human service workers in major disasters.* (DHHS Publication No. ADM 77-538). Washington, DC: U.S. Government Printing Office.

Farberow, N. L., & Gordon, N. S. (1981). *Manual for child health workers in major disaster.* (DHHS Publication No. ADM 86-1070). Washington, DC: U.S. Government Printing Office.

Fullerton, C., Ursano, R., Tzu-Cheg, K., & Bhartiya, V. (1999). Disaster-related bereavement: Acute symptoms and subsequent depression. *Aviation, Space, and Environmental Medicine, 70,* 902–909.

Gleser, B., Green, B., & Winget, C. (1981). *Prolonged psychosocial effects of a disaster.* New York: Academic Press.

Green, B. L., & Lindy, J. D. (1994). Post-traumatic stress disorder in victims of disasters. *Psychiatric Clinics of North America, 17,* 301–309.

Green, B., Lindy, J., Grace, M., Gleser, G., Leonard, A., Korol, M., et al. (1990). Buffalo Creek survivors in the second decade: Stability of stress symptoms. *American Journal of Orthopsychiatry, 60,* 43–54.

Havenaar, J., Rumyantzeva, G., van den Brink, W., Poelijoe, N., van den Bout, J., van Engeland, H., et al. (1997). Long-term mental health effects of the Chernobyl disaster: An epidemiologic survey in two former Soviet regions. *American Journal of Psychiatry, 154,* 1605–1607.

Huerta, F., & Horton, R. (1978). Coping behavior of elderly flood victims. *The Gerontologist, 18,* 541–546.

Kilijanek, T., & Drabek, T. (1979). Assessing long-term impacts of a natural disaster: A focus on the elderly. *The Gerontologist, 19,* 555–566.

LaGreca, A. M., Silverman, W. K., Vernberg, E. M., & Prinstein, M. J. (1996). Symptoms of post-traumatic stress in children after Hurricane Andrew: A prospective study. *Journal of Consulting and Clinical Psychology, 64,* 712–723.

Lonigan, C., Shannon, M., Taylor, C., Finch, A., & Sallee, F. (1994). Children exposed to disaster: II. Risk factors for the development of post-traumatic symptomatology. *Journal of the American Academy of Child and Adolescent Psychiatry, 33,* 94–105.

Lystad, M. (Ed.). (1985). *Innovations in mental health services to disaster victims.* (DHHS Publication No. ADM 85-1390). Washington, DC: U.S. Government Printing Office.

Melnick, M., & Logue, J. (1985–1986). The effect of disaster on the health and well-being of older women. *International Journal of Aging and Human Development, 21,* 27–38.

Mexico City earthquake. (March 24, 2000). Retrieved June 7, 2001, from http://www.geo.arizona.edu/K-12/azpepp/education/history/mexico/index.html

Mitchell, J. T., & Everly, G. S., Jr. (2001). *Critical incident stress management: The basic course workbook* (3rd ed.). Ellicott City, MD: International Critical Incident Stress Foundation.

Myers, D. (1989). *Training manual: Disaster mental health.* Unpublished manuscript. California Department of Mental Health.

Myers, D. (1990). *Older adults and disaster.* Unpublished disaster mental health training material. Monterey, CA.

Myers, D. (1995). *Just a reminder.* Unpublished disaster mental health training material Monterey, CA.

Myers, D. (1998). *Cultural considerations in disaster: Factors to keep in mind in working with various cultures.* Disaster mental health training material.

Myers, D., & Zunin, L. (1992). *Coping with a traumatic event.* Unpublished educational brochure. Miami, FL: Federal Emergency Management Agency.

Norris, F. J., Friedman, M. J., Watson, P. J., Byrne, C. M., Diaz, E., & Kaniasty, K. (2002a). 60,000 disaster victims speak: Part I. An empirical review of the empirical literature, 1981–2001. *Psychiatry, 65,* 207–239.

Norris, F., Kaniasty, K., Conrad, M., Inman, G., & Murphy, A. (2002b). Placing age differences in cultural context: A comparison of the effects of age on PTSD after disasters in the U.S., Mexico, and Poland. *Journal of Clinical Geropsychology, 8,* 153–173.

Norris, F., & Murrell, S. (1988). Prior experience as a moderator of disaster impact on anxiety symptoms in older adults. *American Journal of Community Psychology, 16,* 665–683.

Norris, F., & Murrell, S. (1990). Social support, life events, and stress as modifiers of adjustment to bereavement in older adults. *Psychology and Aging, 5,* 429–436.

Norris, F., Pfifer, J., & Kaniasty, K. (1994). Individual and community reactions to the Kentucky floods: Findings from a longitudinal study of older adults. In R. Ursano, B. G. McCaughey, & C. S. Fullerton (Eds.), *Individual and community responses to trauma and disaster.* Cambridge, UK: Cambridge University Press.

Norris, F., & Uhl, G. (1993). Chronic stress as a mediator of acute stress: The case of Hurricane Hugo. *Journal of Applied Social Psychology, 23,* 1263–1284.

North, C., Nixon, S., Shariat, S., Mallonee, S., McMillen, J., Spitznagel, E., et al. (1999). Psychiatric disorders among survivors of the Oklahoma City bombing. *Journal of the American Medical Association, 282,* 755–762.

North, C., Smith, E., & Spitznagel, E. (1994). Posttraumatic stress disorder in survivors of a mass shooting. *American Journal of Psychiatry, 151,* 82–88.

Ollendick, D., & Hoffman, M. (1982). Assessment of psychological reactions in disaster victims. *Journal of Community Psychology, 10,* 157–167.

Pynoos, R. S., & Nader, K. (1993). Issues in the treatment of post-traumatic stress in children and adolescents. In J. P. Wilson & B. Raphael (Eds.), *International handbook of traumatic stress syndromes.* New York: Plenum Press.

Saylor, C., Swenson, C., & Powell, P. (1992). Hurricane Hugo blows down the broccoli: Pre-schooler's post-disaster play and adjustment. *Child Psychiatry and Human Development, 22,* 139–149.

Shannon, M., Lonigan, C., Finch, A., & Taylor, C. (1994). Children exposed to disaster: I. Epidemiology of post-traumatic symptoms and symptom profiles. *Journal of the American Academy of Child and Adolescent Psychiatry, 33,* 80–93.

Solomon, S. (2002). Gender differences in response to disaster. In G. Weidner, S. Kopp, & M. Kristenson (Eds.), *Heart disease: Environment, stress, and gender.* NATO Science Series I: Life and Behavioral Sciences, Volume 327. Amsterdam: IOS Press.

Solomon, S., Bravo, M., Rubio-Stipec, M., & Canino, G. (1993). Effect of family role on response to disaster. *Journal of Traumatic Stress, 6,* 255–269.

Stein, B., & Myers, D. (1999). Emotional intervention after trauma: A guide for primary care physicians. *Journal of the American Medical Women's Association, 34,* 60–64.

Thompson, M., Norris, F., & Hanacek, B. (1993). Age differences in the psychological consequences of Hurricane Hugh. *Psychology and Aging, 8,* 606–616.

Ticehurst, S., Webster, R., Carr, V., & Lewin, T. (1996). The psychological impact of an earthquake on the elderly. *International Journal of Geriatric Psychiatry, 11,* 943–951.

Ursano, R., Fullerton, C., Kao, T., & Bhartiy, V. (1995). Longitudinal assessment of posttraumatic stress disorder and depression after exposure to traumatic death. *Journal of Nervous and Mental Disease, 183,* 36–42.

U.S. Administration on Aging & Kansas Department on Aging. (1995). *Disaster preparedness manual for the aging network.*

Vernberg, E. M., LaGreca, A. M., Silverman, W. K., & Prinstein, M. J. (1996). Prediction of post-traumatic stress symptoms in children after Hurricane Andrew. *Journal of Abnormal Psychology, 105,* 237–248.

Wasserstein, S., & La Greca, A. (1998). Hurricane Andrew: Parent conflict as a moderator of children's adjustment. *Hispanic Journal of Behavioral Science, 20,* 212–224.

Young, B. H., Ford, J. D., Ruzek, J. I., Friedman, M. J., & Guzman, F. D. (1998). *Disaster mental health services: A guidebook for clinicians and administrators.* Menlo Park, CA and White River Junction, VT: Department of Veterans Affairs and National Center for Post-Traumatic Stress Disorder.

II
SERVICES, PROGRAMS, AND WORKERS

3

CODE-C: A Model for Disaster Mental Health Service Delivery

INTRODUCTION

CODE-C DISASTER MENTAL HEALTH SERVICE MODEL (CODE-C DMHSM) is a comprehensive, integrated, multiservice model that can be used effectively to address the wide range of mental health needs in communities following disasters. CODE-C is an acronym that can be used as a tool by mental health practitioners. CODE-C DMHSM facilitates communication between disaster mental health practitioners, emergency managers, and persons who will receive services by using a standard nomenclature. The CODE-C DMHSM also defines service components and communicates the differences between disaster mental health services and other more traditional approaches to mental health service delivery.

The CODE-C DMHSM has been used extensively by the authors since the model's development in November 1992. The CODE-C model has been used to plan, organize, and provide disaster mental health services, as well as in the training of disaster workers. CODE-C was first developed and used after Hurricane Andrew to plan and implement a comprehensive stress management program for state and federal workers at the Disaster Field Office in Miami, Florida (Myers, 1992). It was used as a model for disaster worker stress management programs for the Federal Emergency Management Agency (FEMA) after the 1993 Florida winter storms (Myers & Zunin, 1993a), the 1993 great Midwest flood (Myers & Zunin, 1993b), and the 1994 Northridge earthquake (Myers & Zunin, 1994a). The model was the basis of the FEMA Disaster Worker Stress Management Program implemented in 1994 to support federal and state disaster workers in the line of duty (Myers, 1993; Myers & Zunin, 1994b; Federal Emergency Management Agency [FEMA], 1998).

The CODE-C model is included as a component in the City of Berkeley Disaster Mental Health Plan and the City of Berkeley Response Plan for Weapons of Mass Destruction. The model was used during consultations by the authors with the city of Seattle following the 2001 Nisqually earthquake, the 1995 California winter storms, the Sutter and Yuba City evacuation and floods of 1997, and, most recently, the Southern California fires of 2003.

The CODE-C model has been used in training disaster mental health workers following numerous natural disasters in California, and is also taught to citizens in community crisis response training in California. It is currently included in course materials in the following courses at the California Governor's Office of Emergency Services California Specialized Training Institute: Earthquake Recovery, Managing Sustained Operations, Terrorism, and Disaster Medical Operations (Myers, 2002a, 2002b, 2002c). It is taught in the course Disaster Mental Health: Response and Interventions at the University of California, Berkeley Extension, and in lectures at the School of Social Welfare, University of California, Berkeley. It has been used to teach American Red Cross disaster workers psychological response to terrorist events both before and after the terrorist attacks of September 11, 2001 (Myers, 2001a; Myers, 2001b). The model has been presented by the authors during over 200 presentations on disaster mental health, mental health issues in terrorism, bioterrorism, and in presentations to emergency management professionals.

The fundamental differences between disaster mental health and traditional mental health services are incorporated into the CODE-C DMHSM described in this chapter. Key differences in the model include goals and objectives, guiding concepts of disaster mental health programs, range of services provided, duration of services provided, and linkages with other providers. Disaster mental health programs must have core components including needs assessment, *consultation, outreach, debriefing, education,* and *crisis counseling.*

Consultation includes advice, education, training, and assessment services to decision makers, managers, supervisors, and line workers. Consultation is directed at solving problems involving policy, organization functioning, and service provision. *Outreach* is important in reaching as many people possible. Outreach is provided to victims, survivors, disaster workers, and members of the community in their natural environments. *Debriefings and defusings* are group crisis intervention tools for disaster mental health workers in serving survivors and disaster workers following community disasters and violence. Debriefings and defusings are psychoeducational groups that address stress reactions by providing participants with opportunities to receive information on normal reactions by normal people to abnormal events and obtain information on coping strategies and recovery resources (see chapter 5 for a full discussion of CISM services). *Education* services provide information and training on topics specific to disaster psychology and mental health. These services may include workshops, presentations, conferences, written materials, and intensive use of the media. Education services support individual, family, and community recovery. *Crisis counseling* consists of brief interventions with people impacted by disasters. The objective of crisis counseling is to identify disaster-related distress and problems in living and to provide support. Interventions include crisis intervention, problem solving, and development of individual, family, and community support systems.

Disaster mental health services and programs comprehensively target populations at various levels: the community, organizations, groups, and individuals. In the United States, disaster mental health services are provided by a variety of organizations: private and public mental health programs, mental health professional organizations, disaster relief organizations, employee assistance programs, corporations, and local, state, and federal agencies. Federal government programs include those sponsored by FEMA (FEMA Crisis Counseling Program for disaster survivors and workers), the U.S. Public Health Service National Disaster Medical System (NDMS), the military (e.g., U.S. Navy Special Psychiatric Rapid Intervention Team [SPRINT]), and the Department of Veteran Affairs. Other groups that provide special training and volunteers in disaster mental health include the American Psychological Association, American Psychiatric Association, National Association of Social Workers, California Association of Marriage and Family Therapists, American Red Cross, International Critical Incident Stress Foundation, International Association of Trauma Counseling, International Society for Traumatic Stress Studies, and Green Cross. Numerous universities and graduate programs now offer programs in traumatology and disaster mental health.

DISASTER MENTAL HEALTH SERVICES

Disaster mental health services differ from traditional mental health services in their goals, objectives, methods, and settings. These differences are based on how people perceive their disaster-related problems and the resources they are willing to use to cope with these problems. Table 3.1 shows the differences between disaster mental health services and traditional mental health services in relation to goals, objectives, methods, and the settings in which the services are provided.

TABLE 3.I: COMPARISON OF DISASTER MENTAL HEALTH SERVICES
AND TRADITIONAL MENTAL HEALTH SERVICES

	DISASTER MENTAL HEALTH SERVICES	TRADITIONAL MENTAL HEALTH SERVICES
Goals	Prevention of disaster-related stress reactions and restoration to predisaster level of functioning	Assessment, treatment planning, and treatment, leading to reduction in or management of symptoms and long-term change in the person
Target Population	Normal persons affected by disaster	Persons identified as having a diagnosed mental disorder
Objectives	Support, education, and development of resources	Identification of illness that can be treated, managed, or cured
Methods	CODE-C	Psychotherapy, medication, case management
Settings	Community-based, where people live, work, congregate, or seek assistance	Office-, clinic-, or hospital-based.

COMPARISON OF DISASTER MENTAL HEALTH AND TRADITIONAL MENTAL HEALTH SERVICES

The goal of disaster mental health services is to mitigate disaster-related stress reactions and to assist persons and communities impacted by disaster to return as soon as possible to their predisaster level of functioning. In contrast, the goal of traditional mental health services is to provide treatment to mentally ill individuals, with the goal of change in the individual and management or cure of the individual's mental disorder. The target population of disaster mental health services is those in the community affected by the disaster. Persons living in the community are considered normal and are not generally considered mentally ill or suffering from mental disorders that are clinically significant. Traditional mental health services provide intensive assessment, diagnosis, treatment planning, and treatments including individual, group, and psychiatric services. These mental health services are provided to persons who are self-identified or referred by the family or community as mentally ill and needing mental health treatment. The objectives of disaster mental health programs include providing crisis counseling, education, support, and development of community resources. Traditional mental health objectives include the identification of the mental illness and definition of appropriate treatment leading to symptom reduction or cure. The methods used in disaster mental health include needs assessment, consultation, outreach, debriefing, education, and crisis intervention and brief crisis counseling (CODE-C). The methods used in traditional mental health services include individual and group psychotherapy, psychiatric and medication services, milieu therapy, and case management. The settings where disaster mental health services are provided might, at times, include an office setting, but most frequently are community-based and are in locations where people affected by the disaster are located. Persons impacted by disaster seldom seek out mental health services following the disaster. Traditional mental health services are typically office, clinic, or hospital based.

COMPARISON OF CRISIS COUNSELING AND PSYCHOTHERAPY

Another way to address the differences between disaster mental health services and traditional mental health services is to compare the differences in core activities found in crisis counseling programs and psychotherapy. Crisis counseling is proactive. Crisis counselors seek out and actively interact with persons impacted by disasters, inquiring about the person's disaster experiences, disaster-related stress, family functioning, coping strategies, and resources that might be needed. Although it is impossible to generalize across the wide variety of modalities of psychotherapy, many approaches to psychotherapy are more passive, allowing the individual the opportunity to self-disclose events, memories, and meanings that are important to the client. Crisis counseling seeks to restore the individual's ability to cope with the additional stress brought on by disaster. Enhancement of coping might include education, problem solving, specific suggestions on coping based on the experiences of other disaster survivors, teaching of coping skills, use of community resources, and referral for more in-depth assessment or psychotherapy. Traditional psychotherapy emphasizes exploration of the client's feelings and experiences, with the client providing the solutions to the problems he or she faces. Crisis counselors gather history strategically with the priority on current problems and challenges faced by the disaster-impacted persons. The strategic history is largely current and disaster-specific, although a history of previous trauma and loss should be included. Traditional psychotherapy, in contrast, usually includes an in-depth historical approach. The traditional psychotherapist will want information on the client's early childhood experiences, development, schooling, social history, medical history, and psychiatric history. Traditional psychotherapy may be insight-oriented, with the clients (with the guidance of the psychotherapist) learning about their inner lives and about how this discovered truth can help them find true meaning and purpose in life. Psychotherapy may also take a biopsychological approach, utilizing such techniques as biofeedback or psychopharmacology to treat specific conditions and to help clients manage their symptoms. Crisis counselors assist clients with the problems of daily living, such as the stress of relocation due to damage or destruction of their homes. Crisis counseling is oriented toward prevention of mental problems through education and intervention before a disaster-impacted person's disaster problems result in the person's needing intensive treatment. Traditional psychotherapy, on the other hand, involves treatment to alleviate suffering and work toward management or cure of the mental disorder.

TABLE 3.2: COMPARISON OF CRISIS COUNSELING AND
TRADITIONAL PSYCHOTHERAPY

CRISIS COUNSELING	TRADITIONAL PSYCHOTHERAPY
Active	Passive
Restoration and enhancement of coping and problem-solving	Explorative
Strategic history	In-depth historical approach
Educational	Insight oriented
Problems of daily living	Psychological understanding
Prevention	Intensive treatment or case management or both

DISASTER MENTAL HEALTH SERVICE GOALS AND CONCEPTS

The goals of disaster mental health services are to identify disaster-related mental health problems, to educate the community about disaster mental health reactions, and to mitigate psychological reactions to disasters. Disaster mental health services have specific concepts of service delivery that are central to their accessibility and effectiveness in the community.

The first concept is that disaster victims are, for the most part, normal people experiencing normal reactions to an abnormal event. They are usually not suffering from mental disorders. Likewise, they usually do not seek out mental health services following disasters. For many people in the community, there is still a stigma attached to the concept of mental health intervention. Following disasters, most people experience brief stress reactions or increased stress associated with disaster; they do not view themselves or their family members as having a mental illness needing assessment or psychotherapy at a mental health clinic. Although most people do not seek out mental health services, they are usually receptive to information and education about disaster stress reactions, stress management and coping techniques, and crisis counseling services. Disaster mental health services are provided to people in their natural environment, disaster-impacted neighborhoods, homes, workplaces, supermarkets, lines, neighborhoods, shelters, encampments, meal sites, on-scene at damaged or destroyed buildings, service centers, family assistance centers, respite centers, food distribution centers, schools, religious centers, community centers, emergency operations centers, emergency services facilities, emergency services staging areas, first aid sites, hospitals, emergency rooms, casualty collection points, the morgue, and, rarely, at mental health centers.

The second concept is that it is helpful for disaster mental health programs to have names and an identification that is culturally and socially acceptable to the community impacted by the disaster. Disaster mental health programs historically have avoided names with the words "mental health" in the title or name of the program. Names such as "Project COPE" (Counseling Ordinary People in Emergencies), Project Rainbow (a flood recovery mental health program), Project Heartland (the Oklahoma City Bombing Crisis Counseling Program), or Project Liberty (New York City's Crisis Counseling Program following the September 11, 2001, terrorist attacks) are examples. The American Red Cross, on the other hand, is quite straightforward in using Disaster Mental Health (DMH) as the name of their mental health service function. Leaders in the Red Cross DMH function believe that the stigma sometimes attached to mental health services following disaster, and avoidance of these services, are diminishing, and that disaster victims are coming to accept DMH services as important disaster resources.

The third concept is that services and programs must be creative and innovative in providing services. Disaster survivors may be overwhelmed with the demands of the postdisaster environment. Traditional "talk therapy" may not be high on their list of priorities for how to use their time. Combining disaster recovery services with disaster mental health services provides the disaster survivor with information and resources critical to their recovery as well as information and educational material that can help with disaster-related psychological reactions.

The fourth concept is that a disaster mental health program must have community acceptance and support. This involves developing partnerships, collaborations, and coordination of services before, during, and after a disaster strikes. Disaster mental health programs and established community institutions can partner to provide services. This type of partnering builds upon the existing long-term relationships among the community institutions. Disaster mental health programs must also be culturally competent, providing services that are culturally relevant in the languages that are used in the community.

Confidentiality is also important in providing disaster mental health services. Confidentiality is a right that is held by the client, and it involves maintaining information concerning the client's identity and information about the services they receive. Confidential information should not be disclosed to any third party without permission of the individual.

Disaster mental health programs following disasters focus on education, information, assistance with resources, and crisis intervention. Citizens experiencing reactions that are more intense, severe, and disabling may need referral to a higher level of care, including psychotherapy and contemporary trauma therapies. Thus, an important role of disaster mental health programs is to identify and refer those individuals who need or would benefit from psychotherapy.

The destruction that is caused directly and indirectly by disasters leads to complex human and community needs. Disaster mental health services must be based on a comprehensive, integrated multiservice model to effectively address the wide range of community needs. The CODE-C DMHSM is presented here to assist in the assessment, development, and provision of disaster mental health services.

RATIONALE FOR THE CODE-C DMHSM

The CODE-C DMHSM was developed by David Wee, Diane Myers, and Leonard Zunin in 1992 during disaster recovery activities following Hurricane Andrew. It is a tool that can be used to develop comprehensive disaster mental health programs that are specific, appropriate, and effective. The model promotes the development, identification, and standardization of core service components that are essential in disaster mental health programs and disaster worker stress management programs. The definition of a service model and designation of its name facilitates communication between emergency planners and responders by identifying and defining the key service components. The model can assist managers in making strategic decisions concerning deployment of resources to meet rapidly changing conditions during disaster response and recovery. It provides a common language, parameters for data collection, program monitoring and evaluation, and program reporting, and also includes emphasis on prevention, education, crisis intervention, and programming that is assertive, creative, and innovative.

THE CODE-C MODEL

The CODE-C DMHSM includes essential disaster mental health services, including needs assessment, consultation, outreach, debriefing, education, and crisis counseling.

NEEDS ASSESSMENT

Comprehensive needs assessment must be conducted before implementing disaster mental health programs. Needs assessment is the systematic evaluation of information from a variety of sources in order to identify the complex and diverse needs of a disaster-impacted area. Identification of disaster-related mental health needs begins with understanding the demographics of the area, including population statistics (persons in different age groups, persons in different ethnic groups, languages spoken, and income ranges). Types of housing, occupations of residents, and economy of the area are important. A useful source of information is key community informants, who can be religious leaders, community leaders, members of the medical and mental health communities, and business and political leaders. Another important source of information is key indicator data. Key indicator data include information about the disaster impact: the number of people killed or injured, homes and businesses damaged or destroyed, and associated infrastructure damage. A number of factors are associated with disaster-related mental health reactions and the mental health needs arising from the cause and characteristics of the disaster (Cummock, 1995). Some factors to be considered in the needs assessment include the following: type of disaster, presence or absence of warning, scope of destruction, duration of impact, threat of recurrence, exposure to death or gruesome sights and sounds, death or injury of loved ones, and complexity of recovery and the recovery environment. These factors are discussed at length in chapter 1.

The needs assessment activities change as the social and psychological reactions of the impacted community change. The short-term, mid-term, and long-term disaster phase mental health reactions and needs assessment activities are displayed in Table 3.3.

During the short-term, from the time of disaster impact until approximately 3 months postdisaster, needs assessment activities include review of disaster data and interviews with community leaders, disaster response managers, key informants, and victims of the disaster. During the mid-term disaster phase, from approximately 4 months to 1 year, continuing needs assessment may include surveys, questionnaires, empirical research, interviews with key persons, and review of emerging data about the health and mental health impact of the event (e.g., increased utilization of health or mental health resources, increases in calls to stress-related hot lines, increase in domestic violence, and so on). During the long-term disaster phase (1 year and longer), needs assessment strategies and activities will include interviews with survivors and providers, continued review of emerging data, and ongoing identification of long-term needs.

TABLE 3.3: DISASTER MENTAL HEALTH SERVICES FOR DISASTER RECOVERY

TIME FRAME AND PSYCHOLOGICAL REACTIONS	NEED ASSESSMENT	CONSULTATION	OUTREACH	DEBRIEFING (GROUP WORK)	EDUCATION	CRISIS COUNSELING
Short Term (0–3 months) Shock, numbing, distress, sleep, anger, heroic, disruption, disorganization (see mid- and long-term reactions)	Community leaders, disaster-response managers, key informants, victims of the disaster, community damage assessment reports	Emergency service and disaster managers, key service providers, community leaders, schools, community agencies, and service providers	People whose loved ones died or were injured, those with property loss, those exposed to traumatic stimuli; those with barriers to resources, children, frail elderly	Law enforcement, fire service, EMS, high impact groups, groups most at risk	Television, radio, the Internet, print media, public meetings, fliers and brochures, bulletin boards	Individuals, couples, and families unable to use group services
Mid-Term (4 months–1 year) Depression, disappointment, disillusionment, isolation, illness, organizational stress	Formal need assessment, questionnaires, interviewing key persons	Local officials and service providers	Survivors of greatest impact, areas surrounding impacted area	Support groups	Target groups, mailings, emergency service personnel, media, public meetings	Individuals, couples, and families unable to use group services
Long Term (1 year and above) Fatigue and long-term persistent stress, family conflict	Survivors, interviews, and needs	Local officials and service providers	First anniversary	Support groups	Special needs, stress management, public meetings, community	Individuals, couples, and families unable to use group services.

Note. This table shows the relationship between the CODE-C disaster mental health services model and the disaster-phase-specific psychological and behavior responses during disasters and disaster recovery. Each of the CODE-C service components has lists of target populations which a disaster mental health program may try to serve. From *Disasters: Impact on the law enforcement family*, by D. Wee. In *Law Enforcement Family: Issues and Answers*, J. T. Reese and E. Scrivner (Eds.), 1994, Washington, DC: US Department of Justice, Federal Bureau of Investigation.

Needs assessment is an ongoing process in disaster mental health and is necessary to ensure the development of disaster mental health services that are appropriate and effective throughout the phases of disaster recovery. Once the initial needs assessment is completed, the services components of the CODE-C DMHSM can be implemented by the disaster mental health worker.

NEEDS ASSESSMENT CASE EXAMPLE: OKLAHOMA CITY BOMBING   Each of the facts listed below had mental health implications for the survivors and their loved ones. A thorough mental health needs assessment must examine these kinds of statistics. Each fact must then be assessed according to implications for the mental health of those involved. Then, the needs assessment becomes the framework for the design of a responsive and effective mental health program.

On April 19, 1995, at 9:02 A.M., the Alfred P. Murrah Federal Building was torn apart by a bomb that resulted in the following statistics:

- 168 people were killed.
- Approximately 700 individuals were injured in the building and nearby areas.
- The daycare center within the federal building premises was destroyed.
- An estimated 646 people thought to have been in the building when the bomb exploded were profoundly affected.
- Four of the deaths occurred in the Athena Building across the street from the federal building.
- Two deaths occurred in the Oklahoma Water Resources Building.
- One death occurred at the Journal Record Building.
- Three of the fatalities were dead on arrival at local hospitals.
- Three died in hospitals following delays of from 2–23 days (Jordan, 1997).
- Over 16,744 people work or reside in the area impacted by the bomb, and many of the injured were on the streets in the neighborhood or in nearby buildings.
- Many of the injured were children in the federal building's childcare center and in the nearby YMCA's daycare center. There were approximately 50 children in the two daycare centers combined. A total of 13 children died in these centers (Flynn, 1996).
- Over 220 square blocks surrounding the federal building sustained damage. Some 800 buildings received damage ranging from major structural damage to broken windows.
- Nine structures, including the federal building, suffered partial collapse (FEMA, 1995; Oklahoma City Public Works Department, 1995).
- The town of Guthrie lost 11 persons.
- Seven deaths occurred in the town of Norman, just south of Oklahoma City.
- Individuals flocked to Oklahoma City from all areas of the nation, searching for news of loved ones who worked in or near the building.
- 271 children lost one or more parents in the blast.
- Of those children, 60 were left orphaned.
- 80% of the schools within the Oklahoma City School District had children who had immediate family members injured or killed in the bombing.
- Over 12,000 rescue workers from throughout the state of Oklahoma and the nation participated in the recovery effort.

- One nurse was killed by falling debris, and an additional 26 rescuers were hospitalized with injuries.
- During the first 8 days, over 100 tons of rubble were dug out by hand every 12 hours, using small military shovels, and removing it in increments of 5-gallon buckets at a time.
- Urban search and rescue teams worked 12 hours a day for up to 10 days, averaging about 4 hours of sleep per night (Oklahoma City Fire Department, 1995).
- Only by May 25, 36 days after the blast, had all bodies been recovered.
- The Compassion Center was established to provide a safe haven for family members awaiting news of the status of their loved ones. The center was run by the American Red Cross, in cooperation with numerous agencies and organizations.

CONSULTATION

The first *C* in CODE-C represents consultation. Consultation is defined as situation evaluation, advice, and collaboration with decision makers, managers, supervisors, community leaders, providers of recovery services, survivors, and disaster workers regarding mental health needs and issues. Consultation is oriented toward reducing stress and enhancing the coping of individuals, families, organizations, and the community.

The purposes of consultation are to facilitate the work of other professionals in assisting disaster victims, to encourage other professionals and programs to incorporate mental health principles and approaches into their services, and to assist other professionals in linking disaster survivors with appropriate resources including mental health. It is important to first establish trust and collaboration with consultees so that the consultant understands their mission and methods, does not threaten their methodology, and eliminates unrealistic expectations or perceptions of what mental health services can do.

There are two types of consultation-case-oriented and program-oriented. Case-oriented consultation usually involves interviewing a client or providing consultation to a professional regarding the needs of a client and the kind of disaster mental health services that can address the needs. Program consultation is oriented toward influencing programs, administrative structures, processes and allowing for early detection of and intervention with mental health problems, and increasing coordination and linkages among programs, decreasing fragmentation of services, and making services as responsive to as many needs of disaster victims as possible.

Consultation activities change as the social and psychological reactions of the disaster-impacted community change. The short-term, mid-term, and long-term disaster phase mental health reactions and consultation activities are displayed in Table 3.3. During the short-term disaster phase, consultation will be provided to emergency service and disaster managers, key service providers, community leaders, schools, community agencies, and service providers. During the mid-term, consultation will shift to local officials involved in disaster response and recovery as well as to other service providers. The consultation relationships established during the mid-term disaster phase will continue with local officials, service providers, and other new disaster resources that emerge during this period, and continue into the long-term phase of recovery.

Consultation Case Example

During stress management programs with federal and state governmental agencies in numerous disasters, disaster mental health professionals have provided consultation to management on such topics as mitigating environmental stressors in workspaces; accessibility of healthy food and beverages for workers; policies regarding days off, breaks, and length of shifts; stressful personnel situations, including the intrusion of personal and family problems into the workplace; upcoming changes in work assignments or duties; the need for first aid or medical service to be available for staff; the need for new workers to be orientated to the community and to the disaster; worker safety; training needs, including stress management training; employee recognition programs and activities; and the need for respite and recreational activities for workers.

OUTREACH

Outreach is a basic skill for workers providing disaster mental health services and represents O in the CODE-C DMHSM. Outreach is defined as taking services to the recipient in the environment in which they live, work, and spend time. Outreach involves activities undertaken by workers going out to the community to identify victims, to assess problems, and to develop relationships and provide services to victims. It can be a precursor to individual assessment and treatment, or it can be an effective, beneficial intervention by itself.

There are different types of outreach activities. The primary purpose of the outreach is to take the services to the recipient in the environment. Outreach activities include casefinding and outreach to individuals, public education and information, mental health training, meeting with community organizations, and advocacy. Outreach objectives are information, education, normalization of feelings, support, assistance with problem solving, prioritizing, coping, and obtaining of resources. Outreach workers also assist recipients with the opportunity to engage and become affiliated with community members (Cohen & Ahearn, 1980; Myers, 1989; Myers, 1994; Myers, Spofford, & Young, 1996).

Successful outreach workers and programs will establish early presence and visibility, show willingness to engage in whatever needs to be done (resulting in establishment of trust and credibility), and use indigenous workers. Indigenous paraprofessionals can establish peer relationships, understand and empathize with the disaster survivor's style of life, listen sympathetically, and provide emotional support (Solomon, 1986). This is particularly important because many disaster survivors will shun traditional mental health services. Indigenous workers also use their status as reference group members to transmit norms to community members, such as the appropriateness of help seeking. Indigenous workers can help disaster survivors to perceive help seeking as acceptable and sanctioned by their own group members. Indigenous workers also know how to utilize community and social network analyses to identify where and how to disseminate information, to identify and use advice of key local activists, community caretakers, and neighborhood leaders and use them as "key informants." Indigenous workers also have access to local leaders who can assist with dissemination of information, assist with making referrals, and provide leaders with consultation regarding disaster problems that may come to them, information about resources, and backup for problems beyond their capacity to handle alone. Other attributes of outreach workers and indigenous workers who are trained in disaster mental health services are that they can assist in recognizing phases of recovery, phase-appropriate interventions in the community, and identify and target vulnerable, at-risk populations; also, they are appropriate culturally, with language, and are able to identify and overcome barriers (such as distance, transportation, bureaucratic procedures, cultural insensitivities, and local anomalies, etc.).

The outreach activities change as the social and psychological reactions of the disaster-impacted community change. The short-term, mid-term, and long-term disaster-phase mental health reactions due to disaster and outreach activities are displayed in Table 3.3. During the short-term phase, outreach activities will focus on loved ones of the dead, injured, persons who experienced property loss, those exposed to traumatic stimuli, those with barriers to resources, children, and the frail elderly. During the mid-term disaster phase, outreach activities will focus on the survivors among those who experienced the greatest impact of the disaster as well as survivors from areas surrounding the disaster-impacted area. During the long-term disaster phase, outreach activities will target populations identified during the short-term and mid-term disaster phases in preparation for the first anniversary of the disaster.

Outreach Case Example

The East Bay firestorm in 1991 resulted in the evacuation of over 10,000 people and the destruction of 3,354 homes and 456 apartments, leaving over 5,000 people homeless. The City of Berkeley Crisis Counseling Program used a variety of outreach strategies to provide information, education, and referral services to persons affected by the fire. In the immediate aftermath, mental health workers were stationed at check points with police officers. The role of the police officers was to initially keep all people out of the burn area and then to check the identification of people to ensure that only residents were allowed into the area. The role of the mental health workers was to provide support and assistance to the officers in dealing with distressed citizens, information about disaster mental health, and on-scene support when needed. Mental health workers were also paired with public works staff who issued access permits to residents of the area. Mental health workers were able to provide outreach services to at least one or two members of each household in the impacted area. Later outreach activity included door-to-door outreach to homes and apartments in the impacted area to provide information about disaster mental health services available at the Berkeley Fire Resource Center and education about "the normal reactions normal people have following abnormal events." The door-to-door outreach was identified as the best practice by the Center for Mental Health Services. The door-to-door outreach contacted groups of people who had not used disaster mental health services before and identified unmet disaster mental health needs which might not have been identified if this method of outreach had not been utilized (Center for Mental Health Services, 2000).

DEBRIEFING AND DEFUSING

Debriefing and defusing is the third core service component in the CODE-C DMHSM and is represented by D in the acronym. In the CODE-C model, debriefing is defined as structured, time-limited, therapeutic group interactions to help survivors and workers cope with crisis-related stress. Debriefing is important because it provides for the efficient screening, support, and education of large numbers of people. Debriefing may be provided to citizens who self-identify their need for psychological support and refer themselves to debriefing groups offered in the community. It is most frequently used as an intervention to assist emergency and disaster workers with work-related stress and trauma issues. Debriefing is a psychoeducational intervention process provided in groups to address disaster-related reactions. Debriefings utilize intervention models such as the International Critical Incident Stress Foundation (ICISF) model of Critical Incident Stress Debriefing described in chapter 5. Debriefing may also follow support group models described in chapter 6. Disaster survivors' primary concerns often discussed in debriefings include locating and reuniting with family, caring for family members who are sick or injured, establishing housing, food, safety, and stress management.

Debriefings and defusings are provided during the short-term phases of a disaster, typically in the days following a disaster up until several months later. As the needs of disaster workers and survivors change, the model used for debriefing changes. Debriefings may evolve into ongoing support groups that can help to meet the psychological and social needs that emerge during mid-term and long-term disaster recovery. Chapter 6 covers this topic in depth. Groups can be an important, primary service component for disaster mental health programs. Groups are based on key concepts including normalization, universalization, education, sharing of resources, understanding of victims' reactions, optimizing recovery, and reduction of later pathology.

The debriefing and defusing activities change as the social and psychological reactions of the disaster-impacted community change. The short-term, mid-term, and long-term disaster-phase mental health reactions and consultation activities are displayed in Table 3.3. During the short-term disaster phase, the focus of debriefing services is on law enforcement, fire service, EMS, medical workers, disaster workers, and other groups that experienced high impact from the disaster. Other risk groups that could benefit from debriefing might include survivors of the dead, injured, persons who experienced property loss, those exposed to traumatic stimuli, those with barriers to resources, children, and the frail elderly. During the mid-term disaster phase, debriefing and support groups will be developed for persons experiencing long-term disaster-related stress associated with disaster-recovery activities. These groups can be beneficial through the long-term disaster phase, that is, through the first anniversary and longer, depending upon the needs of the group participants and funding if needed to continue the groups. The following debriefing case example illustrates the use of debriefing following the Los Angeles civil disturbances and an evaluation of the effectiveness of the debriefing.

Debriefing Case Example: The 1992 Los Angeles Civil Disturbances

The 1992 Los Angeles civil disturbances was "the worst urban riot in contemporary United States history . . ." (Meyers, Thomas, Webb, & Mitchell, 1992). The civil disturbances began on the afternoon of April 29, following the announcement of the acquittal of four Los Angeles Police Department officers tried for using unreasonable force to subdue Rodney King, an African American motorist. A videotape, recorded by a witness, of the police officers repeatedly hitting King had been distributed worldwide prior to the trial.

Following the trial, civil disturbances occurred throughout the United States and Canada. The cities hardest hit by the violence were Los Angeles, San Francisco, Las Vegas, Atlanta, Tampa, Seattle, Washington, DC, and Toronto, Canada. Los Angeles experienced the greatest destruction with 51 deaths, 2,283 people injured, 10,000 fire calls (for the city and county of Los Angeles and for Long Beach), 5,200 buildings destroyed including 1,600 stores or offices damaged or burned, and 17,000 arrests. The estimated cost of damage resulting from the civil disturbance approached $1 billion.

Critical Incident Stress Debriefings (CISDs) were provided to emergency medical technicians responding into south central Los Angeles during the crisis. These organizations participated in a study providing debriefings for personnel responding to the Los Angeles civil disturbances. CISD was provided from April 30, 1992, to May 12, 1992. The CISD teams consisted of mental health professionals, emergency medical technicians, and firefighter peer support staff. The personnel providing the CISD averaged 2–5 years of experience in delivering CISD. All teams used the seven-stage ICISF model of CISD (Mitchell, 1983). The issue of race, trust, and fear were prominent in the CISD following the disturbances (Scott & Jordan, 1993).

The Emergency Medical Services Survey for the South Central Los Angeles Civil Disturbance (Koehler, Isbell, Freeman, Smiley, & Morales, 1993), which surveyed emergency medical technicians who responded into south central Los Angeles, provides a description of the critical incident stress encountered by the emergency medical technicians. Emergency medical technicians experienced less than adequate law enforcement protection, attacks by crowds when providing medical care, increased number of dispatches, greater number of fractures treated and transported, and a larger number more than expected of injuries and deaths. All these stressors were associated with an increase in emergency medical technicians' stress response. The study also found that 3 months following the civil disturbance, the stress response of emergency medical technicians who were debriefed was significantly lower than that of emergency medical technicians not debriefed. The debriefed group showed significantly lower arousal, and intrusion, fewer reported stress-related problems, and fewer than expected injuries and deaths (Wee, Mills, & Koehler, 1999).

EDUCATION

Education is the fourth core service component in the CODE-C DMHSM. It involves information or training or both for survivors, responders, disaster workers, service providers, and community leaders on common reactions to disaster, disaster stress management strategies, disaster mental health issues and interventions, and resources. Education services involve dissemination of information and training on topics specific to disaster psychology and mental health to disaster mental health workers, service providers, and members of the community. Educational services are provided at the individual, group, neighborhood, organizational, and community level using a variety of strategies that include fliers and brochures, mass media, the Internet, brief presentations, workshops, trainings, and conferences.

The education strategies change as the social and psychological reactions of the disaster-impacted community change. The short-term, mid-term, and long-term disaster phase mental health reactions and consultation activities are displayed in Table 3.3. During the short-term disaster phase, education services will use electronic and print media, the Internet, posters, bulletin boards, fliers and brochures, and public meetings to distribute information about "the normal reaction normal people have to abnormal events." During the mid-term disaster phase, education services target high-need groups such as emergency service personnel, using mailings, media, public meetings, and training. In addition, community caregivers such as doctors, nurses, school personnel, religious leaders, social service workers, and others may be provided with training that will enable them to be sensitive, responsive, and helpful to the mental health aspects of healing their constituents and clients. Such training can help these professionals to develop skills and confidence, foster collaboration with mental health agencies and professionals, and create a broad-based involvement of community professionals in the mental health efforts toward disaster recovery (Myers, 1989; Myers et al., 1996). Long-term disaster-phase education services will focus on special needs, stress management, public meetings, and community events.

EDUCATION CASE EXAMPLE: A CONFERENCE ON DISASTER-PSYCHOLOGICAL
RESPONSE AND RECOVERY: PERSPECTIVES ON THE EAST BAY FIRESTORM

> The East Bay firestorm had a catastrophic impact on the Berkeley and Oakland areas. The Alta Bates Medical Center Mental Health Services and The City of Berkeley Mental Health Services together conducted a conference designed to educate the local mental health community about the impact of the firestorm. The keynote address featured the videotape "Beyond the Ashes," a documentary of disaster survivor's reactions to the fire. Keynote speaker was Diane Myers, R.N., M.S.N., on "Patterns of Psychological Response to Disasters: Loma Prieta Earthquake, Los Angeles Riots, East Bay Firestorm." Plenary sessions were titled Responses to the East Bay Fire: The Berkeley Mental Health East Bay Firestorm Project; Children: Intervention, Expression, and Research; Psychological Aspects of Physical Recovery: Patients and Staff; Healing the Healers; Critical Incident Stress Debriefing; Fire Victims Dream Journal Study; and Relationships: The Psychological Impact of Trauma. Persons participating in the conference found the material presented of value and were, overall, very satisfied. "A Conference on Disaster-Psychological Response and Recovery: Perspectives on the East Bay Firestorm" was designated a "best practice" in the Crisis Counseling Program Best Practices Document by the Center for Mental Health Services, U.S. Department of Health and Human Services (Center for Mental Health Services, 2000).

CRISIS COUNSELING

Crisis counseling is the fifth core service component in the CODE-C model. In the model, crisis counseling is defined as therapeutic, crisis-oriented intervention with survivors for the purpose of stabilization, crisis intervention, stress management, problem-solving, and referral for treatment. Crisis counseling includes interviews conducted by disaster mental health personnel for the purpose of identification of disaster-related distress and problems of living for crisis intervention and problem-solving.

The goals of crisis counseling include the following:

- Helping the person deal with the *current* situational crisis
- Protecting the person from additional stress or harm
- Instilling a sense of hope
- Assisting the person in organizing and mobilizing resources, both internal and external
- Helping people return to at least their precrisis level of functioning: to restore and enhance coping abilities; to restore and enhance problem-solving capabilities; and to restore and enhance use of social support
- Doing everything possible to promote growth as an outcome
- Preventing negative or destructive outcomes (Hafen & Frandsen, 1985; Hoff, 1984; Mitchell & Resnick, 1981; Myers, 1989; Myers et al., 1996)

The goals of crisis counseling are not the following:

- Psychological testing
- Personality reconstruction
- Reconstruction of defense mechanisms
- Development of insight
- Working-through of unconscious conflicts
- Working-through of historical issues or prior trauma
- Family therapy
- Treatment of mental disorders
- Long-term psychotherapy (Myers et al., 1996)

Crisis counseling strategies in disaster include sensitive, active listening; facilitating; ventilation; clarification; validation of feelings; not undermining defenses; normalization of feelings; reframing; and relabeling (Hoff, 1984; Myers, 1989; Myers et al., 1996). Crisis counseling strategies also include assisting survivors in understanding and accepting reality of situation, use of education and anticipatory guidance to help survivors understand crisis reactions and phases of the recovery process, and teaching and reinforcing constructive coping strategies, as well as identifying negative coping strategies (Hoff; Myers et al.). The teaching done as a crisis counseling strategy also includes the teaching of practical, appropriate stress management techniques. Grief counseling around tangible and not-so-tangible losses and the encouragement to use or develop rituals to deal with losses are important (Hoff; Myers, 1989; Myers et al.).

Crisis counseling also involves assisting survivors with problem solving and decision making, as well as helping them obtain resources and advocacy. Advocacy involves providing direct action on behalf of a survivor when the individual is unable to carry out the action alone, when direct action is to assist the individual with psychological recovery, and when the action will not contribute to dependency of the individual on the counselor. Crisis counseling helps in encouraging survivors to develop and use social support systems, and in reinforcing positive changes they have experienced (Hoff, 1984).

The crisis counseling activities change very little as the social and psychological reactions of the disaster-impacted community change. The short-term, mid-term, and long-term disaster-phase mental health reactions and crisis counseling activities are displayed in Table 3.3. During any disaster phase, individuals, couples, and families may be provided with brief crisis counseling or support group services or both.

It is important to emphasize that crisis counseling is to psychotherapy what first aid is to surgery (Everly, Mitchell, Myers, & Mitchell, 2002). That is, crisis counseling is a brief form of individual therapy intended to stabilize the situation and restore or enhance adaptive coping. For individuals whose symptoms are more serious mental illness or whose stress is of a severity or duration that is disabling, referral for a more extensive mental health assessment, diagnosis, and treatment is essential.

CRISIS COUNSELING CASE EXAMPLE

Following Hurricane Andrew in 1992, the Federal Emergency Management Agency established stress management services in its disaster field office in Miami. The mission of the stress management services was to provide needs assessment, consultation, outreach, debriefing, education, and crisis counseling to persons working in the office. Crisis counseling services were available on a drop-in or scheduled basis in the stress management office.

One morning a young man of Cuban descent requested to be seen for a crisis counseling interview.

Crisis counselor: What brings you in today?
Man: I am having problems with control. I am concerned about violence, my temper, [and] I am afraid I will snap.
Cc: What is happening that leads up to your fears about losing control. What about it?
Man: It's with my girlfriend. We have arguments.
Cc: Did you argue before Hurricane Andrew?
Man: Yes, about money.

Crisis counseling focuses on the disaster-related mental health reactions of the individual, group, or family. It is important to inquire about psychological and behavioral changes the person experienced before the disaster.

Cc: Have the arguments been worse since Hurricane Andrew?
Man: Yes.

This young man confirms that psychological and behavioral changes have happened since Hurricane Andrew. The objective is to identify specific disaster-related experiences that have contributed to the current distress.

Cc: What happened during Hurricane Andrew?
Man: I was in a room with my girlfriend. She was going into shock [and] my mother was screaming; the dog was with us. I lost everything. I tried to keep them calm, but they freaked out. I was the man. I thought that I could keep everyone calm but I am only 18.

He makes three important statements:
He has lost everything.
He describes role conflict. His role in the family as "the man" during the hurricane conflicted with his role expectations and needs as the child of his mother and as the boyfriend of his girlfriend.
He also had the belief that he could or should have kept everyone calm during the hurricane when his, his girlfriend's, mother's, and dog's lives were threatened. He had the unrealistic belief that his role was to keep people calm and that he had failed. By hearing himself describe what happened, he realized how unrealistic this belief and his role expectations were.

Cc: Was there another part of you that [was] hurt? Maybe a child part of you?
Man: That is it. I was really scared. They freaked out; I couldn't do anything.
Cc: You protected your family, but you still want to feel safe and nurtured by your mother and girlfriend. Have you talked to them?

The focus is on clarifying and reinforcing adaptive and positive role functioning coupled with specific suggestions to initiate communication about the man's needs. Talking with his mother and girlfriend will help him access support and meet his needs.

Man: Maybe I should.

Using the man as the best informant about what activities are most helpful and consistent with his culture and experience, I ask him about the interaction and exchange between his mother and himself.

Cc: What does your mother do to sooth you and comfort you?
Man: We spend special time together and she cooks special things.
Cc: Maybe you could do that. What about your father?
Man: He is divorced and remarried and has two children. I feel like a big brother to them. My mother and brother are my other family.

The man emphasizes his positive role function as the "big brother" and the importance of his family. I choose to use these relationships to reinforce the positive supports he has in his familial network. In some cultures, a person's wealth is described in terms of family. I use this concept. He responds very strongly to this connection with his support system.

> Cc: With so many family [members], you are a very rich man.
>
> Man: I guess I am. (His eyes fill with tears. As he leaves, he asks for a Kleenex because of his "cold," and says, "I feel better . . . I want to make another appointment next week."
>
> *Several days later, I passed him in the hallways of the Disaster Field Office. As I came closer to him, I noticed that the strain on his face was not there. He appeared cheerful and less preoccupied. As he walked by, he stopped me, extended his hand, and shook my hand warmly.*

PROGRAM EVALUATION AND RESEARCH

The CODE-C model aids in the development of standardized data collection systems and evaluation of disaster mental health services, and can assist in such functions as continuing quality management, administration, budget, and research and evaluation. Data collection systems should also allow for collection of information important to local mental health providers. Program activities could be compared over time and across programs which would aid in program monitoring, consultation, and training.

The evaluation of disaster mental health services in the postdisaster environment is challenging and complex. During disasters, the overriding priority is providing disaster response, recovery intervention, and services as quickly and efficiently as possible. There are overwhelming needs with often inadequate resources and management of resources. Although saving lives, property, and alleviating suffering are priorities, systematic research and evaluation of disaster mental health service are rarely perceived as a high priority. Research and evaluation should best be planned in advance and discussed with stakeholders to prevent misunderstandings and distrust. Evaluation of disaster mental health services and service components is important to continuing to build the knowledge base that forwards the efforts to provide more effective services that help people cope.

CONCLUSION

CODE-C DMHSM is a comprehensive, integrated, multiservice model to effectively address the wide range of disaster mental health problems of communities following disasters. Disaster mental health services differ from traditional mental health service delivery in nondisaster times. Disaster mental health services and traditional mental health services are unique because of different goals, objectives, and methods, and settings. The CODE-C DMHSM is a tool that can be used by planners, managers, and workers to develop comprehensive disaster mental health programs that are disaster-phase specific, use appropriate services, and are effective. The CODE-C model can also serve as a model for the development of immediate services and regular services applications for the Crisis Counseling Program administered by the Center for Mental Health Services. The CODE-C model promotes the development, identification, and standardization of core service components that are critical and essential in disaster mental health programs and disaster worker stress management programs. The CODE-C model includes the essential disaster mental health services of needs assessment, consultation, outreach, debriefing, education, and crisis counseling. The CODE-C Disaster Mental Health Service Delivery Model can be used as an important tool in designing disaster mental health services and programs following disasters, and as a tool for designing research and evaluation studies to examine the need, satisfaction with services, effectiveness, and impact of disaster mental health services.

REFERENCES

Center for Mental Health Services. (2000). *Crisis counseling program: Best practices document.* Washington, DC: Department of Health and Human Services, Substance Abuse, and Mental Health Services Administration, and U.S. Government Printing Office.

Cohen, R. E., & Ahearn, F. L. (1980). *Handbook for mental health care of disaster victims.* Baltimore: Johns Hopkins University Press.

Cummock, M. V. (1995). The necessity of denial in grieving murder: Observations of the victim's families following the bombing in Oklahoma City. *NCP Clinical Quarterly, 5,* 2–3.

Everly, G. S., Jr., Mitchell, D. J., Myers, D., & Mitchell, J. T. (2002). *National Guard Critical Incident Stress Management (CISM): Terrorism and disaster response. Trainer's guide.* Ellicott City, MD: International Critical Incident Stress Foundation.

Federal Emergency Management Agency. (1995). *Building Inspection Area.* Oklahoma City, OK: FEMA-GIS.

Federal Emergency Management Agency. (1998). *Stress management program training manual.* Washington, DC: Author.

Flynn, B. W. (1996). *Psychological aspects of terrorism.* Paper presented at the 1st Harvard Symposium on the Medical Consequences of Terrorism, Boston, MA.

Hafen, B.Q., & Frandsen, K. J. (1985). *Psychological emergencies and crisis intervention: A comprehensive guide for emergency personnel.* Englewood, CO: Morton.

Hoff, L. A. (1984). *People in crisis: Understanding and helping.* Menlo Park, CA: Addison-Wesley.

Jordon, F. B. (1997). The role of the medical examiner/coroner in mass fatality disaster management. *National Foundation for Mortuary Care Disaster Management News, 1,* 1–3.

Koelher, G., Isbell, D., Freeman, C., Smiley, D., & Morales, J. (1993). *Medical care for the injured: The emergency medical response to the April 1992 Los Angeles civil disturbance.* (EMSA No. 393–01). Sacramento, CA: Emergency Medical Services Authority.

Meyers, T., Thomas, T., Webb, H., & Mitchell, P. (May 10, 1992) Path of destruction. *Los Angeles Times,* p. A31.

Mitchell, J. T. (1983). When disaster strikes. *Journal of Emergency Medical Services, 8,* 36–39.

Mitchell, J. T., & Resnick, H. L. P. (1981). *Emergency response to crisis.* Bowie, MD: Robert J. Brady.

Myers, D. (1989). *Training manual: Disaster mental health*. California Department of Mental Health.

Myers, D. (1992). *Hurricane Andrew disaster field office stress management program: After action report*. Miami, FL: Federal Emergency Management Agency.

Myers, D. (1993). *Disaster worker stress management: Planning and training issues*. Federal Emergency Management Agency and Center for Mental Health Services.

Myers, D. (1994). *Disaster response and recovery: A handbook for mental health professionals*. Rockville, MD: Center for Mental Health Services.

Myers, D. (2001a). *Weapons of mass destruction and terrorism: Mental health consequences and implications for planning and training*. Paper presented at the American Red Cross Weapons of Mass Destruction/Terrorism Orientation Pilot Program, Pine Bluff, AR.

Myers, D. (2001b). *Weapons of mass destruction and terrorism. The ripple effect from ground zero*. New York: American Red Cross.

Myers, D. (2002a). Mental health response to terrorism. In *Disaster medical operations: A challenge for emergency management*. San Luis Obispo, CA: Governor's Office of Emergency Services, California Specialized Training Institute.

Myers, D. (2002b). Psychological impacts of terrorist events. In *Criminal justice: Terrorism*. San Luis Obispo, CA: Governor's Office of Emergency Services, California Specialized Training Institute.

Myers, D. (2002c). Psychological impacts of terrorist events. In *Terrorism: The current threat to California: A POST special seminar for the California highway patrol*. San Luis Obispo, CA: Governor's Office of Emergency Services, California Specialized Training Institute.

Myers, D., Spofford, P., & Young, B. (1996). *Responding to traumatic events: A training manual*. Pacific Grove, CA: National Disaster Mental Health Consultants.

Myers, D., & Zunin, L. M. (1993a). *After action report: 1993 Florida winter storms disaster field office stress management program*. Tampa, FL: Federal Emergency Management Agency.

Myers, D., & Zunin, L. M. (1993b). *After action report: 1993 Midwest floods stress management program*. Kansas City, MO: Federal Emergency Management Agency.

Myers, D., & Zunin, L. M. (1994a). *Stress management program after-action report: 1994 Northridge earthquake*. Pasadena, CA: Federal Emergency Management Agency and California Governor's Office of Emergency Services.

Myers, D., & Zunin, L. M. (1994b). *Stress management program for disaster workers: A national cadre of stress management personnel. Training manual*. Atlanta, GA: Federal Emergency Management Agency.

Oklahoma City Fire Department. (1995, July). *Oklahoma City disaster: Initial city and fire department response*. Paper presented at a training symposium on the Carlos, CA.

Oklahoma City Public Works Department. (1995). *Building inspection area*. Oklahoma City, OK: Geographic Information Systems.

Scott, R. T., & Jordan, M. J. (1993, April). *The Los Angeles riots April 1992: A CISD challenge*. Paper presented at the 2nd World Congress on Stress, Trauma, and Coping in the Emergency Services. A meeting of the International Critical Incident Stress Foundation, Baltimore.

Solomon, S. D. (1986). Mobilizing social support networks in times of disaster. In C. R. Figley (Ed.), *Trauma and its wake: Vol 2. Traumatic stress theory, research, and intervention*. New York: Brunner/Mazel.

Wee, D. (1994). Disasters: Impact on the law enforcement family. J. T. Reese & E. Scrivner (Eds.), *Law enforcement family: Issues and answers*. Washington, DC: U.S. Department of Justice, Federal Bureau of Investigation.

Wee, D. F., Mills, D. M., & Koehler, G. (1999). The effects of Critical Incident Stress Debriefing (CISD) on emergency medical services personnel following the Los Angeles civil disturbances. *International Journal of Emergency Mental Health, 1*, 33–38.

4

STRESS MANAGEMENT AND PREVENTION OF COMPASSION FATIGUE FOR PSYCHOTRAUMATOLOGISTS

THE MANAGEMENT OF STRESS AND PREVENTION OF SECONDARY TRAUMATIZATION or *compassion fatigue* for psychotraumatologists is an important issue in disaster mental health. Studies of emergency service workers, disaster workers, and disaster mental health workers have identified stress reactions to the disaster work that can result in patterns of mental and physical distress. Traumatologists' experiences of working with disasters and violence in the community sensitize them to the experiences, pain, challenges, and successes of the community on its road to recovery. The traumatologist who is also a survivor of the same event has even more empathy with other survivors and is often acknowledged by other survivors as "truly knowing," one of the few who truly understands the experience of the disaster survivor. Although trauma therapists can help others heal, they can also be affected by the pain and suffering they share with the survivors they attempt to help.

This chapter will present stress management strategies for psychotraumatologists during disaster, which include predisaster briefings, supervision, consultations, continuing education, and psychotherapy. Also important in the prevention of compassion fatigue are organizational support, workplace strategies, and defusing and debriefing. Team work, professional development strategies and personal strategies are equally important. The stress which can accompany the closure of a specialized disaster mental health program can be mitigated by planning for the end of services, program closure activities, critique of services, debriefing of staff, recognition of staff, and follow-up of staff some months later. Preserving the physical, mental, and social health of traumatologists during disaster response and recovery and maintaining quality services to disaster survivors, other disaster workers, and citizens of the community are also important.

INTRODUCTION

Since the 1970s, professional publications in the field of mental health, emergency services, and disaster management have abounded with reports and studies on the effects of trauma intervention on the responders. During the 1980s and 1990s, much of that literature focused on the psychological effects of trauma exposure on primary victims and among *first responders*— firefighters, police officers, and emergency medical personnel. Simultaneously, as the number of natural and technological disasters was on the rise, studies on the effects of large scale disaster events upon both the victims and the disaster responders increased. Charles Figley (1995) provided a groundbreaking exploration and focus on those professionals who provide services to trauma survivors: crisis workers, trauma counselors, nurses, physicians, and other caregivers who become victims themselves of secondary traumatic stress disorder (STS) or compassion fatigue. A very small number of studies have further narrowed the focus of research to examine the psychological impacts of providing mental health counseling in the specialized context of large scale disasters (Bartone, Ursano, Wright, & Ingraham, 1989; Berah, Jones, & Valent, 1984; Frederick, 1977; Hodgkinson & Shepherd, 1994; Raphael, Singh, Bradbury, & Lambert, 1984; Winget & Umbenhauer, 1982; Wee & Myers, 1997).

The body of literature on the *primary victims* of disasters is extensive. Disasters are overwhelming events that test the capability of the community and individuals to respond and can temporarily lead to massive disruption (Raphael, 1986). Humans have been victims of disasters throughout recorded history (Lystad, 1988). Populations affected by natural disasters show a variety of responses to the event. The responses can range from adaptive restoration of functioning, normal stress response syndromes, resilient recovery, or serious and persisting psychological responses consistent with posttraumatic stress disorder (PTSD) (Horowitz, Stinson, & Field, 1991). Disaster survivors experiencing psychological reactions to disaster are viewed as normal people in abnormal circumstances. Stress responses that would be excessive at other times are now viewed as normal (Myers, 1994b).

Psychological reactions can continue long after the disaster (Green & Gleser, 1983; Linderman, 1944). For example, some individuals who experienced the Loma Prieta earthquake continued to identify symptoms of distress 6 months after the earthquake (Wee, 1991a). Individuals who lost their homes in the East Bay firestorm also showed a persistent and significant stress response 15 months after the fire (Wee & Mills, 1993).

Families are also affected by a multitude of stressors following natural disasters, including evacuation; changes in roles, relationships, and routines;

economic losses; and destruction of home and surrounding environment. Children may exhibit psychological and behavioral symptoms, some of which may become long-term (Frederick, 1985). In addition, disaster worker families can also become a source of stress if the family feels excluded or deprived by the worker's absence and involvement in the disaster work (Raphael, 1986). But even when struck by catastrophe, the family is a critical support system during and following a traumatic event (Figley, 1983).

There is considerable information about the psychological effects of trauma exposure among emergency service and disaster workers. This group of workers often experience the intensity of the disaster directly and can experience psychological reactions for overly prolonged time periods (Lystad, 1988). The psychological impact on disaster workers and emergency service personnel has been examined by a number of investigators (Durham, McCammon, & Allison, Jr., 1985; Lanning & Fannin, 1988; McFarlane, 1988; Miles, Demi, & Mostyn-Aker, 1984; Mitchell, 1986; Moran & Britton, 1994; Robinson, 1989; Taylor & Frazer, 1982; Wee, 1991b). Disasters can cause psychological effects on the workers and influence those closest to them (Wee, 1994a; Hartsough & Myers, 1985; Wraith & Gordon, 1988).

The existing literature on stresses of long-term recovery workers focuses primarily on the stress among American Red Cross and Federal Emergency Management Agency (FEMA) staff. Myers (Hartsough & Myers, 1985) described the typical phases involved in disaster work and the stressors inherent in each phase for the workers, including the "letdown" involved after long-term disaster assignments. Eby (1984) outlined some sources of stress for Red Cross workers involved in small, local disasters, as well as for those workers who responded repeatedly to major disasters. The Center for Mental Health Services (CMHS, formerly the National Institute of Mental Health) and FEMA have developed many publications and training materials on management of disaster worker stress (Department of Health and Human Services [DHHS], 1988a, 1988b; Federal Emergency Management Agency [FEMA], 1987a, 1987b).

Rosenschweig and Vaslow (1992) conducted a study to identify sources of stress among FEMA Disaster Assistance Program employees. A total of 500 FEMA employees were surveyed, and the resulting report made specific recommendations on stress reduction for them. Myers (1992, 1993a, 1993b, 1994a, 1994b), Myers and Zunin (1993a, 1993b, 1994a,1994b), and Zunin, Myers, and Cook (1995) incorporated many of Rosensweig and Vaslow's ideas into the stress management programs they developed and directed for FEMA workers in many disasters including Hurricane Andrew, the Midwest floods of 1993, the Northridge earthquake of 1994, and the Oklahoma City bombing. Armstrong, O'Callahan, and Marmar (1991) described stressors experienced by Red Cross relief personnel working in the 2-month period following the Loma Prieta earthquake, and described a multiple stressor debriefing model developed for the personnel and to be used in exit debriefings before they returned home.

A small number of studies have examined the impact of disaster recovery work upon mental health staff who provide postdisaster counseling. These studies recommend that this specialized group of disaster recovery workers pay special attention to their vulnerability to stress and posttrauma sequelae, so they do not become "victims-by-proxy" (Bartone et al., 1989; Berah et al., 1984; Frederick, 1977; Hodgkinson & Shepherd, 1994; Raphael et al., 1984; Winget & Umbenhauer, 1982).

Hartsough and Myers (1985) describe numerous stressors for disaster workers, of which two types are most prominent in long-term recovery efforts: (a) event stressors and (b) occupational stressors. Event stressors include the type of disaster, personal loss and injury of disaster workers who are primary victims of the disaster, fatigue, exposure to traumatic stimuli, sense of mission failure, or human error. These stressors influence the postimpact recovery environment and worker stress during the long-term recovery phase.

Occupational stressors impacting disaster workers have much to do with the work itself and include time and responsibility pressures and the emotional demands of survivors. The emotional reactions and behavior of disaster victims change over time. Different phases of disaster recovery have different impacts on disaster workers. Immediate positive responses can occur in what are called the "heroic" and "honeymoon" phases, and include a high level of energy and a generally optimistic outlook for a swift recovery. In the "disillusionment" phase, the emphasis for long-term recovery workers shifts more to the aspects that are hard to affect; workers are vulnerable to strong identification with the feelings of the survivors, which in the disillusionment phase include grief, fatigue, irritability, and anger. Workers are also often the target of displaced emotions of the victims, particularly anger.

Symptoms of acute, delayed, and cumulative stress among emergency workers have been extensively covered in the literature (Hartsough & Myers, 1985; Mitchell & Bray, 1990; Mitchell & Everly, 1993; Myers & Zunin, 1994a). For the most part, stress reactions experienced by long-term disaster recovery workers fit those in the cumulative stress category. Symptoms commonly observed by stress management consultants and by crisis counseling staff working with disaster personnel are fatigue and depression;

concentration, memory, and cognitive problems; irritability and interpersonal conflicts; anxiety, especially related to how long the disaster work will continue and related to obligations at home or in their regular job that are not being met; feeling unappreciated; distancing from others and from the job; cynicism and negativity; use of derogatory labels; "sick" or gallows humor; blaming others; poor job performance; absences; physical complaints and illness; accident proneness; and alcohol and substance abuse.

Little empirical research has been done on long-term disaster mental health workers and the effects of their work-related stressors. The research that exists suggests that workers continue to experience significant levels of symptomatology during their entire tenure of disaster support work. Hodgkinson and Shepherd (1994) in their study of disaster crisis counselors found significant levels of symptomatology 12 months into the disaster recovery work. Symptoms most frequently reported included cognitive difficulties, depression, and feelings of inadequacy and insecurity. Wee and Myers (1997) conducted research comparing a group of disaster mental health workers with a group of mental health professionals who were not working in disaster mental health. They found that providing mental health services to disaster victims during long-term recovery appears to be associated with increased levels of stress for the workers doing this work. The disaster mental health workers group were significantly more distressed than the nondisaster mental health workers. Despite current knowledge about the impact of trauma on the primary victims, little has been empirically researched or written about the "cost of caring" (Figley, 1982; 1989, 2002). It is vitally important to know how disaster mental health counselors are affected and, in many cases, traumatized as a result of their exposure to victims. By understanding this process we can not only prevent additional, subsequent traumatic stress among this population, but can also increase the quality of care that they provide for the victims they help (Figley, 1995).

The following case study of disaster mental health workers who provided crisis counseling following the Alfred P. Murrah Federal Building bombing illustrates the impact of this terrorist attack on the community, the psychological impact of the bombing on the workers, the psychological impact of disaster mental health work, and the level of risk the workers had for compassion fatigue.

ALFRED P. MURRAH FEDERAL BUILDING BOMBING

On April 19, 1995, at 9:02 A.M., the Alfred P. Murrah Federal Building was torn apart by a bomb that killed 168 and injured approximately 700 individuals in the building and nearby areas. The shock waves from the blast traveled at 40,000 ft/s, sending shards of metal and glass through walls and bodies. The 30,000-ft^2, 9-story building with its 5-story garage had housed 19 federal agencies and 3 private agencies. One of the agencies most directly hit by the blast was the daycare center within the federal building premises.

An estimated 646 people were thought to have been in the building when the bomb exploded. Four of the deaths occurred in the Athena building across the street from the federal building, two deaths occurred in the Oklahoma Water Resources Building also across the street from the federal building, and one death occurred at the Journal Record Building. Three of the fatalities were dead on arrival at local hospitals, and three died in hospitals from 2 to 23 days after admission (Jordan, 1997). Over 16,744 people work or reside in the area impacted by the bomb, and many of the injured were on the streets in the neighborhood or in nearby buildings. Many of the injured were children in the federal building's childcare center and in the nearby YMCA's daycare center. There were approximately 50 children in the two daycare centers combined. Thirteen children died in these centers.

Several square blocks required search and rescue activities. Over 220 square blocks surrounding the federal building sustained damage. A total of 800 buildings received damages ranging from major structural damage to broken windows. Nine structures, including the federal building, suffered partial collapse (FEMA, 1995; Oklahoma City Public Works Department, 1995). Following the bombing, the federal building and 29 other damaged structures were demolished (Oklahoma City Fire Department, 1995). The replacement value of the federal building was estimated at $30 million.

The emotional devastation was even greater than the physical devastation of the bombing. Although most of the victims were from Oklahoma County, in which Oklahoma City is located, many neighboring towns and counties suffered losses. The town of Guthrie, north of Oklahoma City, lost 11 persons, and there were 7 deaths from the town of Norman, just south of Oklahoma City. Individuals flocked to Oklahoma City from all areas of the nation, searching for news of loved ones who worked in or near the building.

The emotional impact on children extended far beyond the deaths of the 13 children killed in the bombing. A total of 271 children lost one or more parent in the blast. Of those children 60 were left orphaned. Eighty percent of the schools within the Oklahoma City School District had children who had immediate family members injured or killed in the bombing.

In addition to those people who were emotionally impacted by the injury or death of a loved one, over 12,000 rescue workers from throughout the state of Oklahoma and the nation participated in the recovery effort. They were exposed to unspeakable hardship and horror as they persevered to recover every body and body fragment. In addition, their own lives were threatened by the unstable condition of the building and its hazardous contents. Firefighters took off their helmets and put them over the heads of nurses who were trying to start intravenous fluids on victims in the rubble (Oklahoma City Fire Department, 1995). One nurse was killed by falling debris, and an additional 26 rescuers were hospitalized with injuries. Work conditions were grueling. For the first 8 days, over 100 tons of rubble were dug out manually every 12 hr, using small military shovels, and removed in increments of 5-gallon buckets at a time. Urban search and rescue teams worked 12 hr a day for up to 10 days, averaging about 4 hr of sleep per night (Oklahoma City Fire Department). When there was no longer any hope that live survivors would be found, rescue efforts changed to recovery efforts, and heavy equipment was brought in to remove the debris. On May 4, recovery efforts were halted because of the unstable condition of the building. Three bodies could not be recovered until after the implosion of the building on May 23. On May 25, all bodies had been recovered.

In addition to the search, rescue, recovery, and body identification personnel, dozens of agencies and hundreds of workers provided healthcare, mental health counseling, pastoral care, social services, and compassion to the survivors and the families of victims. Much of the care was provided at the Compassion Center, established in the first hours of the disaster at the First Christian Church in Oklahoma City. Under the auspices of the medical examiner's office, the compassion center was established to provide a safe haven for family members awaiting news of the status of their loved ones. The center was run by the American Red Cross, in cooperation with numerous agencies and organizations. A wide range of supportive services were provided, along with regular, daily briefings by the fire department and medical examiner's office, on the status of the recovery activities. When positive identification of a victim was made, formal death notification to family members was conducted by a team consisting of a medical examiner's representative, clergy, a healthcare professional (usually a registered nurse), and a mental health counselor.

CRISIS COUNSELING PROGRAM: MENTAL HEALTH SERVICES IN A PRESIDENTIAL DECLARED DISASTER

When it is determined that in a large-scale disaster the needs of the impacted community will exceed those resources available locally and at the state level, the governor of the state may request the president of the United

States to declare the situation a major disaster. This disaster declaration makes available to the community a wide range of federal assistance. Section 416 of the Robert T. Stafford Disaster Relief and Emergency Assistance Act (Public Law 93-288, as amended) authorizes funding for mental health services following a presidential declared disaster (Federal Emergency Management Agency [FEMA] and Center for Mental Health Services [CMHS], 1992):

> The Crisis Counseling Assistance and Training Program for survivors of major disasters provides support for direct services to disaster survivors and disaster workers. A training component in disaster crisis counseling for direct services staff of the project and for other disaster services workers may be included. This program has been developed in cooperation with FEMA and the CMHS within the Substance Abuse and Mental Health Services Administration (SAMHSA) (Myers, 1994b).

Assistance under this program is limited to presidential declared major disasters. Moreover, the program is designed to supplement the available resources and services of state and local governments. Thus support for crisis counseling services to disaster victims may be granted if these services cannot be provided by existing agency programs. The support is not automatically provided, and a grant application with a needs assessment and program plan must be prepared and submitted through the state mental authority to FEMA (Myers, 1994b). The program must provide plans for outreach to impacted populations, crisis counseling, referral, consultation, public education, and training of crisis counselors. The program must also reflect attention to cultural, ethnic, or geographic needs or other special factors unique to the disaster or indigenous to the area (Myers).

On May 8, 1995, the Oklahoma Department of Mental Health and Substance Abuse Services opened the Project Heartland Center, funded by the FEMA Crisis Counseling Assistance and Training Program. Services that had been provided by a variety of agencies at compassion centers started the transition to Project Heartland by the second week after the bombing. Project Heartland provided crisis intervention, crisis counseling, support groups, and outreach to individuals affected by the bombing. Project Heartland and its contract agencies had a total of 74 staff.

The Project Heartland crisis counseling staff were exposed regularly to the pain, loss, anger, and anguished stories of the survivors, family members of victims, and disaster response workers. Because of the intensity of the emotional climate in which the crisis counselors worked, the program employed a private consultant to provide stress management services to the crisis counselors. It is this group of crisis counselors that has been surveyed for this study.

BOMBING DISASTER REACTION STUDY

The Alfred P. Murrah Federal Building Bombing Reaction Study examined the effects of disaster crisis counseling work on mental health workers. The primary focus of the study is the disaster experiences, postdisaster stress response, perception of social support, and reactions of mental health workers providing crisis counseling services to victims of the Oklahoma City bombing disaster. The purpose of the research was to identify variables which may be associated with vulnerability to the development of postdisaster stress response in workers involved in long-term mental health recovery activities. The result of such assessment can assist mental health workers, who provide disaster crisis counseling services, in identifying their vulnerabilities, stress responses, and effective interventions to mitigate stress responses during long-term disaster mental health recovery activities.

VOLUNTEER SUBJECTS OF STUDY

Subjects for this study consist of volunteers from the Oklahoma Department of Mental Health and Substance Abuse Services working in the Alfred P. Murrah Federal Building Bombing Crisis Counseling Program. A total of 74 mental health personnel provided crisis counseling, outreach, and educational services to persons impacted by the bombing. All subjects were over 21 years of age and employed by the Oklahoma Department of Mental Health and Substance Abuse Services or contract agencies. The Alfred P. Murrah Federal Building Bombing Reaction Questionnaire included an informed consent statement and an explanatory cover letter which described its general purpose, the intent of the study, and its confidential nature. Consultation was offered to anyone who might experience anxiety aroused in the retelling of disaster experiences.

STUDY QUESTIONNAIRE PROCEDURES

Disaster mental health workers received the 179-item self-report questionnaire packet on the 9th month following the bombing. It included items concerning demographic information, personal experiences with the bombing, experiences with the crisis counseling program, empathy received from people involved or not involved with this incident, involvement in stress management activities, and several open-ended questions. Instrumentation included three standardized measures.

The Compassion Fatigue Self-Test for Helpers (Figley, 1995) was used to identify the presence and degree of severity of experiences associated with secondary traumatic stress and burnout. Secondary traumatic stress (used interchangeably with the term compassion fatigue) is defined as ". . . the natural consequent behaviors and emotions resulting from knowing about a traumatizing event experienced by a significant other—stress resulting from helping or wanting to help a traumatized or suffering person" (Figley, 1993). Burnout can be defined as a gradually progressive process with key features being physical exhaustion, emotional exhaustion, depersonalization, and reduced personal achievement, with work-related and interpersonal symptoms. The Compassion Fatigue Self-Test for Helpers is still being developed and is reported to have good psychometric properties (Figley, 1995, 2002).

The Frederick Reaction Index A (Frederick, 1985, 1988) was used to examine the presence of symptoms and degree of severity of posttraumatic stress disorder ranging from doubtful, mild, moderate, severe, and very severe. The scale has been found to have a reliability coefficient yielding an inter-rated reliability of .77 for a single rater, in which 50 cases were given anonymous clinical ratings including levels of severity by three raters. A Greenhouse–Geisser probability of .92 and Huy–Feldt probability of .95 were found when epsilon factors for degrees of freedom adjustment were applied (Frederick, 1985, 1987).

The Symptom Checklist 90—Revised (SCL-90-R) (Derogatis, 1994) was used to evaluate the presence and severity of psychological symptoms of distress experienced by the respondents. The Symptom Checklist-90-R is a 90 item self-report symptom inventory that has nine primary symptoms dimensions and three global indices of distress. The SCL-90-R was designed to reflect psychological symptom patterns in community, medical, and psychiatric respondents and has been used in an extensive number of cases (Derogatis, 1993).

Questionnaires were returned to the researchers for coding, data entry, and analysis. The Statistical Package for the Social Sciences (SPSS, 1993) was used to analyze the data. The analysis contained descriptive and inferential statistics using univariate, bivariate, and multivariate procedures including: crosstabs, analysis of variance, one-way analysis of variance, t-test, chi-square, and Kappa and Pearson correlation.

RESULTS OF STUDY

- A total of 34 questionnaires were returned for a return rate of 45.9%. The workers returning the questionnaires were mostly female, middle aged, ethnically diverse, with master's degrees, and involved in doing crisis counseling work.
- Counselors were psychologically impacted by their work whether or not they personally experienced the bomb blast.
- Many of the respondents (61.8%, $n = 21$) reported that they feared someone they knew might die as a result of the bombing.

- 64.7% of the counselors exhibited some degree of severity for post-traumatic stress disorder, as measured by the Frederick Reaction Index (Frederick, 1988).
- 44.1% of counselors exhibited "caseness" on the SCL-90-R Global Severity Index score or two dimensional T scores greater than or equal to a T score of 63. Caseness refers to the subjects who are considered to be at risk or a positive case for a psychiatric disorder (Derogatis, 1994).
- 73.5% of counselors were rated as being at moderate risk or greater for compassion fatigue: moderate risk (23.5%), high risk (29.4%), or extremely high risk (20.6%), as measured by the Compassion Fatigue Self-Test for Psychotherapists (Figley, 1995).
- 76.5% of counselors were rated as being at moderate risk or greater for burnout: moderate risk (35.3%), high risk (26.5%), or extremely high risk (14.7%), using the same compassion fatigue self-test.
- Over half (52.9%) of the counselors evaluated disaster mental health work as more stressful than other jobs they had under-taken.
- Longer duration of work providing counseling services to disaster victims was significantly related to higher mean distress scores.
- Certain categories of counselors had higher levels of distress than that of their coworkers: administrators of the counseling program, males, and ethnic groups other than Caucasian.

STRESS MANAGEMENT REPORTED BY DISASTER WORKERS

Practicing personal stress management activities was reported by 82.4% ($n = 28$) of respondents. Frequency of personal stress management activities was reported by 2.9% ($n = 1$) as every other month; 5.9% ($n = 2$) as monthly; 44.1% ($n = 15$) as several times per week; 17.6% ($n = 6$) as daily; 11.8% ($n = 4$) as several times per day; and 14.7% ($n = 5$) as never practiced.

When counselors were asked to describe the types of activities that they used in managing personal stress, the following were their responses:

"Friday night is my designated 'de-stress' time. I spend it with a close friend. We have supper, then do crafts, and watch TV or movies or talk. I also listen to relaxing music on my way to, and from, work."

"I went for a weekend in the woods twice, without a phone or other people. I did not have my home phone or my answering machine on for several months."

Other frequently listed personal stress management activities include the following:

- Leisure and "diversion" activities—dinner, movies, social activities, reading, crocheting, making time for old hobbies, and outdoor activities such as walking or fishing
- Family time—communication with a spouse regarding personal feelings; time with family, especially children; games
- Exercise—walking (most frequently mentioned), weightlifting, aerobic exercise and weight training, running, swimming, bicycling, and dancing
- Relaxation and meditation—listening to relaxation tapes or music, deep breathing, positive visualization, daydreaming, going through journals, crafts, painting or drawing, and rest
- Informal group therapy with coworkers; brainstorming; sharing of information; consulting with other counselors
- Personal counseling and personal sessions with the family doctor
- Spiritual activities—attending church or spirituality growth groups, reading philosophy
- Humor

Participation in stress management training activities sponsored by the crisis counseling program was reported by 53% ($n = 27$). Not participating in the stress management services of the crisis counseling program was reported by 38.2% ($n = 13$) of the respondents. Counselors reported utilizing the following types of program-sponsored stress management services:

- Debriefings with or without facilitator (Some counselors went to one or two debriefings. Others attended regularly, with a frequency of twice a week to once a month.)
- Informal debriefing and defusing among coworkers
- Training (frequently mentioned, with a wide variety of topics listed as being helpful and supportive)
- Consultation and professional support
- Staff meetings

EVALUATION OF STRESS AMONG OKLAHOMA CITY CRISIS WORKERS

The Alfred P. Murrah Federal Building bombing resulted in many respondents experiencing fear that someone they knew might die as a result of the bomb blast. This anxiety might be the most significant psychological feature of this bombing disaster. Although the bombing impacted the mental health workers, it appeared not to have impacted any subgroups of these workers significantly more than other workers. Job classification of an administrator and the number of months providing disaster mental health services to bombing survivors were significantly associated with increased degree of severity of stress disorder.

Sample mean scores for the Risk of Compassion Fatigue and Burnout test suggest high risk for both compassion fatigue and burnout. Increased number of months working with bombing survivors is significantly associated with higher risk for compassion fatigue and burnout. This indicates that there may be a close relationship between disaster mental health work and compassion fatigue and burnout. Increased duration of time providing crisis counseling and educational services to victims of the bombing appears related to increased compassion fatigue. Sloan, Rozensky, Kaplan, and Saunders (1994) in their study of medical, mental health, and public safety personnel following a school shooting found that three of five job stress dimensions, described by Hartsough and Myers (1985), were significant predictors of traumatic stress response 6 months postincident. Time pressure was most predictive, followed by quantitative work load, and then qualitative work load, corroborating the findings of this study related to quantity or "dose" of work contributing to risk of compassion fatigue and burnout.

A higher level of generalized distress for workers belonging to the classification "Other Ethnic Groups" (Latino, African American, Native American, and others), as measured by the Global Severity Index on the SCL 90-R, approached significance. The higher generalized distress for ethnic groups other than Caucasians was not found to originate in response to this disaster or disaster mental health work but may have been present prior to the bombing. The predisaster generalized level of distress may be associated with situations and conditions experienced by other ethnic groups (and not experienced by Caucasians) and may be associated with the need for continuous forbearance by these groups to cope with racism, sexism, and community violence (Snowden, 1997. Personal communication. Professor, School of Social Welfare, University of California Berkeley).

The findings in this study are quite important in comparison to other studies of disaster mental health workers. This study found the highest proportion of disaster mental health workers with some degree of severity for stress disorder compared to disaster mental health workers in other studies reported in the literature. Lindstrom and Lundin (1982) found that 4 out of 13 (31%) people who provided rescue and healthcare assistance following a fire had General Health Questionnaire scores suggesting psychological disturbance. Hodgkinson and Shepherd (1994) found that 60% of social workers experienced significant levels of symptoms during their 1st year of disaster social work. A study of disaster social workers providing counseling to individuals and families following the Piper Alpha North Sea oil production and platform explosion and the Clapham rail crash, found higher mean and subscale Hopkins Symptom Checklist for the disaster social workers than for the general population. The differences found were small but highly significant. Nine months following the Northridge earthquake, disaster mental health workers were surveyed for their reactions to the earthquake and to providing disaster mental health services during a Federal Emergency Management Agency Crisis Counseling Program. The proportion of disaster mental health workers with some degree of severity for stress disorder was 60.5%. The proportion of mental health workers who did not do disaster mental health work but experienced the earthquake was 52% (Wee & Myers, 1997). The proportion of disaster mental health workers providing services following the Alfred P. Murrah Federal Building bombing with some degree of severity for stress disorder is 64.7% ($n = 22$). Among disaster mental health workers 44.1% ($n = 15$) have caseness.

Perhaps the most significant finding of this study is the severity of distress among disaster mental health workers as compared to the distress reported among emergency service workers in other studies. Since 1983, with the publication of Mitchell's seminal work on stress management for emergency service workers (Mitchell, 1983) a multitude of research projects have studied the effects of disaster on the responders. For example, in a study of disaster workers following the Piper Alpha disaster, a comparison of police officer controls and mortuary worker groups showed no significant changes in individual officers (Alexander & Wells, 1991). Jenkins and Sewell (1993) in a study of distress and health among paramedics in the Killeen shooting incident found significantly increased levels of distress post event. Questionnaires were completed by 37 EMTs, paramedics, and firefighters 1 week postincident and as a 1-month follow-up. Depression, anxiety, hostility, and general symptom index scales increased significantly during the 8–10 days postevent. The mean severity of reported health problems was significantly higher in the month after the event than the month before. In a study of stress response of emergency personnel responding to the I-880 collapse, researchers found 9% were above thresholds established for case identification and would be considered moderate to high distress responders averaging 1.5 years postevent (Marmar, Weiss, Metzler, Ronfeldt, & Foreman, 1996). A study of the psychological reactions of rescue workers following a tornado found 17% would qualify for PTSD diagnosis (McCammon, Durham, Allison, & Williamson, 1986). Scott and Jordan (1993), in a study of Los Angeles County firefighters after the Los Angeles civil disturbances, found that 27% of the firefighters who responded reported continuing symptoms of distress 6 months after the incident. Wee, Mills, and Koehler (1999), in a survey 3 months following the Los Angeles civil disturbances, found that 42% of the EMTs surveyed had some degree of severity of stress response. Deahl, Gillham, Thomas, Searle, and Srinivasan (1994), in a study of British soldiers whose duties include handling and identification of bodies following the Gulf War, found that 50% had evidence of psychological disturbance suggestive of posttraumatic stress disorder (PTSD). A study 6 months following a massacre found that 50% of the officers present at the incident had some degree of mild to severe PTSD (Mantel, Dubner, & Lipson, 1985). One month after the Bradford fire disaster, a study of police officers found 35% would have met four criteria, and 21% met three of four criteria for DSM III diagnosis of PTSD (Duckworth, 1986). These findings suggests that 56% of the Bradford fire disaster police officers had some level of stress response following this event. Rescue and disaster workers following a railroad accident showed 70% expressing evidence of some strain and 35% finding at least moderate strain intensity (Raphael et al., 1984). Following the Alfred P. Murrah Federal Building incident, 64.7% of the disaster mental health workers providing services had some degree of severity for stress disorder.

The findings of this study suggest that the nature of the Alfred P. Murrah Federal Building bombing as a terrorist act, exposure to the bomb blast and its aftermath, the length of time providing disaster mental health services, and job duties providing disaster mental health services during long-term disaster recovery appear to have a similar and even more intense severity of stress response compared to the shorter term, high-intensity rescue, disaster, and emergency work done by emergency service workers. This severity of stress among the disaster mental health workers is higher than the distress levels found in almost all other groups of emergency and rescue workers studied in the last 16 years. These results strongly suggest that serious attention needs to be paid to developing effective stress management and prevention programs for these at-risk workers.

The disaster mental health workers of the Alfred P. Murrah Federal Building Bombing Crisis Counseling Program, Oklahoma City, Oklahoma, faced enormous challenges in providing crisis counseling following what was called the worst terrorist attack in United States history prior to the terrorist attacks of September 11, 2001. The disaster mental health workers were pioneers in the effort to bring support, understanding, reassurance, encouragement, and crisis counseling to the people of Oklahoma City and beyond who were impacted by this bombing. The crisis counseling program provided stress management services and resources to the counselors involved, without which the level of stress could have gone even higher. The presence of levels of stress and distress among the disaster mental health workers should in no way be interpreted as judgment or criticism of their efforts to ease human suffering. Rather, the risk for compassion fatigue and burnout might be viewed as evidence of the extraordinary empathy, sympathy, understanding, and energy devoted to caring for the children, mothers, fathers, sisters, brothers, families, neighbors, emergency service workers, and fellow human beings struck by this catastrophic disaster.

The findings of this study must be interpreted in the light of its methodological limitations, which include disaster mental health workers in a crisis counseling program following a terrorist event; limited generalizability to other groups of disaster mental health workers in other types of disasters; nonavailability of data on the disaster mental health workers' predisaster experiences, levels of posttraumatic stress disorder, compassion fatigue, and general levels of distress; and absence of a control group for comparison to mental health workers from Oklahoma City. Although comparisons were made with results from other studies, there are difficulties comparing the degree of severity for stress disorder in this sample of disaster mental health workers with that found in other studies of disaster mental health workers, emergency service workers, and disaster workers. The instruments used in this study may under- or overestimate the presence and degree of severity of stress disorder when compared with other studies using other instruments at other points in time, postdisaster.

In addition, Wee and Myers (2002) found that both the severity of distress as well as the proportion of distressed workers in this group of counselors were higher than those in most other studies of trauma workers reported in the literature. One other study reporting a high proportion of disaster counselors with some degree of severity for posttraumatic stress disorder (60.5%) examined the counselors providing disaster mental health services in Los Angeles' Project Rebound following the 1994 Northridge earthquake (Wee & Myers, 1997, 2002).

AFTERMATH STRESS MANAGEMENT

The counselors studied by Wee and Myers in both the Oklahoma City bombing and the Northridge earthquake are a unique group of disaster workers, in the sense that their work is long term. The counselors were employed by local mental health agencies through funding of the Federal Emergency Management Agency (FEMA) Crisis Counseling Program. Similar long-term mental health programs for persons affected by disasters are also often established by local agencies or by university medical centers. The counselors' work usually begins in the first days after the disaster and may extend for a year or more into the recovery period.

SOURCES OF STRESS

There are multiple stressors that affect these long-term disaster counselors. Myers (Hartsough & Myers, 1985) outlined some of the stressors that impact disaster workers. Some factors are related to the individual, such as health, socioeconomic situation, preexisting stresses, previous trauma and loss, coping skills, identity and self-expectations, culture, spiritual beliefs, and perceptions and interpretations of the event. Interpersonal factors include relationships, social supports, and impact of the disaster on the individual and their family. Community factors include size and nature of the community, degree of social solidarity, prior disaster experience, response of the community to the disaster, and amount of initial and ongoing disruption due to the disaster. Finally, factors related to the disaster itself will impact the workers (whether there was a warning, the type of disaster, the scope of the disaster, to name a few). Some of these factors may serve to strengthen and support the worker, while other factors may put a worker at risk for compassion fatigue and traumatic stress. All of these factors need to be considered in an assessment of how each individual worker will be affected in the long-term.

Several factors, however, are specific for counselors working in the long-term disaster aftermath in their own community. First, regardless of whether or not counselors sustained personal losses in the disaster, they will most likely be impacted merely by being a part of the affected community. Myers (Hartsough & Myers, 1985) points out that "a disaster is an awesome event. Simply seeing massive destruction and terrible sights evokes deep feelings. Often, residents of disaster-stricken communities report disturbing feelings of grief, sadness, anxiety, and anger, even when they are not themselves victims. . . . Such strong reactions confuse them when, after all, they were spared any personal loss. These . . . reactions are normal in every way; everyone who *sees* a disaster is, in some sense, a victim (Myers, 1994b)."

Bolin and Bolton (1986) explain communities as a complex social whole, which constitute symbolic objects that provide orientation for residents (Hunter, 1974, 1975; Fried, 1966) and are the basis of residents' "cognitive maps" (Suttles, 1972; Trainer & Bolton, 1976). These mental maps keep the local community safe, familiar, and readily accessible to the residents. Residents identify themselves with their communities and, in doing so, incorporate them as part of their self-concept (Hunter, 1974). In effect, the "wounding" of the community itself can disrupt an individual's sense of self-identity and feeling of safety, regardless of whether the individual suffered personal losses. In short, disaster counselors who reside in the damaged community will inevitably be affected themselves and come to their work bearing personal pain from the event.

In addition to being personally impacted by a disaster in their own community, traumatologists helping disaster survivors face many of the same stressors common to all professionals working with disaster-affected individuals beyond the immediate crisis stage. Unlike crisis workers (e.g., psychiatric crisis intervention staff, debriefers, and hot line counselors), whose response is to the immediate effects of a catastrophic event on the survivor, long-term disaster counselors are faced with the prolonged, and usually compounded, aftermath of the disaster.

Counseling people in the aftermath of disaster involves repeated exposure to the event through the client's recounting and reexperiencing of the event in the counselor's presence. It also involves repeated exposure to the survivor's intense emotional reaction to the disaster (e.g., pain, fear, rage, despair, and hopelessness) (Dutton & Rubinstein, 1995).

In addition, the disaster counselor is exposed to the institutional and other social responses that revictimize the survivor and over which the trauma counselor may have little control (Dutton & Rubinstein, 1995).

The process of obtaining temporary housing, replacing belongings, getting permits to rebuild, applying for government assistance, seeking insurance reimbursement, and acquiring help from private or voluntary agencies is often fraught with rules, red tape, hassles, delays, frustrations, and disappointment (Myers, 1994b). Individuals who felt competent and effective before the disaster may experience a serious erosion of self-esteem and confidence, and feelings of helplessness and anger are common, both in the survivors and in those who counsel them (Myers, 1994b). Disaster traumatologists become, to some extent, bystanders and helpless (although not silent) witnesses to damaging events and ongoing strife (Pearlman & Saakvitne, 1995). This helplessness to change what the disaster and its aftermath wreak on the victims challenges the therapist's helper identity (Staub, 1989).

In addition, since the disaster counselor's task is often quite complex, the results of the therapists' work can be mixed and very slow to appear. Consequently, the disaster traumatologist is exposed to traumatic events repeatedly and over a significant period of time (Dutton & Rubinstein, 1995), often with minimal feelings of efficacy. This helplessness on the part of the therapist to "fix" the situation that causes intense suffering for the client may be a significant contributor to the disaster traumatologist's risk for compassion fatigue and STS, as helplessness is one of the key criteria for the development of PTSD (Wee & Myers, 2002).

THE NATURE OF TRAUMAS

In addition to exposure to the client's experience, another source of trauma for therapists dealing with a client's victimization is the nature of the injury itself (Danieli, 1985). Through exposure to the client's trauma, therapists not only become aware of the client's pain, but also come to the stark realization that traumatic events can occur, have occurred, perhaps repeatedly, and can recur (Dutton & Rubinstein, 1995). When traumatologists enter their clients' worlds, it is no longer possible to deny the potential for trauma in their own lives. The experience of even one survivor client is an inescapable reminder of the therapist's own personal vulnerability to traumatic loss (Pearlman & Saakvitne, 1995). Having once counseled a flood survivor, a therapist never again sees a river as totally benign, and an earthquake counselor, forever after, eyes bridges with a measure of doubt.

It is for these reasons that therapists working with the trauma of disaster survivors are at such high risk to become traumatized themselves. Because of this high risk for compassion fatigue, this chapter focuses on what can be done before, during, and after disaster assignments to maintain the psychological health and well-being of these trauma counselors. It will provide recommendations for the prevention of compassion fatigue, based upon the research and practice reported in the literature to date with the following groups of workers: therapists providing treatment to trauma casualties, emergency service workers (first responders), and disaster workers in general. In addition, it will draw from the author's personal experiences in developing stress management protocols, educational materials, and training programs for mental health counselors in over a dozen presidentially declared disasters.

The strategies for prevention and treatment of compassion fatigue and secondary traumatic stress will be organized into categories of what can be done in predisaster, during disaster, and postdisaster assignments.

PREDISASTER

This section describes actions that can be taken by a mental health agency or group before a disaster strikes to ensure that mental health staff are ready and well-prepared in case they are required to engage in disaster work. Naturally, many of these strategies will contribute to an efficient and effective disaster mental health response. However, the primary purpose for discussing these actions in this chapter is the prevention or minimization of compassion fatigue in the workers by providing them will the necessary knowledge, skills, tools, and supports they need to perform a difficult and risky job as safely as possible. This section will discuss the following predisaster approaches: personal emergency preparedness; designing an appropriate mental health disaster plan; selection of disaster mental health staff; predisaster stress assessment of disaster mental health workers; education and training of disaster mental health staff; and orientation to the disaster assignment.

PERSONAL EMERGENCY PREPAREDNESS

Having a personal and family emergency plan will help any worker who has potential disaster responsibilities to cope with whatever emergencies may occur while they are at home. Every emergency worker should be familiar with hazards and likely emergencies inherent in the local geographic area and should have contingency plans for self and family. This is important to the safety of the family and to the availability of the worker for disaster assignment. The more quickly things can be taken care of at home, the more quickly the worker can report to work with some worries about the family taken care of. Similarly, if the worker is at work when a disaster occurs, peace of mind and concentration will be enhanced if the family is prepared and able to cope with problems at home (Myers, 1994b).

DESIGNING AN APPROPRIATE DISASTER MENTAL HEALTH PLAN

By realistically designing disaster mental health programs based on models known to be effective, mental health planners, administrators, and clinicians can avoid the frustration and potential burnout inherent in misdirected efforts following a disaster.

It is important to base a disaster mental health response on some important key concepts of disaster mental health. Individuals and the community will pass through a variety of phases on the road to recovery, and mental health approaches must be appropriate to the phase of a disaster.

A crisis intervention approach and active outreach into the community are essential in the immediate aftermath of the disaster. Community-based outreach continues to be a key to reaching disaster-affected individuals throughout the long-term recovery process, as most disaster survivors do not see themselves as needing mental health services following disaster and usually do not seek such services. Community mental health programs provide public information and education about expected stress responses in adults, children, and families, usually framing symptoms as "the normal reactions of normal people to an abnormal situation" and suggesting ways to cope and where to go for help.

Direct mental health services to individuals are often more practical than psychological in nature. Counselors are often most helpful and relevant to survivor needs by assisting them with problem solving, decision making, and obtaining resources, rather than providing psychotherapy.

Beyond the immediate crisis stage of the disaster, mental health staff, continuing their active outreach approach and collaboration with other helping agencies, will begin to identify individuals with more serious psychological problems such as posttraumatic stress reactions, depression, and exacerbation of prior trauma or prior stresses. Relationship and marital problems may surface or exacerbate, including domestic violence. Substance abuse may increase. It is these individuals who will likely require more intensive psychological counseling and for whom mental health professionals with skill in trauma treatment will be necessary. Myers (1994b) provides a more detailed look at key concepts of disaster psychology as they apply to program design in the various phases of disaster response and recovery.

SELECTION OF DISASTER MENTAL HEALTH STAFF

Much of the confusion and stress at the time of disaster impact can be minimized if a mental health agency or professional group has predesignated staff trained as a disaster response team, with call-up and deployment procedures in place (Myers, 1994b).

Not all mental health professionals are well-suited for disaster work. Various phases of response and varying tasks require a special "fit" of the worker. In the crisis phase, mental health workers need to use an active outreach approach. They must go out to community sites where survivors are involved in the activities of their daily lives. Such places include impacted neighborhoods, schools, disaster shelters, disaster recovery centers (DRCs), family assistance centers (FACs), meal sites, hospitals, churches, community centers, and the like. The traditional office-based approach is of little use in these sites. Very few people will come to an office or approach a desk labeled "mental health." However, they will usually be eager to talk about what happened to them when approached with warmth and genuine interest. The most effective approach is to informally engage survivors in conversation, often dubbed by experienced disaster mental health workers as the "over-the-cup-of-coffee approach." Staff who do well in these roles must be comfortable with an extroverted, outgoing approach. They need to be flexible, able to focus, good at "thinking on their feet," and have a common-sense, practical, and often improvisational method of dealing with problems.

Later, as more serious psychological difficulties arise, trauma therapists with treatment skills are necessary. However, they must be willing and able to "be with" survivors who are suffering tragedy, concrete losses, and ongoing life disruption without becoming frustrated at not being able to "fix" the situation for the victim (Myers, 1994b).

Choosing and assigning staff to program areas where their unique skills are needed, utilized, effective, and appreciated will contribute greatly to prevention of burnout.

Disaster traumatologists must also be selected to match the demographic needs of the population. Counselors with special expertise in working with children, older adults, and particular ethnic groups must be included in the disaster team. Cultural competency is essential for staff working in the post-disaster environment. The primary reason for attending to these issues, of course, is to provide appropriate services to the community.

PREDISASTER STRESS ASSESSMENT

A systematic assessment of workers' personal and job stress prior to placing them in disaster mental health assignments can help to screen out those who might be at high risk for compassion fatigue or STS. To measure job-related stress, Bailey, Steffen, and Grout (1980) developed a stress audit questionnaire to identify "stressors" and "satisfiers" among nurses in intensive care units (McCammon & Allison, 1995). Similarly, Rosenschweig and Vaslow (1992) studied FEMA disaster workers and developed a list of top "stress producers" and "stress reducers." The tools used in both of these studies have potential for modification into a tool for risk assessment before assigning mental health staff to disaster work. Dunning (1988) suggests looking carefully at possible indicators of psychological injury including illness, turnover patterns within a work group, requests for transfer, absenteeism, and job performance. The presence of such factors could indicate that a work unit or individual workers are at a high level of risk or are suffering actual burnout. Assigning these workers to disaster mental health responsibilities might be moving them "from the frying pan into the fire." It might also provide them with a much needed change of pace and responsibility, but they should be monitored closely and provided with appropriate supervision and support to ensure that cumulative stress from their prior job and current disaster work does not result in compassion fatigue or STS.

In addition to predisaster measurement of personal and professional stress levels, consideration should be given to assessment of compassion fatigue, burnout, and STS in workers already engaged in trauma intervention before assigning them to disaster work. Figley's Compassion Fatigue Self Test for Psychotherapists (Figley, 1995, 2002) is an excellent tool. More research on formal assessment and diagnosis of STS is still needed, but a wide range of PTSD assessment tools exists that could be used or modified to measure STS. Carlson (1997) offers a comprehensive guide to PTSD assessment tools.

There will be times when mental health staff themselves have sustained direct losses from the disaster. There have been many situations in which disaster survivors—staff have heroically participated in mental health response activities without letting coworkers or supervisors know of their own losses. While this is likely a mixture of denial and altruism commonly occurring after the impact of a disaster, it may put the worker at real risk if personal, family, and financial needs are not attended to. Every mental health agency should determine which of its workers have been directly affected in order to support the workers and to make appropriate work assignments. The organization can support its own workers by providing formalized debriefing, counseling services, and support groups for those workers who were personally impacted (Myers, 1994b).

If a disaster mental health counselor does have a personal trauma history, either as a survivor of the disaster at hand or of other trauma, support and supervision will be important for early identification and intervention with STS (Pearlman & MacIan, 1995). The question must be asked as to whether personally impacted mental health workers can and should be involved in the mental health disaster response. They will likely need some time off from work, both initially and over the long run, to attend to their own personal and family needs. A disaster work assignment should be initially and regularly evaluated with workers to assess how disaster work may affect them on a personal level, and how their personal situation may affect their disaster work. An important factor will be the worker's ability to separate personal coping styles from those of other survivors, and not to impose, consciously or unconsciously, their own values and methods of coping upon others. The ability to empathize with survivors may be enhanced by the worker's own losses. However, the worker must be able to maintain perspective and avoid the hazards of overidentification with survivors. Taking too much control in a desire to help, playing down others' crises, or avoiding listening to intense feelings because they are too painful for the worker can be potential problems (Myers, 1994b).

Another group of counselors to identify predisaster are new therapists, who may be very vulnerable to compassion fatigue and STS and who could benefit from extra supervision and support. Pearlman and MacIan (1995) found that the newest therapists in trauma work had the most difficulties. This finding is consistent with the burnout literature, which shows that being younger or newer to the work is correlated with the highest levels of burnout (Ackerley, Burnell, Holder, & Kurdek, 1988; Deutsch, 1984) and with the most negative reactions to doing therapy (Rodolfa, Kraft, & Reilley, 1988). Pearlman & MacIan also found that the newest trauma therapists were often working with the most acutely distressed patients, and less than 20% of them were receiving supervision. Their work clearly recommends the need for more supervision and more support for newer therapists working in the trauma field. Identifying these staff at the beginning of a disaster assignment will assure that they can be provided with appropriate supervision and support. Student interns will require similar support.

In addition to identifying potentially "at risk" therapists, Pearlman and Saakvitne (1995) advise that in employment and training settings, those who interview applicants, whether for graduate school, internships, postdoctoral fellowships, or staff positions, should inform them of the risks related to doing trauma work. They emphasize the harm that can be done by offering a position to someone who does not have the self capacities, ego resources, and access to do this type of work. This "duty to warn" must be taken seriously by managers and supervisors who hire or assign staff to disaster mental health response teams.

EDUCATION AND TRAINING OF DISASTER MENTAL HEALTH STAFF

Mental health professionals working in any field of trauma must have initial and ongoing specialized training. First, it is essential that graduate and professional schools of social work, psychiatry, psychology, and psychiatric nursing include course work and supervised practice in the field of trauma assessment and treatment. In addition, conferences, workshops, and other continuing education forums are necessary, both to maintain and update knowledge and skills, as well as to provide professional, collegial support.

Specialized training is essential, even for experienced trauma therapists, before working in the field of disaster mental health. Mental health professionals frequently assume that their clinical training and experience are more than sufficient to enable them to respond adequately in disaster. Unfortunately, traditional mental health training does not address many issues found in disaster-affected populations (FEMA, 1988). While clinical expertise, especially in the field of crisis intervention, is valuable, it is not enough. Mental health personnel need to adopt new procedures and methods for delivering a highly specialized service in disaster. Training must be designed to prepare staff for the uniqueness of disaster mental health approaches (Myers, 1994b). Ideally, graduate and professional programs that train mental health professionals should include course work specifically on disaster mental health. Most, however, do not.

Because disaster mental health work requires a perceptual shift from traditional mental health service delivery, the acquisition of new skills and information is essential (Myers, 1994b). A thorough discussion of disaster mental health training is the topic of chapter 3.

An important component of disaster mental health training involves education about potential compassion fatigue, burnout, STS, stress management, and self-care. Such training helps to create a work environment in which secondary stress reactions are to be anticipated and recognized as a common component of the work, and in which detection and intervention with these conditions can be facilitated (Dutton & Rubinstein, 1995).

Stress management training developed by Myers (1989a, 1989–1997, 1992, 1993a, 1994a), Myers and Zunin (1993a, 1993b, 1994a, 1994b), and Wee (1994b) for mental health and other workers in numerous federally declared disasters have included the following stress management topics:

- Phases of disaster for workers
- Factors that influence disaster workers' stress reactions (factors related to the worker, the role, the setting, the community, and the disaster itself)
- Sources of stress for disaster workers
- Stressors in specific work environments
- Stressors in specific roles, for example, outreach worker, crisis counselor, treating trauma therapist, supervisor, and manager
- Personal coping strategies for disaster workers before, during, and after the disaster assignment
- Stress management techniques:
  1. Stress inventory
  2. Breathing
  3. Stretching
  4. Cognitive techniques
  5. Relaxation
  6. Meditation
  7. Imagination
  8. Humor
  9. Creative expression
  10. Time management
  11. Conflict resolution
  12. Resistance building and lifestyle: work schedule, rest, nutrition, exercise, social support, relaxation, and recreation

In addition to the above training curricula, Pearlman and Saakvitne (1995) offer a paradigm of stress prevention strategies for trauma workers that includes personal strategies, professional strategies, organizational strategies, and interventions by helping professionals. Yassen (1995) presents a framework that utilizes concepts of primary prevention, secondary prevention, and tertiary prevention, and has developed a comprehensive, ecological model for the prevention of STS. Munroe, Shay, Fisher, Makary, Rapperport, and Zimering (1995) have developed a team model for use in prevention of STS. Each of these models could well serve, pre-disaster, as a curriculum for disaster mental health worker stress management training.

ORIENTATION TO THE DISASTER ASSIGNMENT

Before reporting for disaster orientation, every worker being assigned to a disaster-impacted area should have up-to-date immunizations for hepatitis B and diphtheria/tetanus (DT). In addition, during the flu season in winter months (November to April), immunization for influenza should be considered for all disaster workers because of the degree of public exposure they experience. For international disaster assignments, recommended immunizations for the country to be visited should be up-to-date. Staying healthy and energetic on the job will certain help to minimize fatigue and burnout.

Before deployment to the disaster assignment, personnel should be oriented and briefed as thoroughly as possible about what they will encounter in their disaster assignment location and role. This forewarning can help personnel to anticipate and to prepare emotionally for what they may experience in their assignment (Hartsough & Myers, 1985; Myers, 1994b). It also provides them with concrete information that will be essential to them in their work and crucial to their well-being and safety. A comprehensive discussion of orientation to the disaster assignment is contained in chapter 3.

STRATEGIES AGAINST COMPASSION FATIGUE DURING DISASTER

This section outlines strategies that can be taken by the mental health agency, by supervisors, and by disaster mental health workers themselves to prevent compassion fatigue during the actual disaster mental health assignment. Suggested approaches include briefing of disaster mental health staff before deployment; supervision of staff; consultation; continuing education and training; psychotherapy; organizational support and workplace strategies; defusing and debriefing; working as a team; mental health worker professional strategies; and mental health worker personal strategies.

BRIEFING OF DISASTER MENTAL HEALTH STAFF

Several approaches to stress prevention and management during disaster have already been discussed in the predisaster section of this book. The first is to continue to brief workers before they begin any new assignment. During ongoing disaster recovery, if work sites, roles, or responsibilities change, briefing the worker on the new situation can reduce anxiety and ease the transition into the new assignment.

SUPERVISION OF STAFF

The importance of supervision for disaster workers was discussed in the predisaster section. During the immediate postimpact phase of disaster, workers respond with enthusiasm and often heroism to the immediate needs of the situation. It is the rule, rather than the exception, that mental health staff, like other disaster responders, tend to overextend themselves in their efforts. Disaster workers are usually not the best judges of their level of functioning, and usually underestimate the effects of stress and fatigue on their health and performance. Thus, good on-scene supervision is helpful. The following suggestions may be helpful to supervisors in dealing with compassion stress among disaster traumatologists (Myers, 1994b):

1. Remember that early identification and intervention with stress reactions is the key to preventing compassion fatigue. Review stress symptoms with workers before they go into the field. Provide handouts for workers regarding stress management and self-care.
2. Assess workers' appearance and level of functioning regularly. It is not uncommon for workers to deny their own level of stress and fatigue. For example, they may say they are doing "fine" but may be exhibiting multiple stress symptoms and appear very fatigued.
3. Try to rotate workers among low-stress, moderate-stress, and high-stress tasks. Limit workers' time in high-stress assignments (such as working with families identifying the deceased at the morgue) to an hour or so at a time, if possible. Provide breaks and personal support to staff in such positions.
4. If possible, limit the length of shifts to 12 hr maximum. A 12-hr shift should be followed by 12 hr off duty.
5. Ask workers to take breaks if effectiveness is diminishing; order them to do so if necessary. Point out that the worker's ability to function is diminishing due to fatigue, and that they are needed functioning at full potential to help with the operation. Allow the worker to return to work if rest is taken and functioning improves.

6. On breaks, try to provide workers with the following:

Bathroom facilities

A place to sit or lie down away from the scene; quiet time alone

Food and beverages

An opportunity to talk with supervisor or coworkers, if they wish

Supervision is important not only on-scene in the immediate disaster after-math. Its importance continues and magnifies as staff move into long-term recovery work with the community and with clients. Cerney (1995) notes that much secondary trauma can be avoided or its effects ameliorated if therapists use regular supervision or consultation. Within the process of supervision, blind spots can be detected, overidentification can be corrected, alternative treatment approaches can be discussed and evaluated, and, especially important in prevention of compassion fatigue, the therapist's overextension or overinvolvement can be analyzed and understood. Pearlman and MacIan (1995) emphasize the special importance of good supervision for those therapists with a trauma history and those who are newer therapists. It is important to continue to monitor the needs of those disaster mental health staff who are also survivors of the disaster. Appropriate supervision, consultation, and support can help to ensure that they do not become overwhelmed, and that their personal needs and professional roles do not become blurred. Supervision should include not only clinical guidance and oversight. It must also ensure that treatment and supportive approaches are appropriate to the phase of disaster, are appropriate to the goals and objectives of the disaster mental health program, and are culturally and ethnically fitting.

CONSULTATION

In numerous postdisaster mental health projects, project administration staff have provided or brought in outside consultants and trainers specifically to provide stress management services and education to mental health personnel (Varblow, 1994; Wee & Myers, 2002). Consultants with prior experience from other disasters and other mental health projects can offer refreshing insights and concrete ideas that can assist staff in reaching their goals. More importantly, consultants can suggest approaches to stress management and STS prevention that have been used elsewhere in the field and that have proven to be helpful.

CONTINUING EDUCATION AND TRAINING

Hand-in-hand with the importance of good supervision is the necessity for continuing education and training throughout the duration of the disaster mental health program. Goals and topics of continuing education in disaster are discussed in detail in chapter 3. Both initial training and continuing education training provide rewards for staff that have tangible positive effects on morale (Myers, 1994b).

PSYCHOTHERAPY

In addition to supervision and training, personal psychotherapy can be important to preventing compassion fatigue and intervening with STS in disaster mental health staff. Dutton and Rubinstein (1995) emphasize that trauma workers with personal histories of traumatization are likely to require deliberate personal attention to their own healing process in order to manage most effectively the difficult task of coping with their own STS reactions. Pearlman and Saakvitne (1995), in emphasizing the helpfulness of personal psychotherapy for the trauma therapist, point out that, among other things, it provides a regular opportunity to focus on oneself, one's own needs, and the origins of one's responses to the work. They also underscore the explicit acknowledgment that psychotherapy provides: that one is deserving of care and that one's personal needs are valid and important.

Individual expressive therapy such as art, music, or movement can help therapists to become and remain centered and to reclaim their emotional lives in the chaotic postdisaster environment. Group therapy and support groups can also be of help to disaster mental health workers, providing a safe space both for healing and for exploring the interaction of a therapist's past with his or her current work with survivor clients (Pearlman & Saakvitne, 1995). Group therapy and support groups for disaster mental health workers are particularly effective in dealing with the unique aspects of disaster work, which other trauma therapists have not encountered and may have a hard time understanding.

ORGANIZATIONAL SUPPORT AND WORKPLACE STRATEGIES

In addressing organizational approaches to prevention of STS, Pearlman and Saakvitne (1995) emphasize the importance of creating an atmosphere of respect for both clients and employees. This is important in the early phases of disaster, where mental health staff may be working with survivors in chaotic, field-based situations, as well as in long-term recovery work, where staff may work with clients in both field and office settings. Organizational support and respect is conveyed to staff by providing assistance with concrete, disaster-related needs (e.g., time off, on-site childcare, etc.); adequate briefing of workers; work-related supplies; official identification; well-designed procedures for management of telephone calls, communications, paperwork; transportation; food and housing on disaster assignment, if necessary; policies regarding maximum duration of shifts (no longer than 12 hr maximum) and frequency of breaks (every 2 to 4 hr); excellent training, supervision, consultation, support, and recognition of staff efforts (Myers, 1994b). Pearlman and Saakvitne (1995) also underscore that mental health staff should have adequate employee benefits, such as health insurance with provision for mental health care and time off for vacations, in order not to endanger themselves with compassion fatigue and STS.

Yassen (1995) describes the symbolic as well as actual value of such physical perks as having an office, good lighting, privacy, environmental safety and security, employee amenities (e.g., access to food and fluids, office supplies, places to take breaks), and availability of colleagues. She also outlines the important, but less tangible, aspects of the work environment, related to the values, expectations, and culture characterizing the setting. Harvey (1985), for example, identified the importance of a clear philosophical value base as being a key element in comparing rape crisis centers. Workers must understand the organization's implicit as well as explicit demands upon them, and Yassen (1995) lists important aspects for the organization to clarify to its personnel:

- Value system
- Tasks: job descriptions, philosophy, expectations, task variety, adequacy of supervision, in-service and career opportunities, training and orientation, job security, and pay
- Managerial: lines of authority, accessibility of leaders who are open to feedback, role models, accountability, and ability to motivate/build morale
- Interpersonal: personnel guidelines, respect for differences, value of social support and mutual aid, trust among staff, and sensitivity to the needs of individuals (e.g., personal days, stress management training)

Dutton and Rubinstein (1995) suggest other workplace strategies for preventing and responding to STS. They advise adjusting workers' caseloads to include a diversity of clients, thus reducing one's amount of contact with severely traumatized clients, and diversifying work-related activities beyond direct contact with victims (e.g., teaching, supervision, research, and consultation).

CRITICAL INCIDENT STRESS MANAGEMENT

Critical incident stress management is a comprehensive, integrated multi-component crisis intervention system (Mitchell & Everly, 2001). It is designed to support personnel through traumatic events that have the potential to disrupt homeostasis, disrupt coping, and produce distress or functional impairment. CISM interventions include one-to-one support, small group interventions (defusing and debriefing), large group interventions, family support services, and pastoral care interventions. CISM interventions have an enormous potential in assisting in the prevention of compassion fatigue in disaster personnel. They are discussed in more detail in chapter 6. Slight modifications to the basic CISM model are often used for providing support to mental health staff doing long-term disaster work (Myers & Zunin, 1994b).

WORKING AS A TEAM

Building a team approach to disaster mental health work can provide both prevention and active intervention with secondary traumatization (Munroe et al., 1995). Social support is a known source of significant psychological benefit for trauma survivors (Keane, Scott, Chavoya, Lamparski, & Fairbank, 1985; Solomon, 1986). A strong team approach can provide the same social support for trauma mental health professionals (Munroe et al.). Stress management training materials for disaster workers (Hartsough & Myers, 1985; Myers, 1989a, 1989b–1997, 1994b; National Institute of Mental Health [NIMH], 1987a, 1989b) have long emphasized the importance of working in a "buddy system" in disaster, utilizing teams of at least two workers to ensure that staff can serve as check-and-balance for each other and monitor each others' stress level while providing support and encouragement.

MENTAL HEALTH WORKER PROFESSIONAL STRATEGIES

A multitude of publications offer suggestions for disaster worker self-care during the immediate response phase of disaster (Hartsough & Myers, 1985; Myers, 1989a, 1989b, 1994b; NIMH, 1987a, 1987b; Wee, 1994b). The following are suggestions for mental health staff, summarized from the above publications, for management of stress while working on a disaster operation:

1. Request a briefing at the beginning of each shift to update yourself and coworkers on the status of various situations since your last shift. This can help you gear up for what you may be encountering during your shift.
2. Develop a "buddy" system with a coworker. Agree to keep an eye on each other's functioning, fatigue level, and stress symptoms. Tell the buddy how to know when you are getting stressed ("If I start doing so-and-so, tell me to take a break"). Make a

pact with your buddy to take a break when he or she suggests it, if the situation allows.

3. Encourage and support coworkers. Listen to each other's feelings. Don't take anger too personally. Hold criticism unless it is essential. Tell each other "You're doing great" and "Good job." Give coworkers a pat on the back. Bring each other a snack or something to drink.

4. Try to get some activity and exercise. Even something as simple as using the stairs instead of the elevator can provide exercise during a busy work day. Gently stretch out muscles that have become tense.

5. Eat regularly. If not hungry, eat frequently, in small quantities. Try to avoid excessive sugar, fats, and caffeine. Drink plenty of liquids.

6. Humor can break the tension and provide relief. Use it with care, however. People are highly suggestible in disaster situations, and survivors or coworkers can take things personally and be hurt if they feel they are the brunt of "disaster humor."

7. Use positive "self-talk," such as "I'm doing fine" and "I'm using the skills I've been trained to use."

8. Take deep breaths, hold them, then blow out forcefully.

9. Take breaks if effectiveness is diminishing, or if asked to do so by your supervisor. At a minimum, take a break every 4 hr.

10. Use a clipboard or notebook to jot things down. This will help compensate for the memory problems that are common in stressful situations.

11. Try to keep noise to a minimum in the worksite. Gently remind others to do the same.

12. Try to avoid unnecessarily interrupting coworkers when they are in the middle of a task. Think twice before interrupting.

13. Let yourself defuse at the end of each shift by taking a few minutes with coworkers to talk about your thoughts and feelings about the day.

14. When off duty, enjoy some recreation that takes your mind off the disaster. Draw on supports that nurture you. This may include friends, meditation, reading, or religion.

15. Pamper yourself in time off. Treat yourself to a special meal, get a massage, or take a long bath.

16. If needed, give yourself permission to spend time alone after work. However, don't totally withdraw from social interaction.

17. Get adequate sleep. Learn relaxation techniques that can help you fall asleep.

18. On long disaster assignments, attend periodic debriefing or worker support groups to talk about the emotional impact upon yourself and coworkers. Use stress management programs if they are available. If such programs are not offered, try to get them organized.

19. On disaster assignments away from home, remember the following:

- Try to make your living accommodations as personal, comfortable, and homey as possible. Unpack bags and put out pictures of loved ones.
- Bring familiar foods and snacks from home that will not be available on your disaster assignment.
- Make new friends. Let off steam with coworkers.
- Find local recreation opportunities and make use of them.
- Remember things that were relaxing at home and try to do them now; take a hot bath or shower, if possible; read a good book; go for a run; listen to music.
- Stay in touch with people at home. Write or call often. Send pictures. Have family visit if possible and appropriate.
- Avoid excessive use of alcohol and caffeine.
- Keep a journal.

Yassen (1995) emphasizes the importance of balance and boundaries for the prevention of professional STS. Disaster mental health workers need to have balance in both the quantity and quality of tasks in their work life, paying close attention to the proportion of their work that involves direct trauma treatment, and balancing it with other professional responsibilities. Finding a satisfactory and healthy balance between professional and personal life is also important. Setting time boundaries, professional boundaries, and personal boundaries is essential. Cerney (1995) writes that to maintain boundaries necessary for good health, disaster mental health staff may need to prioritize their commitments, and even terminate some of them. She also notes the importance of therapeutic realism, emphasizing that mental health personnel must not allow themselves to fall into the belief that they must be able to handle every kind of patient or to handle an unlimited number of patients. Studies continuously find that many mental health staff hold the irrational belief that they must operate at peak efficiency and competence at all times with all people (Deutsch, 1984; Forney, Wallace-Schutzman, & Wiggers, 1982), which can be a key contributing factor for STS in disaster mental health workers.

MENTAL HEALTH WORKER PERSONAL STRATEGIES

Personal strategies include lifestyle choices such as exercise, a healthy diet, and a balance between work, play, and rest (Myers, 1994b). Also important are creative expression, meditation and spiritual replenishment, self-awareness, and humor (Yassen, 1995). Other informal strategies such as maintaining strong personal support networks of family and friends, developing diverse interests, limiting trauma exposure and media coverage of the disaster outside work hours, and seeking positive experiences outside of (disaster) work can be helpful (Dutton & Rubinstein, 1995; Edelwich & Brodsky, 1980). Other activities that contribute to disaster mental health worker self-care and health promotion include being willing to talk about events and feelings; practicing yoga or meditation; practicing deep breathing and other relaxation techniques; prayer; using "self-talk" and positive self-encouragement; maintaining meaningful practices and rituals; reading; keeping a journal; creative pursuits such as art and writing; music; dancing; getting a massage; taking a warm bath or shower; attending the theater or movies; going out to dinner; spending time with family, children, friends, pets, nature; traveling; and pursuing hobbies (Hartsough & Myers, 1985; Myers, 1994b; Myers & Zunin, 1994b; Pearlman & Saakvitne, 1995; Wee & Myers, 2002).

POSTDISASTER

Postdisaster strategies for mitigating stress for workers include planning for the ending of their assignment, program closure activities, critique of the project, debriefing of staff, follow-up, and recognition of staff.

PLANNING FOR THE ENDING

There is a certain amount of work to be done in ending what has been a long-term but time-limited disaster mental health program such as a FEMA Crisis Counseling Program. Typically, such programs last from 1 to 2 years following the disaster. Staff should receive consultation and training and hold planning sessions about how they will end the program. Whether staff were involved for short-term (a few weeks or months) or long term (months to years), they usually experience a mixture of emotions at the end of the work: relief that it is over, and sadness and guilt at leaving it behind. In addition, there is often a sense of "letdown" and some difficulty in transitioning back into regular job and family responsibilities. Mental health personnel working in disaster can be helped to anticipate these mixed emotions through education and training about common reactions and coping strategies that can help with the changes.

PROGRAM CLOSURE ACTIVITIES

Ending the services of a well-accepted, effective disaster mental health recovery program requires time and planning. Both community and staff must be prepared for it. Terminating the program in a thoughtful, professional, and responsible manner will help staff to feel pride in their accomplishment, rather than feeling guilt at "abandoning" the survivors. The following suggestions can be helpful (Myers, 1989b):

- Plan a timeline for phase-down activities, starting at least 3 months before the program will end.
- Conduct case reviews to identify individuals or families who will need continuing assistance; plan appropriate referrals.
- Develop a resource list of ongoing services and distribute list to clients.
- Provide training to mental health staff about common reactions of disaster staff at termination of their work assignment (guilt, sadness, depression, fatigue, disillusionment, boredom, detachment, anxiety, need for closure).
- Provide consultation and support for staff who will be unemployed at the end of the project.
- Critique and review achievements of the project.
- Inform the public of project termination date and plan public closure activity, if any is to be provided.
- Consider a conference, symposium, or workshop where professional staff can present lessons learned from the program and implications for future practice or research.
- Thank the community for its support of the program.
- Write final reports and program evaluations.
- Debrief staff.
- Provide recognition for staff.
- Develop follow-up protocols and resources for staff experiencing compassion fatigue or STS in the aftermath of the project.

CRITIQUE OF THE PROJECT

A critique can be helpful to staff by bringing closure to a disaster mental health project. A critique is a critical evaluation of the project, its difficulties, and its successes. It is different and separate from a debriefing, which attends to the psychological and emotional impact of the work on personnel. A critique can result in positive changes in the disaster plan, policies, and procedures to improve approach of the staff members in the next situation (Myers, 1994b). A critique can also help staff to take pride and feel a sense of ownership in the project. It helps them to see the positive effect of their efforts in the disaster recovery.

DEBRIEFING OF STAFF

The purpose of a formal debriefing is to address the emotional and psychological impact that the disaster assignment has had on the worker. McCammon and Allison outline the conceptual components of a variety of posttrauma debriefing models (1995). Important to all of the models is the empathy, understanding, and peer support generated when the debriefing is conducted for a group of people who have worked together. The debriefing should be run by a mental health facilitator with experience in disaster and specialized training in debriefing techniques. It allows staff to identify and talk about the feelings associated with the disaster project, provides "normalization" of their responses, and lends peer support as the project comes to a close. Debriefing serves an educational purpose, informing workers of the common stress and grief reactions and transition issues to expect when the project is over. Resources to assist them with transitional issues, compassion fatigue, or STS in the aftermath of their assignment should be discussed.

In long-term disaster assignments, debriefings may be used on a regular basis to assist staff with the feelings and stresses involved in their work. These debriefings, as well as a final or exit debriefing at the end of a long project, will require modification of Mitchell's debriefing model used in circumscribed "critical incidents" (Mitchell, 1983). Mitchell & Everly (1995) present a variation of CISD called the "mass disaster/community response CISD" that encourages participants to explore the most negative impacts of the entire experience, while also exploring with participants any lessons learned and anything positive they will take away from the experience. The multiple stressor debriefing model developed by Armstrong et al. (1991) and the disaster worker debriefing model developed by Myers and Zunin (1994b) also work well for the purpose of intermittent stress management and exit debriefing. Both of these models, while based on the prototype of Mitchell's model, include the added dimension of encouraging participants to discuss any of a large number of incidents that they might have experienced in the weeks or months of their disaster work. In these models, questions are framed to encourage discussion of incidents that were "challenging" or "difficult," with participants discussing the events themselves as well as the thoughts, feelings, stress reactions, and coping approaches associated with the events.

In addition to the above, Myers and Zunin invite debriefing participants to share not only a positive experience that they experienced during the disaster, but one that had a meaningful or profound effect on them. This inquiry is based on their belief that disaster work is not only traumatic, but is also profoundly meaningful and often very touching for workers. Debriefing staff about only the negative and stressful aspects does not allow them to fully process the many facets of what the disaster meant to them. Brian Flynn, Ed.D., chief of the Emergency Services and Disaster Relief Branch, Center for Mental Health Services (U. S. Department of Health and Human Services), is a 17-year veteran of disaster mental health. Following his work in the aftermath of the Oklahoma City bombing, he wrote,

> What I witnessed and experienced in Oklahoma City deeply moved me. Many people assume that the experience traumatized me and, to some extent, it did. However, in many ways, it was one of the most profoundly positive experiences in my personal and work life. I am so deeply moved by the experience that, even now, tears sometimes accompany my attempts to tell the story . . . When I received a psychological debriefing on leaving Oklahoma City, I was asked to identify the single most positive event of my experience there. This is the story I told.
>
> I did not enter the highly secure site of the bombing until all of the rescue and body recovery work was complete. A chain link fence was surrounding several city blocks outside which people gathered to stand vigil and leave mementos (flowers, notes, religious icons, teddy bears). Inside the perimeter, in the medical supply area, I talked with several workers who were in the process of dismantling that operation. When they became aware of my mental health role, one woman to whom I had been speaking said, "Wait here. I want you to see something. I'll be right back." She returned carrying a rather worn and limp brown teddy bear. The bear had on a silly yellow hat on which was written "Hug Specialist." Around its neck was a stethoscope and it wore a hospital wristband stating to whom it should be returned if lost.
>
> This woman explained to me that one of her roles was to have workers inside the perimeter hug the bear. She then took the bear outside the fence where people from the community hugged it. And she repeated the process. The bear thus became the link between those inside who were involved in some of the most difficult work imaginable and those who stood vigil outside, wanting so much to help. It was the *bearer* of their connection, their affection, their hope. Who could have thought of such a simple, but moving, way to connect people necessarily separated by role, steel, and troops yet connected by their common hopes and persistence? Symbols. Rituals. Although

I have received much recognition in my 25-year federal career and it means a great deal to me, none means more to me than when she asked me that morning to hug the bear (Flynn, 1995).

The accomplishments of disaster mental health counseling are less visible and tangible than the physical rebuilding of bridges and buildings. Mental health staff often feel frustration at the slow pace of their work, question the efficacy of their efforts, and feel there is little to show for the long months of their work. Specially designed small group exercises can augment debriefing by helping staff to recognize and appreciate their contribution to the community's healing, to understand the personal meaning of their experiences, and to begin the transition to other endeavors. Two examples follow (Myers, 1989b–1997):

AS THE PROJECT ENDS . . .

In small groups, staff discuss the following questions, then report some of their key points back to the larger group.

1. How has this disaster mental health assignment been different from other jobs you have had?
2. What have been the most challenging aspects of the work?
3. What have been the special rewards of the work?
4. How have you been changed by the work? What are some things you will be taking with you from this job?
5. Describe a meaningful, profound, or touching incident that happened to you during your work.
6. What do you anticipate your transition will be like as you leave the disaster project and move on? What will help you with this transition?

"LEGACY" EXERCISE

In small groups, staff discuss the following questions, recording their answers on flip charts (the charts will later help in writing a final report of the project's accomplishments). When they are done, they report their key points back to the larger group.

Despite your knowledge that the community healing process is not over and will go on long after this project has ended, what is the legacy you have left behind?

1. What has the project given to individual survivors?
2. How has the project helped our community in the healing process?
3. What will the project behind in the community?

FOLLOW-UP

Knowing what we know about the risks of compassion fatigue for trauma intervention workers, it would be both prudent and compassionate to provide follow-up to disaster traumatologists after the completion of their disaster assignments. While resources for any problems that develop or continue from their disaster work should be discussed during worker debriefing, a formalized follow-up in the form of a questionnaire or stress assessment should be considered. The Compassion Fatigue Self Test for Psychotherapists or a PTSD assessment scale can be used at the end of the assignment and at periodic intervals in the first year following disaster work. If the same tests were also used predisaster to evaluate worker stress, they would provide a useful analysis of the impact of the work. Assessments can indicate the need for additional debriefing, support, or psychotherapy to treat the compassion fatigue or STS resulting from the assignment. Support and treatment services should be offered as a matter of course to workers whose test results indicate a significant level of distress.

RECOGNITION OF STAFF

Recognition of the efforts and accomplishments of mental health staff will assist in bringing closure to their disaster experience and in validating the value of their work. A plaque, a letter of appreciation, a declaration from local or state government, or a souvenir such as an official disaster photograph will have much meaning for personnel.

Those outside the field of mental health may not recognize the risks inherent in psychological trauma intervention. However, disaster traumatologists routinely place themselves in positions of risk for compassion fatigue and STS in order to assist the community in its recovery. A small thank you goes a long way.

SUMMARY

The research and literature focusing on the impact of trauma on first responders, disaster workers, and trauma counselors indicates that these personnel are at risk for PTSD, compassion fatigue, burnout, and STS. Wee and Myers' research (1997, 2002) with disaster mental health workers following the Oklahoma City bombing and the Northridge earthquake clearly indicate that disaster traumatologists, a highly specialized group of professionals, are at high risk for compassion fatigue and STS in the course of their work with disaster survivors. This chapter has outlined strategies and interventions that can be utilized predisaster, during disaster, and after disaster to mitigate and intervene with compassion fatigue and STS.

REFERENCES

Ackerley, G. D., Burnell, J., Holder, D. C., & Kurdek, L. A. (1988). Burnout among licensed psychologists. *Professional Psychology: Research and Practice, 19,* 624–631.

Alexander, D. A., & Wells, A. (1991). Reactions of police officers to body-handling after a major disaster: A before-and-after comparison. *British Journal of Psychiatry, 159,* 547–555.

Armstrong, K, O'Callahan, W. T., & Marmar, C. R. (1991). Debriefing Red Cross disaster personnel: The multiple stressor debriefing model. *Journal of Traumatic Stress, 4,* 581–593.

Bailey, J. T., Steffen, S. M., & Grout, J. W. (1980). The stress audit: Identifying the stressors of IC nursing. *Journal of Nursing Education, 19,* 15–25.

Bartone, P., Ursano, R., Wright, K., & Ingraham, L. (1989). Impact of a military air disaster. *Journal of Nervous and Mental Disease, 177,* 317–328.

Berah, E., Jones, H., & Valent, P. (1984). The experience of a mental health team involved in the early phase of a disaster. *Australia and New Zealand Journal of Psychiatry, 18,* 354–358.

Bolin, R., & Bolton, P. (1986). *Race, religion, and ethnicity in disaster recovery* (Monograph No. 42). Boulder: University of Colorado, Program on Environment and Behavior.

Carlson, E. B. (1997) *Trauma assessments: A clinician's guide.* New York: Guilford Press.

Cerney, M. S. (1995). Treating the "heroic treaters." In C. R. Figley (Ed.), *Compassion fatigue: Coping with secondary traumatic stress disorder in those who treat the traumatized.* New York: Brunner/Mazel.

Danieli, Y. (1985). The treatment and prevention of long-term effects and intergenerational transmission of victimization: A lesson from Holocaust survivors and their children. In C. R. Figley (Ed.), *Trauma and its wake: The study and treatment of post-traumatic stress disorder.* New York: Brunner/Mazel.

Deahl, M. P., Gillham, A. B., Thomas, J., Searle, M. M., & Srinivasan, M. (1994). Psychological sequelae following the Gulf War: Factors associated with subsequent morbidity and the effectiveness of psychological debriefing. *British Journal of Psychiatry, 165,* 60–65.

Department of Health and Human Services. (1988a). *Prevention and control of stress among emergency workers: A pamphlet for team managers.* (DHHS Publication No. ADM 88-1496). Washington, DC: U.S. Government Printing Office.

Department of Health and Human Services. (1988b). *Prevention and control of stress among emergency workers: A pamphlet for workers.* (DHHS Publication No. ADM 88-1497). Washington, DC: U.S. Government Printing Office.

Derogatis, L. (1993). *SCL-90-R bibliography of research reports.* Minneapolis, MN: National Computer Systems.

Derogatis, L. (1994). *SCL-90-R administration, coding, and procedures manual.* Minneapolis, MN: National Computer Systems.

Deutsch, C. J. (1984). Self-reported sources of stress among psychotherapists. *Professional Psychology: Research and Practice, 15,* 833–845.

Duckworth, D. (1986). Psychological problems arising from disaster work. *Stress Medicine, 2,* 315–323.

Dunning, C. (1988). Intervention strategies for emergency workers. In M. Lystad (Ed.), *Mental health response to mass emergencies.* New York: Brunner/Mazel.

Durham, T. W., McCammon, S. L., & Allison, E. J., Jr. (1985). The psychological impact of disaster on rescue personnel. *Annals of Emergency Medicine, 14*(7), 664–668.

Dutton, M. A., & Rubinstein, F. L. (1995). Working with people with PTSD: Research implications. In C. R. Figley (Ed.), *Compassion fatigue: Coping with secondary traumatic stress disorder in those who treat the traumatized.* New York: Brunner/ Mazel.

Eby, D. L. (1984). A disaster worker's response. In *Role stressors and supports for emergency workers.* (DHHS Publication No. ADM 85-1408). Rockville, MD: National Institute of Mental Health.

Edelwich, J., & Brodsky, A. (1980). *Burn-out: Stages of disillusionment in the helping professions.* New York: Human Sciences Press.

Federal Emergency Management Agency. (1987a). *FEMA workers can be affected by disasters* (Brochure L-156). Washington, DC: Federal Emergency Management Agency and National Institute of Mental Health.

Federal Emergency Management Agency. (1987b). *Returning home after the disaster: An information pamphlet for FEMA disaster workers* (Brochure l-157). Washington, DC: Federal Emergency Management Agency and National Institute of Mental Health.

Federal Emergency Management Agency. (1988). *Disaster assistance programs: Crisis counseling programs: A handbook for grant applicants* (DAP-9). Washington, DC.

Federal Emergency Management Agency and Center for Mental Health Services. (1992). *Crisis counseling programs for victims of presidential declared disasters.* Washington, DC.

Federal Emergency Management Agency. (1995). *Building Inspection Area.* Oklahoma City, OK: FEMA-GIS.

Figley, C. R. (1982). Traumatization and comfort: Close relationships may be hazardous to your health. Keynote presentation, *Families and close relationships: Individuals in social interaction.* Conference held at Texas Tech University, Lubbock.

Figley, C. R. (1983). *Stress and the family: Vol. II. Coping with catastrophe.* New York: Brunner/ Mazel.

Figley, C. R. (1989). *Helping traumatized families.* San Francisco: Jossey-Bass.

Figley, C. R. (1993). Compassion stress and the family therapist. *Family Therapy News, 1–8.*

Figley, C. R. (Ed.). (1995). *Compassion fatigue: Coping with secondary traumatic stress disorder in those who treat the traumatized.* New York: Brunner/Mazel.

Figley, C. F. (Ed.). (2002). *Treating Compassion Fatigue.* New York: Brunner-Routledge.

Flynn, B. (1995). Thoughts and reflections after the bombing of the Alfred P. Murrah Federal Building in Oklahoma City. *Journal of the American Psychiatric Nurses Association, 1,* 166–170.

Forney, D. S., Wallace-Schutzman, F., & Wiggers, T. T. (1982). Burnout among career development professionals: Preliminary findings and implications. *Personnel and Guidance Journal, 60,* 435–439.

Frederick, C. J. (1977). Current thinking about crisis or psychological interventions in United States disasters. *Mass Emergencies, 2,* 43–49.

Frederick, C. J. (1985). Children traumatized by catastrophic situations. In S. Eth & R. S. Pynoos (Eds.), *Post-traumatic stress disorder in children* (pp. 71–100). Washington, DC: American Psychiatric Press.

Frederick, C. J. (1988). *Frederick reaction index (Form A).* Unpublished manuscript.

Fried, M. (1966). Grieving for a lost home. In J. Q. Wilson (Ed.), *Urban renewal.* Cambridge, MA: MIT Press.

Green, B. L., & Gleser, G. C. (1983). Stress and long standing psychopathology in survivors of the Buffalo Creek disaster. In D. Ricks & B. S. Dohrenwend (eds.), *Origins of psychopathology: Problems in research and public policy* (pp. 73–90). Cambridge, MA:

Harvard University Press.

Hartsough, D. M., & Myers, D. G. (1985). *Disaster work and mental health: Prevention and control of stress among workers.* (DHHS Publication No. ADM 85-1422). Rockville, MD: National Institute of Mental Health.

Hodgkinson, P. E., & Shepherd, M. A. (1994). The impact of disaster support work. *Journal of Traumatic Stress, 7,* 587–600.

Horowitz, M. J., Stinson, C., & Field, N. (1991) Natural disasters and stress response syndromes. *Psychiatric Annals, 21*(9), 556–562.

Hunter, A. (1974). *Symbolic communities.* Chicago: University of Chicago Press.

Hunter, A. (1975). The loss of community: An empirical test through replication. *American Sociological Review, 40,* 537–552.

Jenkins, S. R., & Sewell, K. W. (1993, March). *Distress and health among paramedics in the Killeen shooting incident.* Paper presented at the Annual Meeting of the Society for Behavioral Medicine, San Francico, CA.

Jordan, F. B. (1997). The role of the medical examiner/coroner in mass fatality disaster management. *National Foundation for Mortuary Care Disaster Management News, 1,* 1–3.

Keane, T. M., Scott, W. O., Chavoya, G. A., Lamparski, D. M., & Fairbank, J. A. (1985). Social support in Vietnam veterans with post-traumatic stress disorder: A comparative analysis. *Journal of Consulting and Clinical Psychology, 53,* 95–102.

Lanning, J. K. S., & Fannin, R. A. (1988). It's not over yet. *Chief Fire Executive, 40–44,* 58–62.

Lindemann, E, (1944). Symptomatology and management of acute grief. *American Journal of Psychiatry, 101,* 141–148.

Lindstrom, B., & Lundin, T. (1982). Stress reactions among rescue and health care personnel after a major hotel fire. *Nord. Psykiatr. Tidss, 36* Suppl. 6.

Lystad, M. (1988). Perspectives on human responses to mass emergencies. In M. Lystad (Ed.), *Mental health response to mass emergencies: Theory and practice* (pp. 22–51). New York: Brunner/Mazel.

Mantel, M. R., Dubner, J. S., & Lipson, G. S. (1985) *San Ysidro massacre: Impact on police officers.* San Diego, CA: San Diego Police Department.

Marmar, C. R., Weiss, D. S., Metzler, T. J., Ronfeldt, H. M., & Foreman, C. (1996). Stress responses of emergency services personnel to the Loma Prieta Earthquake Interstate 880 freeway collapse and control traumatic incidents. *Journal of Traumatic Stress, 9*(1).

McCammon, S. L., & Allison, E. J. (1995). Debriefing and treating emergency workers. In C. R. Figley (Ed.), *Compassion fatigue: Coping with secondary traumatic stress disorder in those who treat the traumatized.* New York: Brunner/Mazel.

McCammon, S., Durham, T., Allison, E., & Williamson, J. (1986). *Emotional reactions of rescue workers following a tornado.* Paper presented at the 94th annual convention of the American Psychological Association, Washington, DC.

McFarlane, A. C. (1988). The longitudinal course of post traumatic morbidity: The range of outcomes and their predictors. *Journal of Nervous and Mental Disease, 176*(1), 30–39.

Miles, M. S., Demi, A. S., & Mostyn-Aker, P. (1984). Rescue workers' reactions following the Hyatt Hotel disaster. *Death Education, 8,* 315–331.

Mitchell, J. T. (1983). When disaster strikes . . . the Critical Incident Stress Debriefing process. *Journal of Emergency Medical Services, 8,* 36–39.

Mitchell, J. T. (1986). Critical Incident Stress Management. *Response,* 24–25.

Mitchell, J., & Bray, G. (1990). *Emergency services stress: Guidelines for preserving the health and careers of emergency services personnel.* Englewood Cliffs, NJ: Prentice Hall.

Mitchell, J., & Everly, G. S., Jr. (1993). *Critical Incident Stress Debriefing: An operations manual for the prevention of traumatic stress among emergency services and disaster workers.* Ellicott

City, MD: Chevron.

Mitchell, J. T., & Everly, G. S. (1995). *Innovations in Disaster and Trauma Psychology, Volume 1: Applications in Emergency Services and Disaster Response.* Ellicott City, MD: Chevron Publishing Co.

Moran, C., & Britton, N. R. (1994). Emergency work experience and reactions to traumatic incidents. *Journal of Traumatic Stress, 7*(4).

Munroe, J. F., Shay, J., Fisher, L., Makary, C., Rapperport, K., & Zimering, R. (1995). Preventing compassion fatigue: A team treatment model. In C. R. Figley (Ed.), *Compassion Fatigue: Coping with secondary traumatic stress disorder in those who treat the traumatized.* New York: Brunner/Mazel.

Myers, D. (1989a). *Training manual: Disaster mental health.* Sacramento, CA: California Department of Mental Health.

Myers, D. (1989b–1997). Unpublished training materials.

Myers, D. (1992). *Hurricane Andrew disaster field office stress management program: After action report.* Miami, FL: Federal Emergency Management Agency.

Myers, D. (1993a). *Disaster worker stress management: Planning and training issues.* Washington, DC: Federal Emergency Management Agency and Center for Mental Health Services.

Myers, D. (1993b). *After action report: 1993 California winter storms.* Washington, DC: Federal Emergency Management Agency.

Myers, D. (1994a). *A stress management program for FEMA disaster workers: Program description, operational guidelines, and training plan.* Washington, DC: Federal Emergency Management Agency and Center for Mental Health Services.

Myers, D. (1994b). *Disaster response and recovery: A handbook for mental health professionals.* Rockville, MD: Center for Mental Health Services.

Myers, D., & Zunin, L. M. (1993a). *After action report: 1993 Florida winter storms disaster field office stress management program.* Tampa, FL: Federal Emergency Management Agency.

Myers, D., & Zunin, L. M. (1993b). *After action report: 1993 Midwest floods stress management program.* Kansas City, MO: Federal Emergency Management Agency.

Myers, D., & Zunin, L. M. (1994a). *Stress management program after action report: 1994 Northridge earthquake.* Pasadena, CA: Federal Emergency Management Agency and California Governor's Office of Emergency Services.

Myers, D., & Zunin, L. M. (1994b). *Stress management program for disaster workers: A national cadre of stress management personnel: Training manual.* Atlanta, GA: Federal Emergency Management Agency.

National Institute of Mental Health. (1987a). *Prevention and control of stress among emergency workers: A pamphlet for managers.* Rockville, MD: Author.

National Institute of Mental Health. (1987b). *Prevention and control of stress among emergency workers: A pamphlet for workers.* Rockville, MD: Author.

Oklahoma City Fire Department. (1995, July). *Oklahoma City disaster: Initial city and fire department response.* Presentation at a training symposium on the Oklahoma City Disaster sponsored by the Industrial Emergency Council of San Carlos, CA.

Oklahoma City Public Works Department. (1995). *Building inspection area.* Oklahoma City, OK: Geographic Information Systems.

Pearlman, L. A., & MacIan, P. S. (1995). Vicarious traumatization: An empirical study of the effects of trauma work on trauma therapists. *Professional Psychology: Research and Practice, 26,* 558–565.

Pearlman, L. A., & Saakvitne, K. W. (1995). Treating therapists with vicarious traumatization and secondary traumatic stress disorders. In C. R. Figley (Ed.), *Compassion fatigue: Coping with secondary traumatic stress disorder in those who treat the traumatized.* New York: Brunner/Mazel.

Raphael, B. (1986). *When disasters strike. How individuals and communities cope with catastrophe.* New York: Basic Books.

Raphael, B., Singh B., Bradbury, B., & Lambert, F. (1984). Who helps the helpers? The effects of a disaster on the rescue workers. *Omega, 14,* 9–20.

Robinson, R. (1989). Critical incident stress and psychological debriefing in emergency services. *Social Biology Resources Center Review, 3*(3), 1–4.

Rodolfa, E. R., Kraft, W. A., & Reilley, R. R. (1988). Stressors of professionals and trainees at APA-approved counseling and VA medical center internship sites. *Professional Psychology: Research and Practice, 19,* 43–49.

Rosenschweig, M. A., & Vaslow, P. K. (1992). *Recommendations for reduction of stress among FEMA disaster workers.* Rockville, MD: National Institute of Mental Health.

Scott, R. T., & Jordan, M. J. (1993, April). *The Los Angeles riots April 1992: A CISD challenge.* Paper presented at the 2nd World Congress on Stress, Trauma, and Coping in the Emergency Services. A meeting of the International Critical Incident Stress Foundation, Baltimore.

Sloan, I. H., Rozensky, R. H., Kaplan, L., & Saunders, S. M. (1994). A shooting incident in an elementary school: Effects of worker stress on public safety, mental health, and medical personnel. *Journal of Traumatic Stress, 7,* 565–574.

Snowden, L. R. (1997). Personal communication. Professor, School of Social Welfare, University of California Berkeley.

Solomon, S. (1986). Mobilizing social support networks in times of disaster. In C. R. Figley (Ed.), *Trauma and its wake: Vol. 2. Traumatic stress theory, research, and intervention.* New York: Brunner/Mazel.

SPSS. (1993). SPSS for Windows. Release 6.0. Chicago: SPSS.

Staub, E. (1989). *The roots of evil: The origins of genocide and other group violence.* Cambridge, UK: Cambridge University Press.

Suttles, G. (1972). *Social construction of communities.* Chicago: University of Chicago Press.

Taylor, Ph. D., & Frazer, A. G. (1982). The stress of post-disaster body handling and victim identification work. *Journal of Human Stress, 8*(12), 4–12.

Trainer, P., & Bolin, R. (1976). Persistent effects of disasters on daily activities: A cross-cultural comparison. *Mass Emergencies, 1,* 279–290.

Varblow, P. (1994). Stress management. In *Project Rebound, 2nd quarterly report.* Los Angeles, CA: Los Angeles County Department of Mental Health.

Wee, D. F. (1991a). Earthquake Reaction Survey. Unpublished report. Available from Berkeley Mental Health, 2640 Martin Luther King Jr. Way, Berkeley, CA.

Wee, D. F. (April 1991a). San Francisco Earthquake and Other Disasters: Research Study of Emergency Workers at the Cypress Structure Collapse. Paper presented at the meeting of the International Critical Incident Stress Foundation, Baltimore, MD.

Wee, D. F. (1994a) Disasters: Impact on the law enforcement family. In J. T. Reese & E. Scrivner (Eds.), *Law enforcement family: Issues and answers.* Washington, DC: U.S. Department of Justice, Federal Bureau of Investigation.

Wee, D. (1994b). *Disaster training for crisis counselors.* Unpublished training materials.

Wee, D. F., & Mills, D. (1993). Satisfaction Survey. City of Berkeley crisis counseling program: Eastbay firestorm FEMA 919-DR. Available from Berkeley Mental Health, 2640 Martin Luther King Jr. Way, Berkeley, CA. 94704.

Wee, D. F., Mills, D. M., & Koehler, G. (1999). The effects of critical incident stress debriefing (CISD) on emergency medical services personnel following the Los Angeles civil disturbances. *International Journal of Emergency Mental Health, 1,* 33–38.

Wee, D., & Myers, D. (1997). Disaster mental health: Impact on workers. In K. Johnson, *Trauma in the lives of children.* Alameda, CA: Hunter House Press.

Wee, D. F., & Myers, D. (2002). Stress response of mental health workers following disaster: The Oklahoma City bombing. In C. R. Figley (Ed.), *Treating compassion fatigue*. New York: Brunner/Mazel.

Wee, D. F., & Myers, D. (2002). Research findings focusing on Oklahoma City bombing disaster workers. In C. R. Figley (Ed.). *Treating Compassion Fatigue*. New York: Brunner-Routledge.

Winget. C. N., & Umbenhauer, S. L. (1982). Disaster planning: The mental health worker as "victim-by-proxy." *Journal of Health and Human Resources Administration, 4,* 363–373.

Wraith, R., & Gordon, R. (1988). *Workers' responses to disaster*. Melbourne, Australia: Department of Child and Family Psychiatry, Melbourne Royal Children's Hospital.

Yassen, J. (1995). Preventing secondary traumatic stress disorder. In C. R. Figley (Ed.), *Compassion fatigue: Coping with secondary traumatic stress disorder in those who treat the traumatized*. New York: Brunner/Mazel.

Zunin, L. M., Myers, D., & Cook, C. (1995). *Stress management final report: Oklahoma City federal building bombing*. Washington, DC: Federal Emergency Management Agency.

Government publications referenced in this chapter are in the public domain and are not copyrighted. They may be reproduced or copied without permission from the government agency or from the authors. Citation of the author and source is requested.

5

CRITICAL INCIDENT STRESS MANAGEMENT IN LARGE-SCALE DISASTERS

INTRODUCTION

LARGE-SCALE DISASTERS PRESENT EXTRAORDINARY CHALLENGES TO PROFESSIONALS who are responsible for providing critical services before, during, and after a disaster strikes. Effective disaster mental health response requires a preplanned, coordinated, and comprehensive program of services that must be effectively integrated into the overall community response coordinated by the local emergency management organization. Over the past 30 years, knowledge of the psychological impacts of disaster on individuals and communities has grown tremendously (see chapters 1 and 2). Likewise, the knowledge of what constitutes an effective disaster mental health program has been fine-tuned through field-based observations, clinical experience, program evaluation, and empirical research on services delivered by a wide range of providers. Numerous training manuals (Farberow & Frederick, 1978; DeWolfe, 2000; Myers, 1994b; Young, Ford, Ruzek, Friedman, & Gusman, 1998) have been published describing methods for assessing community needs and developing and delivering mental health services proven to be effective in prior disasters. One could argue that a "standard of care" has developed in which effective methods of disaster mental health service delivery have been identified, standardized, provided, and evaluated over time.

Critical incident stress management (CISM) is a comprehensive and organized form of crisis intervention originally designed by Jeffrey Mitchell in the mid-1970s to mitigate the harmful effects of traumatic stress and cumulative traumatic stress among emergency responders. Since its inception, CISM has also been provided to a variety of populations, including both citizens and responders, following disasters and large-scale community tragedies. It is our belief that CISM as a system of early crisis intervention and psychological first aid can play an important role in an effective disaster mental health program. A substantial body of research exists that validates the efficacy of CISM when applied as a comprehensive system of crisis intervention, which has as its goals stabilization of individuals and their situation, return to adaptive functioning, and facilitation of access to continued care when needed. However in recent years critical incident stress debriefing (CISD, one of the core components of CISM) has been the target of skepticism and criticism in some professional circles and in a number of research publications. A key issue in the "debriefing controversy" is whether the group intervention of CISD prevents the development of posttraumatic stress disorder and whether, in some individuals, participation in a CISD may actually cause increased distress. Hull (2001) wisely advises that "The humane wish to assist individuals at the point of major trauma or disaster is not helped by a closed debate, with advocates and antagonists retreating to their enclaves. Consensus can only be reached by further research and open discussion" (p. 564). It is our belief as authors of this chapter and as disaster practitioners and researchers that CISM has much to offer as a comprehensive system of crisis intervention for disaster situations. However, it is also our belief that continued research and dialogue are essential as we explore the questions of how best to screen populations to identify those needing intervention, to identify the goals of intervention, and to identify which interventions are most effective and when to apply them.

An important consideration in providing any group or one-to-one crisis intervention services is whether or not individuals want to talk about their experience, and if they do, at what point in time and in what type of format? Various research findings seem to suggest that helping people ventilate their emotions soon after a critical event will hasten recovery from posttraumatic stress, and most trauma therapies emphasize the importance of talking about one's feelings and thoughts about the trauma (McNally, Bryant, & Ehlers, 2003). However, in the immediate days and even weeks after a traumatic event, people appear to alternate between phases of avoidance and phases of processing their experience. Raphael, Wilson, Meldrum, and McFarlane point out that "an individual may or may not be in a state in which he or she wishes, or is prepared, to discuss what has happened" (1996, p. 466). Thus, encouraging survivors to discuss their thoughts and feelings right away when they are disinclined to do so may increase the risk that they will be overwhelmed by the experience, which will be counterproductive (McNally et al., 2003). For this reason, facilitating telling of the trauma story and ventilation of feelings must be *appropriate to the needs and wishes of the particular individual.* Thus, any form of psychological first aid must respect an individual's wishes regarding whether to talk about the trauma (McNally et al.). Litz, Gray, Bryant, and Adler (2002) suggest that anyone not wishing to participate in a group should be given the option of meeting with an individual trauma therapist.

Thus, in introducing this chapter on crisis intervention, stress management, and CISM, we wish to emphasize the importance of *offering* but not *requiring* survivors or personnel to partake of our services. Defusings, debriefings, and individual sessions should never be made mandatory. As Foa (2001) suggests, professionals should listen actively and supportively but not probe for details and emotional responses, nor push for more information than survivors are comfortable providing.

In addition, special care should be taken when conducting group interventions. Individuals should be triaged and assigned to groups according to their level of exposure to the traumatic event and traumatic stimuli. It is contraindicated to mix individuals with a mild level of exposure with those who have had more serious, frightening, or gruesome exposure, thus "contaminating" them with images and emotions they had never experienced during the actual event.

This chapter will describe the crisis intervention system known as CISM, the core components (interventions) of the system, and the application of those components in disaster mental health response. It will emphasize the importance of services being provided by specially trained mental health professionals and peer counselors; services being provided within an integrated, comprehensive, multi-component, organized crisis intervention *system*; and services following the highest standards of care based on experience, evaluation and research. The section on debriefing, one of the components of CISM, will describe several models of debriefing that have been used in disaster, including the International Critical Incident Stress Foundation (ICISF or Mitchell) model, the multiple stressor debriefing model (Armstrong et al., 1991), and the disaster worker stress debriefing model (Myers & Zunin, 1994b). The chapter will explore research on the effectiveness of CISM, including an overview of research involved in the debate about the effectiveness of CISD. Readers are encouraged to explore the referenced research firsthand for a more in-depth presentation of specific findings and to stay abreast of continued research as it evolves beyond the publication of this book.

We begin this chapter with the following case examples illustrating the use of CISM in a large-scale disaster and in a hostage-taking incident, with comments from the people who participated in these services.

LOMA PRIETA EARTHQUAKE

On October 17, 1989, at 5:04 P.M., an earthquake measuring 7.1 on the Richter Scale occurred along the San Andreas Fault in the Santa Cruz

Mountains of northern California. The strong ground motions caused serious damage in Santa Cruz, Santa Clara, San Mateo, San Francisco, Alameda, Monterey, and San Benito counties. Presidential declarations of disaster were issued for all seven counties. The strong ground motions caused three quarters of a mile of the bi-level section of the I-880 Cypress Structure to collapse 60 miles to the north in the City of Oakland. There were 42 people killed, 109 injured, and 116 vehicles involved. Earthquake support groups were offered by the City of Berkeley Disaster Mental Health Program during the weeks following the earthquake. The critical incident stress debriefing model was used during the earthquake support groups. The support groups were offered on a drop-in basis to people who wanted emotional support and information. The people who participated in the support groups were mailed a self-report satisfaction survey 6 months following the groups. Of the respondents participating in the earthquake support group who returned the surveys, 90% reported that the group reduced their distress, 96.7% found the CISM personnel to be supportive, 80.6% found the information provided was useful, and 87.5% were satisfied with the earthquake support group (Wee, 1991).

The earthquake survivors who participated in support groups following the Loma Prieta earthquake wrote comments on their questionnaires. Their comments illustrate the benefits that participants experienced from the support groups:

"Work helped, friends, and the support group. I was very scattered, anxious and didn't know that it was a common reaction until I went to the group. The group helped because I saw it was a natural reaction that was happening to many people."

"It gave me the chance to talk (and listen) to a broader group of people than just my friends—also, finding out more about what kind of reactions are common (through the discussion and through handouts) helped me to understand what I was going through and not minimize it or blame myself for it."

"It helped to hear of other people's fears and also to be able to verbally express my own fears to sympathetic and supportive people."

"It helped to hear that others were having the same feelings and reactions, to know that I wasn't 'crazy.'"

"Nice to know I'm not alone in my feelings, fear—that I am normal."

"Supplied needed information about typical symptoms and reactions to a disaster of this magnitude. Also helped me in 'coping' with the stresses of the quake."

HENRY'S BAR HOSTAGE INCIDENT

Critical incident stress debriefing was offered to former hostages following the Henry's Bar hostage incident in Berkeley, California. The incident involved a gunman who entered a crowded bar and opened fire on the people in the bar. By the time this event ended hours later, the perpetrator had killed 1 person, injured 7 others including a police officer, and held 33 hostages. The gunman made bizarre demands, terrorized the hostages, and was killed when he acted aggressively toward the hostages after police officers ordered him to surrender. Mental health services, including critical incident stress debriefing (CISD) and specialized support groups, were provided to the former hostages during the days that followed their release. A follow-up questionnaire was mailed 6 months later. The comments of the former hostages illustrate their experiences in the support group.

"It brought all of us together who shared a common tragedy/event, and gave us a direction to release our feelings and thoughts into. They helped us to understand what we felt and why, what we may experience in the future, and even symptoms to look for in our selves as well as the others there. It enabled expression, or the option of just listening. It gave those of us there a chance to not be strangers, and to understand each other and what we felt, so that we could help each other, and not have it be awkward. It got people to talk. It brought out what people kept inside. It alleviated fears and addressed issues, including male–female issues."

"I can say that I'm glad the support group was there. You have no idea, looking back, how beneficial it was to have people there, professionals, who could relate and know what we were going thru [sic]. It helped greatly to piece everything together and get our lives back on track. It is a service that makes a difference. I hope everyone takes advantage of it if they go thru [sic] trauma, because everyone needs help. I only wish I could've talk to those hostages in Sacramento from last month, because talking to someone who can relate makes all the difference in the world. Thank you one and all!!!"

"Talking to other hostages helped me to cope the most just through being able to air the experience with people who understood where I was coming from. Also to let me know that it wasn't just a light experience capable of being shrugged off easily, others were having serious problems posttraumatically and that made me feel more comfortable and less guilty about mine. Because I was not physically injured or molested I felt like my mental repercussions were uncalled for and should be controlled easily, but knowing others were having trouble made me realize my problems were real and acceptable. Counselors also helped in that they understood the gravity of the situation. Family and friends didn't realize that at all . . ."

CRITICAL INCIDENT STRESS MANAGEMENT

Critical incident stress management is an integrated, comprehensive, multicomponent program focusing on crisis intervention with traumatic stress. Originally developed as a system of crisis intervention and stress management for emergency service workers, it has since been expanded to use with disaster workers and citizens impacted by disaster. CISM may include, but is not limited to, the following: preincident education and preparation, continuing stress education, consultation to administrators and supervisors, significant-other support services, family support services, individual crisis intervention, peer counseling, on-scene support services, demobilization, crisis management briefing, defusing, critical incident stress debriefing (CISD), pastoral crisis intervention, follow-up, referral, research and development, and other services as required.

HISTORY OF CRITICAL INCIDENT STRESS MANAGEMENT

The origins and foundations of Critical Incident Stress Management are found in a number of areas. The military has a long history of using psychoeducational methods, including debriefing, during and following military combat. From the work of T. W. Salmon (1919) in World War I, and Kardiner and Spiegel (1947) in World War II, the three principles of crisis intervention—immediacy, proximity, and expectancy—were formulated. CISM as an organized method of crisis intervention was developed by Mitchell in the mid-1970s to intervene with traumatic stress experienced in the line of duty by emergency medical services (EMS), fire, and police personnel. The Mitchell model of critical incident stress debriefing was first published and standardized in 1983 (Mitchell, 1983). While CISD was never intended to be a "one intervention fits all" technique, it was not until 1986 that Mitchell began publishing and teaching about the more comprehensive critical incident stress management model of crisis and stress management interventions. In 1989, the International Critical Incident Stress Foundation (ICISF) formalized an international network of over 350 crisis response teams trained in the standardized and comprehensive crisis intervention model known as critical incident stress management (Mitchell & Everly, 2001).

In government disaster service and emergency management agencies, the stress experienced by disaster response personnel has been addressed with a range of stress management interventions, (Myers, 1992, 1993a, 1993b, 1993c, 1994b, 1995; Myers & Zunin, 1993a, 1993b, 1994a, 1994b; Myers, Zunin & Zunin, 1990; Sword, Myers, & Iona, 1992). Likewise, the American Red Cross has recognized the importance of defusing and debriefing among the crisis interventions of its disaster mental health services (DMHS) for both disaster victims and Red Cross disaster workers (American Red Cross, 1995).

Since its inception as a model of crisis intervention for emergency workers, and its subsequent expansion into use with disaster service workers, CISM has been utilized in a wide variety of settings, including schools and colleges, health care facilities, private business and industry, the military, and other community settings.

STRESS REACTIONS

CISM focuses on two types of human stress response: traumatic stress and cumulative traumatic stress. Traumatic stress response occurs when there is an event that is outside the usual realm of human experience and is distressing. Traumatic stressors include events that can occur to an individual, such as sexual assault or abuse, robbery, serious physical injury or abuse, an automobile accident, severe injury or death of one's own child, suicide of a family member or friend, homicide, line of duty injury or death for first responders, and the like. Community-wide traumatic stressors include natural disasters, large-scale environmental pollution, multiple fatality accidents, terrorism, and so forth. Traumatic stress response may involve psychological, physiological, behavioral, cognitive, or spiritual reactions that can overwhelm the coping ability of the normal individual. Cumulative traumatic stress is a stress reaction that builds as a result of a series of traumatic events that are experienced by individuals over a period of time, overwhelm individuals' ability to cope with their stress reactions, and prohibit them from returning to their prestress level of functioning. Cumulative stress is an important concern for citizens following disaster, for they are not only exposed to the original disaster event but to subsequent stress in the postdisaster environment. It is also a significant concern for emergency service workers repeatedly exposed to traumatic stress in the course of their job responsibilities.

Emergency service workers in the course of their work are often exposed to a series of traumatic stressors, each causing a traumatic stress response. There may be insufficient time between stressful events to allow for the restoration of normal coping ability or mitigation of the traumatic stress response in each succeeding traumatic event. The resulting increase in intensity of stress response can put the emergency service worker at greater risk of emotional, cognitive, behavioral, and physical signs and symptoms of distress.

For an emergency worker, cumulative traumatic stressors might be: (a) the line-of-duty-death of a fellow worker, (b) a grisly car wreck with children killed, (c) a police shooting of a citizen. For a citizen after disaster, cumulative traumatic stressors might be: (a) a 6.9 magnitude earthquake severely damaging a house and personal belongings, (b) all family members not being located for over 24 hr, (c) the building inspector "red-tagging" the house (deeming it unlivable), (d) the insurance company informing the family that their deductible on earthquake insurance is $72,000, and they do not have that kind of liquid assets, and (e) months later, the planning department declaring their lot to be on unsafe soil and not issuing a building permit to rebuild.

Cumulative traumatic stress can lead to psychological and physical distress. Cumulative stress response might initially be experienced as feeling anxious, overwhelmed, and exhausted. Cumulative stress without opportunities to rest and restore coping skills can result in chronic fatigue, somatic symptoms such as high blood pressure, muscle tension, headaches, gastrointestinal distress, and sleep disturbance. Deterioration of job performance may occur, with symptoms such as procrastination, lateness, absenteeism, withdrawal, and avoidance. Ultimately, cumulative stress may result in feelings of hopelessness or helplessness or both, depression, change of job, consideration of change in personal living situation (e.g., divorce), contemplation of self-destructive actions such as suicide, and substance abuse (Mitchell & Everly, 2001).

CRITICAL INCIDENTS

A critical incident is defined as any situation entailing a high level of stress that causes unusually strong emotional reactions that have the potential to interfere with functioning either at the time or later. Types of events likely to cause trauma to an individual or group might include the following:

- Significant loss (death of loved one, serious injury to self or loved one, loss of home), especially under unexpected or traumatic circumstances
- Serious injury or death of one or more children
- Witnessing trauma, injury, or death
- A situation where there is strong identification with victims
- Exposure to traumatic sights, sounds, smells, or activities
- A situation that seemingly could have been prevented (real or perceived human cause, error, or negligence)
- A situation in which people are unable to take effective action
- Serious physical or psychological threat, such as a hostage situation
- A situation in which recovery is unlikely or pain and suffering will likely be great
- A tragic ending after a prolonged expenditure of effort in an attempted rescue

- A situation that attracts a great deal of media attention (Mitchell, 1983; Myers, 1985; Young, 1989)

Entire communities can be affected by certain types of events that can leave a portion of the members of the community traumatized. These events usually have the following characteristics: numerous people are killed or injured, the event alters the community environment via damage or destruction, and the event is outside community members' expectations and experience or is perceived to be deliberately caused by a human being. Community-wide events that are potentially traumatizing are the following:

- Natural disasters (earthquake, hurricane, fire, and flood, etc.)
- Technological or human-caused disaster (large-scale environmental pollution, structural collapse, explosion, etc.)
- Health disasters (famine, epidemic, etc.)
- Multiple injury/fatality accidents
- Hostage situation
- Violence in the workplace
- Terrorism
- Riot, civil disturbances
- Child-related traumatic events
- Homicide or suicide
- High publicity crime of violence, sex, or other unethical or illegal activity
- Organizational traumatic events (layoffs, reorganizations, takeovers, public censure, etc.)

CRITICAL INCIDENT STRESS RESPONSE

Critical incident stress responses have physical, cognitive, emotional, behavioral, and spiritual signs and symptoms that can occur immediately or may be delayed in onset. Some individuals may experience a stress response during the incident, others immediately following the event, and others in the hours, days, and sometimes weeks, months, and years following the incident. Some of the common physical, cognitive, emotional, and behavior signs and symptoms of critical incident stress response are listed in Table 5.1. Those reactions that are considered "normal reactions of normal people to abnormal events" are listed. Also listed are those symptoms that are potentially serious, and that should be referred for further assessment and intervention. There may be other critical incident stress responses that will be experienced that do not appear on this list.

TABLE 5.1: CRITICAL INCIDENT STRESS RESPONSES[a]

Physical reactions:
- Increased pulse, respiration, blood pressure
- Nausea, indigestion, diarrhea
- Psychogenic sweating or chills
- Tremors, especially of hand, lips, and eyes
- Muffled hearing
- Visual focusing ("tunnel vision")
- Headaches
- Feeling uncoordinated
- Lower back pain
- Feeling a "lump in the throat"
- Faintness or dizziness
- Exaggerated startle reaction
- Fatigue, exhaustion
- Appetite change
- Change in sexual desire
- Frequent colds, allergies

Physical reactions to consider for immediate referral to healthcare personnel:
- Severe shortness of breath
- Chest pain
- Irregular heartbeat
- Dizziness, collapse
- Sudden weakness, numbness (especially of face, arm, and leg)
- Difficulty speaking or being understood
- Sudden severe headache
- Heat stroke
- Seizure
- Continuing vomiting or diarrhea
- Blood in vomit, stool, urine, and sputum
- Loss of consciousness
- Worsening of chronic health conditions

Cognitive reactions:
- Memory problems
- Difficulty naming objects
- Slight disorientation
- Slowness of thinking, difficulty comprehending
- Mental confusion, difficulty calculating
- Difficulty using logic, making judgments and decisions, problem solving
- Loss of ability to conceptualize alternatives or to prioritize tasks
- Loss of objectivity
- Time distortion
- Preoccupation with thoughts of the event, intrusive memories
- Recurring dreams or nightmares

Cognitive reactions to consider for referral to a mental health professional:
- Dangerously diminished alertness to surroundings
- Serious disorientation (to self, others, place, time)

- Significant disturbance of memory
- Preoccupation with a single thought
- Inability to make simple decisions
- Delusional or psychotic thinking
- Suicidal or homicidal ideation
- Significant amnesia
- Episodes of dissociation

Emotional reactions:
- Shock, numbness, disbelief
- Feeling "high," heroic, invulnerable
- Feelings of gratefulness for being alive, relief, euphoria
- Anxiety, fear
- Identification with victims
- Anger, resentment
- Irritability, restlessness, hyperexcitability
- Sadness, grief, depression, moodiness
- Despair, hopelessness
- Recurrent dreams of the event or other traumatic dreams; other sleep problems
- Guilt, self-doubt
- Feeling isolated, detached, lost, or abandoned
- Apathy, diminished interest in usual activities
- Denial or constriction of feelings; numbness
- Worry about safety of others
- Feeling overwhelmed, helpless
- Unpredictable mood swings

Emotional reactions to consider for referral to a mental health professional:
- Reactions so intense as to endanger safety of self or others
- Excessively "flat" emotion
- Persistent emotion out of context (e.g., hysterical laughing)
- Depression and hopelessness with suicidal ideation
- Anxiety that impairs functioning
- Phobias

Behavioral reactions:
- Change in ordinary behavior patterns
- Difficulty communicating
- Sleep problems
- Decreased efficiency and effectiveness of activity
- Outbursts of anger; increased conflict with others
- Hyperactivity; inability to rest or let up
- Crying easily or frequently
- Increased use of alcohol, tobacco, other drugs
- Changes in eating or sleeping patterns
- Social withdrawal, distancing, limited contacts with others
- Avoiding reminders of the event
- Hypervigilance for danger; startle reactions

(Continued)

TABLE 5.1:   CONTINUED

Behavioral reactions to consider for referral to a mental health professional:
- Inability to care for self or carry out everyday functions
- Extreme hyperactivity
- Immobility, muteness
- Extreme regression
- Repetition of ritualistic acts
- Abuse of alcohol or drugs
- Persistent sleep problems
- Inappropriate anger/abuse of others
- Violence (or serious threat)
- Loss of control
- Self-destructive or antisocial acts
- Frequent accidents

Spiritual reactions[b]:
- Crisis of faith (anger at God, no longer practicing faith, withdrawal from faith community)
- Strengthening of faith
- Newfound faith

Spiritual reactions to consider for referral to a spiritual care or mental health professional:
- Crisis of faith
- Obsessive religious thoughts
- Compulsive religious acts

Note: [a]From *Key Concepts of Disaster Mental Health*, by D. Myers, 2003a, City and County of San Francisco: Division of Mental Health and Substance Abuse. [b]From *National Guard Critical Incident Stress Management (CISM): Terrorism and Disaster Response*, by G. S. Everly, Jr., D. J. Mitchell, D. Myers, and J. T. Mitchell, 2002, Ellicott City, MD: International Critical Incident Stress Foundation.

PREPLANNING FOR CRISIS INTERVENTION AND STRESS MANAGEMENT SERVICES IN DISASTER

Disaster mental health and CISM services are most efficiently provided when disaster mental health planning is done before the disaster happens. Disaster mental health planning involves evaluation of local hazards and impact scenarios, the diverse needs of various demographic and occupational groups, the mental health needs that usually emerge in each phase of disaster, disaster mental health resources that are available, and how these resources will be identified, trained, activated, and coordinated with other disaster response resources.

Disaster mental health preparedness planning should build on lessons from previous disasters and build on existing programs, personnel, and skills. Disaster mental health managers should use established relationships with disaster mental health resources and CISM teams that already exist in the area. Disaster mental health and CISM responders should not only be trained in disaster mental health and CISM but also in response to specific hazards such as earthquakes, meteorological disturbances, floods, fires, hazardous materials, and terrorism. Cross-training of mental health and CISM personnel with other disaster response units in the disaster plan should also be provided to familiarize mental health personnel with other disaster workers and their roles and responsibilities. Likewise, disaster mental health personnel should provide orientation and training to other disaster response personnel on phases of disaster, normal human response in each phase, disaster mental health needs of various populations in the community, and stress management for disaster personnel.

The disaster mental health plan and the local disaster plan should include disaster mental health managers and stress management personnel in the emergency operations center (EOC) when a state of emergency is declared and the emergency operation center is opened. The role of the disaster mental health manager is to ensure the appropriate community-wide mental health response to the emergency. The role of stress management personnel in the EOC is to make sure that EOC personnel are recognizing and coping effectively with their own stress responses.

Preplanning for disaster mental health response will ensure that appropriate service capability can be maintained throughout the duration of disaster response and recovery. During long-term recovery, the disaster mental health program should be prepared to make available psychological support services for personnel and citizens for as long as 18 months to several years. The disaster mental health plan should include the capacity to provide needs assessment, consultation, outreach, debriefing, education, and crisis counseling services (the CODE-C model of disaster service delivery described in chapter 3).

The disaster mental health plan should also anticipate the specialized needs that will emerge following specific types of disasters. For example, it is anticipated that following a mass fatality event, reactions of grief and loss will be intense and long lasting, and mental health professionals specializing in grief counseling will be particularly important. Likewise, specific psychological reactions in emergency personnel, their families, and the community will occur following terrorist events. Disaster plans need to recognize the unique psychological impacts of various types of events, train their personnel accordingly, and preplan strategies to mitigate the impacts on the community.

The disaster mental health plan must also include procedures for alerting mental health personnel and activating the services so that disaster mental health and CISM services are provided in an efficient, organized, coordinated, and deliberate manner.

CRITICAL INCIDENT STRESS MANAGEMENT INTERVENTIONS

Critical incident stress management interventions range from providing information prior to disasters, to interventions that can be provided to targeted groups or individuals at different time intervals during and imme- diately after the disaster, to interventions after the disaster is over and disaster recovery begins. CISM may include, but is not limited to, the following: preincident and postincident education, organizational consultation, on-scene support services, demobilization, crisis management briefing, defusing, individual crisis intervention, critical incident stress debriefing, family and significant-other support services, pastoral crisis intervention, follow-up, referral, research and development, and other services as required.

PREDISASTER AND POSTDISASTER EDUCATION

Emergency managers, emergency service workers, and disaster workers require specialized training to competently and effectively perform their disaster responsibilities. An essential component of all disaster training is information about psychological reactions to disaster, disaster stress and stress management (including self-care, buddy-care, and organizational interventions), critical incident stress, and CISM. Information should be provided on the standard procedures for accessing all stress management, CISM, and follow-up services.

Disaster drills or exercises provide an excellent opportunity to educate disaster workers about disaster stress management. All workers who partici- pate in exercises of the disaster plan should receive information on disaster stress and stress management at the conclusion of the disaster exercise and prior to the operational critique. Postdisaster exercise education includes observations about participants' experience during the exercise, comments about what additional challenges emergency service workers and disaster workers would have if this exercise were a real disaster, description of com- mon psychological reactions to disaster exercises, and, finally, a description of coping activities people might try in the coming days. This brief pre- sentation is best done by disaster worker peer support personnel and should include a disaster stress handout.

Over recent years, the benefits from providing this type of education have been evident. Numerous disaster exercise participants reported surprise at the intensity of their postexercise reactions, and they found that it was helpful to have anticipatory guidance about potential reactions before they experienced them. Information about the impact of disasters on the disaster worker's family should also be included (Wee, 1994). Preincident education about critical incident stress and stress management should also be provided in the basic training academies for public safety dispatchers, law enforcement officers, firefighters, emergency medical services personnel, and any other group with roles during disasters.

Predisaster education can also be provided to community-based groups of citizens and citizen emergency response teams (Wee, 1995a), school personnel (including administrators, staff, and teachers) (Johnson, 1998), and employees of corporations and nongovernmental agencies that have roles during disaster. Predisaster education for such groups includes information about disaster stress reactions, phases of disaster reactions, self-help and assisting others during disaster, and disaster mental health programs and services. This predisaster education also includes demonstrations and the practice of helping techniques that are appropriate for citizens to use to help their friends, families, and colleagues.

Postdisaster education on critical incident stress reactions, available services, and coping suggestions should be provided to emergency responders, disaster workers, citizens, and community caregivers (doctors, nurses, clergy, school personnel, etc.) who will help the community recover over the long term. This postdisaster education can be in the form of articles, fliers, brochures, media coverage, and training sessions.

ORGANIZATIONAL CONSULTATION

Organizational consultation involves collaboration with and advice to decision makers, managers, supervisors, community leaders, providers of recovery services, spiritual care providers, disaster workers, survivors, and others on matters related to mental health needs and issues, facets of recovery, mental health resources, integration of mental health with other services, and stress management and coping for survivors, responders, families, organizations, and the community (Myers, 2003b).

ON-SCENE SUPPORT SERVICES

On-scene support involves taking crisis intervention services to survivors and responders in the environments in which they live, work, and spend time (Myers, 2003b). The objective is to provide an opportunity for distressed people to talk about their reactions to the disaster or incident, to help stabilize their condition, to provide support and stress related information, and to help move them toward a return to their previous level of functioning. On-scene support services puts into practice the three primary components of crisis intervention: proximity, immediacy, and expectancy. Proximity involves providing the assistance close to the physical location where the person is experiencing the distress. Immediacy means that the assistance is provided close to the time when the person experiences the stress. Expectancy entails the positive, optimistic attitude and expectation that the individual will return to more stabile functioning as soon as possible following the provision of assistance and support.

ON-SCENE SUPPORT FOR EMERGENCY WORKERS

There is increasing research that indicates that emergency workers experience on-scene support as helpful. A follow-up survey of emergency service workers who responded to the Cypress Structure Interstate 880 Freeway collapse in Oakland, CA (1989) found high levels of satisfaction with on-scene services (Wee, 1995c). A total of 366 questionnaires were distributed 6 months after the Loma Prieta earthquake with 124 usable questionnaires returned for a total response rate of 34%. Of the emergency workers receiving on-scene support services ($n = 25$), 85% evaluated the service as effective in reducing their level of distress, 89% reported the staff providing services were supportive, and 91% found the information provided about stress reactions to be useful (Wee, 1995c).

Two key considerations in on-scene support are authorization and safety. A primary rule in providing on-scene support services is not go to the scene of an incident unless such services are requested by an authorized organization. Uninvited, "spontaneous" volunteers have no place at the scene of an emergency unless requested and authorized to be there for a specific purpose, working as part of a coordinated response team.

The second rule is that safety comes first. Stress management teams should report to command staff and usually work under, or in conjunction with, the safety officer at the scene. CISM personnel who have been requested to provide on-scene support must stay out of the active operations area in order to be safe and not interfere with the work that is going on. If they are asked by command personnel to provide support within the internal perimeter of operations, they must be equipped with the same safety equipment as operational personnel, and they must be given instructions on both operation of the equipment and how to proceed safely within the area.

Safety considerations are also psychological in nature. Emergency response operations are hazardous environments that require knowledge, judgment, and experience to effectively provide psychological support without being injured or being in the way and causing injury to someone else. In addition, CISM personnel at the scene of a traumatic event are exposed to the same traumatic sights, sounds, and emotions as the victims. CISM professionals and emergency service peer-support persons are at risk of primary and secondary critical incident stress reactions while providing on-scene support at the scene of a disaster or critical incident. For this reason, only the most experienced CISM professionals and peers who have developed and fine-tuned their own strategies for dealing with traumatic stress should provide on-scene support services.

Stress management personnel who provide on-scene support for emergency personnel should have cross-training in emergency operations and disaster management in order to have familiarity with the nature of the work being done. Ride-alongs with emergency personnel will further orient mental health professionals to the reality of emergency operations. It is important for mental health professionals to understand both the stressors and the coping strategies of emergency personnel in order to provide on-scene support that is relevant and effective. It is essential that mental health professionals not overreact to emergency service stress in the field. For this reason, it is ideal for on-scene CISM services to be provided by a team of mental health professionals and emergency service peers.

Stress management functions in the field include observation of personnel at the scene, advice to command staff, and support of individuals showing obvious signs of distress. If a specific request is made to the stress management team, every effort should be made to meet the request, unless the team member believes the request is contraindicated, can explain the reason, and give an alternative suggestion to the person making the request.

Team members maintain a low profile, stay outside of the internal perimeter, do not get actively involved in operations, and do not interfere with investigations that may be taking place. They maintain the confidentiality of their interactions with workers. They do not speak with the media unless cleared by the public information officer (PIO), and media contact is only for the purpose of public education about disaster stress and coping techniques.

Usually, on-scene support services are provided to workers not actively engaged in service at the moment and at a location at least somewhat removed from operations. Rest areas and food service areas, first aid stations, respite centers for workers, and staging areas are locations where CISM teams may provide support without disrupting operations.

On-scene support interventions are always done one-to-one, not in groups. Team members must be familiar with the obvious and subtle cognitive, physical, emotional, and behavioral signs and symptoms of distress. Interventions are kept short—usually 5 to 15 min. Interventions include focusing on the here and now and on the worker's immediate needs, listening, asking open-ended questions, providing feedback, being discreet and providing whatever privacy is possible, reassuring and encouraging, orienting, problem solving, suggesting, guiding, allowing the worker to rest, reassessing, planning next steps with the worker, and referring if necessary (Mitchell & Everly, 1994).

The objective of on-scene support is to maintain personnel in service, or to return personnel to service as soon as possible after intervention and rest. However, on-scene support may also serve to identify workers who are fatigued or stressed to the point where they require transfer to new or lighter duty or relief from duty. On-scene CISM personnel do not make command decisions about removing someone from duty. Their role is to provide consultation and advice to command personnel or the incident safety officer regarding any workers who, in the judgment of the CISM worker, needs rest, a change of assignment or relief from duty.

ON-SCENE SUPPORT FOR VICTIMS

CISM or disaster mental health teams may be asked to provide support to victims and their families at the scene of a disaster or at a location near the disaster scene. Disaster survivors gather at many sites following a disaster: the site of impact, mass care locations and shelters, casualty collection points, first-aid sites and hospitals, family assistance centers, distribution centers (for food, water, clothing), disaster application centers, Red Cross service centers, etc. Very effective CISM services have been provided at sites of police barricades (keeping people out of unsafe areas), where people are distraught at being prevented from returning to their neighborhood and homes; outside the perimeter of a mass casualty such as an explosion or plane crash or school violence, where people are upset and desperately seeking information about the whereabouts and well-being of loved ones; at a shelter or family assistance center, where victims are housed because they cannot return to their homes or where they are awaiting information on the status of loved ones. Myers (1994b) has written in depth about providing mental health services in a disaster shelter, Sitterle (1995) and Blakeney (1996, 2002) have written about family support at the Family Assistance Center for families of Oklahoma City bombing victims, Teahen and LaDue (2000) have written about on-scene support and family assistance centers in mass fatality events, and Myers (2003c) has written about on-scene support and family assistance centers in terrorist events.

Ground rules for on-scene deployment to assist citizens are similar to those for providing on-scene support to workers: Do not go unless officially requested; wear ID and appropriate clothing and protective gear; be alert to safety; be an integrated component of the overall disaster response team effort.

The objectives of on-scene interventions with victims include the following: to begin to establish a sense of psychological safety; to protect victims from further psychological trauma; to acknowledge victims' distress; to assist with reduction of stress, if possible; to help victims begin to reestablish a sense of calm and control; and to assist with referrals to continuing support services.

On-scene interventions are usually brief in duration and more practical and pragmatic than psychological. Myers (2000) developed a model for delivery of on-scene support to citizens following disaster that includes four components: detect, direct, protect, connect.

Detect involves a quick assessment of the immediate needs: What has happened? What is the cause? How serious is it? Is the scene safe? Who is involved? Who is in most need of mental health assistance? What are their needs? What resources are available?

Direct: Most disaster victims are shocked, dazed, and at least somewhat disoriented in the immediate aftermath. They are very suggestible and respond well to directions. By being self-assured and in control of themselves, CISM staff can help to provide a sense of control while providing structure and direction. Be brief, clear, repetitive if necessary. Direct people where to go and what to do, to safe and secure areas, to medical care, to food, clothing, or shelter as needed.

Protect people from further harm. Help to find them shelter from the elements (rain, hot sun). Protect them from exposure to traumatic stimuli, from emotionally distraught victims, from onlookers, from the media. Try to establish a quiet, private, neutral environment. If a building is not available to shelter and protect people, try to remove them at least a short distance from the scene of any deaths, injuries, or traumatic sights and sounds. This may mean moving people down the block, around the corner, or to a nearby park. It may mean simply turning a person around so that they are facing away from a traumatic scene instead of looking at it. It may involve telling onlookers to move along or to take their children elsewhere so they will not be traumatized by what is going on. One might suggest that law enforcement expand the perimeter around the disaster operation to keep citizens more distant from the scene and its traumatic stimuli. For example, in a recent drowning tragedy at a crowded and popular lake, hundreds of families and their children gathered on the beach to watch search and recovery divers attempting to find the body of the young drowning victim. The on-scene CISM consultant suggested to the incident commander that the beach be closed until the body was recovered, taken from the water, and removed from the scene. This action prevented a large number of vulnerable children and adults from witnessing a scene that could cause them considerable distress and traumatic memories. Protecting individuals from witnessing or hearing traumatic stimuli can indeed prevent posttraumatic stress reactions in the aftermath.

Connect individuals to whatever assistance or resources they need, either at the scene or in the future. Providing these connections may require that on-scene CISM personnel consult with those in charge of the scene about the needs of the victims, pointing out needs and suggesting possible solutions or resources. People may need to be connected with accurate information on the status of their loved ones, their homes, their community. They may need referral to community resources (having a resource list in the form of a hand-out is a useful tool when working at a disaster scene). Connect people to each other—ask if there is someone they can call to be with them or, if they are unable to make such a call, offer to make it for them. Connecting victims to victims at a disaster scene can provide comfort—for example, asking an adult to look after a child while the parent is busy or having someone who is reasonably well-functioning to look after someone who is more distraught. Connect victims to whatever comfort can be provided—water, food, shade or shelter, blankets, telephones, a pat on the back or a hug if the person seems receptive. Reassuring people that their reactions are the "normal reactions of normal people to an abnormal event" can provide comfort and assurance that they are not going crazy, and can be an opportunity to connect people with suggestions about coping strategies and resources for support as they move forward through the recovery process.

On-scene mental health interventions can have a powerful, positive effect on victims' recovery by providing evidence that caring assistance is available, by protecting victims from further emotional trauma, by connecting victims with resources, and by setting a positive expectation that recovery can and will occur.

DEMOBILIZATION

A demobilization is provided after large-scale events involving many (100+) responders, who may be local responders or from outside the area who have assisted under a mutual aid agreement. Its only use is in a large-scale event. A similar intervention for large groups of citizens—a Crisis Management Briefing—will be discussed in a later section.

Demobilization is a brief group intervention that provides information on critical incident stress and gives anticipatory guidance regarding postincident stress management. It provides a much-needed transition from large-scale events back into normal routines (Mitchell & Everly, 2001). It usually consists of a 10-min stress education presentation, followed by rest and some nutritious refreshments. Thus, it provides both informational and "rest and recharge" opportunities for personnel. It also allows stress management staff to screen large groups of responders and to identify groups who may need additional services when they return home. A well-conducted, effective demobilization can help personnel to leave the disaster feeling well taken care of and with positive expectations for their recovery from any traumatic stress they have suffered on the job.

A demobilization should be done after work teams have been released from the disaster or incident and will not be returning to the operation, and before returning to normal duty. The demobilization should be done for teams of workers (engine or truck companies, search teams, dog teams, etc.). Each team receives its own demobilization and work groups are not mixed. The demobilization is provided by trained stress management personnel—mental health professionals, chaplains, or emergency service peers not involved in the disaster operation. It is not essential for a mental health professional to be present (Mitchell & Everly, 2001). If possible, a member of the disaster operation command staff should be present to meet and greet groups as they arrive for demobilization and to thank them for their work. The command staff member does not, however, attend the demobilization.

Because of the sheer size of the event, demobilization requires coordination, communication, planning, and logistical finesse in order to be successfully carried out. Coordination with the incident commander or safety officer is necessary to assess the need and timing for demobilization. In addition, specific information about the experiences of the emergency service worker crews during the operation, the crew's level of preincident critical incident stress education, and the availability of CISM services in the teams' areas of origin are useful information for the stress management team conducting the demobilization.

Demobilization is ideally done in a building with at least two large rooms (one for informational talks, one for rest and food), moveable chairs and tables, food service (or space for catering service), and parking for many vehicles. Chairs in the meeting room are arranged in small circles to accommodate individual teams who will be attending the demobilization. It is important to assign personnel to manage the demobilization center, to check personnel in and out, to manage and serve food, and to provide media liaison and control.

In the demobilization, the CISM leader provides a 10-min informational talk on critical incident stress, typical reactions and signs and symptoms, returning home following a disaster, brief stress management suggestions, and the availability of CISM follow-up services after returning home. Handouts covering these topics are very useful, as teams are usually tired and anxious to leave, and their concentration may be impaired. Attendees are given the opportunity to make any comments or ask any questions they may have, but no one is required to speak and no questions are asked of them. They are then encouraged to have some refreshments and fluids in the next room before returning home or returning to normal duty. Stress management team members may also be available in the refreshment area to circulate and chat with personnel or answer questions, but they should be very low key and conversational, not probing. Remember, the purpose of this part of the demobilization is for personnel to rest and replenish themselves.

RESPITE CENTERS: AN INNOVATION IN DEMOBILIZATION

Following the terrorist attacks of September 11, 2001, in New York City, it was evident that recovery workers at Ground Zero would be spending weeks and, in many cases, months working at the scene. The American Red Cross, in collaboration with the City of New York and various charities, established a new variation of the demobilization intervention, "respite centers." Established at several locations near Ground Zero and open 24 hours a day, the centers provided an environment where recovery workers could relax, receive hot meals, clean clothes, massages, mental health support, and pastoral crisis intervention from spiritual care providers of many faiths (Crick, 2001). Jill Hofmann, coordinator of one of the respite center teams, described the stress on the recovery workers: "Every day they find human remains, they're listening to the pounding of the machines, they're constantly in danger, they're inhaling things that may be toxic. All of that is potential for stress, not to mention looking for their family members, friends, brothers, or civilians" (Salmon & Sun, 2001). The mental health counseling and support at the respite centers was very informal, often at the table as workers were eating. Pet therapy was also available, coordinated by the K-9 Disaster Relief Organization. A favorite at the respite center tent a half-block from Ground Zero was Nike, a 120-pound golden retriever often brought into the tent during night shifts to comfort workers. "They pet him, they hug him. Nike rolls over, and they scratch him and pull his ears. And a lot of times, he's doing the most work when it looks like he's not doing any work," said Nike's owner, Frank Shane (Salmon & Sun). In addition to counseling and pet therapy for recovery workers, Red Cross Mass Care volunteers served more than 12.8 million meals and snacks, mostly to emergency workers at Ground Zero (not all of the meals were served in the respite centers) (Irby, 2001). Red Cross nursing staff in the respite centers operated first aid rooms where bandages, pain relievers for aching muscles, eye drops, and other items were available. There were "oasis" rooms with television sets, a bank of computers where people could read their email, games to play, and newspapers to read. There were soft recliners to relax in, plus rooms with cots for naps. On each cot was a teddy bear, a piece of candy, and often a note from a child. The respite centers contained banners and stacks of letters from school children across America praising what the workers were doing (Crick).

The respite center was not an entirely new concept that developed in New York City. A similar center was established for rescue and recovery personnel at the Myriad Center convention complex in Oklahoma City following the 1995 Murrah Federal Building bombing. The center was collaboratively run by the Red Cross, FEMA, city and state agencies, various charities, and private businesses. It provided dormitory sleeping, 24-hour meals and snacks, massages, haircuts, hot tubs, pet therapy, free telephones, recreation, socialization, banners and cards from well-wishers around the world, spiritual care professionals, and stress management and CISM personnel for informal counseling and support. A similar concept of mini respite areas for workers has been followed in other disaster settings, usually in conjunction with worker meal sites. In those settings, such as the staff cafeteria in the New York Family Assistance Center at Pier 94, chaplains, CISM personnel, Red Cross disaster mental health staff, pet therapy animals and their handlers, and other supportive services are available to interact informally with workers during their breaks.

The respite center concept has successfully adapted the goals and functions of demobilization to numerous disaster situations involving long-term assignment of rescue and recovery workers, where the more traditional form of demobilization was not a precise "fit." Much can be learned from studying this prototype model for application in other large-scale disasters.

The effort to provide a demobilization is worth the time and effort because of the potential benefits to the workers who participate. The first benefit is that the worker's experiences are vivid and immediate, and the worker is receptive to information and education relevant to experiences they are having presently or could have in the future. Thus, the second benefit is in the form of anticipatory guidance, preparing the worker for any physical, emotional, cognitive, and behavioral reactions they or their coworkers might have during the hours, weeks, and months following the event. The third benefit is the acknowledgment of workers' efforts by command staff.

A follow-up survey of emergency service workers who responded to the Interstate 880 Cypress Structure Collapse during the 1989 Loma Prieta earthquake in California found high levels of satisfaction with the demobilization services. Of the respondents receiving demobilization services who completed the survey ($n = 37$), 84% evaluated the service as effective in reducing their level of distress, 100% reported the CISM staff were supportive, and 91% found the information provided was useful (Wee, 1995c).

Demobilization can be difficult to carry out if personnel coming off duty are tired and anxious to be on their way home. Following the 1990 East Bay Hills (California) fire, hundreds of fire personnel were to be demobilized at the staging area at Alameda Naval Air Station. However, few crews wanted to participate, and most did not go into the demobilization center. Stress management personnel utilized one of the most important of disaster mental health skills—flexibility. They followed a basic tenet of disaster mental health: take the services to the people, do not wait for the people to come to you. Instead of waiting inside the demobilization center for crews to come to them, staff went onto the tarmac of the air station and circulated from crew to crew, providing information, handouts, and listening to stories of what the crews had been through. The stress management staff reported that they felt their services were very well received and much more effective than if crews had been required to come in to the demobilization center and sit through a meeting.

CRISIS MANAGEMENT BRIEFING

The crisis management briefing (CMB) is a CISM service that can be used appropriately and effectively following large natural disasters, terrorism incidents, and mass disasters and violence (Mitchell & Everly, 2001; Everly et al., 2002). Whereas demobilization is designed for large groups of *workers*, the crisis management briefing is designed to be used with *citizens*. The crisis management briefing is a large group crisis intervention designed for use with groups of up to 300 citizen participants. The goals of CMB are to provide information, reduce the sense of chaos, provide coping resources, and engender increased cohesion and morale. The CMB has four phases. The first phase is to assemble participants who have experienced a common crisis event. Participants can be assembled in a large room such as an auditorium or school gymnasium. The CMB is advertised using a variety of methods including posters, radio, television, and newspaper announcements. The second phase involves providing the facts of the crisis event by an appropriate, credible, and authoritative source. This person or panel of experts provides credible information that serves to control destructive rumors, reduce anticipatory anxiety, provide citizens with advice on responding to the crisis, and return a sense of control to the victims. For example, after the anthrax attacks of 2001, the speaker or panel would consist of public health or communicable disease experts to provide information about anthrax, how it is spread, what to do if a citizen thinks they have been exposed, etc. Phase three is conducted by a credible mental health professional who discusses the common psychological reactions that can occur following a crisis event. The fourth phase is to for the mental health professional to provide personal coping and self-care information that assists individuals to help themselves, their friends, and family mitigate the normal stress reactions that can occur during and after a crisis event. Specific stress management strategies should be discussed that are consistent with the cultural practices of the people attending the crisis management briefing. Information about organizational and community resources that are available to support the participants and help in their physical and psychological recovery should be described. A period of time for questions from the participants should also be made available to demonstrate that the authoritative source and mental health professional are interested and responsive to the needs of the crisis management briefing participants. Printed information sheets should be made available that provide information about the crisis event (e.g., information about anthrax), as well as handouts that describe the normal cognitive, emotional, behavioral, and physical reactions that might occur, coping activities, and community resources.

DEFUSING

The goals of defusing are to mitigate the impact of a traumatic event and accelerate the normal recovery process by providing an opportunity for discussion and providing information on stress reactions and stress management soon after the critical incident. It also provides opportunity for assessment of the need for other CISM services (Mitchell & Everly, 2001), including referral to a higher level of care if symptoms or conditions warrant further assessment and possible treatment.

Defusing is different from demobilization in several ways. First, it is smaller in size. Second, it is longer, usually lasting from 20 minutes to an hour. Third, it allows (but does not require) those who wish to talk about their experience to do so.

Defusing is provided to small groups of about six to eight individuals. Groups usually include people who worked as a team on an incident (e.g., engine companies, ambulance crews, etc.) or who experienced the same event in the same place at the same time (e.g., apartment dwellers whose apartment building collapsed in an earthquake). Defusing is frequently used with citizen groups (for example, with bank tellers following a robbery) in addition to being used with emergency service and disaster worker groups.

Defusing, ideally, should be done immediately, preferably 1 to 2 hours after the incident, and no longer than 8 hours after the incident (Mitchell & Everly,

2001). The 8-hour guideline is based on defusing done with groups in the workplace; the intervention should take place before the work shift is over. If the shift is 12 hours in duration, the defusing should be done within 12 hr.

Defusing may be used in disaster to support emergency personnel until their tour of duty is completed and any additional needed services can be provided. In this situation, a defusing can be provided at the conclusion of a shift, followed by on-scene support during subsequent shifts. The emphasis on the defusing is to allow discussion about the work experience and to provide information about stress and stress management. This is to assist personnel with issues around self-care and colleague care during periods of work as well as off-duty periods of rest. When personnel will be returning to the operation on subsequent shifts, they will benefit from staying in cognition, rather than being led into deep emotion during a defusing. It is a disservice to lead them into deep emotion and then return them to doing the same work that generated the emotion. More extensive exploration of thoughts, emotions, and symptoms can be made available during additional stress management forums in the weeks that follow the end of their duty at the disaster site.

Defusing is conducted by trained stress management team members, usually a peer or chaplain for emergency services groups and a mental health professional for citizen groups. Peer support personnel are individuals who are members of a CISM team and have completed the CISM basic training, peer counseling training, and training in crisis intervention. The peer support person can do the defusing alone or with a mental health professional or chaplain. When the defusing is done without a mental health professional, the peer support person should consult with a mental health professional after the defusing to ensure that any worker in the group who is at risk is referred for appropriate care.

A defusing ideally should be conducted in a location that is private and comfortable, but in mass disaster, such locations may be hard to come by. Quite effective disaster defusing has been conducted in parking lots, on street corners, in the corner of large rooms in shelters, in mass feeding tents, and in employee cafeterias. The key is to gather together the group and find a place that is at least somewhat removed visually and auditorily from other people. For example, in a large, noisy, mass care shelter, a small group of people meeting in the corner will have reasonable privacy from others in the room. In one mass fatality disaster, a very successful defusing was conducted in a ladies' restroom, where several employees had retreated in a flood of tears. Privacy was not a concern, as everyone in the building had been traumatized, and when someone came in to use the restroom, they either ignored or joined the group.

The primary components of the defusing are as follows:

- *Introduction.* To introduce the intervention team, explain the process, and set expectations
- *Exploration.* To allow but not probe for discussion of the traumatic experience via participants' disclosure of facts, cognitive and emotional reactions, and symptoms of distress related to the traumatic event; to assess the need for further services
- *Information.* To cognitively normalize and educate with regard to stress, stress management, and trauma

As with demobilization, people in a defusing may speak or may choose to remain silent. Facilitators explore the impact of the event by using noninvasive, nonprobing questions: What happened? What was that like for you? What other aspects would you like to discuss? What part are you having the most difficulty with now?

The well-executed defusing can fulfill several functions. It can eliminate the need for a CISD, especially in groups that have attended defusings before and used them efficiently and effectively. A defusing also provides an opportunity to assess whether the group could benefit from a CISD. If most group members still have things to talk about at the end of the defusing, if they are exhibiting numerous signs and symptoms of traumatic stress, or if the event itself was particularly powerful and traumatic, a CISD or individual follow-up should be done, usually a day or several days later. Having done a defusing first may enhance a debriefing by familiarizing participants with the CISM approach, reducing their anxiety about the intervention, and starting the ventilation and education process.

A follow-up survey of emergency service workers who responded to the Cypress Structure freeway collapse found high levels of satisfaction with defusings. Of the respondents receiving Defusing Services ($n = 15$), 56% evaluated the service as effective in reducing their level of distress, 90% reported the CISM staff were supportive, and 91% found the information provided was useful (Wee, 1995c).

INDIVIDUAL DEFUSING: FOUR-STEP GUIDE TO HEALING CONVERSATION

In the CISM literature, defusing is taught and practiced as a group intervention. However, in their work with bereavement, trauma, and disaster, Myers, Zunin, and Zunin (1990) have developed an adaptation of Mitchell's defusing that they call a "Four-Step Guide to Healing Conversation." The simple steps of this approach can be used to guide an individual conversation with anyone affected by trauma, crisis, or loss. The method has been taught both to professionals and to the general public. Teaching the technique to members of the general public before or after disaster can help to strengthen the natural social support network in the community. Traumatized people often rely on family, friends, and church groups rather than seeking professional counseling (McNally et al., 2003). The framework of the conversation gives people the confidence to talk comfortably and helpfully with those in trauma or grief. Of course, as was mentioned in the introduction to this chapter, if the person seems disinclined to talk, it is important not to probe.

In a workshop on loss for educators given by Hilary Zunin, one teacher noted the following:

> I've always been afraid that I'd put my foot in my mouth if I reached out to someone in grief. But this four-step guide made sense from the start. I've begun responding with much more self-confidence and have been able to "be there" with my heart instead of listening to my mind busily wondering what to say next (Myers et al., 1990).

The four-step guide has been used successfully in a wide variety of settings following disaster: in disaster shelters, disaster application centers and service centers, at mass feeding stations, in first-aid stations and hospitals, in neighborhoods, on home visits, and in schools. The four-step conversation can last anywhere from a few minutes (in a very abbreviated form) to an hour or more.

The simplicity of the four practical steps may be deceiving. First, the interviewer needs to be prepared to listen authentically. This can be difficult in the chaotic environment of a disaster. However, once one's ears and heart are open, the practice of this process can have enormous value in providing comfort and support in the face of trauma and loss.

1. *Gather facts.* Early after the impact of an overwhelming event, it is easier for most people to talk about facts than feelings. Preoccupied with trauma and grief, most people are disconnected from their feelings and may be uncomfortable, irritable, or confused with questions about their emotions. Since facts are foremost in the individual's mind in early trauma and grief, the four-step process begins here. Stating and restating facts is grounding, and is a process that most people can handle with success. A gentle inquiry into the specifics of who, what, when, where, and how is the natural way to begin (Myers et al., 1990).

    Who was with you when the earthquake struck? Who were you worried about? Who helped you? *What* was the situation? What did you see? Hear? What did you do? What did others do? What happened to your loved ones? To your home?

When did help get to you? When were you able to locate your loved ones? When do you expect to be able to return home?

Where were you when the quake struck? Where were your other family members? Where did you take cover? Where are you living now?

How is your family doing? How are you sleeping? How is your appetite? How have your daily activities changed? How is your work (or studies) affected? How is your concentration? How are you coping? (Myers, 1999).

Once the person feels comfortable speaking, they may retell their story, and may seem preoccupied with details. This is a normal form of ventilation. Conversation centered around facts seems less threatening and invasive and requires less trust than conversation about feelings. This phase of the conversation helps to set the event in a realistic perspective (Myers et al., 1990).

2. *Inquire about thoughts.* Several areas to explore are

First thoughts: What were your first thoughts when the earthquake started? When the shaking stopped? When your home was red-tagged? When you returned to work (or school)?

Current thoughts: What have you been thinking about these days?

Repetitive thoughts: Is there anything that keeps running through your mind?

Disturbing or bothersome thoughts: Is there a thought that keeps coming to mind that is disturbing to you?

Comforting thoughts or thoughts that help you cope: Is there a thought that "keeps you going" or brings you strength? (Myers et al., 1990; Myers, 1999).

3. *Acknowledge feelings.* Having talked about some facts and some of their thoughts, the traumatized person is then usually more trusting and open to talking about emotions. They may start talking about feelings spontaneously or the interviewer may ask some questions about their emotional reactions. This part of the conversation may also be guided into discussion of stress reactions that may be bothering the individual. Some questions might include: What has been the hardest part for you? What has affected you most? Bothered you most? How can you tell this has

been affecting you? How has this been affecting your health (sleep, relationships, work, etc.)? How are you feeling about _____? (Fill in the blank with a fact they have told you that seems to be emotional for them) (Myers, 1999).

4. *Encouragement.* As the conversation moves to a close, the interviewer briefly reviews, summarizes, and paraphrases what they have heard the person say, accepting their thoughts and feelings. This phase of the talk validates the normalcy of their reactions. Often in the intensity of trauma and grief, people question the normalcy of their feelings, and will welcome sensitive reassurance that their feelings are normal and they are not "losing touch with reality" (Myers et al., 1990). This closing phase is also an opportunity for teaching and anticipatory guidance about the phases of disaster recovery and phases of grief. Help the individual to identify and reinforce positive coping strategies. (What has helped you to cope in past crises?) It is likewise a good time to identify and steer the person away from any unhelpful or destructive coping strategies. (Is there any behavior or attitude that might get in the way of your healing?) Emphasize social supports and resources. (Who can you rely on? Who can help you get through this?) Make a referral if needed, and make yourself available as a resource if appropriate. It is helpful to remind the individual to take care of themselves, to ask one or two ways they do so, and to reinforce those self-care behaviors. The conversation can be ended by giving thanks and appreciation for the individual's sharing and for their courage (or whatever else touched you in your conversation).

CRITICAL INCIDENT STRESS DEBRIEFING

Critical incident stress debriefing (CISD) is an organized approach to the management of stress responses following a critical incident or disaster. Originally developed by Jeffrey T. Mitchell for the management of traumatic stress reactions among high risk emergency service personnel (Mitchell & Everly, 2001), the process has subsequently been adapted and adopted by other occupational groups, employee assistance programs, and disaster service organizations for use with both disaster workers and citizens. Numerous models of debriefing exist, and this chapter will present several: the *ICISF model* (Mitchell & Everly), the *multiple stressor debriefing model* (Armstrong, O'Callahan, & Marmar, 1991), and the *disaster worker debriefing model* (Myers & Zunin, 1994b).

All of the debriefing models presented in this chapter maintain the same focus of intervention: to assist workers and survivors in dealing with the intense thoughts, feelings, and reactions that occur after a traumatic event, and to decrease the impact and facilitate the recovery of "normal people having normal reactions to abnormal events." It is important to note that all of the models utilize group crisis intervention techniques. In the field of CISM, the term *debriefing* is never used to refer to a one-on-one intervention but always to a group intervention. This distinction will be especially important in the evaluation of research conducted on the efficacy of debriefing, which will be covered later in this chapter.

Debriefing is designed to utilize a number of therapeutic strategies. First, it is designed to provide the earliest possible intervention, before traumatic memories may become solidified and perhaps distorted and overgeneralized (Mitchell & Everly, 2001). Titchener (1988) emphasizes the importance of early intervention in the traumatic stress arising from disasters. He points out that after the passage of time, the therapeutic work becomes much more difficult as defenses and resistance harden, and "the stress response disorders may be transformed from the easiest psychological conditions to treat to the impossible to treat" (p. 175).

Debriefing provides an opportunity for *catharsis*, or ventilation of emotions (Mitchell & Everly, 2001). In a review of studies investigating the relationship between catharsis and stress, Pennebaker and Susman (1988) concluded that disclosing traumatic events leads to reduced stress arousal and improved immune functioning. In addition to catharsis, CISD provides the opportunity to *verbally reconstruct* and express specific traumas, fears, and regrets (Mitchell & Everly). In a review of traumatologist Pierre Janet's work, van der Hart, Brown, and van der Kolk (1989) recount that the successful treatment of posttraumatic reactions is based not solely upon catharsis, but upon the individual's ability to reconstruct and integrate the trauma by discussing it verbally.

Debriefing provides a structure for discussing, reconstructing, and integrating the trauma. The intervention has a finite beginning and a finite end, superimposing structure on the chaos of the trauma experience (Mitchell & Everly, 2001). It also provides group support. Yalom (1985), in his classic work on the therapeutic group process, notes that the group format itself has numerous intrinsic healing properties. Among them are the exchange of useful constructive information, catharsis, the dissolution of the myth of a unique weakness or abnormality among individuals, the modeling of constructive coping behavior, the opportunity to derive a sense of group caring and support, the opportunity to help oneself by helping others, and the generation of feelings of hope. When CISD is used among a group of peers (in the workplace, for example), peer-group support is an added therapeutic element. Carkhuff and Truax (1965) and others have frequently demonstrated the effectiveness of peer/lay support models, especially when the peer group views itself as being highly unique, selective, or otherwise "different" from the general population, (Mitchell & Everly), as is the case with emergency responders, disaster workers, and disaster victims.

Finally, the CISD process provides a mechanism for *screening* traumatized individuals, identifying those who are more highly symptomatic and would benefit from more intensive psychological care, and for making appropriate *referral.*

Critical incident stress debriefing should not be used following ordinary events. This intervention is designed for use after traumatic events, where critical incident stress responses are experience by the people involved. Trained CISM teams or mental health teams with CISM training are the appropriate resource to provide CISD. A follow-up survey of emergency service workers who responded to the 1989 California Interstate 880 Cypress Structure freeway collapse found high levels of satisfaction with the debriefing services. Of the respondents receiving CISD ($n = 41$), 81% evaluated the service as effective in reducing their level of distress, 95% reported the CISM staff were supportive, and 88% found the information provided was useful (Wee, 1995c).

Critical incident stress debriefings are not operational critiques. The process and procedures of the incident are not the focus of discussion, but rather the personal *thoughts* and *reactions* of those attending the debriefing. Obviously, participants will discuss the operation during the debriefing, and it is not unusual for participants in a debriefing to learn more about what happened during the incident. This often means they did not have a complete picture of what was happening in other parts of the operation, and it can be very helpful to them to "fill in the blanks" in their picture of what took place. For this reason, an operational critique of a disaster operation is an important component of healing. However, it should be held as a separate meeting from the CISD. If facilitators allow the CISD to turn into an operational critique, there is the danger that only facts will be discussed, and that participants' thoughts, emotions, and stress reactions will not be dealt with. It is recommended that, if the debriefing is turning into an operational critique, the facilitator remind participants that the purpose of the group is to discuss members' *personal* reactions to the event, and gently steer the debriefing back on course.

While therapeutic, a debriefing is not psychotherapy. This is where most psychotherapists have trouble when new to CISD. They must remember that CISD does not allow time for taking in-depth histories, psychological testing, passive responding, personality change, reconstruction of defense mechanisms, or working through of unconscious conflicts. The pace of the intervention is brisk, as the group is usually concluded in 2 to 3 hr, maximum. While follow-up may be provided in the form of a follow-up debriefing or a referral, there is no psychotherapeutic contract between facilitator and participant, and no guarantee of another contact in which the facilitator can continue working with the individual.

In addition, debriefing is not a job performance or fitness-for-duty evaluation. Confidentiality is maintained, and the facilitator does not report back to management or to a specific supervisor about any one individual. If management is seeking such an evaluation, the CISM team member should suggest that a psychological evaluation, not CISD, is the appropriate route to follow.

Unlike defusing and demobilization, which can be performed by a CISM-trained peer counselor, debriefing is always conducted by a licensed mental health professional with CISM training, in conjunction with trained peers for specialized groups such as emergency services organizations. When CISD is provided to citizen groups in a disaster, trained mental health professionals usually facilitate the groups, without the assistance of emergency-service peers. The most effective CISD facilitators are those who have experience and skills in group process, crisis intervention, posttraumatic stress, grief and bereavement, and stress management.

Usually, CISDs are provided 24 to 72 hr after a critical incident. CISDs may be provided much later following a mass disaster—sometimes days, weeks, and even several months later. Disaster survivors are overwhelmed with concerns following a disaster, including locating and reuniting family, caring for family members who are sick or injured, establishing housing, food, and safety, and dealing with concrete, financial, and symbolic losses. Mental health and stress management concerns are not usually at the top of their hierarchy of needs until later, when stress has become evident and even painful. While the earliest possible intervention should be the goal, disaster survivors may not be ready to receive CISD until later in their recovery. Titchener (1988) maintains that the window of opportunity for early intervention is quite large (up to 2 years following a traumatic event) before the trauma becomes "cemented" and difficult to treat. While every disaster recovery program aims to provide the earliest possible services to survivors, Titchener's findings imply that CISD may be effective "early intervention" up to the 2-year mark.

CRITICAL INCIDENT STRESS DEBRIEFING: ICISF MODEL

Mitchell and Everly (1994, 1996, 1997b, 1998a, 2001) divide the CISD process into seven phases. The phases are designed and timed to progress from the cognitive domain (introduction and fact phases) to a transitional phase from cognition to affect (thought phase), to a strongly affective phase (reaction phase), back through a transition phase (symptoms phase), ending with cognition again (teaching and reentry phases). The phases include the following objectives (Mitchell & Everly, 2001):

- Introduction: To introduce intervention team members, explain the process, and set expectations
- Fact Phase: To describe the traumatic event from each participant's perspective on a cognitive level
- Thought Phase: To allow participants to describe cognitive reactions and to transition to emotional reactions
- Reaction Phase: To identify the most traumatic aspect(s) of the event for the participants and to identify emotional reactions
- Symptom Phase: To identify personal symptoms of distress and transition back to a cognitive level
- Teaching Phase: To educate regarding normal reactions and adaptive coping mechanisms and stress management
- Reentry Phase: To clarify ambiguities, answer questions, prepare for termination and follow-up

Step-by-step guidelines for how CISD is conducted according to the ICISF model are found in Mitchell and Everly's publications (1994, 1996, 1997b, 1998a, 2001).

MULTIPLE STRESSOR DEBRIEFING MODEL

During the 1989 Loma Prieta earthquake in Northern California, Red Cross, Federal Emergency Management Agency (FEMA), and other disaster personnel faced multiple stressors over an extended period of relief operations. The Department of Veterans Affairs (DVA) consulted with the American Red Cross, and offered the San Francisco DVA's Posttraumatic Stress Disorder Clinical Team as debriefers for Red Cross personnel. The team of experienced group therapists reviewed five intervention models in existence at the time: Crisis Intervention (Cohen & Ahearn, 1980), National Organization of Victim Assistance (NOVA) Debriefing (NOVA, 1987), Didactic Debriefing (Dunning, 1988), Critical Incident Stress Debriefing (Mitchell, 1983, 1984, 1986), and Psychological Debriefing (Raphael, 1986). Mitchell's work, advocated by disaster relief personnel, appeared most relevant to the needs of Red Cross workers (Armstrong et al., 1991). Nonetheless, modifications to the ICISF model were clearly needed.

The ICISF model, developed for first responders (fire, police, emergency medical services), debriefs work that is intensive, focused, and usually brief.

For Red Cross and FEMA workers, there is no clearly defined "critical incident" in a disaster relief operation. The majority of the work for these personnel continues for weeks and months, postimpact (Armstrong et al., 1991; Myers, 1995). Stressors include high public and self-expectations; the need to adapt to constant change; multiple contacts with trauma victims; long hours; poor work environment and living conditions; changing policies and priorities; inexperience of some personnel; being away from home; politics; public scrutiny; and loss and letdown when the assignment is over (Armstrong et al., 1991; Myers, 1995). Debriefings for Red Cross workers and FEMA personnel may be held as periodic stress management groups for personnel in ongoing work assignments. They can also be held at the end of a tour of duty, as workers are demobilized and prepare to go home or to another work assignment (Myers, 1995). In these types of disaster relief organizations, some of the workers may have been working since the first day of the disaster, while others come in weeks later, at a different phase of the disaster, and have a very different experience and perspective on the work. The differing job roles of the workers also affect the process of debriefing, some workers being in administrative roles, others working directly with victims, etc. Consequently, the events that were most stressful to one worker might be very different from those that were stressful to another (Armstrong et al., 1991).

The multiple stressor debriefing model has four stages: (a) *disclosure of events*, (b) *feelings and reactions*, (c) *coping strategies*, and (d) *termination.*

In the *disclosure of events* stage, the purpose and rules of the group are outlined and leaders ask about events that were most troubling to participants. Because of the varied experience in the group, workers are given time to discuss several incidents that affected them (Armstrong et al., 1991).

In the *feelings and reactions* stage, workers are asked about feelings and reactions linked to the difficult incidents they were involved with. A whiteboard or flip chart is often used to write down the different members' feelings about their incidents within the disaster. This visual aid provides a helpful tool for education and normalization about the common stress reactions during disaster work. As the list is formed, it seems to help others in the group to bring up or to elaborate upon their own stress reactions in the discussion (Armstrong et al., 1991).

In the *coping strategies* phase, the visual aid and handouts are used to educate about normal or unusual responses to stress. Participants talk about their past and current experiences in coping with stressors. They identify practical coping strategies for use while still in the stressful environment, as well as what can be done to prepare to return home. Disaster workers often express reluctance and even guilt about spending time caring for themselves, and it is helpful to emphasize how much more helpful they can be to others if they manage their own stress effectively. Talking with group members about how they coped with other disasters can be helpful in identifying ways for the group to best cope with the current catastrophe (Armstrong et al., 1991).

In the *termination* stage of the debriefing, participants are encouraged to discuss feelings about leaving the disaster and returning home. Because the development of close relationships in disaster work is inevitable, this phase emphasizes saying goodbye to coworkers, as leaving behind friendships and rewarding assignments can contribute to letdown and depression after returning home. Participants discuss a plan of action to prepare them for returning to home and regular job responsibilities, as well as a plan for obtaining support in processing the disaster or for any transitional difficulties. The need for workers to continue to talk about their experience after returning home is emphasized. Follow-up individual or family counseling is encouraged if workers continue to have problems (Bergmann & Queen, 1986). Final questions are answered, and referrals are provided as needed (Armstrong et al., 1991).

Because disaster relief workers usually have two to three week assignments, it can be very helpful to build weekly group debriefings into their schedules. The initial group would be an *entry briefing*, with information on the numerous expected stressors for the specific disaster, as well as discussion of coping strategies and resources. A mid-assignment group would focus on the effects the work is having on personnel, allow for identification of anyone needing a new, less stressful assignment, and help members focus on self-care. A final *exit debriefing* allows for processing of the entire disaster experience and preparation for the transition home. Because multiple experiences and stressors are discussed, 2-hr sessions are recommended, with the group being kept to about 12 to 15 workers (Armstrong et al., 1991).

In addition to its usefulness with disaster workers on long-term assignments, the MSDM can be helpful in working with other groups that have high exposure to long-term, chronic stress (Armstrong et al., 1991).

DISASTER WORKER STRESS DEBRIEFING MODEL

In the mid-1980s the federal government began to seriously examine the psychological and emotional impact of disaster work on its employees. Several publications and video training tapes (Center for Mental Health Studies of Emergencies [CMHSE], 1985; Hartsough & Myers, 1985; Myers, O'Callahan, & Peuler, 1984) explored and described the impact of disaster work on personnel. In 1991, FEMA and the National Institute of Mental Health (NIMH) initiated a study to identify sources of stress among FEMA Disaster Assistance Program employees and to make specific recommendations for a stress reduction program for disaster workers (Rosensweig & Vaslow, 1992). Following Hurricane Andrew in 1992, FEMA engaged the services of several mental health consultants to develop and pilot test a stress management program for FEMA disaster employees, consistent with the literature on disaster worker stress and the findings of Rosensweig and Vaslow. The stress management program was developed and fine-tuned over the course of several large-scale disasters (Myers, 1992, 1993a, 1993b, 1993c, 1994a, 1995; Myers & Zunin, 1993a, 1993b, 1994a; Sword et al., 1992). The program was formally implemented in 1994 with the training of a national cadre of stress management personnel to serve FEMA disaster workers (Myers, 1994a; Myers & Zunin, 1994b). The FEMA stress management program follows the CODE-C model described in chapter 3 of this text, and contains the program elements of needs assessment, consultation, outreach, debriefing/defusing, education, and crisis counseling.

Over a period of several years, numerous large disasters, and the debriefing of several thousand FEMA employees, Myers and Zunin (1994b) adapted and fine-tuned the debriefing process to more accurately and effectively address the needs of workers in large-scale disasters. They found that neither the ICISF model nor the multiple stressor debriefing model exactly fit the needs of the workers they were debriefing. The existing models did not take into consideration one vital aspect of the disaster worker experience, namely, that for many of these personnel, their disaster work provided some of the most meaningful experiences of their lives. The work has a multitude of rewards: It is filled with action, challenges, excitement, pride, appreciation, a sense of doing important work, helping people, learning new skills, and forming new (and often deep) relationships. The work encourages the development of a multitude of new skills and strengths: dedication, endurance, sensitivity, patience, flexibility, adaptability, versatility, creativity, collaboration, problem solving, and people skills. A first-time disaster worker often goes home with a whole new sense of self and self-esteem. These meaningful aspects of the experience contribute to difficulties for many disaster workers in the termination of their assignment and the transition back into "normal" or "routine" home and work life. For many, the ending of the disaster assignment is a huge loss. The trauma-focused debriefing models in existence failed to explore thoroughly the positive aspects of the disaster worker experience and the sense of loss in termination of the assignment, leaving much of the experience unprocessed.

Myers and Zunin adapted the ICISF and multiple stressor debriefing models to incorporate an exploration of the positive and meaningful aspects of the disaster experience for the workers. The model consists of seven phases: (a) *introduction*, (b) *facts*, (c) *thoughts*, (d) *challenges*, (e) *meaning*, (f) *teaching*, and (g) *transition*.

In the *introduction* phase, facilitators introduce themselves and give a very brief synopsis of their relevant experience. The facilitators then define and describe debriefing and its goals. The following script illustrates how the process is typically explained:

> Disaster work can be exciting and rewarding, but it is also demanding and stressful. It engages workers in activities that may be intensely meaningful as well as difficult and painful. After working in a disaster, it is not unusual for staff to feel some ambivalence about giving up their disaster roles. Personnel often feel that their lives have been changed by their experience, but have not had time to reflect on how they have been changed. They may feel a sense of loss that the job is over, and concern about returning to their regular lives. They may finish their work in a state of physical and emotional fatigue, and may feel relief that the assignment is ending. The mixture of relief and sadness can be confusing.
>
> Debriefing is a structured group meeting to enhance the experience of disaster work and to facilitate the transition out of the assignment and back into the routine of daily life. It provides an opportunity for workers to discuss some of their experiences in the disaster, to acknowledge the stresses and rewards of the assignment, to discuss the personal impact of the disaster on their lives, and to honor the relationships that have been formed during the job. It allows workers to address the issues that may arise out of the ongoing commitment to disaster work. It also provides workers with practical information about disaster stress management, and helps them to identify healthy, adaptive coping techniques (Myers & Zunin, 1994b, pp. 95–96).

Ground rules are also presented in the *introduction* phase. Confidentiality is discussed and emphasized. The length of the group session is presented (usually 1 to 2 hours), and the fact that all participants must stay until the end. Group members are told that they are free to talk as much or little as they want, but participation is encouraged. A positive group tone is established, and criticism of others is disallowed. The difference between a debriefing and an operational critique is outlined, with a clear explanation that the debriefing is not an operational critique. Pagers and cell phones are turned off or given to someone outside the room for the duration of the meeting. Participants are then asked if they have any questions about the process, and all questions are answered.

In the *fact* phase, participants are asked to introduce themselves by name, and are asked to give a brief description of their job or role in the disaster. In a small sized group (under 20 or so), this is done round-robin, the only time in the session that the round-robin format is used. If the group is too large to accommodate round-robin introductions, members are asked to introduce themselves, their job, and role the first time they speak in the group.

In the *thought* phase, participants are asked several questions:

- What were your thoughts when the disaster happened?
- What thoughts did you have when you were asked to respond to the disaster?
- What were your thoughts when you first arrived at the disaster?
- Any hopes or expectations you had as you began your assignment?
- Any prominent or recurring thoughts as you went about your assignment?
- How did you feel as you approach termination of your assignment?

In the *challenges* phase, participants are asked to describe any major challenges they faced in the course of their disaster assignment. These might include difficult or unusual demands made upon them, struggles, or activities that involved a great deal of emotion. To facilitate this phase, leaders might ask "What was the hardest part (or biggest challenge or most difficult part) of this job for you?"

In the *meaning* phase, participants are asked to describe a significant, meaningful, rewarding, or profound incident that happened to them during their assignment. They are asked to explore what touched them or affected them most about the incident, and how the incident changed them. In exploring one specific challenging incident and one specific meaningful incident in these two phases of the debriefing, workers are taking their first steps toward working through the full measure of the personal impact of the disaster.

In the *teaching* phase, group members are asked about the feelings and reactions that they experienced during their assignment. These may be listed on a flipchart or whiteboard if facilitators desire. The reactions are then discussed, normalized, and healthy, adaptive coping strategies are explored.

The importance of referral is discussed for reactions that are unusual, of long duration, disruptive, or of uncomfortable intensity for any individual. Handouts about common reactions, coping strategies, and resources for follow-up are helpful in this phase.

In the last phase, *transition*, participants are asked to explore their reactions to termination of their assignment and to anticipate the transition back to "normal" life, relationships, and work. Some education may be done about what a transition involves—an ending and letting go (of roles and relationships), a period of confusion or distress, a period of working through, and a new beginning (Bridges, 1980). Education is also done about some of the common transition difficulties for disaster workers leaving a disaster: difficulty gearing down to a more normal pace, the need to rest, wanting or not wanting to talk about the disaster with family and friends, irritation with people's problems that seem "trivial" in comparison to those seen in disaster, mood swings, etc. (FEMA, 1987). Participants are asked to think about what difficulties they usually have with transitions and to identify strategies to make their leave-taking and homecoming as smooth as possible. If the debriefing group consists of people who have worked together for the duration of all or part of their assignment, members are asked to look around the room and make any statements of appreciation, closure, or goodbye that they wish to make. The debriefing then closes with the customary wrapping up of loose ends, answering of questions, and discussion of resources for referral or follow-up.

The three types of debriefing presented in this chapter are included in table 5.2.

FOLLOW-UP DEBRIEFINGS FOR DISASTER WORKERS

All groups receiving CISM services following large-scale disasters should receive follow-up services if possible. When deployment has been for 5 or more days of work, follow-up individual or group sessions should ideally be scheduled for about 5 days after ending the disaster assignment. If additional follow-up is needed, it is usually recommended to be done 2 to 3 weeks after the first follow-up. A third follow-up is recommended 3 months later (Young et al., 1998). Mitchell and Dyregrov (1993) recommend the following questions for discussion in the follow-up group or one-on-one sessions with individuals:

- "How are things since the debriefing?"
- "Is anyone stuck on any particular part of the incident?"
- "How have things been on your own (or off-duty) time?"

TABLE 5.2: COMPARISON OF TARGET POPULATIONS AND STAGES OF CRITICAL
INCIDENT STRESS DEBRIEFING, MULTIPLE STRESSOR MODEL, AND DISASTER
WORKER DEBRIEFING MODELS

	DEBRIEFING MODELS		
Comparison Categories (Stage/Phase)	ICISF model Critical Incident Stress Debriefing	Multiple Stressor Debriefing Model	Disaster Worker Debriefing Model
Target population	Emergency and Disaster Workers	Disaster Workers/Red Cross Disaster Workers	Disaster Workers
1	Introduction	Disclosure of Events Stage	Introduction Phase
2	Fact Phase	Feeling and Reactions Stage	Facts Phase
3	Thought Phase	Coping Strategies Stage	Thoughts Phase
4	Reaction Phase	Termination Stage	Challenges Phase
5	Symptom Phase		Meaning Phase
6	Teaching Phase		Teaching Phase
7	Reentry Phase		Transition Phase

ICISF Model (Mitchell & Everly, 2004, the *Multiple Stressor Debriefing Model* (Armstrong, O'Callahan, & Marmar, 1991), and the *Disaster Worker Debriefing Model* (Myers & Zunin, 1994b).

- "What else do you feel you might need to get you past this particularly bad event?"

Young et al. (1998) recommend some additional discussion questions:

- "What, if any, changes have you noticed in your work habits since the disaster?"
- "How has the disaster affected your personal relationships?"
- "What stress management strategies have you used?"
- "Which stress management techniques work for you?"
- "Which ones don't?"
- "Has this experience resulted in any positive changes in your professional or personal life?"

Additional follow-up meetings can be conducted by CISM professionals, peers, and chaplains during the next 1 to 3 years, depending upon the impact of the disaster and its continuing effect on personnel. Individuals whose reactions continue to be intense, uncomfortable, or interfere with their work or relationships should be referred for more intensive counseling or psychotherapy.

Large-scale disasters are complex political, cultural, social, and economic events that go through predictable phases. Special attention should be paid to times of "reminders" of the disaster that intensify memory and stress. Such events include the anniversary (or anniversaries) of the disaster, reminders of the disaster (the hurricane season returns), and hearings, trials, sentencing, imprisonment or execution of perpetrators in human-caused events or terrorism. Some individuals or families may benefit from CISM services, including debriefings, during these times.

Follow-up may also be provided by recontacting a group that has received service or by contacting individual service recipients. In past disasters, this contact has been done by phone, in person, by mail, and by email. Follow-up is also achieved through ongoing public education and outreach in the months and, sometimes, years following the disaster. Brochures and fliers, public service announcements, and human interest news stories can continue to emphasize that recovery is a long process, that various phases are involved, and that most reactions are "normal." They can suggest coping strategies and remind people of available resources and how to contact them. Critical incident stress management services should always be provided in the context of ongoing community needs assessment.

SPECIAL NEEDS OF DISASTER RESPONDERS DURING IMPACT AND RESPONSE PHASES

Emergency service workers who respond during the impact and immediate response phases of the disaster are a priority population because of the intensity and danger of the work, the magnitude of need for their services, fatigue and cumulative stress, and role conflict regarding professional and family responsibilities. It is normal for emergency-service workers to experience intense reactions to the disaster during and immediately following impact. However, workers usually suppress their reactions and respond heroically to the situations that require their knowledge and skills to save lives. During California's 1989 Loma Prieta earthquake, many firefighters reported that during the earthquake they feared they would be killed or injured, and experienced intense concern for the safety of family and friends. Just after the quake, despite these concerns, they immediately responded to such emergencies as the Interstate 880 Cypress Structure freeway collapse. During the rescue work on the collapsed highway, firefighters worked in the pancaking space between the upper and lower levels of the freeway. During their work, there were strong aftershocks and subsequent compression of the levels. As the space compressed, the escape route became smaller, increasing the risk that workers would become trapped. Gasoline was leaking from crushed vehicles, increasing the risk of an explosion if extrication tools caused sparks. Personnel were exposed to traumatic stimuli, hearing cries for help become dim as time passed, or witnessing extraordinary procedures such as a necessary limb amputation with a chainsaw to extricate one of the persons trapped.

Cumulative stress is an additional factor for emergency personnel during and immediately after impact. The operation to save lives and protect property will continue for several days and weeks until the immediate response phase moves into the recovery phase. Such intensive work for days to weeks can expose emergency-service workers to repeated traumatic incidents, threats to personal safety, organizationally induced stress, and physical fatigue. While the disaster workers are performing these work duties, they also have competing demands for their time, emotional presence, and physical presence in helping their family during the impact and immediate response phase of the disasters. The competing work and personal demands from family and friends can create stress and disaster related problems (Wee, 1994).

It is also important for CISM teams to offer support to family members of personnel deployed to lengthy disaster operations. Family support could include information about the operation and its mission, objectives for the operational period, and planning estimates concerning when units will be released. Family support can also include assistance to families with immediate needs following the impact of the disaster. This might include information about disaster assistance, resources to assist with protecting property, helping families to maintain or secure housing, and other concrete needs that might emerge.

DISASTER WORKERS FROM OUTSIDE THE AREA

Large-scale disasters, by definition, are events that overwhelm the resources of the local area. If the resources required to protect lives, property, and meet the needs of the population impacted by the disaster are beyond the resources and capability of the local area, the local area will request assistance from the region, state, federal government, and nongovernmental agencies in the form of mutual aid. Planning for the mental health and stress management needs of mutual aid personnel is essential. Disaster workers arriving from outside the disaster area are faced with a variety of stressors including logistical stress associated with transportation and finding lodging, food, medical care, and personal needs; organizational coordination or confusion; and stress from exposure to the disaster and its victims.

Resources must be found for providing CISM services for workers from outside the impacted area. Ideally, mutual aid personnel units should activate and deploy members of their own CISM team when deployed to a disaster. Peer support, clergy, and mental health professionals should accompany the unit to provide psychological support if needed, rather than depending upon the already overtaxed resources in the disaster area. If mutual aid teams do not have their own CISM teams to bring with them, other resources must be found. Often, there are CISM teams ready and willing to help. Following the Oklahoma City bombing, CISM teams from across the nation offered their services to the citizens and to responding disaster personnel. The Oklahoma Critical Incident Stress Management network took on the task of coordinating volunteer CISM teams from across the state and nation, linking them with the needs of local and mutual aid personnel. Special care must be taken to ensure that mutual aid personnel have access to CISM care when they return home. Each team should receive a demobilization or an exit debriefing before leaving, during which follow-up services at home should be discussed. If a local CISM team does not exist for the homecoming workers, an attempt should be made to locate a team in a nearby jurisdiction. The International Critical Incident Stress Foundation maintains a directory of teams nationwide and can assist. Their number is 410-750-9600.

The CISM program for mutual aid disaster workers should include a number of services. An important service is predeployment briefing at the staging area that is well away from the scene of operations. The predeployment briefing should include information about the operational objectives and general psychological issues that have been encountered by the previous shifts. On-scene in-briefings are held outside the inner perimeter to allow for briefing on specific roles and tasks required of the emergency workers, as well as more specific psychological issues. Information about stressors encountered as well as specific coping strategies and stress management information from previous shifts is provided. On-scene support personnel are identified and should assist in the staged in-briefing where appropriate. Additional job task and coping skills coaching may be required, depending upon the complexity and stress of the operation.

On-scene support and defusing should be provided for mutual aid workers as well as local disaster workers. When the decision is made to use mutual aid personnel, preparations should begin for the worker demobilization. Planning should be coordinated between the local CISM team and the psychological support services that accompanied the mutual aid teams. Demobilization activities, worker recognition, and any other psychological support services should be developed so as not to be viewed as intrusive, inconvenient, or inappropriate to the workers. Timing of recognition ceremonies, demobilization, departure from the disaster area and arrival home should be carefully considered so that already tired workers are not further fatigued by the process. One approach used by the Los Angeles County Search and Rescue Team upon return from providing heavy search and rescue at the Oklahoma City Federal Building bombing in 1995 was to provide demobilization during the bus trip to family reunification sites (Wirth, 1997). While the demobilization was held on the bus, a briefing for family members was done at the reunification site. A socialization event was provided with food and beverages when families were reunited. The critical incident stress debriefing was done after 5 days, with follow-up debriefing in 3 weeks.

SELF-CARE FOR CISM PERSONNEL

Peer support personnel and mental health professionals who provide CISM services need to be aware of the potential impact of the work. Practitioners in the field of traumatology have observed secondary stress reactions in themselves and their colleagues. Figley (1995), in his research and work on "compassion fatigue," or secondary traumatization of persons caring for victims of trauma, notes that nearly all of the hundreds of reports focusing on traumatized people exclude those who were traumatized indirectly or secondarily. The Diagnostic and Statistical Manual IV (APA, 1994) (American Psychological Association) clearly indicates that mere knowledge of another's traumatic experience can be traumatizing. Peer support personnel and mental health professionals providing CISM services to personnel and citizens who have experienced critical incidents and disasters would clearly be "at risk" for secondary traumatization, making self-care, buddy-care, and team-care important aspects of providing CISM services.

In one of the few studies on compassion fatigue and CISM, Wee and Myers (2003) examined the potential for compassion satisfaction, compassion fatigue, and burnout in a sample of persons attending a workshop on prevention of compassion fatigue at an international conference of providers of CISM services. In the study, more than half (58%) of the respondents reported experiencing psychological reactions after providing CISM services, including an array of behavioral, emotional, cognitive, and physical symptoms of psychological stress. Of the respondents 40% were found to have moderate, high, or extremely high risk for compassion fatigue. At the same time, 89% of respondents were found to have a good, high, or extremely high potential for compassion satisfaction, and 87% were found to be at extremely low risk for burnout. The results appear to indicate that, while the CISM practitioners recognize the stress associated with their work (as reflected in the reported symptoms), the work provides significant rewards (as measured by compassion satisfaction) that outweigh the stress and mitigate against burnout. Likewise, while 40% tested positive for compassion fatigue (or secondary traumatic stress) as a result of their empathy with CISM recipients, the rewards of the work again appear to mitigate the negative effects of the work. This type of data can help to establish a normative sample for which other groups of people who help survivors of critical incidents and traumatic events can evaluate their degree of potential for compassion satisfaction, fatigue, and burnout. By so doing, they can develop organizational, group, lifestyle, self-care, and buddy-care strategies to help themselves and their colleagues. Prevention of compassion fatigue among disaster mental health, CISM, and crisis intervention personnel is discussed in detail in chapter 4.

EFFECTIVENESS OF CISD AND CISM: RESEARCH ISSUES AND FINDINGS

There is an increasingly large body of research on the effectiveness of debriefing, psychological debriefing, critical incident stress debriefing, and critical incident stress management. Before reviewing the research, it is useful to review terminology. *Debriefing* is a generic term that has been used for a wide range of crisis interventions. It is also used in some circles to refer to an operational critique of an event, causing further semantic confusion. *Psychological debriefing* (PD) is a Scandinavian term originally coined to describe small-group crisis intervention. However, both debriefing and PD are often used to refer to any of a wide range of interventions, including 1:1 interventions. CISD is a 7-phase, small-group crisis intervention following a specific protocol outlined by the International Critical Incident Stress Foundation. Some researchers have attempted apply this group protocol to individuals, with limited success, as reported in their research. CISM is an integrated, multicomponent crisis intervention system with 10 core elements, one of which is CISD. Unfortunately, each term has been used as a synonym for every other term, creating considerable confusion both in research and in practice (Everly & Wee, 2003).

It is important to note that debriefing research is particularly challenging. First, it is not possible to predict when and where a potentially traumatizing event may occur, making it virtually impossible to assess individuals prior to exposure to a trauma. In addition, it is difficult to conduct randomized controlled trials; randomization has historically been considered unethical because it would mean withholding a potentially useful intervention from acutely distressed individuals (Litz et al., 2002).

There have been a number of recent research studies that have questioned the effectiveness of the interventions being called *debriefing* in preventing or mitigating symptoms of PTSD. Some studies have found either partial or no support for debriefing as an intervention (Flannery & Everly, 2001). The conclusions of other studies have been mixed with regard to overall effectiveness of debriefing (Everly & Boyle, 1999). A number of studies have found positive results of CISD and CISM (Everly & Boyle; Flannery & Everly; Mitchell, 2003). McNally et al. (2003) summarize the situation by stating:

> The need for controlled evaluations of early interventions has only recently been widely acknowledged. Psychological debriefing—the most widely used method—has undergone increasing empirical scrutiny, and the results have been disappointing. Although the majority of debriefed survivors describe the experience as helpful, there is no convincing evidence that debriefing reduces the incidence of PTSD, and some controlled studies suggest that it may impede natural recovery from trauma. Most studies show that individuals who receive debriefing fare no better than those who do not receive debriefing. Methodological limitations have complicated interpretation of the data, and an intense controversy has developed regarding how best to help people in the immediate wake of trauma (p. 45).

There is a sizable body of research, and it would be beyond the scope of this chapter to provide a comprehensive review of all the existing studies. There are numerous reviews of existing studies to which the critical and interested reader is directed for further evaluation of the research, namely Bisson, McFarlane, and Rose (2000); Everly and Boyle (1999); Flannery and Everly (2001); Mitchell (2003); Ormerod (2002); Litz et al. (2002); and McNally et al. (2003). Raphael and Wilson in *Psychological Debriefing: Theory, Practice, and Evidence* (2000) present a thorough discussion of debriefing in 25 chapters, including key concepts, the background and evolution of debriefing, models of debriefing, the shortcomings and difficulties of conducting research on debriefing, and the adaptation and use of debriefing models with various groups of recipients, including debriefing in different cultural frameworks.

In conducting a brief overview of the relevant research, we begin by addressing the studies that have found either partial or no support for the effectiveness of debriefing. Unfortunately, most of the studies fail to clearly define and distinguish the operational nature of the independent variable being studied; that is, the specific form or model of intervention used (Everly & Boyle, 1999). An essential component of any research is a clear and restrictive definition of the independent variable (Mullen, 1989). In those research publications not supportive of the efficacy of debriefing, the type of debriefing interventions studied is not clear, the training of the interventionists is not described (Flannery & Everly, 2001), and there is controversy as to whether the outcomes studied (e.g., reduction in psychiatric symptomatology) are the appropriate measures of success for a crisis intervention.

Of the research studies reporting limited or negative outcomes associated with debriefings, the most frequently referenced, and the basis of much of the negative reaction in the literature, is the Cochrane Review (Wessley, Rose, & Bisson, 1998). While the Cochrane Review is intended to be an entirely independent review of prior research, two of the authors of this article were primary investigators on two negative studies contained within the report, thus building in bias and compromising the independence of the review. The study reviewed 11 randomized controlled trials (RCTs) on debriefing sessions consisting of one-to-one counseling sessions with medical patients in hospital settings, some of the patients in pain and on medication. None of the debriefings studied were group sessions, the standard of practice for CISD. Thus, the study examined interventions different from CISD as it is taught and practiced in numerous countries following ICISF guidelines. Two authors of the Cochrane Review article did note later that the research on debriefing may not have studied debriefings using standard debriefing practices (Everly & Wee, 2003). The authors of the original review and a subsequent review (Rose, Bisson, & Wessely, 2002) report that "We are unable to comment on the use of group debriefing, nor the use of debriefing after mass traumas" (p. 10). The patients in their study did not receive a range of crisis interventions applicable to their situation, violating the standard of practice of CISM; services must be part of a multicomponent *system* offering an array of crisis intervention services pertinent to the client's needs. In summary, this study examined interventions that do not resemble the CISD and CISM standards of care, found negative results in the interventions studied, and generalized the negative findings to imply negative results from CISD and CISM. The authors of the Cochrane Review reported that single-session individual debriefing did not reduce psychological distress nor prevent PTSD, and concluded on the basis of this research that compulsory debriefings should be discontinued as a crisis intervention (Everly & Wee, 2003; Flannery & Everly, 2001). The conclusions caused considerable alarm among readers who did not carefully read the review and recognize its limitations and fanned the flames of what subsequently became known as "the debriefing controversy." It is worthy to note that the quality of a sample of Cochrane Reviews was independently examined by ten methodologists in 1998, and was reported by Olsen et al. in *The British Medical Journal* (2001). Major problems were identified in 29% of the reviews. The major problem for 17% of the studies was that the evidence did not support the conclusions drawn. In 23% of the reviews, the conduct of the review or the reporting of the findings was unsatisfactory. Olsen's study concludes that users of the Cochrane Reviews "should interpret the reviews cautiously. . . . Errors occur, and potential biases may emerge . . . [and] some Cochrane Reviews have need of correction and improvement" (p. 830).

Dr. Martin Deahl of St. Batholomew's and Royal London School of Medicine and Dentistry and the University of London cautions against using only randomized controlled trials (RCTs) in measuring the effectiveness of CISM interventions (Mitchell, 2003). He wrote the following as a reaction to the Cochrane Review:

> Outcome research into the effectiveness of acute interventions such as debriefing raises important questions about the ethics as well as the status of conventional RCT methodology as the imprimatur of Evidence Based Medicine (EBM). RCTs have become the dominant paradigm of treatment outcome studies to the virtual exclusion of observational or case studies. CISD was designed for groups of emergency services workers following traumatic events. Conducting a methodologically rigorous RCT of group debriefing would be extremely difficult given that group trauma generally only occurs in unpredictable and often chaotic circumstances such as war or disaster. In emergency situations such as these the operational imperative is paramount and investigators must do the best they can with the available material under difficult and at times extremely fraught circumstances. Irrespective of whether or not debriefing reduces long-term morbidity many individuals find it subjectively helpful at the time. Under these circumstances can it therefore be ethically justifiable to employ "non-intervention" controls denying individuals short term support whatever the long-term outcome? In conflict, following disaster or accident, naturalistic studies, often conducted opportunistically remain useful and have considerable heuristic value despite methodological shortcomings particularly relating to sample selection and randomization to different treatment conditions. Applying the stringent criteria demanded by the arbiters of EBM such as the Cochrane library to trials of preventive interventions

means that much useful work might go unpublished. Clinicians might well lament that in attempting to satisfy such rigorous methodological criteria RCTs have become so divorced from clinical reality that their findings become meaningless . . . RCTs are not the sine qua non of EBM and debriefing studies which challenge their hegemony and lend credibility to observational studies have important implications for the ways in which the quality and value of research evidence is assessed both in social psychiatry and empirical science in general (Mitchell, 2003, pp. 15–16).

Another frequently referenced study reporting that CISD did not improve natural recovery from trauma-related disorders was published in *Lancet* (van Emmerik, Kamphuis, Hulsbosch, & Emmelkamp, 2002). The article incorrectly states that "single session debriefing is standard clinical practice after traumatic events" (standard of practice for debriefing is a group intervention). The meta-analysis included seven studies, mixing such interventions as five "CISDs" (none resembled the standard model for CISD), three "non-CISD interventions" (one of these was the only group intervention closely modeling standard CISD format), and six "no-intervention control groups." The authors' description of interventions leads the reader to conclude that the interventions included individual consultations, counseling or therapy sessions, and group interventions. The terms "counseling," "psychotherapy," and "crisis intervention" were used as if they were synonymous. Thus, the major flaw in the *Lancet* review is that the interventions assessed are not all the same. If a study measures different interventions while erroneously claiming that they are the same, one cannot draw any legitimate conclusions (Mullen, 1989). The most interesting finding of the *Lancet* study is that the one and only group intervention resembling the CISD model in group structure, time frame of intervention, and length of intervention (Shalev, 1998) was included in the "non-CISD" intervention group. The *Lancet* study concludes that "non-CISD interventions resulted in a medium-to-large reduction in the severity of symptoms of posttraumatic stress disorder and a small-to-medium reduction in other symptoms." Thus, the *only intervention resembling actual CISD*, although included in the *Lancet's* "non-CISD group," was found to have a medium-to-large effect in reducing symptoms.

Other studies reporting to find negative or no value to debriefings include the following: Bisson, Jenkins, Alexander, and Bannister, 1997; Carlier, Voerman, and Gersons, 2000; Conlon, Fahy, and Conroy, 1999; Creamer, Burgess, Buckingham, and Pattison, 1989; Deahl, Gillham, Thomas, Searle, and Srinivasan, 1994; Griffiths and Watts, 1992; Hobbs,

Mayou, Harrison, and Worlock, 1996; Kenardy et al., 1996; Lavender, 1998; Lee, Slade, and Lygo, 1996; Matthews, 1998; Mayou, Ehlers, and Hobbs, 2000; McFarlane, 1988; Rose and Bisson, 1998; Rose, Berwin, Andrews, and Kirk, 1999; Rose et al., 2002; Searle and Bisson, 1992; Small, Lumley, Donohue, Potter, and Waldenstrom, 2000; Weisaeth, 1989.

Mitchell's review of the research on CISM (2003) finds that many of the studies reporting negative or neutral findings examined interventions that demonstrated a clear violation of the acceptable standards of practice within CISM. Most of the studies were conducted on one-on-one, single-session interventions (CISD is intended to be a group intervention). Many of the interventions were done with individual hospitalized primary victims of burns, traffic accidents, house fires, childbirth, sexual assault, and the like (CISD was designed to be used on teams of emergency workers and members of homogeneous groups who have experienced a traumatic event). In almost all of the studies, the interventions were not part of a package of services designed to meet all of the client's needs (CISD is intended to be but one intervention within the CISM system of care). The interventions were much shorter than standard debriefings. (The average time of interventions was 43 minutes, with some being as short as 5 minutes. CISD usually runs for 1 to 2 hours; interventions in the studies were much shorter in duration.) Interventions were often provided under inappropriate conditions, such as in a patient's room in a burn center, often with seriously ill persons on medication. CISD was never designed to be utilized on single severely injured primary victims. In fact, it should only be used cautiously with those who are healing from physical wounds since physical healing takes precedence over emotional healing (Tehrani, 1998). Persons conducting the interventions had unspecified credentials and training (CISM requires a minimum of a 2-day basic course in group interventions; additional courses are recommended). While Mitchell's neutrality might be questioned in his review of the research (he is founder and former president of the International Critical Incident Stress Foundation), a careful reading of the research publications themselves shows his analysis of these studies in question to be accurate.

Litz et al. (2002) also point out that many of the studies of CISD have been studies of primary victims of trauma who would be excluded from CISD if the CISM model were used. They concede that proponents of CISD could argue that negative findings on the efficacy of debriefing confirm the CISD principle that individual primary victims of trauma are inappropriate for debriefing. They further emphasize that controlled study of group-administered CISD to emergency services personnel exposed secondarily to trauma is needed to test the CISD model.

In an extensive review of studies on the efficacy of debriefing, Bisson et al. (2000) reported that studies vary greatly in quality, "but, overall, the quality of the studies, including randomized controlled trials, is poor" (p. 53). They report that common methodological shortcomings include small sample size, absence of control group, absence of randomization, varying degrees of trauma, ignoring other confounding variables, low response rates, sampling bias, and lack of uniformity of intervention and timing variance. They report that there has been a bias in the research toward the systematic study of *individual PD* as a stand-alone intervention, as opposed to *group PD* as part of a more comprehensive traumatic stress management program that has been argued as being most effective by numerous authors (Dyregrov, 1998; Everly & Mitchell, 2000; Flannery & Everly, 2001; Mitchell & Everly, 2001) and is the standard of care practiced in CISM. Bisson et al. (2000) note that, while numerous studies show little evidence that debriefing prevents psychopathology, it is well-received by participants and may very well be a useful intervention to facilitate the screening of individuals who are at risk, to disseminate education and referral information, and to assist organizational morale. They note that to focus solely on the reduction of PTSD and other psychological symptoms is probably too simplistic an approach to take to determine whether or not PD is beneficial as an early intervention. They summarize that "it would therefore be premature at present to conclude that PD should be discontinued as a possible intervention following trauma" (p. 55). They further emphasize that the beneficial aspects of debriefing are particularly evident when employed as part of a comprehensive stress management program such as CISM.

Let us turn now to some of the studies finding positive results of CISD and CISM. The primary goals of crisis intervention within the CISM model are to mitigate the impact of a critical incident (or disaster) and to accelerate recovery processes of normal people having normal reactions to abnormal events (sometimes referred to as primary prevention). CISM does not have as its goals the complete elimination of stress symptoms, depression, anxiety, PTSD, or any other psychiatric disorder (Mitchell, 2003). Most of the studies reporting limited or no support for debriefing use psychiatric symptomatology as their measure of success or failure of the interventions. Ormerod (2002) writes that evidence-based practice founded on rigorous research is important in providing guidelines and evaluating the effectiveness of debriefing; however, the value of clinical experience should not be ignored and factors other than reduction in symptoms may be important to consider in evaluating debriefing, such as the process of an intervention, level of satisfaction, quality of support, cost-benefits, reducing sickness, and performance criteria. Likewise, satisfaction questionnaires given to recipients of CISM services indicating perception of support from interventions, satisfaction with interventions, usefulness of the interventions, and self-reports of reduction in stress levels following interventions should not be discounted.

As an example of Ormerod's position, Robinson, Mitchell, and Murdoch (1995) found that, in a survey of ambulance officers in Victoria ($n = 823$), 14% stated that debriefing had enabled them not to take sick leave, 18% not to leave their job, 11% not to take out frustrations at work, and 26% not to take out frustrations at home.

Tehrani, Walpole, Berriman, and Reilly (2001) studied employees exposed to the Paddington Rail Crash who attended a group debriefing session. They observed several benefits of the debriefing, including an increased shared understanding and a change in attitude to recognizing positive outcomes. In a 4-month follow-up, a significant reduction in Impact of Event Scale (IES) scores and anxiety and depression scores was found for all subjects, and all employees demonstrated an improvement in performance (Ormerod, 2002).

Three months following the 1992 Los Angeles civic disturbances, emergency medical technicians who responded at South Central Los Angeles crisis area were surveyed, with 66 usable questionnaires were returned for a response rate of 59%. A portion of the emergency medical technicians received CISD and a portion did not (with no systematic assignment to CISD or no CISD). The emergency medical technicians who received CISD were significantly less distressed than the emergency medical technicians who did not receive CISD (Wee, Mills, & Koehler, 1999). Not participating in a critical incident stress debriefing was the strongest predictor of post-civil-disturbance stress response of the emergency medical technicians (Wee, 1996c).

Bohl (1991) performed a naturalistic randomized study of 40 police officer who received CISD within 24 hr of a critical incident, compared to 31 who did not receive CISD within 24 hr. When evaluated 3 months later, those who received CISD were less depressed, less angry, less anxious, and had less PTSD symptoms. In a similar study in1995, Bohl evaluated 30 firefighters who received CISD within 24 hr of a critical incident and 35 who did not. At 3 months, anxiety symptoms and stress symptoms were less in the CISD group than in the non-CISD group.

Burns and Harm (1993) conducted a study of 219 Emergency Department nurses who experienced critical incidents. Of these, 193 reported that CISD had been personally helpful to them, 86.6% reported that talking about the incident helped, 85.1% said it helped to know they were not alone in their reactions to the incident, and 83% said it was helpful to hear others talk about the incident. On the negative side, 26.9% said it was not helpful if group leaders had no relevant experience, 23.1% said they were not comfortable with some of the people in the group, and 19.2% said the CISD was done too long following the incident.

Richman (1998) conducted a study of various traumatic events impacting emergency personnel in Australia between 1988 and 1998. Of the 586 personnel participating in the study, 90% of personnel evaluated CISD as moderately valuable, 67% found it very valuable, and 55.6% of the participants felt that CISD had brought them relief from or lessening of symptoms.

Robinson and Mitchell (1993) studied 288 emergency workers in Australia between 1987 and 1989. Evaluation forms were given to CISD participants within two weeks of the CISD. 96% of emergency services personnel and 77% of welfare or hospital staff reported symptom reduction because of the CISD.

Everly and Boyle (1999) conducted a meta-analysis of five previously published investigations of the CISD model of psychological debriefing, revealing a large effect size (Cohen's $d = .86$), attesting to the effectiveness of CISD in mitigating symptoms of psychological distress. The beneficial effect was revealed despite a wide variety of subject groups, a wide range of traumatic events, and a diversity of outcome measures in the studies.

Other studies reporting positive outcomes associated with debriefings include Dyregrov 1998; Everly, Boyle, and Lating, 1999; Feldman and Bell, 1991; Ford et al., 1993; Hytten and Hasle, 1989; Jenkins, 1996; Meehan, 1996; Lanning, 1987; Nurmi, 1999; Richards, 2001; Robinson, 1994; Robinson and Mitchell, 1993; Robinson, Mitchell, and Murdoch, 1995; Rogers, 1992; Shalev, 2000; Shapiro and Kunkler, 1990; Sloan, 1988; Smith and de Chesnay, 1994; Stallard and Law, 1993; Turnbull, 1997; Turner, Thompson, and Rosser, 1993; and Ursano, Fullerton, Vance, and Wang, 2000. There have also been a number of studies which report positive outcomes and include comparison groups (Chemtob, Tomas, Law, & Cremmiter, 1997; Ersland, Weisaeth, & Sund, 1989; Jenkins; Nurmi, 1997; Wee, Mills, & Koehler, 1993; Yule, 1991).

This chapter's review of the research on CISD has identified a number of conditions under which CISD may not be effective:

1. Use by untrained and unskilled providers
2. Failure to adhere to standards of care (e.g., applying CISD to individuals instead of to groups, for which it was developed)
3. Application of the intervention to inappropriate populations (e.g., to individual primary victims)

4. Application of the intervention in inappropriate circumstances (e.g., in emergency rooms or hospital units with people in pain and sometimes medicated)
5. Use of the intervention for purposes it was never designed for (e.g., to treat PTSD or depression)
6. Use of the intervention as a "stand-alone" intervention outside a multicomponent system of care
7. Unrealistic expectations of what CISD can be expected to achieve (Mitchell, 2003)

Let us now turn our attention to studies of the effectiveness of CISM. Numerous studies have examined the effects of multicomponent crisis intervention programs (CISM). Chemtob et al. (1997) evaluated CISD combined with traumatic stress education using two groups in a time-lagged design. The impact of event scores (Horowitz, Wilner, & Alvarez, 1979) for both groups were significantly reduced when compared with preintervention levels (Mitchell & Everly, 1998b).

Leeman-Conley (1990) studied an Australian bank following armed robbery, and found that the impact of a CISM approach appeared to reduce sick leave by 60% and workers' compensation by 68%.

Brom, Kleber, and Hofman (1993) found the groups of Dutch victims of traffic accidents that received CISM intervention had fewer symptoms than a control group.

Amir, Weil, Kaplan, Tocker, and Witzum (1998) found that CISM services (CISD, brief therapy, and family support) for women victims of a terrorist attack led to total Impact of Event Scores (IES) showing a decrease in PTSD symptoms.

Flannery and colleagues have published numerous studies on the use of the Assaulted Staff Action Program (ASAP), a structured program of CISM for healthcare providers of child and adult services in emergency rooms, inpatient, outpatient, day programs, homeless shelters, and community-based settings (Flannery, 1998, 1999, 2000; Flannery, Fulton, Tausch, & DeLoffi, 1991; Flannery, Hanson, & Penk, 1994; Flannery, Hanson, Penk, Flannery, & Gallager, 1995; Flanner et al., 1998; Flannery & Penk, 1996; Flannery, Pen, & Corrigan, 1999). The program was found to be effective in returning staff to functioning and has resulted in sharp declines in facility-wide violence (by 63%), as well as dollar cost savings in terms of less sick leave, less medical and legal expense, less industrial accident claims, less staff turnover, and sustained productivity (Flannery & Everly, 2001).

Western Management Consultants (1996) evaluated a comprehensive CISM program for nurses in the Canadian provinces from British Columbia to Ontario. The nurses were affected by such serious traumatic events as the death of a patient, violent death of a colleague, patient suicides, and patient assaults on staff. The study found that of those who were debriefed following critical incidents, 82% reported that the CISM services had met or exceeded their expectations, 89% indicated that they were satisfied with the CISM services, and 99% indicated reduced absence from work because of CISM interventions. Of the nurses who had experienced a critical incident and contemplated leaving their jobs, 24% did not resign after a CISM intervention. Estimates are that a single nurse replacement would have cost $38,000. The cost savings attributed to CISM services were determined to be $7.09 for every dollar spent to establish the program (Mitchell & Everly, 1998b), or a 700% return on the investment of the Canadian government in the CISM program.

The American Psychological Association (1997) wrote an extensive report on the mental health response to the 1995 Oklahoma City bombing. The report recognized that the long-term impact of the bombing on first response and rescue and recovery teams was not known at the time of the writing of the report, and it acknowledged that the success of CISM in ameliorating those long-term impacts would require scrutiny. Nonetheless, the report made the following recommendations (pp. 26–28):

1. Mandatory CISM/mental health services for first response teams following all terrorist and mass casualty incidents
2. Inclusion of mental health and CISM in incident command protocols
3. Need for more CISM-trained mental health professionals
4. Disaster mental health services/CISM for spouses and families of first response and rescue and recovery teams
5. Need for better information regarding federal funds to assist with disaster mental health and CISM
6. Interstate mutual aid agreements for CISM
7. Debriefing for first response and rescue and recovery team supervisory and administrative personnel
8. Consider careful assignment of personnel to centers where death notification occurs
9. State worker's compensation laws must provide coverage for psychological as well as physical injuries
10. Continued research on the efficacy and adequacy of CISM

Hokanson (1997) found that of the 600 debriefed participants in a study of the effectiveness of CISM with Los Angeles County Fire Department,

56% reported a significant reduction in symptoms within 72 hr and 14% had less persistent PTSD symptoms (Everly, Flannery, & Mitchell, 1999).

Busuttil et al. (1995) studied 34 Royal Air Force personnel with traumatic exposures resulting in PTSD symptoms. CISM interventions were conducted in a 12-day residential model, and highly significant improvement was demonstrated at follow-up points in 6 weeks, 6 months, and at 1 year.

In a randomized treatment control study of 106 British soldiers returning from a United Nations peace keeping mission in Bosnia, Deahl, Srinivasan, Jones, Neblett, and Jolly, (2000) found the group who received critical incident stress debriefing had significantly lower alcohol misuse than nontreated controls. CISD group members had lower scores on psychometrically assessed anxiety, depression, and PTSD than non-CISD groups. In a paper in 2001, the same group of authors suggested that future trials of CISD and CISM should measure a broader range of outcome measures than PTSD symptomatology. They recommended measuring sick leave, substance abuse, group morale, motivation to work, and ability to function.

Everly, Flannery, and Eyler (2000) completed a meta-analysis of seven studies that evaluated critical incident stress management as an integrated multicomponent crisis intervention program, finding an extremely large effect size and a fail-safe number of sufficient magnitude. These findings attest to the power of CISM to mitigate symptoms of psychological distress (Everly et al., 2000).

Everly and Eyler (2000) conducted a meta-analytic review of seven CISM studies. Their meta-analysis yielded a sufficiency criterion of 868 (minimal sufficiency criterion is 45). Their number is far in excess of the minimum required to deem CISM an effective method of crisis intervention. They conclude that future research should stop asking if CISM works, but rather should focus on fine-tuning which CISM interventions are best used, when, and administered by whom.

Self-reports of the perceived helpfulness of CISM in dealing with traumatic stress have been conducted by Wee (1995b, 1995c, 1996a, 1996b, 1996c). In a study of emergency workers who responded to the Cypress Structure I-880 freeway collapse following the Loma Prieta earthquake in 1989, participants had received a variety of CISM services, including on-scene support, demobilization, defusing, and CISD. Participants were asked to complete a questionnaire 6 months after the disaster. The questionnaires indicated that receiving CISM services resulted in high levels of satisfaction, decreased distress, perception of the services as supportive, and assessment that the stress management information was useful (Wee, 1995c).

92% of participants indicated that they would want CISM services in future critical incidents or disasters (Wee, 1995c). The American Academy of Orthopaedic Surgeons (1996), in a study of 350 emergency medical responders, found similar results, with 314 (90.8%) reporting that CISD was beneficial to them. Litz et al. (2002) counter that perceived helpfulness of debriefing is not associated with positive change in psychological status. However, they also concede that the beneficial elements of respectful listening and validation, which may have a positive influence, have not been measured in studies of debriefing to date.

Other studies finding positive effectiveness of CISM include Everly, Flannery, Eyler, and Mitchell, 2001; Harbert, 1992; Hokanson, 1997; Jarero and Artigas, 2002; Manzi, 1995; Mitchell, Schiller, Eyler, and Everly, 1999; North et al., 2002; Ott and Henry, 1997; Richards, 2001; and Tehrani, 1995, 1998.

CONCLUSION

It would be impossible to summarize all of the literature and research on debriefing in a brief statement. A variety of themes has run through many of the studies and articles evaluating debriefing, CISD, and CISM, whether the studies have concluded pro or con for the interventions. One theme is that semantics need to be clarified. The word *debriefing* has so many meanings that it has no meaning. We suggest that interventions be clearly described when being studied. Further, the terms CISD and CISM should only be used within the clear definitions given for those interventions by the International Critical Incident Stress Foundation. Third, early interventions such as debriefing should not be made mandatory. Rather, the individual's personal coping style, which in the early aftermath of trauma may include suppression and avoidance of overwhelming traumatic memory, should be respected unless or until it appears to be counterproductive for the individual.

There has been a strong theme in the literature as well as this book that there needs to be a flexible approach to disaster interventions, allowing for the needs as well as the strengths and coping styles of individuals to define type and timing of interventions. Hiley-Young and Gerrity (1994), while acknowledging the usefulness of CISD procedures for some disaster victims, cautioned against having an unreasonable expectation of any single intervention. Ormerod (2002) describes the need for people to be more realistic about what can actually be achieved in the aftermath of trauma. She also describes the need for an acknowledgment that any early intervention cannot expect to prevent later posttrauma, but can certainly provide support and resources for individuals following exposure to critical incidents and disasters. Raphael concludes that,

> The belief in debriefing must sit alongside knowledge and be informed by it. Its positive and hopeful aspects should be recognized and further developed. It is a powerful social movement that should be understood and assessed. Where it is not effective, practice must change. . . . The debate about debriefing to find and use its truths must continue at both popular and scientific levels (Raphael, 2000, p. 358).

The enormous body of literature on trauma clearly reflects the complex array of vulnerability factors and resiliency factors at play in the posttrauma environment. It makes sense, then, that an equally rich array of early interventions should be at the fingertips of the experienced clinician intervening with trauma and disaster. The National Institute of Mental Health (2002) clearly supports a comprehensive, systematic, and multicomponent approach to early intervention. It is based on this reasoning that we favor such an approach.

Continuing research in the field of trauma and disaster mental health is essential to better understanding the impact of disasters and the impact of disaster mental health services, including debriefing and critical incident stress management, on citizens and responders affected by disasters. Future research needs to continue to identify and define what interventions, administered by whom, and at what time phase, are most helpful in producing which desired results. Disaster mental health practitioners need to stay abreast of current research literature and ever-evolving research findings in order to make the best possible applications of models and interventions as they evolve.

REFERENCES

American Academy of Orthopaedic and Scientific Affairs. (1996). Tales from the front: Huge response to sound off on CISD. *EMT Today, 1,* 3.

American Psychological Association. (1997). Final report: Task force on the mental health response to the Oklahoma City bombing. Retrieved June 21, 2004 from: http://www.mipt.org/pdf/FinalRptOKCBombAPAJuly1997.pdf.

American Psychiatric Association. (1994), *Diagnostic and statistical manual of mental disorders* (4th Ed.). Washington, DC: Author.

American Red Cross (1995). *Disaster mental health services (ARC 3043).* Washington, DC: American National Red Cross.

Amir, M., Weil, G., Kaplan, Z., Tocker, T., & Witzum, E. (1998). Debriefing with group psychotherapy in a homogeneous group of non-injured victims of a terrorist attack: A prospective study. *Acta Psychiatrica Scandinavia, 98,* 237–242.

Armstrong, K., O'Callahan, W., & Marmar, C. (1991). Debriefing Red Cross disaster personnel: The multiple stressor debriefing model. *Journal of Traumatic Stress, 4,* 581–593.

Bergmann, L., & Queen, T. (1986). Critical incident stress, part 2. *Fire Command,* May, 52–56.

Bisson, J., Jenkins, P., Alexander, J., & Bannister, C. (1997). Randomized controlled trial of psychological debriefing for victims of acute burn trauma. *British Journal of Psychiatry, 171,* 78–81.

Bisson, J. I., McFarlane, A. C., & Rose, S. (2000). Psychological debriefing. In E. B. Foa, T. M. Keane, & M. J. Friedman (Eds.), *Effective treatments for PTSD: Practice guidelines from the International Society for Traumatic Stress Studies.* New York: Guilford.

Blakeney, R. (1996). *Family assistance center.* Oklahoma City, OK: Oklahoma Office of the Chief Medical Examiner.

Blakeney, R. (2002, November). Providing relief to families after a mass fatality: Roles of the medical examiner's office and the family assistance center. *Office of Victims of Crime Bulletin.* Retrieved April 29, 2003, from http://www.ojp.usdoj.gov/ovc/publications/bulletins/prfmf_11_2001/welcome.html

Bohl, N. (1991). The effectiveness of brief psychological interventions in police officers after critical incidents. In J. Reese, J. Horn, & C. Dunning (Eds.), *Critical incidents in policing* (Rev. Ed., pp. 31–88). Washington, DC: Department of Justice.

Bohl, N. (1995). Measuring the effectiveness of CISD. *Fire Engineering, 148,* 125–126.

Bridges, W. (1980). *Transitions.* Reading, MA: Addison-Wesley.

Brom, D., Kleber, R., & Hofman, M. (1993). Victims of traffic accidents: Incidence and prevention of post-traumatic stress disorder. *Journal of Clinical Psychology, 49,* 131–140.

Burns, C., & Harm, N. (1993). Emergency nurses' perceptions of critical incidents and stress debriefing. *Journal of Emergency Nursing, 19,* 431–436.

Busuttil, W., Turnbull, G. J., Nal, L. A., Rollins, J., West, A. G., Blanch, N., et al. (1995). Incorporating psychological debriefing techniques within a brief group psychotherapy programme for the treatment of post-traumatic stress disorder. *British Journal of Psychiatry, 167,* 495–502.

Carlier, I. V. E., Voerman, A. E., & Gersons, B. P. R. (2000). The influence of occupational debriefing of posttraumatic stress symptomatology in traumatized police officers. *British Journal of Medical Psychology, 73,* 87–98.

Carkhuff, R., & Truax, C. (1965) Lay mental health counseling. *Journal of Consulting Psychology, 29,* 426–431.

Center for Mental Health Studies of Emergencies. (1985). *Role stressors and supports for emergency workers.* (DHHS Publication No. ADM 85-1408). Washington, DC: U.S. Government Printing Office.

Chemtob, C., Tomas, S., Law, W., & Cremniter, D. (1997). Postdisaster psychosocial intervention: A field study of the impact of debriefing on psychological distress. *American Journal of Psychiatry, 154,* 415–417.

Cohen, R., & Ahearn, F. (1980). *Handbook for mental health care of disaster victims.* Baltimore and London: Johns Hopkins University Press.

Conlon, L., Fahy, T. J., & Conroy, R. (1999). PTSD in ambulant RTA victims: A randomized controlled trial of debriefing. *Journal of Psychosomatic Research, 46,* 37–44.

Creamer, M., Burgess, P., Buckingham, W., & Pattison, P. (1989). *The psychosocial aftermath of the Queen Street shootings.* Melbourne: University of Melbourne, Department of Psychology.

Crick, B. (2001, December 10) WTC workers find sense of family at respite centers. *In the news.* Retrieved February 27, 2001, from http://www.redcross.org/news/ds/0901wtc/011210respite.html

Deahl, M. P., Gillham, A. B., Thomas, J., Searle, M. M., & Srinivasan, M. (1994). Psychological sequelae following the Gulf War: Factors associated with subsequent morbidity and the effectiveness of psychological debriefing. *British Journal of Psychiatry, 165,* 60–65.

Deahl, M. P., Srinivasan, M., Jones, N., Neblett, C., & Jolly, A. (2001). Evaluating psychological debriefing: Are we measuring the right outcomes? *Journal of Traumatic Stress, 14*, 527–529.

Deahl, M., Srinivasan, M., Jones, N., Thomas, J., Neblett, C., & Jolly, A. (2000). Preventing psychological trauma in soldiers: The role of operational stress training and psychological debriefing. *British Journal of Medical Psychology, 73*, 77–85.

DeWolfe, D. (2000). *Training manual for mental health and human service workers in major disasters* (2nd ed.). (DHHS Publication No. ADM 90-538). Available at http://www.mentalhealth.org/publications/allpubs/ADM90-538/index.htm

Dunning, C. (1988). Intervention strategies for emergency workers. In M. Lystad (Ed.), *Mental health response to mass emergencies* (pp. 284–307). New York: Brunner/Mazel.

Dyregrov, A. (1998). Psychological debriefing—an effective method? *Traumatology, 4,* Article 1.

Ersland, S., Weisaeth, L., & Sund, A. (1989). The stress upon rescuers involved in an oil rig disaster: "Alexander L. Kielland," 1980. *Acta Psychiatrica Scandinavica, 80* (Suppl. 355), 38–49.

Everly, G. S., Jr., & Boyle, S. (1999). Critical Incident Stress Debriefing (CISD): A meta-analysis. *International Journal of Emergency Mental Health, 1*, 165–168.

Everly, G. S., Jr., Boyle, S., & Lating, J. (1999). Effectiveness of psychological debriefing with vicarious trauma: A meta-analysis. *Stress Medicine, 15*, 229–233.

Everly, G. S., Jr., & Eyler, V. A. (2000, April). *Sufficiency criterion in empirically-validated psychological interventions: The case of critical incident stress management.* Invited paper, 3rd International Conference, Psychological and Social Services in a Changing Society, Kuwait City, Kuwait.

Everly, G. S., Jr., Flannery, R. B., Jr., & Eyler V. (2000). *Effectiveness of comprehensive crisis intervention system: A meta-analysis.* Paper presented at the 3rd International Conference, Psychological and Social Services in a Changing Society, Kuwait City, Kuwait.

Everly, G. S., Jr., Flannery, R. B., Jr., Eyler, V., & Mitchell, J. T. (2001). Sufficiency analysis of an integrated multicomponent approach to crisis intervention: Critical incident stress management. *Advances in Mind-Body Medicine, 17*, 174–183.

Everly, G. S., Jr., Flannery, R. B., Jr., & Mitchell, J. T. (1999) Critical Incident Stress Management (CISM): A review of the literature. *Aggression and Behavior: A Review Journal, 5*(1), 23–40.

Everly, G. S. Jr., & Mitchell, J. T. (2000). The debriefing "controversy" and crisis intervention: A review of lexical and substantive issues. *International Journal of Emergency Mental Health, 2*, 211–225.

Everly, G. S., Jr., Mitchell, D. J., Myers, D., & Mitchell, J. T. (2002). *National Guard Critical Incident Stress Management (CISM): Terrorism and disaster response. Trainer's guide.* Ellicott City, MD: International Critical Incident Stress Foundation.

Everly, G. S. Jr., & Wee, D. F. (2003, May). *A review of effectiveness and "best practices" in emergency mental health within the military environment.* Paper presented at the 11th Annual National Tri-Service Combat Stress Conference and Critical Incident Stress Certificates Training Courses, Camp Pendleton, CA.

Farberow, N. L., & Frederick, C. J. (1978) *Training manual for human service workers in major disasters.* (DHHS Publication No. ADM 77-538). Rockville, MD: National Institute of Mental Health, 1978.

Federal Emergency Management Agency. (1987). *Returning home after the disaster: An information pamphlet for FEMA disaster workers.* (FEMA and NIMH Publication L-157). Washington, DC: U.S. Government Printing Office.

Feldman, T. B., & Bell, R. A. (1991). Crisis debriefing of a jury after a murder trial. *Hospital and Community Psychiatry, 43,* 79–81.

Figley, C. R. (1995). Compassion fatigue as secondary traumatic stress disorder: An overview. In C. R. Figley (Ed.), *Compassion fatigue.* New York: Brunner/Mazel.

Flannery, R. B., Jr. (1998). *The Assaulted Staff Action Program (ASAP): Coping with the psychological aftermath of violence*. Ellicott City, MD: Chevron.

Flannery, R. B., Jr. (1999). Critical Incident Stress Management and the assaulted staff action program. *International Journal of Emergency Mental Health, 1,* 103–108.

Flannery, R. B., Jr. (2000). Debriefing health care staff after assaults by patients. In B. Raphael & J. P. Wilson (Eds.), *Psychological debriefing, theory, practice, and evidence*. Cambridge, UK: Cambridge University Press.

Flannery, R. B., Jr., & Everly, G. S. (2001). Crisis intervention: A review. In J. T. Mitchell & G. S. Everly (Ed.), *The basic Critical Incident Stress Management course: Basic group crisis intervention* (3rd ed., pp. 111–118). Ellicott City, MD: International Critical Incident Stress Foundation.

Flannery, R. B., Jr., Fulton, P., Tausch, J., & DeLoffi, A. (1991). A program to help staff cope with the psychological sequelae of assaults by patients. *Hospital and Community Psychiatry, 42,* 935–938.

Flannery, R. B., Jr., Hanson, M. A., & Penk, W. E. (1994). Risk factors for psychiatric inpatient assaults on staff. *Journal of Mental Health Administration, 21,* 24–31.

Flannery, R. B., Jr., Hanson, M. A., Penk, W. E., Flannery, G. J., & Gallager, C. (1995). The Assaulted Staff Action Program (ASAP): An approach to coping with the aftermath of violence in the work place. In L. R. Hurrell, Jr., S. L. Souter, & G. P. Keita (Eds.), *Job stress interventions* (pp. 199–212). Washington, DC: American Psychological Association.

Flannery, R. B., Jr., Hanson, M. A., Penk, W. E., Goldfinger, S., Pastva, G. P., & Navon, M. A. (1998). Replicated declines in assault rates after the implementation of the Assaulted Staff Action Program. *Psychiatric Services, 49,* 241–243.

Flannery, R. B., Jr., & Penk, W. E. (1996). Program evaluation of an intervention approach for staff assaulted by patients: Preliminary inquiry. *Journal of Traumatic Stress, 9,* 317–324.

Flannery, R. B., Jr., Penk, W., & Corrigan, M. (1999). Assaulted Staff Action Program (ASAP) and a decline in assault rate: Community based replication. *International Journal of Emergency Mental Health, 1,* 19–22.

Foa, E. B. (2001). *Guidelines for response to the recent tragic events in the U.S.* Unpublished manuscript. Philadelphia: University of Pennsylvania.

Ford, J. D., Shaw, D., Sennhauser, S., Greaves, D., Thacker, B., Chandler, P., et al. (1993). Psychological debriefing after Operation Desert Storm: Marital and family assessment and intervention. *Journal of Social Issues, 49,* 73–102.

Griffiths, J., & Watts, R. (1992). *The Kempsey and Grafton bus crashes: The aftermath*. East Lismore, Australia: Instructional Design Solutions.

Halbert, K. (1992). *The development and use of CISM team within a rural tertiary hospital*. Paper presented at the meeting of the Agency for Health Policy and Research, Atlanta, GA.

Hartsough, D. M., & Myers, D. (1985). *Disaster work and mental health: Prevention and control of stress among workers*. Rockville, MD: National Institute of Mental Health.

Hiley-Young, B., & Gerrity, E. T. (1994). Critical Incident Stress Debriefing (CISD): Value and limitations in disaster response. *National Center for PTSD Clinical Quarterly, 4,* 17–19.

Hobbs, M., Mayou, R., Harrison, B., & Worlock, P. (1996). A randomized controlled trial of psychological debriefing for victims of road traffic accidents. *British Medical Journal, 313,* 1438–1439.

Hokanson, M. (1997). *Evaluation of the effectiveness of the Critical Incident Stress Management program for the Los Angeles County Fire Department*. Paper presented at the 4th World Congress on Stress, Trauma, and Coping in the Emergency Services Professions, Baltimore, MD.

Horowitz, M., Wilner, N., & Alvarez, W. (1979). Impact of event scale: A measure of subjective distress. *Psychosomatic Medicine, 41,* 208–218.

Hull, A. (2001). Psychological debriefing: Theory, practice, and evidence [Book Review]. *The British Journal of Psychiatry, 179,* 564. Retrieved October 27, 2003, from http://bjp.rcpsych.org/cgi/content/full/179/6/564

Hytten, K., & Hasle, A. (1989). Firefighters: A study of stress and coping. *Acta Psychiatrica Scandinavica, 80* (Suppl. 335), 50–55.

Irby, D. (2001, December 19). *Red Cross relief going strong 100 days after attacks.* [Chapter Information Bulletin]. Retrieved February 27, 2002, from https://corpweb.redcross.org/comm/ds/fy02/cib/121901.html

Jarero, I., & Artigas, L. (2002). *Traumatic stress after natural or human provoked disaster: The seven phase model: An approach for mental health interventions in disaster situations.* Mexico City: Asociacion Mexicana para Ayuda Mental en Crisis, A.C. [Mexican Association for Crisis Therapy].

Jenkins, S. R. (1996). Social support and debriefing efficacy among emergency medical workers after a mass shooting incident. *Journal of Social Behavior and Personality, 11,* 477–492.

Johnson, K. (1998). *Trauma in the lives of children: Crisis and stress management techniques for counselors, teachers, and other professionals.* Alameda, CA: Hunter House Books.

Kardiner, A., & Spiegel, H. (1947). *War, stress, and neurotic illness.* New York: Hoeber.

Kenardy, J. A., Webster, R. A., Lewin, T. J., Carr, B. J., Hazell, P., & Carter, G. L. (1996). Stress debriefing and patterns of recovery following a natural disaster. *Journal of Traumatic Stress, 9,* 37–49.

Lanning, J. K. S. (1987*). Post trauma recovery of public safety workers for the Delta 191 Crash: Debriefing, personal characteristics, and social systems.* Unpublished doctoral dissertation, University of Michigan, Ann Arbor, MI.

Lavender, T. W. (1998). Can midwives reduce postpartum psychological morbidity? *Birth, 25,* 215–219.

Lee, C., Slade, P., & Lygo, V. (1996). The influence of psychological debriefing on emotional adaptation in women following early miscarriage: A preliminary study. *British Journal of Medical Psychology, 69,* 47–58.

Leeman-Conley, M. (1990 April/May). After a violent robbery . . . *Criminology Australia,* 4–6.

Litz, B., Gray, M., Bryant, R., & Adler, A. (2002). Early interventions for trauma: Current status and future directions. *Clinical Psychology: Science and Practice, 9,* 112–134.

Manzi, L. A. (1995). *Evaluation of the on site academy's residential program.* Research investigation submitted to Boston College.

Matthews, L. R. (1998). Effect of staff debriefing on posttraumatic stress symptoms after assaults by community residents. *Psychiatric Services, 49,* 207–212.

Mayou, R. A., Ehlers, A., & Hobbs, M. (2000). Psychological debriefing for road traffic accident victims: Three-year follow up of a randomized controlled trial. *British Journal of Psychiatry, 176,* 589–593.

McFarlane, A. C. (1988). The longitudinal course of posttraumatic morbidity: The range of outcomes and their predictors. *The Journal of Nervous and Mental Disease, 176,* 30–39.

McNally, R. J., Bruant, R. A., & Ehlers, A. (2003). Does early psychological intervention promote recovery from posttraumatic stress? *Psychological Science in the Public Interest, 4,* 45–78.

Meehan, D. (1996). Critical Incident Stress Debriefing. *Navy Medicine, 35,* 4–7.

Mitchell, J. T. (1983). When disaster strikes. *Journal of Emergency Medical Services, 8,* 36–39.

Mitchell, J. T. (1984). The 600 run limit. *Journal of Emergency Medical Services.*

Mitchell, J. T. (1986). Critical Incident Stress Management. *Response,* 24–25.

Mitchell, J. T. (2003, February). *Crisis intervention and CISM: A research summary.* Ellicott City, MD: International Critical Incident Stress Foundation. Retrieved April 18, 2003, from http://www.icisf.org

Mitchell, J. T., & Bray, G. P. (1990). *Emergency services stress: Guidelines for preserving the health and careers of emergency services personnel.* Englewood Cliffs, NJ: Prentice Hall.

Mitchell, J. T., & Dyregrov, A. (1993). Traumatic stress in disaster workers and emergency personnel: Prevention and intervention. In J. P.Wilson & B. Raphael (Eds.), *International handbook of traumatic stress syndromes* (pp. 905–914). New York: Plenum Press.

Mitchell, J. T., & Everly, G. S., Jr. (1994). *Human elements training for emergency services, public safety, and disaster personnel.* Ellicott City, MD: Chevron.

Mitchell, J. T., & Everly, G. S., Jr., (1995). *Innovations in disaster and trauma psychology: Vol. 1. Applications in emergency services and disaster response.* Ellicott City, MD: Chevron.

Mitchell, J. T., & Everly, G. S., Jr. (1996). *Critical Incident Stress Debriefing: An Operations manual for the prevention of traumatic stress among emergency service and disaster workers.* Ellicott City, MD: Chevron.

Mitchell, J. T., & Everly, G. S., Jr. (1997a). *Innovations in disaster and trauma psychology: Vol. 2. A new era and standard of care in crisis intervention.* Ellicott City, MD: Chevron.

Mitchell, J. T., & Everly, G. S., Jr. (1997b). *Critical Incident Stress Debriefing: An operations manual for the prevention of traumatic stress among emergency services and disaster workers.* Elicott City, MD: Chevron.

Michell, J. T., & Everly, G. S., Jr. (1998a). *Critical Incident Stress Management: The basic course workbook* (2nd ed.). Ellicott City, MD: International Critical Incident Stress Foundation.

Mitchell, J. T., & Everly, G. S., Jr. (1998b). Critical Incident Stress Management: A new era in crisis intervention. *Traumatic Stress Points, 12*(4), 6–11.

Michell, J. T., & Everly, G. S., Jr. (2001). *Critical Incident Stress Management: The basic course workbook* (3rd ed.). Ellicott City, MD: International Critical Incident Stress Foundation.

Mitchell, J. T., Schiller, G., Eyler, V. E., & Everly, G. S., Jr. (1999). Community crisis intervention: The Coldenham tragedy revisited. *International Journal of Emergency Mental Health, 1,* 227–236.

Mullen, B. (1989). *Advanced BASIC meta-analysis.* Hillsdale, NJ: Erlbaum.

Myers, D. (1985). Role simplification in disaster: A response. In *Role stressors and supports for emergency workers.* (DHHS Publication No. ADM 85-1408) (pp. 38–47). Washington, DC: U.S. Government Printing Office.

Myers, D. (1992). *Hurricane Andrew disaster field office stress management program: After action report.* Miami, FL: Federal Emergency Management Agency.

Myers, D. (1993a). *After action report: Disaster stress management consultant: 1993 California winter storms.* Pasadena, CA: California Department of Mental Health.

Myers, D. (1993b). Taking care of personnel (Contributor). *Earthquake Recovery: A survival manual for local government.* Oakland, CA: California Governor's Office of Emergency Services.

Myers, D. (1993c). *Disaster worker stress management: Planning and training issues.* Washington, DC: Federal Emergency Management Agency and Center for Mental Health Services.

Myers, D. (1994a). *A stress management program for FEMA disaster workers: Program description, operational guidelines, and training plan.* Washington, DC: Federal Emergency Management Agency and Center for Mental Health Services.

Myers, D. (1994b). *Disaster response and recovery: A handbook for mental health professionals.* Rockville, MD: Center for Mental Health Services.

Myers, D. (1995). Worker stress in long-term disaster recovery efforts. In G. S. Everly, Jr., & J. T. Mitchell (Eds.), *Innovations in disaster and trauma psychology: Vol. 1. Applications in emergency service and disaster work* (pp. 158–191). Ellicott City, MD: Chevron.

Myers, D. (1999). Four-step guide lecture notes and training activities. Unpublished material.

Myers, D. (2000). *Disaster mental health: A review of key concepts.* Unpublished training manual. County of San Mateo, CA: Mental Health Services Division.

Myers, D. (2003a). *Key concepts of disaster mental health.* Unpublished training manual. City and County of San Francisco: Division of Mental Health and Substance Abuse.

Myers, D. (2003b). Psychological impacts of terrorist events. In *Criminal justice: Terrorism.* San Luis Obispo, CA: Governor's Office of Emergency Services, California Specialized Training Institute.

Myers, D. (2003c, February). *Psychology of terrorism: Issues and interventions.* Pre-Congress workshop presented at the 7th World Congress of the International Critical Incident Stress Foundation, Baltimore, MD.

Myers, D., O'Callahan, W., & Peuler, J. (1984). *Human response to disaster: Training human service workers* [Videotape]. Sacramento, CA: California Department of Mental Health, National Institute of Mental Health, and Federal Emergency Management Agency.

Myers, D., & Zunin, L. M. (1993a). *After action report: 1993 Florida winter storms disaster field office stress management program.* Tampa, FL: Federal Emergency Management Agency.

Myers, D., & Zunin, L. M. (1993b). *After action report: 1993 Midwest floods stress management program.* Kansas City, MO: Federal Emergency Management Agency.

Myers, D., & Zunin, L. M. (1994a). *Stress management program after action report: 1994 Northridge earthquake.* Pasadena, CA: Federal Emergency Management Agency and California Governor's Office of Emergency Services.

Myers, D., & Zunin, L. M. (1994b). *Stress management program for disaster workers: A National Cadre of Stress Management Personnel.* Training manual. Atlanta, GA: Federal Emergency Management Agency.

Myers, D., Zunin, H, & Zunin, L. M. (1990). Debriefing and grief: Easing the pain. *Today's Supervisor, 6*(12), 14–15.

National Association for Victim Assistance. (1987). Community Crisis Response Team training materials.

National Institute of Mental Health. (2002). *Mental health and mass violence: Evidence-based early psychological intervention for victims/survivors of mass violence. A workshop to reach consensus on best practices.* Washington, DC: Author.

North, C. S., Tivis, L., McMillen, J. C., Pfefferbaum, B., Cox, J., Spitznagel, E. L., et al. (2002). Coping, functioning, and adjustment of rescue workers after the Oklahoma City bombing. *Journal of Traumatic Stress, 15,* 171–175.

Nurmi, L. (1997). *Experienced stress and value of CISD among Finnish police officers (DVI) and emergency personnel in the Estonia ferry disaster.* Paper presented at the 4th World Congress on Stress, Trauma and Coping in the Emergency Services Professions, Baltimore, MD.

Nurmi, L. (1999). The sinking of the *Estonia:* The effects of Critical Incident Stress Debriefing on rescuers. *International Journal of Emergency Mental Health, 1,* 23–32.

Olsen, O. Middleton, P., Ezzo, J., Gotzsche, P. C., Hadhazy, V., Herxheimer, A., et al. (2001). Quality of Cochrane reviews: Assessment of a sample from 1998. *British Medical Journal, 323,* 829–832.

Ormerod, J. (2002). Current research into the effectiveness of debriefing. In The British Psychological Society (Ed.), *Psychological Debriefing: Professional Practice Board Working Party.* Leicester, UK: St. Andrews House.

Ott, K., & Henry, P. (1997). *Critical Incident Stress Management at Goulburn correctional center: A report.* Goulburn, New South Wales, Australia: New South Wales Department of Corrective Services.

Pennebaker, J., & Susman, J. (1988). Disclosure of traumas and psychosomatic processes. *Social Science and Medicine, 26,* 327–332.

Raphael, B. (1986). *When disaster strikes.* New York: Basic Books.

Raphael, B. (2000). Conclusion: Debriefing—science, belief, and wisdom. In B. Raphael, & J. P. Wilson, (Eds.), *Psychological debriefing: Theory, practice, and evidence*. Cambridge, UK: Cambridge University Press.

Raphael, B., & Wilson, J. P. (2000). *Psychological debriefing: Theory, practice, and evidence*. Cambridge, UK: Cambridge University Press.

Raphael, B., Wilson, J., Meldrum, L., & McFarlane, A. C. (1996). Acute preventive interventions. In B. A. van der Kolk, A. C. McFarlane, & L. Weisaeth (Eds.), *Traumatic stress: The effects of overwhelming experience on mind, body, and society*. (pp. 467–477). New York: Guilford.

Richards, D. (2001). A field study of Critical Incident Stress Debriefing versus Critical Incident Stress Management. *Journal of Mental Health, 10,* 351–362.

Richman, M. (1998). *The Impact of critical incidents and the value of Critical Incident Stress Debriefing*. Hobart, Tasmania, Australia: The Tasmanian Emergency Services Critical Incident Stress Management Program.

Robinson, R. C. (1994). *Follow-up study of health and stress in ambulance services, Victoria, Australia: Part I*. Melbourne, Australia: Victorian Ambulance Crisis Counseling Unit.

Robinson, R. C., & Mitchell, J. T. (1993). Evaluation of psychological debriefings. *Journal of Traumatic Stress, 6,* 367–382.

Robinson, R. C., & Mitchell, J. T. (1995). Getting some balance back into the debriefing debate. *The Bulletin of the Australian Psychological Society, 17,* 5–10.

Robinson, R., Mitchell, J., & Murdoch, P. (1995). The debate of psychological debriefings. *Australasian Journal of Emergency Care, 2,* 6–7.

Rogers, O. W. (1992). *An examination of Critical Incident Stress Debriefing for emergency services providers: A quasi experimental field study*. Unpublished dissertation, University of Michigan, Ann Arbor, MI.

Rose, S., & Berwin, C. R., Andrews, B., & Kirk, M. (1999). A randomized controlled trial of individual psychological debriefing for victims of violent crime. *Psychological Medicine, 29,* 793–799.

Rose, S., & Bisson, J. (1998). Brief early psychological interventions following trauma: A systematic review of literature. *Journal of Traumatic Stress, 11,* 697–710.

Rose, S., Bisson, J., & Wessely, S. (2002). Psychological debriefing for preventing post traumatic stress disorder (PTSD). *The Cochrane Library,* Issue 1.

Rosensweig, M., & Vaslow, P. K. (1992). *Recommendations for reduction of stress among Federal Emergency Management Agency disaster workers*. Washington, DC: FEMA.

Salmon, T. W. (1919). War neuroses and their lesson. *New York Medical Journal, 109,* 993–994.

Salmon, J. L., & Sun, L. H. (2001, December 19). Victims at risk again: Counselors scramble to avert depression, suicides after September 11. *Washington Post*, p. A01. Retrieved February 25, 2002, from http://www.washingtonpost.com/ac2/wp-dyn/A62699-2001Dec18?language=printer

Searle, M. M., & Bisson, J. I. (1992). Psychological sequelae of friendly fire. *Proceedings of Military Psychiatry Conference: Stress, Psychiatry, and War, Paris*.

Shalev, A. Y. (2000). Stress management and debriefing: Historical concepts and present patterns. In B. Raphael & J. P. Wilson (Eds.), *Psychological debriefing: Theory, practice, and evidence* (pp. 17–31). Cambridge, UK: Cambridge University Press.

Shapiro, D., & Kunkler, J. (1990). *Psychological support for hospital staff initiated by clinical psychologists in the aftermath of the Hillsborough disaster*. Sheffield, UK: Sheffield Health Authority Mental Health Services Unit.

Sitterle, K. A. (1995). Mental health services at the compassion center: The Oklahoma City bombing. *National Center for Post-Traumatic Stress Disorder Clinical Quarterly, 5*(4), 20–23.

Sloan, P. (1988). Posttraumatic stress in survivors of an airplane crash-landing. *Journal of Traumatic Stress, 1,* 211–229.

Small, R., Lumley, J., Donohue, L., Potter, A., & Waldenstrom, U. (2000). Randomized controlled trial of midwife led debriefing to reduce maternal depression after operative childbirth. *British Medical Journal, 321,* 1043–1047.

Smith, C. L., Jr., & de Chesnay, M. (1994). Critical Incident Stress Debriefings for crisis management in post-traumatic stress disorders. *Medicine and Law, 13,* 185–191.

Stallard, P., & Law, F., (1993). Screening and psychological debriefing of adolescent survivors of life threatening events. *British Journal of Psychiatry, 163,* 660–665.

Sword, R. M., Myers, D., & Iona, C. C. (1992). *After action report: Stress management advisors, Hurricane Andrew.* Miami, FL: Federal Emergency Management Agency.

Teahen, P. R., & LaDue, L. R. (2000). *Mass fatalities incident response plan.* Cedar Rapids, IA: National Mass Fatality Institute.

Tehrani, N. (1995). An integrated response to trauma in three post office businesses. *Work and Stress, 19,* 380–393.

Tehrani, N. (1998). Debriefing: A safe way to defuse emotion. *The Therapist, 5,* 24–29.

Tehrani, N., Walpole, O., Berriman, J., & Reilly, J. (2001). A special courage: Dealing with the Paddington Rail Crash. *Occupational Medicine, 51,* 93–99.

Titchener, J. L. (1988). Clinical intervention after natural and technological disasters. In M. Lystad (Ed.), *Mental health response to mass emergencies: Theory and practice* (pp. 160–180). New York: Brunner/Mazel.

Turnbull, G. (1997). Hostage retrieval. *Journal of the Royal Society of Medicine, 90,* 478–483.

Turner, S. W., Thompson, J., & Rosser, R. M. (1993). The King's Cross fire: Early psychological response and implications for organizing a "phase-two" response. In J. P. Wilson & B. Raphael (Eds.), *International handbook of traumatic stress syndromes* (pp. 451–459). New York: Plenum.

Ursano, R. J., Fullerton, C. S., Vance, K., & Want, L. (2000). Debriefing: Its role in the spectrum of prevention and acute management of psychological trauma. In R. Raphael & J. P. Wilson (Eds.), *Psychological debriefing: Theory, practice, and evidence* (pp. 32–42). Cambridge, UK: Cambridge University Press.

van der Hart, O., Brown, P., & van der Kolk, B. (1989). Pierre Janet's treatment of post-traumatic stress. *Journal of Traumatic Stress, 2,* 379–396.

van Emmerik, A. A. P., Kamphuis, J. H., Hulsbosch, A. M., & Emmelkamp, P. M. G. (2002). Single session debriefing after psychological trauma: A meta-analysis. *Lancet, 360,* 766–771.

Wee, D. (1991 April). *San Francisco earthquake and other disasters: Research study of emergency workers at the Cypress structure collapse.* Paper presented at the 1st World Congress for Stress, Trauma, and Coping in the Emergency Services Professions, Baltimore.

Wee, D. (1994) Disasters: Impact on the law enforcement family. In J. T. Reese & E. Scrivner (Eds.), *Law enforcement family: Issues and answers.* Washington, DC: U.S. Department of Justice, Federal Bureau of Investigation.

Wee, D. (1995a). *Disaster mental health for citizen emergency response teams.* Berkeley, CA: Berkeley Office of Emergency Services.

Wee, D. (1995b). Research in CISM: Why do research? In *LIFE NET.* Ellicott City, MD: International Critical Incident Stress Foundation.

Wee, D. (1995c). Research in CISM: Part 2. Were they satisfied? In *LIFE NET.* Ellicott City, MD: International Critical Incident Stress Foundation.

Wee, D. (1996a). Research in CISM: Part 3. Did they change? In *LIFE NET.* Ellicott City, MD: International Critical Incident Stress Foundation.

Wee, D. (1996b). Research in CISM: Part 4. How effective is this? In *LIFE NET.* Ellicott City, MD: International Critical Incident Stress Foundation.

Wee, D. (1996c). Research in CISM: Part 5. What predicts EMT post civil disturbance stress response?" In *LIFE NET*. Ellicott City, MD: International Critical Incident Stress Foundation.

Wee, D. F., Mills, D. M., & Koehler, G. (1993). *Stress response of emergency medical services personnel following the Los Angeles civil disturbances.* Paper presented at the 3rd World Congress on Stress, Trauma and Coping in the Emergency Services Professions, Baltimore.

Wee, D. F., Mills, D. M., & Koelher, G. (1999). The effects of Critical Incident Stress Debriefing on emergency medical services personnel following the Los Angeles civil disturbance. *International Journal of Emergency Mental Health, 1,* 33–38.

Wee, D., & Myers, D. (1998). Disaster mental health: Impact on the Workers. In K. Johnson (Ed.), *Trauma in the lives of children.* Alameda, CA: Hunter House.

Wee, D., & Myers, D. (2003). Compassion satisfaction, compassion fatigue, and Critical incident stress management. *International Journal of Emergency Mental Health, 5,* 33–37.

Weisaeth, L. (1989). The stressors and post-traumatic stress syndrome after an industrial disaster. *Acta Psychiatrica Scandinavica, 80*(Suppl. 355), 25–27.

Wessely, S., Rose, S., & Bisson, J. (1998). A systematic review of brief psychological interventions (debriefing) for the treatment of immediate trauma related symptoms and the prevention of post traumatic stress disorder. *The Cochrane Library,* Issue 3. Oxford, UK: Update Softward.

Western Management Consultants. (1996). *The Medical Services Branch CISM evaluation report.* Vancouver, BC: Author.

Yalom, I. (1985). *Theory and Practice of Group Psychotherapy* (3rd. ed.). New York: Basic Books.

Young, B., H., Ford, J. D., Ruzek, J. I., Friedman, M. J., & Gusman, F. D. (1998). *Disaster mental health services: A guidebook for clinicians.* Menlo Park, CA, and White River Junction, VT: Department of Veterans Affairs.

Young, M. (1989). Crime, violence, and terrorism. In R. Gist & B. Lubin (Eds.), *Psychosocial aspects of disaster.* New York: Wiley.

Yule, W., & Udwin, O. (1991). Screening child survivors for post-traumatic stress disorders: Experiences from the *Jupiter* sinking. *British Journal of Clinical Psychology, 30,* 131–138.

6

SUPPORT GROUPS IN DISASTER MENTAL HEALTH PROGRAMS

INTRODUCTION

THIS CHAPTER PRESENTS SUPPORT GROUPS AS A PRIMARY SERVICE FOR DISASTER mental health programs. The chapter is based on key concepts that include normalization, universality, education, resource sharing, understanding of victims' reactions, recovery optimization, and reduction of later pathology. In this chapter, practitioners are guided through support group typologies, development of support groups, group design, group format, promotion of groups, and facilitation of support groups. Support groups that begin during the immediate-response period of disasters must transition to group formats consistent with the psychological and social needs that emerge during long-term disaster recovery. Support group tasks and interventions, and transformation of participants are key issues. Termination strategies must be developed for the support groups provided, during both immediate and long-term recovery.

Support groups for disaster survivors are one of the most powerful and effective interventions available to postdisaster crisis counselors. Support groups provide a positive, warm, supportive, and helping environment for disaster survivors during the lengthy, emotional, and stressful process of physical and psychological recovery. Disaster survivors benefit in many ways from participating in support groups. They experience that they are not alone in their reactions to disaster, they can receive and provide emotional support, and they can learn about helpful personal and community resources.

Disaster survivors are faced with the tasks of dealing with remembrance, loss, and mourning in relation to their disaster experiences. Support groups can recreate a sense of belonging, bear witness and affirm, and help to restore the survivors' humanity. Support group facilitators face the challenge of meeting the changing needs of the group over time. They must also ensure that the groups are culturally sensitive.

Support groups have been found to be useful following a wide range of disasters. Judy Herman (1992, p. 214) comments on the usefulness of support groups following human atrocities:

> Traumatic events destroy the sustaining bonds between individual and community. Those who have survived learn that their sense of self, of worth, of humanity, depends upon a feeling of connection to others. The solidarity of a group provides the strongest protection against terror and despair, and the strongest antidote to traumatic experience. Trauma isolates; the group re-creates a sense of belonging. Trauma shames and stigmatizes; the group bears witness and affirms. Trauma degrades the victim; the group exalts her. Trauma dehumanizes the victim; the group restores her humanity.

Support groups offer a means for healing following war by providing trauma victims with the opportunity to engage in active contact and therapeutic dialogue with other survivors as an important means of promoting their healing process (Gelsomino & Macky, 1988).

Support groups have been found to be useful following technological accidents, as reported by Handford, Martin, and Kales (1988):

> During the acute phase as well as during the period of recovery, group therapy approaches may be particularly useful. Here, members of the group may share suffering in common. Similar experiences and emotions are relived, intellectual understanding of the technological accident is fostered, and coping mechanisms are exchanged and strengthened. Members of such support groups may continue to be of help to one another even after formal therapy sessions have ended.

Following community-wide disasters, support groups help link people together. Utilization and promotion of networks of support can begin at this stage. Even within the early hours or the first few days, it may be very valuable to link victims together in neighborhood shelters or connect them with supportive groups of family, friends, or community members. Those who have been through the experience are likely to derive much benefit from sharing their emotions and perceptions of what has happened, and from talking through and interpreting events together (Raphael, 1986).

THE VALUE OF SUPPORT GROUPS

Numerous disaster handbooks and training manuals emphasize the importance and effectiveness of support groups in dealing with disaster (Myers, 1989, 1994a, 2000; Myers, Spofford, & Young, 1996; Young, Ford, Ruzek, Friedman, & Guzman, 1998). The Center for Mental Health Services (CMHS) (2000), in a report documenting best practices in the federally funded Crisis Counseling Assistance and Training Programs, cites numerous disaster recovery programs that testify to the strength of their support group programs.

One of the crisis counseling programs commended by CMHS was the City of Berkeley Fire Resource Center. Following the East Bay firestorm in 1991, support groups were funded by the Federal Emergency Management Agency (FEMA) crisis counseling program for community members of Oakland and Berkeley, California, impacted by the firestorm. The East Bay firestorm was the worst wildland–urban interface fire in the history of the United States. The fire killed 25 people and injured 237, destroyed 3,354 homes, 456 apartments, and left over 5,000 people homeless. Firestorm survivors were surveyed 15 months after the fire, and 205 survivors (i.e., 28% of the total number surveyed) responded to 739 mailed questionnaires. Persons who had participated in support groups were asked to evaluate their helpfulness. Of the 39 who reported participating in support groups, 36 evaluated the groups as helpful, with 19 of the 36 evaluating the groups as very helpful. Some of the favorable comments by group participants are given below:

> [It helped] to know that other people were having the same feelings that I was. And to be able to talk about the fire with people that experienced it in a similar way that I did.

> The support group did wonders for me, helping me cope with the stress and to communicate with my husband. After each meeting, we would spend 1 to 2 hr talking over fire-related issues and emotions.

> Thank you for offering support groups. I couldn't get into one early on because of work, meetings, classes, etc. But finally was able to join the last one.

SUPPORT GROUP KEY CONCEPTS AND CURATIVE FACTORS

Support groups provide participants with the opportunity to listen and be heard. The key concepts and factors that underlie the purpose and efficacy of support groups include the following:

1. *Catharsis and verbalization of trauma.* Mitchell and Everly (1997) describe that a supportive group provides a safe, structured environment for catharsis or ventilation of emotions, as well as for verbal reconstruction of the trauma. These are important elements in the therapeutic effect of support groups. Lang (1971) showed that expressing emotions lowers levels of arousal, and Pennebaker and Susman (1988) concluded that disclosure of traumatic events leads to reduced stress arousal and improved immune functioning. The group process gives individuals the opportunity not only to release emotions but also to verbally reconstruct and express specific traumas, fears, and regrets (Mitchell & Everly, 2001). Van der Hart, Brown and van der Kolk (1989) review the work of the master traumatologist Pierre Janet. Janet noted at the turn of the 20th century that the successful treatment of posttraumatic reactions was largely based upon the individual's ability to not just express feelings but also reconstruct and integrate the trauma using the verbally expressive medium (Mitchell & Everly, 1987). Pennebaker's work (Pennebaker, 1985; Pennebaker & Beall, 1986) confirms the critical role that verbal reconstruction and expression of the trauma play in the successful resolution of posttrauma syndromes. Pennebaker and Campbell (2000) found that individuals who did *not* talk about traumas were far more likely to suffer from health problems than people who had comparable experiences but talked about them—even when controlling for social support, age, gender, and so forth.

2. *Structure.* Disaster sweeps its victims into a maelstrom of loss, fear, suffering, and unanswered questions. The support group provides a consistent, safe, and enclosed environment that envelops the victims. By meeting at a stated time in a preagreed place with the same facilitators, and by following the same ground rules, the group provides predictability. Each group session has a beginning, middle, and end, superimposing boundaries in a time of chaos. In addition to the sense of safety that group members can attain within the group itself, other benefits may extend beyond the group environment. Borkovec, Wilkenson, Folensbee, and Lerman (1983) found that providing a structured environment within which to worry actually reduced the overall tendency for worry to contaminate or interfere with other activities.

3. *Education.* Support groups provide an opportunity to educate participants about the normal reactions of normal people to

abnormal events and the common psychological reactions that people have during the different phases of disaster recovery. The group enables facilitators to educate members in disaster mental health, and provides survivors with cognitive tools to help cope with their distress. To give one example, group facilitators provided information verbally and in writing concerning the common reactions survivors had to the first anniversary of the East Bay firestorm. The educational materials also provided information and suggestions about dealing with possible reactions, as well as sources of emotional support.

4. *Normalization.* Normalization of symptoms occurs as the educational process leads survivors to discover from each other and the facilitators that the cognitive, emotional, physical, and behavioral symptoms that they are experiencing—however distressing—are normal and usual reactions to a disaster. Symptoms such as difficulty in sleeping may be common to any type of disaster, but other symptoms may be specific to a particular type of disaster. For example, after the collapse of freeway structures in the 1989 Loma Prieta and the 1994 Northridge earthquakes, survivors developed a fear of stopping their cars under freeway overpasses. Support group facilitators provided information and reassurance that both types of symptoms (sleep problems and fear of freeway collapses) were normal reactions. Normalization of reactions occurs as support group members realize that their symptoms are not unusual.

5. *Universality.* Universality refers to the fact that survivors' reactions are not only *normal* but also so common as to be almost *universal.* The Loma Prieta earthquake support group members universally feared they would be injured or killed and expressed anxiety about the safety of loved ones they were not with at the time. Participants were relieved to find that others shared the same fears. Universality diminishes the myths of uniqueness and weakness within an individual (Yalom, 1985). Jones (1985) states, "There is real value, especially for young men, in understanding that others feel the same strong emotions under such circumstances, that each is not alone in the strength of his shock, grief, and anger" (p. 307). A disaster survivor might express universality as "I thought I was going crazy. Now I know I'm not the only one who's felt that way" (Scanlon-Schlipp & Levesque, 1981).

6. *Sharing of resources.* Discussion of available resources and exchange of useful information (Yalom, 1985) are important activities

in support groups. Sharing helps to overcome feelings of help-lessness, increases group cohesiveness, provides opportunities for giving and receiving, and assists in the practical aspects of recovery. Resources that can be shared include information about insurance procedures, experiences with architects and contractors, tips on handling the red tape of financial aid forms, and so forth, as well as information about any government, nonprofit, or grassroots organizations that can help. In the Loma Prieta and Northridge earthquake support groups, members often exchanged phone numbers and helped each other with transportation and commute problems by carpooling to work or in taking children to school.

7. *Group caring and social support.* An important healing factor intrinsic to the group format is the opportunity to derive a sense of group caring and support (Yalom, 1985). The communication and interaction give group members the knowledge that their thoughts, feelings, and experiences are being understood by group members and the facilitator.

Group members who have been traumatized experience disruption in their connections and relationships with others (Erikson, 1972). Disaster relocation and the exhausting activities involved in disaster recovery can also lead to disruption of personal relationships and support systems (Myers, 1994b). At the same time, research indicates that this social support may protect crisis survivors from both physical and mental disorders (Solomon, 1986). An important goal for the mental health professional is to assist in strengthening social ties and building new ones (Solomon; Raphael & Wilson, 1993). Support groups assist in this social support function.

Adding to the sense of isolation that disaster survivors experience is the fact that others have not had the same traumatic experience. Lindy has described this phenomenon as the "trauma membrane" (Lindy & Grace, 1986). The survivor community draws a boundary around itself to safeguard the traumatized members from harm and to promote psychic healing. Trauma comes with its own unique constellation of suffering that can only really be grasped by others who are similarly affected. Regardless of the capacity for empathy of the facilitators, only other survivors know just how they feel. The trauma membrane surrounds the survivors' vulnerable psychological surface. Like a newly developing membrane of an injured cell, the trauma membrane forms to guard the inner reparative process of the organism and protect it from noxious stimuli (Lindy & Grace). The support group environment becomes a safe place for its members. For instance, one of the East Bay firestorm support groups assisted a member who suffered a catastrophic setback while rebuilding her house. The support group members arranged to stay with her until she began to feel she could cope. The sense of being understood in this basic and profound way reduces isolation and is an essential ingredient of recovery. In the words of Seneca, Roman philosopher, political leader, and author of tragedies, "It is sweet to mingle tears with fears; griefs, where they wound in solitude, wound more deeply."

In addition to being cared for by the group, individual members derive satisfaction and a sense of purpose from being able to care for others. This altruism is another healing factor of support groups in trauma recovery (Scanlon-Schlipp & Levesque, 1981).

8. *Identification and guidance.* Disaster survivors resonate deeply with what other survivors are experiencing. The support group consists of *peers* who recognize the opportunity to learn from one another's experiences and to follow each other's examples (Scanlon-Schlipp & Levesque, 1981). The constructive coping of one group member often becomes a model of behavior for others (Yalom, 1985). Carkuff and Truax (1965) long ago demonstrated the value of lay support models. Peer support interventions offer unique advantages over traditional mental health services, especially when the peer group (consisting of disaster-affected persons) views itself as being unique or otherwise different from the general population (consisting of nondisaster-affected persons) (Mitchell & Everly, 2001).

9. *Prevention of pathology.* An intended function of support groups is the prevention or amelioration of possible disaster-related psychological morbidity and more severe impairments in functioning (Bradford, 1994 ; Dembert & Simmer, 2000) and in relationships. Social support, education, stress management, connection to resources, and shoring up of coping capacity; all these assist in mitigating a pathological response to the disaster's stressors and losses.

10. *Recovery optimization.* Support groups link survivors and their families with resources to help them reestablish their predisaster level of functioning. Information about where to obtain assistance

from governmental and nongovernmental programs, temporary housing, taxes, insurance, building codes, rebuilding, health maintenance, helping children cope, impact of disasters on families and couples, and a similar aids can assist survivors in approximating their level of normal daily functioning as soon as possible.

11. *Hope.* As individuals in the group move forward through the recovery process, they begin to feel glimmers of hope that they can go on and that they will reach a new and livable state of normalcy. Scanlon-Schlipp and Levesque (1981) point out that seeing others get better and move forward also gives group members hope.

A support group was provided for family members who lost loved ones in the crash of USAir Flight 427 near Pittsburgh, PA, in 1994. Around the 12th week after the crash, group members first began showing signs of hope, talking of the future and indicating optimism that they would some day feel better (Dembert & Simmer, 2000).

After the bombing of the Alfred P. Murrah Federal Building in 1995, many types of support groups were quickly formed, coordinated by Project Heartland. Two of the groups were provided for U.S. Housing and Urban Development workers and Social Security Administration workers who survived the blast despite being in the building. The groups were conceptualized as going through initial, middle, and later phases. During the later phase, a refined progression of existential awareness led to the realization that a survivor could begin to rebuild a life, and that the group did have a vested interest in caring for the welfare of the individual members. Group members came to realize that while there was no returning to life as it was before the bombing, each member aspired to reach a "new normal" day-to-day life over time (Dembert & Simmer, 2000).

TYPES OF SUPPORT GROUPS

Four types of support groups can be developed to provide participants with a therapeutic group environment: *Support groups led by group facilitators* have the primary function of ventilation, psychological education, and emotional support. Peer-led *self-help groups* help survivors to reestablish their sense of control by providing mutual support, addressing practical postdisaster problems, and developing action plans regarding common concerns (Young et al., 1998). *Topic groups*, organized around recovery topics or issues, may be led by group facilitators or specialists in certain aspects of disaster recovery (e.g., building codes). They may meet once or twice and provide education, group interaction, networking, and support. *Event groups* are large events bringing together groups of disaster survivors to deal with specific recovery phase issues, topics, or community events. The event group allows for informal group interaction, support, and networking.

These different types of groups are designed to meet similar objectives while recognizing varying needs that are often specific to the particular phase of disaster recovery.

FACILITATOR-LED SUPPORT GROUPS

Support groups that are led by a group facilitator can be time limited or ongoing and are often organized around disaster survivor needs or identity. Following the East Bay firestorms in Berkeley, CA, groups included a neighborhood women's group, a couples' group for couples who were dealing with the destruction of their homes, and a teen group for young people enrolled in the local high school. Each group provided a safe, warm, and supportive place to talk about their postdisaster experiences and challenges. A women's group, single women's group, lesbian/gay/bisexual group, nurses group, and Holocaust survivors group were also formed, as disaster recovery needs unique to each group were discovered.

Support groups were also formed for children at the preschool, elementary, junior high and high school age level to provide opportunities for ventilation, psychological education, and emotional support. Support groups involving children are more activity-oriented for younger children and are more verbally oriented for older children (Johnson, 1998). An African American girls' group was developed, as well as a group for preteen girls that used doll making as a focus for building self-esteem and identity in the course of disaster recovery.

SELF-HELP GROUPS

The formation and activities of self-help groups can help survivors to reestablish their sense of control, direct their collective energy into mutual support, address practical postdisaster problems, and develop action plans to address common concerns (Young et al., 1998). These authors describe that self-help groups can serve to

- Provide emotional support, validation, and enhanced sense of community
- Facilitate information sharing
- Provide opportunities for participants to help others
- Provide an enhanced sense of personal control
- Increase political empowerment

Disaster mental health workers can support self-help group establishment and operation by providing consultation to groups, providing specialty knowledge (e.g., stress management), helping with access to resources, helping to publicize groups, helping groups to network, and accepting referrals for more intensive assessment or counseling of participants for whom the self-help group is not sufficient or appropriate. Disaster mental health workers should, however, take care to respect group autonomy and should avoid taking the leadership role. They should also be sure to refer to the group as a self-help group and avoid labeling it as a "mental health" group (Young et al., 1998).

TOPIC GROUPS

Topic groups are organized around specific disaster recovery topics. The topic group typically meets once, though additional meetings may be held for different groups of participants. The topic group allows for presentation of disaster recovery information, psychological education, group interaction, mutual support, networking, and support provided by the group facilitator. Topics for groups are developed through ongoing assessment of disaster survivor needs, and through interviews with key informants, disaster survivors, and support group facilitators. Topic groups that were conducted following the East Bay firestorm included How to Work with Architects and Contractors, Taxes Following Disasters, Dreams of Fire Survivors, Stress Management Training for Emergency Services Personnel, and a community-wide presentation on Disaster Mental Health. A topic group titled Wildfire Crisis Training was presented on wildland–urban interface fire prevention and suppression. In addition to fire prevention and fire fighting topics, the presentation included content on the normal reactions of normal people following disaster and a description of the coping strategies being used by disaster survivors to deal with disaster-related stress.

EVENT GROUPS

Event groups bring large numbers of disaster survivors together to address an entire community's needs and the time phase of disaster recovery or a particular topic or theme (e.g., children's recovery from disaster). The events are presented in community settings. The event group allows for presentation of disaster recovery information, psychological education, informal interaction, support, and networking. Crisis counselors who attend the event and circulate among the participants have opportunities to have therapeutic conversations with them.

The first anniversary of the disaster is an important time for disaster survivors, and is often a very strategic time to develop and provide event groups. A major event group following the East Bay firestorm was a disaster mental health conference that provided information, panel presentions, and workshops on disaster psychological reactions, the impact on specific populations, and mental health issues involved in providing mental health services to disaster survivors. Other event groups included first anniversary events, a children's art display and exhibit, and "Closing House" (when the disaster crisis counseling program ended).

Event groups often require 3 or more months to plan and implement, as opposed to topic groups that require much less time. Effective event groups require developing partnerships with other community agencies and groups that are planning events around the same time. Partnerships can be developed with schools, artist groups, emergency service organizations, and existing community agencies and organizations.

DEVELOPING SUPPORT GROUPS

A number of issues must be carefully considered in the development and implementation of culturally relevant and sensitive support groups. Some of the issues include evaluating the need for support groups in the community, choosing the group format that will be the most useful and effective, promoting the group, beginning the support group, facilitating the mature support group, evaluation of the group, and termination strategies.

EVALUATING THE NEED FOR SUPPORT GROUPS

Evaluating the need for support groups requires a very careful examination of the community impacted by the disaster. Included in this evaluation is a comprehensive understanding of the impact of the disaster on the community, main populations, and subpopulations. The impact of the disaster needs to be assessed in relation to physical damage, housing, disruption of essential services, and economic, social, educational, religious, cultural, and psychological effects. It must be determined if community members accept and feel comfortable with the idea of participating in support groups.

Assessment of the impact of disaster requires evaluating the spatial relationships of the disaster impact. People who died and their families, the injured and their families, persons who had pets that were killed or injured— all of them have to be identified. Persons whose houses were destroyed or damaged must be assessed, including the numbers of homeowners, renters, and predisaster homeless. It is also important to identify subpopulations with special needs such as children, older people, ethnic groups, persons with disabilities, and people with chronic mental illnesses (Speier, Thomas, Carter, DeWolfe, & Rubin, 1996). Other groups to assess include sexual minorities, various professionals such as nurses, artists, domestic workers, and therapists, persons who lost their jobs in the disaster, and other interest groups such as disaster response and recovery personnel, and persons with unique needs.

Also affecting the need for and type of support groups are such issues as the overall short-term and long-term impact of the disaster on the specific community and the extent and magnitude of damage, death, and injury experienced by community members (Herman, 1992).

The type of disaster and its inherent patterns often shape the nature, content, processes, and schedules of the support groups used in disaster recovery (Lystad, 1988). Dembert and Simmer (2000) describe particular issues in the formation and facilitation of relevant support groups in five types of disasters: natural disasters, accidental disasters (transportation and technological accidents are common), disasters caused by intent to harm others, business or industry disasters, and disasters that directly or indirectly traumatize children and adolescents.

DESIGNING SUPPORT GROUPS

In designing support groups, the following issues need to be considered:

- Target group definition
- Disaster-related needs assessment
- Cultural considerations
- Convenience of community location (in terms of physically accessibility and culturally acceptability to the target group, availability of public transit, parking and security, etc.)
- Convenience of meeting time
- Childcare and respite care for attendees

For example, a support group for older adults who survived a disaster could meet an appropriate at community location familiar to seniors, such as a church, senior center, or community center. Support groups for teenagers can be held following the school day, possibly at a school or teen center, or at parks and recreation facilities used by teenagers. Support groups for people who work daytime hours may meet in the early evening. Support groups for nurses or other round-the-clock shift workers may require special scheduling.

GROUP FORMAT

In deciding the format of the group, consideration must be given to the following five factors: drop-in versus pregroup screening, group promotion and recruitment of group members, membership requirements and qualifications

(Dembert & Simmer, 2000), duration and frequency of the group sessions and support group rules.

1. *Drop-in versus pregroup screening.* The drop-in type of support group format is often offered during the early phases of disasters when there is considerable disruption to housing, essential services, and daily routines. Drop-in type groups are usually single session and require more staffing to provide individual crisis counseling to those who are unable to participate in the group processes or those who are disruptive. Pregroup screening prior to multisession support groups requires the development of an intake service that evaluates the needs of individuals, evaluates them in relation to the support group screening criteria, and provides information about the objectives of the group and about group rules. If the support group applicants have to wait for some time prior to the beginning of the support group, a service plan should be developed to support the applicants with services focused on their disaster-related needs.

2. *Group promotion.* Promoting the group involves using the information obtained during needs assessment to advertise the group. Strategies may include developing flyers, contacting key persons and organizations in social networks, getting publicity through newspapers, radio, and television. Referrals from other disaster survivors as well as other from agencies, organizations and health care providers serving disaster survivors can also be used to promote the group.

3. *Membership requirements and qualifications.* The purpose and target population of the group determine membership requirements, which may include age, special needs, demographic considerations, and so forth.

4. *Duration and frequency of group meetings.* The life spans of groups can vary widely: We could have a single-session support group, or a time-limited support group, or even an ongoing group with no designated termination date. When the designated maximum number of members is attained, support group membership can be closed, with new members being taken in only when other members discontinue support group attendance. Another support group membership strategy is to conduct a support group that is closed for membership, but has periodic openings for new members every 2 or 3 months. The frequency of group meetings is usually once a week, but meetings may be more frequent in the early phase of disaster when more support is needed, and less frequent later in disaster recovery as group members become more self-sufficient.

5. *Group rules.* Support groups must have clear group rules in order to promote a safe, comfortable, positive, supportive, and sharing environment. Within such an environment, members can deal with such concerns as their disaster experiences, daily stresses, disaster recovery difficulties, and postrecovery adjustment. The support group rules focus on confidentiality, commitment to attend (including policies on cancellations, rescheduling, vacations, and late arrivals), commitment to talk about problems, and the importance of the group member providing an explanation and saying goodbye prior to dropping out.

FACILITATING SUPPORT GROUPS

The power and effectiveness of a support group stem from the role of the support group leader and the power of the group itself. Herman (1992) states that

> The trauma focused group requires active, engaged leadership. Leaders are responsible for defining the group task, creating a climate of safety, and ensuring that all group member are protected. The role of the group leader is emotionally demanding, because the group leader must set an example of bearing witness. She must demonstrate to the group members that she can hear their stories without becoming overwhelmed. Most group leaders discover that they are no more capable than anyone else of doing this alone. For this reason, shared leadership is advisable (p. 223).

The support group leader is responsible for providing a feeling of safety in the group, facilitating discussion of the management of stress-related symptoms, problem solving, and reviewing with support group members the daily tasks of self-care. The support group leader must also maintain the focus of the group, maintain group work in cognitive and educational as well as active and exploratory modes, engage in active listening, and provide leadership with direction, focus and structure. The support group leader must ensure that each participant has the opportunity to be heard, must provide support and validation to each group member, give encouragement to members to express their feelings, and manage countertransference.

Specific member needs may require specific facilitation skills. For example, Piper, McCallum, and Azim (1992) provide a good theoretical and clinical basis for incorporating loss and mourning into short-term groups. Paolercio (1993) thoroughly describes session-by-session issues in support groups. The facilitator must also know when and how to refer the seriously disturbed group member for urgent or emergent care, as well as know what to do if a group member dies by suicide, illness, or injury (Dembert & Simmer, 2000). The leader must also be aware of and acknowledge community or political events that may affect the group, as well as events such as holidays and anniversary dates of the disaster (Myers, 1994a). The group facilitator must also have an understanding of when documentation and reporting are mandatory for issues brought up in the group (Dembert & Simmer).

The skills and the empathy of the facilitator are vital factors in the success of a support group. However, the empathy that allows the leader to work so well with trauma victims can also put this person at risk for secondary traumatization:

> *Empathy is a major resource for trauma workers to help the traumatized.* Empathy is important in assessing the problem and formulating a treatment approach, because the perspectives of the clients—including the victim's family members—must be considered. Yet as noted earlier and throughout this volume (see Harris, chapter 5) from research on Secondary Traumatic Stress and Secondary Traumatic Stress Disorder we know that empathy is a key factor in the induction of traumatic material from the primary to the secondary victim. Thus the process of empathizing with a traumatized person helps us to understand the person's experience of being traumatized, but, in the process, we may be traumatized as well (Figley, 1986, p. 15).

Disaster support group facilitators must make certain that they debrief after group sessions. This may be done informally with colleagues, or may be done through regularly scheduled debriefings for the group facilitators. Self-care is especially important for professionals providing disaster mental services. The case example at the end of this chapter outlines some of the special needs of support group facilitators. A thorough discussion of approaches for the prevention of compassion fatigue is included in chapter 4.

CRITICAL INCIDENT STRESS DEBRIEFING FOR SUPPORT GROUPS

Support groups during the first months following disasters often use a critical incident stress debriefing model (Mitchell, 1983; Mitchell & Bray, 1990; Mitchell & Everly, 1996; Mitchell & Everly, 1997). Critical Incident Stress Debriefing (CISD) is a psychoeducational support group that has two main goals: mitigation of the impact of a traumatic event such as a disaster and acceleration of the normal recovery process. Key components of CISD include rapid intervention, stabilization of the situation, and mobilization of

personal and organizational resources. CISD also involves encouraging traumatized people to talk about the trauma event, education and normalization
of reactions, restoration of the social network, provision of practical stress
management information, and a return to normal functioning as soon as possible. The best time for CISD is between 24 and 72 hr after the disaster, but
the group may be held sooner or may be delayed, if the situation warrants.
CISD is only provided by a qualified team of mental health professionals,
working with peer support personnel if the group is being provided to emergency service professionals. Group sessions usually last between 2.5 and 3 hr
on the average, and are confidential. CISD is a seven-phase model, and
includes an introduction phase, fact phase, thought phase, reaction phase,
symptom phase, teaching phase, and a reentry phase. The topic of debriefing
groups in disaster is discussed in considerable depth in chapter 3 of this book.

THE MATURE SUPPORT GROUP

Members of support groups will initially need opportunities to share disaster
experiences, fears, and acute stress responses associated with the disaster
impact and the immediate aftermath. Over time, the initial acute stress
response will recede and be replaced by disaster-recovery-oriented stress.
The intervention model changes as the phase of disaster recovery and the
needs of group members change. During each phase of recovery, participants establish concrete trauma-related goals that they wish to accomplish.
An important aspect of disaster recovery groups is that the focus of the
group is on *disaster*, and not on the conflicts and differences among group
members. Focusing on issues other than those that are disaster-related
diverts the support group from its primary task.

The mature support group has seven areas of content around which the
group process centers: assistance in identification of and movement toward
recovery goals, remembrance, mourning, cognitive mastery, stress management, teaching and resource sharing, and follow-up. Herman (1992) points
out that mature support groups are also focused on the transition from
past-time orientation to present-time orientation and are goal-oriented. She
also points out that, with the passage of time (that has made the group
mature), the group has achieved homogeneous membership, closed boundaries, very high cohesiveness and low conflict tolerance. Support group
members will encounter stress in the areas of negotiating with bureaucracy,
financial problems, emotional challenges, time pressures, and physical
demands. Helpful interventions for members include problem solving,
communication, establishment of priorities, stress management, and providing
information on resources such as specialists and community organizations.

DESIRABLE PATTERNS OF INTERACTION

The interactions between group members and group leaders contributes to the power and effectiveness of support groups. Support group members share their stories, thoughts, feelings, goals, struggles, and accomplishments with each other. Successes, validation of experiences, and support from others with common experiences are uplifting and reaffirming to the support group member. Desirable patterns of support group interaction include sensitive and careful listening to what other group members say, communication of empathy between group members, and high levels of member to member interaction. It is desirable to have low levels of leader to coleader and leader to support group member interactions.

GROUP PROBLEMS

Problems can emerge in support groups because of issues with group structures, leadership, and group member behavior. The group members and leaders can identify support group problems that interfere with the group's ability to focus on its tasks. Problems can arise when clear rules are not communicated or maintained, resulting in an unsafe, negative or unsupportive group environment, or a group that is dominated by one or two members. The leadership must maintain the focus of the support group on disaster recovery, with high levels of member to member interaction. The group facilitator also must maintain a low-conflict environment. If support group members engage in problematic behavior in the group and disrupt the environment or task orientation of the support group, use of group normative pressure on the individuals followed by consultation with the support group leaders are indicated. In situations where a seriously disturbed group member is in a support group where other members are not seriously disturbed, individual attention during and after group sessions would be helpful.

Depending upon issues disclosed in the group (child abuse and neglect, for instance), the duty to warn victims of intended violence may become relevant depending upon the law in the particular state. Likewise, group facilitators may need to consider issues of involuntary treatment for group members who meet specific criteria defined by law (e.g., credible homicidal or suicidal risks).

TERMINATION

Termination of the support group requires preparing the participants. The process of preparing the participants must begin 1–2 months before the actual termination date of the group. The support group leader facilitates discussion of the support group members' accomplishments during the period the group was in session, as well as an assessment of each member's needs after the termination of the group. The group members are also given the time and opportunity to provide feedback to the group leader. An approach that has been successful in facilitating termination in disaster support groups is to ask group members to give an imaginary gift to each member of the group. This allows each group member to express their hopes and support to the other group members for the time after the group ends. Additional issues should be addressed within the group, including whether and how to continue individual relationships after the group terminates, the continuation of the group as a self-help group (Dembert & Simmer, 2000), and referrals to other resources. It is also possible under certain circumstances to facilitate the induction of new support group leaders if the original leaders must terminate their role with a group and if the group wishes to continue. It is also important to arrange for follow-up of individuals (or the group as a whole) when funding for the group ends, as in the case of a federal or local grant for a specific time period or for a specific number of sessions (Dembert & Simmer).

FUTURE SERVICES

Many of the disaster survivors who participated in the Loma Prieta earthquake and East Bay firestorm support groups have reported wanting support groups in the future. Of the emergency service workers responding to the Cypress Structure freeway collapse who responded to a mailed survey, 92% wanted psychological support services to be made available and 79% wanted debriefing groups to be provided in the event of future disasters (Wee, 1995a). For citizens who participated in earthquake support groups following the Loma Prieta earthquake (using a critical incident stress debriefing model) and who responded to a mailed questionnaire, 90% stated that it was important for services such as earthquake support groups to be made available in the future (Wee, 1995b). The following comments from some of these support group members illustrate the value these participants attached to the groups:

> I think the support groups are essential! While some died and some were injured, the emotional damage to our generation is immeasurable and crucial, and we are still living with the threat of "the big one" [to come].

> Most of the negative reactions (aside from severe mental health questions) on your questionnaire would have been marked "extremely" had I answered this the first month after the quake. I feel greatly

recovered and feel the group sessions especially influenced this recovery. Thank you.

Please continue support group in the event of another major earthquake. Thank you.

Thank you so much. Your newsletters, your support group, and the group facilitator guided me through the hardest time. I wish there was more time with the group formally but it's established enough that we will keep going for a while. There's so much to get done. I would have liked to partake in other things but it wasn't possible. I appreciated you offering me the chance. If I can be of help, call me.

The support group saved my life—and I don't say that lightly. I was suffering extreme posttraumatic stress and not understanding it until joining the group.

CASE EXAMPLE

The Ben Lomond Community Support Group
Reprinted from Final Report (Peuler, 1983)
Project COPE (Counseling Ordinary People in Emergency)
Santa Cruz, California
(Publication in the public domain)

Sunday, January 3, 1982, promised heavy rain along the coast of California. A significant downpour, perhaps three inches of rain, was expected. While people slept, the storm came ashore. Steep hills which range along much of the Santa Cruz County coastline lifted the warm moist air into the colder atmosphere where a massive condensation took place, dropping up to 20 inches of rain in some areas. The storm caused mudslides and flooding that took 22 lives in Santa Cruz County, severely damaging 3,000 homes and leaving over 100 families homeless. Project COPE evolved out of the mental health community's attempt to meet the psychological needs of the survivors of the disaster. The project was funded by the Federal Emergency Management Agency (FEMA) Crisis Counseling Assistance and Training Program.

An early priority of the project was to have victim support groups available immediately following the disaster. The goal was to provide a forum for residents to vent their feelings and problem-solve on issues related to their traumatic experiences in the storm. Three community support groups were offered in the mountainous area of Santa Cruz County. Locations were chosen on the basis of which parts of the county were most devastated during the disaster. Availability of the groups was publicized through the media. Flyers were distributed to churches, disaster relief centers, schools and parent groups, clubs and organizations, supermarkets and laundromats. Group facilitators made a commitment to continue these groups for as long as the group members expressed a need for them.

Reports from participants and facilitators indicated that, without question, the groups provided a valuable service to the disaster victims. For many, attendance at one to four meetings met their needs. For others, long-term participation in the support group played a critical role in the recovery process.

The Community Support Group in Ben Lomond began on February 2, 1982, four weeks after the storm brought a state of disaster to Santa Cruz County. The group continued to meet every week for two hours until several months past the one-year anniversary of the storm. Meetings were held in a public library building in the small town of Ben Lomond, near the site of the Love Creek mudslide that took the lives of 10 people. It was centrally located in a mountainous area of the county that was particularly devastated during the storm.

There was a core group of eight to ten participants, the majority of whom were women. The maximum attendance was 14 with average weekly attendance of between six and eight members. Group members included individuals who lost family members and neighbors, individuals who nearly lost their own lives, people who sustained major property damage, and others who experienced frightening experiences in the storm.

GROUP FORMAT

During the first 2 months, facilitators followed a similar format each week. This consisted of introductions in which each member told the others in the group where they were living and what happened to them during the disaster. The repetitions seemed necessary and helpful. The facilitators encouraged participants to get more in touch with the emotional content of the experience with each retelling of their stories. Active listening was an effective tool for supporting, validating and drawing out feelings of the participants. Sessions were characterized by an intensity of emotions and by the rapt attention that group members gave each other. Many noted that friends and family had quickly tired of hearing them talk about the storm and that a clear need was met in the group setting. They experienced a unique receptiveness and depth of understanding from other storm victims that they did not receive in most other relationships.

Closure in groups was effected by each member taking a turn at telling how it was for him or her to be in group that night. Participants inevitably expressed feelings of relief and gratitude that they had the opportunity to retell their stories. Facilitators noted that it was important to again emphasize the normalcy of their responses. Groups always ended with hugs. [One of the facilitators] noted that in the beginning she initiated this ritual by asking all group members to give *her* a hug. This simple and reassuring gesture tended to help members reestablish ego boundaries after the re-experiencing of intense emotions and gave physical expression to positive feelings generated by the sharing that had taken place in group.

As the group needs changed, the format was slightly altered. New members continued to be encouraged to go through the process of retelling their experiences. As the need to repeat the story diminished, participants used their turns to give updates on their situations, share information, or ask for help in problem solving. They often shared their frustrations, anxieties, and accomplishments. The focus shifted to preparedness for the winter—evacuation plans, how to feel safe and regain a sense of control.

THE ROLE OF THE FACILITATOR

At each meeting with new participants, facilitators identified themselves and their function in the group. It seemed reassuring to members to have experienced group leaders who were able to provide direction to the group— to have someone in charge. Similarly, providing some structure to groups seemed helpful and reassuring. Co-facilitators perceived their role as that of providing information, support, encouragement, and reassurance. One facilitator noted that her mental health background served to give credibility to her reassurances. She felt that to foster the empowerment of the group and the individuals in the group was a key function of the facilitator. She found that asking questions that projected group members toward a positive future was helpful (e.g., What do you want to have happen? What is the best possible outcome?). Dependence on group facilitators was avoided by strongly reinforcing peer support of members during group and outside of group. Many participants exchanged phone numbers and contacted each other when they felt the need for additional support.

The need for good self-care on the part of the facilitator has been emphasized. [One facilitator] noted that she could not have been adequately prepared, prior to the first meeting, for the tragic and gruesome stories she heard from the group members. It was necessary for her to vent and to take advantage of debriefing sessions in order to be fully available to group participants each week.

DISASTER RECOVERY AS A GRIEF PROCESS

One facilitator observed that there is a need to grieve losses of home and property much as there is a need to grieve the loss of a loved one. Some similarities exist between the psychological reactions to death and dying as outlined by Kubler-Ross and those experienced by disaster victims.

Denial was evident in many group members during the first two months. Many exhibited a kind of euphoria and were just thankful that they were alive. It took time before the full impact of their losses set in. It is noted that the denial seemed a healthy and necessary psychological protection against becoming overwhelmed by their experiences. Anger, directed toward governmental agencies, mortgage companies, toward God, etc., was experienced by most victims at some point. It served as a mobilizing force for many. The bargaining phase was exemplified by struggles with the institutions that held their financial futures in the balance. Bargaining came in a very concrete, rather than symbolic, form. Most disaster victims experienced some form of depression, and most often became stuck in this phase. The depression was often precipitated by a sense of having lost in the bargaining process. Six months following the disaster, depression was the most prevalent emotion in group members.

At the time the crisis counseling project ended, all group members had not yet experienced the closure that comes with acceptance. For those who did, it was represented by a reconciliation with the fact that they suffered unexpected and undeserved misfortune. There was a sense of being able to start "putting to rest" their trauma and to start getting on with their lives. For some, this happened when putting a payment down on a new home. For others, it involved an assessment of lessons learned and a recognition that they did have the strength and inner resources to help survive their disaster experiences. Many group members stated that the group experience played a key role in their reestablishing self-esteem and re-asserting a sense of power in their own lives.

For many group members, the recovery process would be ongoing for many years to come. Many said that getting through the next winter's rainy season was a major hurdle. They found that the anniversary date of the storm evoked strong feelings of grief as well as introspection. For some, it brought a sense of relief that they had gotten through that first year. The commitment to continue the group through the anniversary date and beyond ensured a solid source of support and reassurance as they moved toward resolution.

THE VALUE OF THE GROUP EXPERIENCE

The support groups offered unique value to disaster victims. Hearing each other express thoughts and feelings that they feared were "crazy" helped to normalize their own experiences in a way that reassurance from a non-victim could not have done. The deep sense of emotional isolation that is common following an extraordinary experience was, at least, partially dispelled for group participants. The mutual support and information sharing regarding common financial and legal problems arising from the disaster were invaluable. . . . The group meetings provided consistency and stability in a world that had been fragmented and irrevocably changed by the disaster. The group became "family."

Group members indicated that the presence of experienced and professional therapists was reassuring as they struggled with their fears and was helpful in keeping sessions focused and productive. The example of the Community Support Group in Ben Lomond would indicate that such groups could offer tremendous support to victims and speed up the process of recovering from a disaster. While the group began in response to an immediate crisis, it offered an experience with lasting transformative effects for many of the participants.

SPECIAL NEEDS OF COMMUNITY SUPPORT GROUP FACILITATORS

All of the facilitators involved in leading community support groups for extended periods of time agreed that their own special needs for self-care were an important aspect of the group process. While the group experience was a uniquely rewarding one, it was also a rigorous and difficult one in many ways. The intensity of emotions expressed was enervating at times. While other therapeutic groups often have one or two highly distressed individuals at any one time, all the participants in the recovery groups had just experienced life shattering trauma. Leaders expressed feelings of personal frustration that the problems faced by victims were as complex as they were. There were no simple solutions—they couldn't "fix things up" for group members. The fact that it was easy to identify with the victims, individuals who had been arbitrarily forced to suffer the consequences of a natural disaster, made it difficult to not take on the victims' grief. Because the usual "rules" and approaches to group therapy did not necessarily apply, total flexibility was demanded of group leaders. Because there was no financial compensation (for facilitators), a special type of commitment was required.

Facilitators agreed that it was essential for them to "debrief" after group sessions. This could be done informally with spouses and family members or with other professionals involved in disaster counseling who could provide support by empathetic listening. Co-facilitators provided mutual support to each other. It was also helpful for some to have phone contact and support initiated by Project COPE staff.

It is important to note that many of the same factors that made the groups demanding of the leaders' energies also contributed to making them a richly rewarding experience. Closeness and rapport with group participants was quickly established. There was a sense of playing a very special support role as victims moved toward recovery. Facilitators were an integral part of the "family."

All of the facilitators stated that their lives were enriched by the experience. All agreed with one facilitator's reflection that, for her, the impact of the intense and meaningful experience in the support group was in equal measure to that of the group members: "Their lives will never be the same—and neither will ours."

REFERENCES

Borkovec, T. D., Wilkenson, L., Folensbee, R., & Lerman, C. (1983). Stimulus control applications to the treatment of worry. *Behavioral Research and Therapy, 21,* 247–251.

Bradford, E. (1994). Support Groups. In D. Wee, *Support groups in crisis counseling programs: Training handout* (Vol. 1). Berkeley, CA: Project REBOUND, Northridge Earthquake Crisis Counseling Assistance and Training, Regular Services Program (FEMA 1008-DR-CA).

Carkhuff, R., & Truax, C. (1965). Lay mental health counseling. *Journal of Consulting Psychology, 29,* 426–431.

Center for Mental Health Services. (2000). *Crisis counseling assistance and training program: Best practices document.* Washington, DC: Author.

Dembert, M. L., & Simmer, E. D. (2000). When trauma affects a community: Group interventions and support after a disaster. In R. H. Klein & V. L. Schermer (Eds.), *Group psychotherapy for psychological trauma.* New York: Guilford.

Erikson, K. T. (1972). *Everything in its path: Destruction of community in the Buffalo Creek flood.* New York: Simon & Schuster.

Figley, C. R. (Ed.). (1995). *Compassion fatigue: Coping with secondary traumatic stress disorder in those who treat the traumatized.* New York: Brunner/Mazel.

Gelsomino, J., & Macky, D. W. (1988). Clinical intervention in emergencies: War-related events. In M. Lystad (Ed.), *Mental health response to mass emergencies: Theory and practice.* New York: Brunner/Mazel.

Handford, H. A., Martin, E. D., & Kales, J. D. (1988). Clinical intervention in emergencies: War-related events. In M. Lystad (Ed.), *Mental health response to mass emergencies: Theory and practice.* New York: Brunner/Mazel.

Herman, J. L. (1992). *Trauma and recovery.* New York: Basic Books.

Johnson, K. (1998). *Trauma in the lives of children.* Alameda, CA: Hunter House.

Jones, D. R. (1985). Secondary disaster victims. *American Journal of Psychiatry, 142,* 303–307.

Lang, P. (1971). The application of psychophysiological methods to the study of psychotherapy and behavior modification. In A. Bergin & S. Garfield (Eds.), *Handbook of psychotherapy and behavior change.* New York: Wiley.

Lindy, J. D., & Grace, M. (1986). The recovery environment: Continuing stressor versus a healing psychosocial space. In B. J. Sowder & M. Lystad (Eds.), *Disasters and mental health: Contemporary perspectives and innovations in services to disaster victims.* Washington, DC: American Psychiatric Press.

Lystad, M. (1988). Perspectives on human responses to mass emergencies. In M. Lystad (Ed.), *Mental health response to mass emergencies. Theory and practice* (pp. 22–51). New York: Brunner/Mazel.

Mitchell, J. T. (1983, January). When disaster strikes. *Journal of Emergency Medical Services, 8,* 36–39.

Mitchell, J. T., & Bray, G. P. (1990). *Emergency services stress: Guidelines for preserving the health and careers of emergency services personnel.* Englewood Cliffs, NJ: Prentice Hall.

Mitchell, J. T., & Everly, G. S., Jr. (1996). *Critical Incident Stress Debriefing: An operations manual for the prevention of traumatic stress among emergency service and disaster workers.* Ellicott City, MD: Chevron.

Mitchell, J. T., & Everly, G. S., Jr. (1997). *Innovations in disaster and trauma psychology: Vol. 2. A new era and standard of care in crisis intervention.* Ellicott City, MD: Chevron.

Mitchell, J. T., & Everly, G. S., Jr. (2001). *Critical Incident Stress Management: The basic course workbook* (3rd ed.). Ellicott City, MD: International Critical Incident Stress Foundation.

Myers, D. (1989). *Training manual: Disaster mental health.* Unpublished training manual. Sacramento, CA: California Department of Mental Health.

Myers, D. (1994a). *Disaster response and recovery: A handbook for mental health professionals.* (DHHS Publication No. SMA 94-3010). Washington, DC: U.S. Government Printing Office.

Myers, D. (1994b). Psychological recovery from disaster: Key concepts for delivery of mental health services. *National Center for Posttraumatic Stress Disorder Clinical Quarterly, 4*(2), 1–5.

Myers, D. (2000). *Disaster mental health: A review of key concepts.* Unpublished training manual. County of San Mateo, CA: Mental Health Services Division.

Myers, D., Spofford, P., & Young, B. (1996). *Responding to traumatic events: A training manual.* Unpublished training manual. Pacific Grove, CA: National Disaster Mental Health Consultants.

Paolercio, M. (1993). *We're still quakin'. . .* Hayward, CA: Theodon Books. (Available only through the author at 568 Prentiss Street, San Francisco, CA 94110)

Pennebaker, J. W. (1985). Traumatic experience and psychosomatic disease. *Canadian Psychologist, 26,* 82–95.

Pennebaker, J. W., & Beall, S. (1986). Confronting a traumatic event. *Journal of Abnormal Psychology, 95,* 274–281.

Pennebaker, J. W., & Campbell, R. S. (2000). The effects of writing about traumatic experience. *National Center for Post-Traumatic Stress Disorder Clinical Quarterly, 9,* 17–21.

Pennebaker, J. W., & Susman, J. (1988). Disclosure of traumas and psychosomatic processes. *Social Science and Medicine, 26,* 327–332.

Peuler, J., White, D., Ritter-Splain, S., Bellina, P., & Whiteneck, T. (1983). *Final report: Project COPE (Counseling Ordinary People in Emergency).* Santa Cruz, CA: County of Santa Cruz Community Mental Health Services.

Piper, W. E., McCallum, M., & Azim, H. F. A. (1992). *Adaptation to loss through short-term group psychotherapy.* New York: Guilford.

Raphael, B. (1986). *When disasters strike.* New York: Basic Books.

Raphael, B., & Wilson, J. P. (1993). Theoretical and intervention considerations in working with victims of disaster. In J. P. Wilson & B. Raphael (Eds.), *The international handbook of traumatic stress syndromes.* New York: Plenum.

Scanlon-Schlipp, A. M., & Levesque, J. (1981). Helping the patient cope with the sequelae of trauma through the self-help group approach. *The Journal of Trauma, 21,* 135–139.

Solomon, S. D. (1986). Mobilizing social support networks in times of disaster. In C. R. Figley (Ed.), *Trauma and its wake: Vol. 2. Traumatic stress theory, research, and intervention.* New York: Brunner/Mazel.

Speier, T., Thomas, M., Carter, N., DeWolfe, D., & Rubin, M. (1996). *Responding to the needs of people with serious and persistent mental illness in times of major disaster.* (DHHS Publication No. SMA 96-3077). Washington, DC: U.S. Government Printing Office.

Van der Hart, O., Brown, P., & van der Kolk, B. (1989). Pierre Janet's treatment of post-traumatic stress. *Journal of Traumatic Stress, 2,* 379–396.

Wee, D. F. (April 1991). *San Francisco Earthquake and other disasters: Research study of emergency workers at the Cypress Structure collapse.* Workshop presentation at the 1st World Congress for Stress, Trauma, and Coping in the Emergency Services Professions. International Critical Incident Stress Foundation, Baltimore.

Wee, D. F. (Fall, 1995a). Research in CISM: Why do research? In *LIFE NET.* Ellicott City, MD: International Critical Incident Stress Foundation.

Wee, D. F. (Winter, 1995b). Research in CISM: Part 2. Were they satisfied? In *LIFE NET.* Ellicott City, MD: International Critical Incident Stress Foundation.

Yalom, I. (1985). *Theory and practice of group psychotherapy* (3rd ed.). New York: Basic Books.

Young, B. H., Ford, J. D., Ruzek, J. I., Friedman, M. J., & Gusman, F. D. (1998). *Disaster mental health services: A guidebook for clinicians.* Menlo Park, CA and White River Junction, VT: Department of Veterans Affairs.

III
NEW ISSUES AND
CHALLENGES

Weapons of Mass Destruction and Terrorism: Mental Health Issues and Interventions

RESEARCH ON NATURAL AND HUMAN-CAUSED DISASTERS CLEARLY INDICATES that the psychological reactions following human-caused disasters, such as terrorism, are more frequent, more intense, and more prolonged than psychological reactions following natural disasters. The Institute of Medicine and National Research Council (1999) found that 5 years post-civilian terrorism attack, 30.7% of injured victims and 10.5% of uninjured victims suffered from PTSD. The same study found PTSD rates exceeding 40% in other civilian terrorist attacks. North et al. (1999) studied the psychiatric impact of the Oklahoma City bombing on 182 injured survivors of the direct blast. They found that 45% of the subjects had a postdisaster psychiatric disorder, with 34% having PTSD and 22% having major depression. Norris et al. (2002), in their review of 20 years of research on the mental health impacts of disaster, found mass violence to be the most disturbing type of disaster, with 67% of the population severely impaired compared to 39% who experienced technological disasters and 34% who experienced natural disasters.

The Federal Bureau of Investigation defines terrorism as "the unlawful use of force or violence against persons or property to intimidate or coerce a government, the civilian population, or any segment thereof, in furtherance of political or social objectives" (State of California, Governor's Office of Emergency Services, 2003). Terrorism intends as its primary goal to terrify, to accomplish a political or social or ideological goal through a violent act by the intentional creation of fear and disequilibrium, and perceived personal, community, or government vulnerability, demoralization, and helplessness. Types of terrorism may include chemical weapons such as nerve, blood, vesicant, and respiratory agents; biological weapons such as anthrax, smallpox, plague, and botulism; nuclear weapons and radioactive poisoning; explosive or incendiary devices; and cyberterrorism, such as computer intrusion, theft, erased files, altered websites, shutdowns, viruses, worms, and the like. We do not, however, call terrorist events "chemical-ism" or "poison-ism" or "disease-ism" or "radiation-ism" or "bomb-ism." We call them terrorism because these phenomena derive their power from their ability to psychologically injure, manipulate, and control the behavior of individuals and populations. While psychological trauma is a frequent side effect of other types of disaster, with terrorism, the infliction of psychological pain is the very purpose of the behavior (Flynn, 1998).

While chemical and biological weapons have been used throughout history, primarily in war (State of California, Governor's Office of Emergency Services, 1999, 2003), terrorist attacks using these weapons are relatively new phenomena (Hall, Norwood, Ursano, Fullerton, & Levinson, 2002). Weapons of mass destruction are commonly referred by the acronym CBRNE (chemical, biological, radiological, nuclear, and explosives) (Myers, 2003a).

Understanding the physical properties of weapons of mass destruction and how to respond to their physical effects is vital, but is not enough. In order to effectively understand, prevent, and respond to weapons of mass destruction and terrorism (WMD/T) events, we must understand the centrality of their psychological impact. Psychological conditions will need to be identified, stabilized, and treated. In addition, Holloway, Norwood, Fullerton, Engel, and Ursano (1997) emphasize that government and private agencies need to understand and incorporate social and behavioral impacts into bioterrorism planning. Not only will emergency care of medical and psychological casualties be necessary, but effective education and risk communication by community leaders with the general public will be necessary.

TERRORISM EVENT CHARACTERISTICS

Certain characteristics of disaster increase the magnitude and severity of psychological effects (Hartsough & Myers, 1985; Flynn, 1996). Terrorist events may include the following of these psychologically dangerous event characteristics (Myers, 2001; Myers, 2003a):

Lack of warning. Warning allows people to take psychological and physical protective action. A disaster that strikes without warning produces the maximum social and psychological disruption. In the United States, the general public has not been aware of the risk of WMD/T and was in no way prepared for the attacks of September 11, 2001, and the following anthrax attacks.

Lack of familiarity. Not knowing the type of event, types of agents involved, how to prepare, or how to respond can lead to community-wide feelings of helplessness, vulnerability, and disequilibrium.

For example, fire fighters in New York City had no precedent to warn them that the sudden intensity of the jet fuel fires would melt steel girders and bring the World Trade Center (WTC) buildings down. Likewise, postal authorities, mail handlers, local police, fire, emergency medical services, and public health professionals were initially scrambling for information on anthrax and how to handle real or hoax bioweapons events. At first, government officials and public health experts were not prepared for how to best inform and reassure an anxious public faced with a new and unfamiliar threat, and did almost everything wrong, according to psychologists and other researchers (Goode, 2001).

Weapons that cannot easily be seen or identified. Weapons such as chemical and biological agents are difficult to identify, and may result in fear of contamination and inability to protect oneself. Conventional weapons (e.g., explosive devises) have immediate, tangible consequences, while biological agents, for example, may be invisible.

A widespread perception that government response systems are not prepared. Such perception leads to anxiety and fear on the part of citizens. For example, as public health officials deliberated the appropriate course of preparedness for smallpox (i.e., to conduct mass vaccinations, or no vaccinations, or "ring" vaccinations of exposed persons in the event of an outbreak of smallpox) the anxiety of the general public rose dramatically as "experts" debated pros and cons on television and in the print media, giving the distinct impression that even the experts did not know what to do.

A sudden contrast of scene and an abrupt change in reality. These make an event all the more horrifying. September 11, 2001, was a peaceful fall day with people going to their jobs at the Pentagon and the World Trade Center, and suddenly the horrifying attacks occurred.

Serious threat to personal safety and security. Threats such as these can lead to immediate and long-term psychological symptoms for both citizens and responders.

Scope of destruction. The more injuries, deaths, damages, and spheres of life impacted (home, work, school), the greater the intensity and duration of psychological impact. The Oklahoma City bombing, the U.S. embassy bombings, the 1993 World Trade Center bombing, the bombing of the U.S.S. Cole, the attacks of September 11, 2001, and anthrax attacks that followed, and the 2003 bombings killing Americans in Saudi Arabia had devastating scopes of destruction. The defenselessness of the victims also increases the level of traumatic stress for terrorism victims (U.S. Department of Justice, 2000). Additional factors associated with a mass fatality terrorist attack include the difficulty of finding victim remains, identifying the victims, and, in some cases, the inability to return remains of victims to their families.

Mass fatalities. The large numbers of individuals killed increase the horror. For disaster response and recovery personnel, police investigators, and coroners and medical examiners, the large numbers of killed and missing increase the amount of time expended in body recovery and identification. Recovery of personal effects (wallets, pictures of family members, personal identification cards with pictures of the deceased, jewelry inscribed with messages from loved ones) can be difficult on personnel because of the high degree of identification with the victims and their families.

Exposure to gruesome or grotesque situations. These exposures increase psychological risk for survivors, rescuers, and those involved with body recovery and identification. In some situations, this exposure is of long duration. These stressors are particularly toxic for emergency personnel who are exposed to injuries, death, and bodies in protracted and difficult rescue and recovery efforts. Workers toiled for 16 days searching for bodies in Oklahoma City, and 37.5 weeks at ground zero following the 2001 World Trade Center attacks.

Intentional human causality. The perception that the events were caused deliberately results in complicated and intense emotions of anger, fear, distrust of fellow human beings, and difficulty making meaning out of the event. A premeditated act of purposeful infliction of harm to innocent people is incomprehensible to survivors. The moral justification assigned by perpetrators causes anger and outrage in survivors (Everly, Mitchell, Myers, & Mitchell, 2002). The world of human relationships is no longer benign and predictable. When war follows an act of terrorism, the reality of being at war results in additional confusion, horror, and fear.

Intensity of emotions and psychological reactions. Weapons of mass destruction and terrorist attacks are beyond the life experience of most people in the United States. In addition to being unprepared for the attacks, people are unprepared for the intensity of their emotions. Emotional reactions by survivors and responders are sudden, intense, severe, and profound (Wee, 2001). Emotional reactions can affect decision making and operations. People struggle as they confront difficult issues of anger, desire for justice, retribution, racial profiling, war, and the ethical and moral dilemmas involved with each.

High degree of uncertainty. Terrorist events leave in their wake a high degree of uncertainty regarding recurrence, additional damages, or potential future health effects. In the disaster literature, it is clear that these events are more psychologically traumatic than situations with more visible, immediate, and predictable outcomes. With terrorism, there is no "low point" at which the community and its leaders are reasonably sure the impact is "over" and further damages will not occur. Increased security measures at airports and government buildings are reminders to the public that a real threat exists and that they are vulnerable to additional attacks. The continued "war on terrorism" and United States' ongoing military involvement in Iraq, with daily losses of life, is another facet to the uncertainty—how long, how many more lives will be lost?

Additional uncertainty exists with regard to the long-term effects of terrorism attacks, especially upon future health. Three Mile Island's nuclear accident showed that the most significant long-term health effect was anxiety caused by the potential for long-term and unknown health effects. Experience with hazardous materials and environmental disasters such as Times Beach and Love Canal reinforces this concern—people who fear for the future effect of exposure on their own health or on future generations are at significantly increased psychological risk.

Lack of personal control and accurate information. Control is out of citizens' hands and is in the hands of the government and responders. An editorial cartoon in the *San Jose Mercury News* (Wright, 2001) shows a government worker in full personal protective equipment ("moonsuit") advising a family, "Go about your business, act normal. . . ." The cartoon illustrates the "mixed messages" about the threat of bioterrorism that the public received from the government in the early days of the crisis, resulting in doubt and anxiety among citizens. If the situation was dangerous enough for the responder to have protective gear, why was the public not provided with protective gear? Likewise, in the environment of uncertainty following the September 11 attacks and the anthrax attacks, people yearn for accurate, complete, and reassuring information from public officials. Such certainty and reassurance often is not possible in times of high risk and confusing and contradictory information. However, effective techniques of risk communication by public officials will go far in reducing public anxiety (see U.S. Department of Health and Human Services, 2002).

Immediate and long-term health problems. Health afflictions due to stress, illness, or injury increase psychological risk. The New York Methodist Hospital in Brooklyn found that they treated 35% more heart attacks than usual in the 60 days after the WTC attacks. They also found 40% more cases of serious arrhythmia (heart rhythm irregularities) in the same period. Both findings were attributed by the researchers to be the result of psychological or emotional stress, during which catecholamine levels rise, increasing heart rate and blood pressure, precipitating the heart attacks (Whitney, 2003). Injured survivors of terrorist events often face long-term medical care, pain, rehabilitation, multiple surgeries, loss of the ability to work, financial crisis, loss of dignity and self-esteem, and depression. Health officials are still uncertain about the possible toxicity of substances at ground zero, and are unsure what has caused the chronic lung problems, dubbed "World Trade Center cough," experienced by many of the firefighters who worked there (Union, "WTC Workers Suffering," 2001). Attacks using biological agents have protracted impacts and ongoing risks that are difficult to assess (Hall et al., 2002). Use of biological weapons can cause vulnerability, demoralization, and fear based on lack of information about the agents and their risk, as well as lack of confidence in the health care system's ability to manage a biological attack and its aftermath (Myers, 2003a). Psychological effects of bioterrorism may include fear of illness and its outcome; fear of contagion and therefore of other people; fear of premature death and horrific death (ebola); fear of disfigurement (smallpox); fear of quarantine and separation from family at time of illness or death; fear about dormant agents (e.g., anthrax spores) and enduring threat; and uncertainty and distrust about the effectiveness and safety of vaccination and treatments (Myers, 2003).

Environmental issues. Cleanup of terrorist-impacted buildings and neighborhoods can be compounded by contamination from hazardous materials preexisting in the target site or by contamination from the terrorist weapons themselves (chemical, biological, radiological, nuclear, or explosive weapons). Health impacts on direct victims, on response and recovery personnel, and on the environment itself, in the form of potentially enduring ecotoxicity, must be considered.

Disrupted social support systems. Social support is known to be an important mitigating factor in the impact of and recovery from trauma. Terrorist events may result in separation of loved ones due to hospitalized injuries or death; contagion and quarantine; disruption of relationships and of supportive communities impacted by terrorist attacks (neighborhoods, workplaces, and schools); loss of a sense of "place"; loss of trust in humankind; and often a personal crisis of faith and spirituality.

Impacts on family life. Almost every person who dies in a terrorist attack leaves behind family: a husband or wife, son or daughter, brother or sister, mother or father, lover, partner, or close friend. Countless children lose a parent or are orphaned; Sealey (2001) estimated the number at as great as 10,000 in the aftermath of the WTC attacks. The absence of that relationship is enduring and the grief is enormous. Stressors in the post-terrorist environment may also take its toll on family life, as seen in some of the statistics in the aftermath of the Oklahoma City bombing: a 25–30% increase in the divorce rate in the police department and a 300% increase in the divorce rate in the fire department (Oklahoma Department of Mental Health and Substance Abuse, 1998). In the aftermath of September 11, 2001, a sad if somewhat predictable dynamic has impacted some of the families of surviving firefighters. Following a long-standing fire department tradition, surviving firefighters become "liaisons" to families of their fallen comrades, assisting widows and their children with such diverse activities as managing finances, assisting with obtaining benefits, taking kids to ball games, helping with homework, shopping, and doing home repairs. It was reported by a top New York City Fire Department (FDNY) official at about the 2nd year anniversary of the attacks that as many as eight firefighters had left their wives for widows of firefighters who were killed in the attack (Jerome, Fowler, Cotliar, Herbst, & Haederle, 2003). Mental health professionals must be knowledgeable about the effects of PTSD, anxiety, depression, survivor guilt, and other posttraumatic effects on family systems, and must be proactive in providing education and consultation to organizations in the aftermath of these types of events. Special care and supervision should be given to peer counselors such as family liaisons. It is essential to ensure that their own emotional needs in the aftermath of the event are taken care of, that their own family system stays healthy in the aftermath, and to ensure against blurring of boundaries and overinvolvement with the families of their fallen comrades that they seek to help.

The long duration of the event and its aftermath. The sense of vulnerability and fearfulness may continue for a lifetime. Following the attacks of September 11, 2001, much discussion was in the news about the how long the "war on terrorism" would last. Similar uncertainty surrounds the U.S. military campaign and ensuing efforts in "rebuilding" Iraq.

Symbolism of the terrorist target. The attack on the Pentagon was an attack on a government office that is a symbol of power, stability, and control. The World Trade Center was a symbol of international finance and influence. Embassies were bombed because they are the symbols of the powers of state and international status. The attack on the U.S.S. Cole in Yemen was an attack on a destroyer. A key criterion in the selection of a terrorist target is its symbolic value. Terrorist events in public places give the profound symbolic message, "We can get you anywhere, at any time. There is no one who can protect you."

The other side of this coin is the importance of symbolism in the citizens' response to the attacks. After the attacks of September 11, 2001, American citizens responded by flying the flag; wearing flag pins and red, white, and blue ribbons; wearing the New York City Police Department (NYPD) and FDNY caps and T-shirts; newspapers printing political cartoons showing a firefighter and police officer as the "Twin Towers of New York"; and the donating of blood. These are examples of the patriotism, solidarity, and sense of community that flourished in the aftermath. It is important to note, however, that not everyone experienced the exhibition of patriotism in a positive way. Many people experienced anxiety and fear in its wake, fearing racial profiling, loss of civil liberties, and imprisonment and deportation of those who were not citizens.

A widespread community is affected. The impact of the attacks of September 11, 2001, was nationwide and international. People of all ages in all parts of the United States and the world had reactions to the attacks. Domestically, not only are crisis intervention and counseling services important but also informative, factual, and anxiety-reducing public relations and public education efforts, targeting virtually the entire community and nation. Parents, teachers, and childcare professionals need support and information about how to talk with children about the event. Psychosomatic symptoms to terrorism are widespread, and public health education is essential. Memorials and commemorations are necessary to help the community articulate and express its grief and to commemorate its losses, both at the time of the losses and as anniversaries of the events occur. Preparedness efforts for enduring threats and potential future attacks can raise public anxiety levels, resulting in chronic, pervasive uncertainty. Individuals and communities must find a balance between anxiety and preparedness, and resiliency and optimism, in order to go on with productive and fulfilling lives.

The impact on the community is not all negative and traumatic. The support of the entire nation for New York City, the Pentagon, and Pennsylvania in the aftermath of the September 11 attacks was evident in the heartfelt love demonstrated by letters, donations, and volunteers that poured into the stricken areas. Likewise, citizens of the affected areas poured out their appreciation and support for those who came to help. Altruism, heroism, prayers, and caring abounded. Such events can bring out the best in most human beings.

An example of such giving is seen in the following story. In 1867, the FDNY sent a state-of-the-art hose carriage to Columbia, South Carolina, which was devastated by fire at the end of the civil war. In 2001, 134 years later, the children of South Carolina raised the $354,000 necessary to buy a fire engine for the FDNY, carrying out a promise from Columbia to someday be able to repay the fire department of New York. In addition to losing 344 personnel, the FDNY lost 98 vehicles, including 19 pumpers and 15 ladder trucks (Sack, 2001).

Not all reactions to the attacks were sympathetic and supportive. Many anti-American groups both domestically and internationally reacted with jubilation to the attacks, further fueling the confusion, anger, and resolve of those impacted by the attacks.

Terrorism is a federal crime. Federal agencies are involved in the aftermath, specifically the Department of Homeland Security (DHS), under which umbrella the FBI is the lead response agency (for criminal investigation) and the Federal Emergency Management Agency (FEMA) is the lead consequence management agency (for long-term recovery). Under federal crime mandates, the dead must be identified for purposes of criminal investigation as well as to return bodies of the victims to family for burial or cremation according to their spiritual beliefs. Survivors and victims' families have rights and benefits, including financial assistance and access to other recovery services including counseling. The public and victims have the right to reasonable protection from further attack and from an invasion of privacy. Survivors and victims' families have to be notified of criminal proceedings so they can attend or testify. Because victims of terrorist attacks are often witnesses in criminal proceedings, they may be intimately involved in the trial over an extended period of time. This role can change the course of their recovery, and mental health support may be necessary to help victims in meeting this obligation.

A report from the U.S. Department of Justice (2000) states that "although victims of terrorism have much in common with other violent crime victims and with disaster victims, they appear to experience higher levels of distress that are in part due to the unique issues related to the traumatic elements, and often the magnitude, of these politically motivated events." The report suggests that specific issues related to the criminality of the event increase the level of traumatic stress for terrorism victims and present special challenges to victims and to the professionals charged with responding to them:

- The often extraordinary financial losses associated with the crime
- The intrusiveness of news coverage, especially repetitive broadcast of disturbing visual images
- Speculation about perpetrators, motivations, and the capacity of official agencies to have prevented the act
- The involvement of the criminal justice system, especially when the process is long and convoluted or when the trial is held in another region or country
- The difficulty in obtaining information about compensation, services, and the investigation when the event occurred outside U.S. boundaries
- The difficulty in identifying and taking into custody perpetrators, especially if the event occurred outside U.S. boundaries
- The difficulty in finding victim services and mental health professionals with experience and expertise in dealing with the issues and needs of terrorism victims.

It is essential that mental health professionals and agencies seek training and expertise in dealing with the issues and needs of terrorism victims. While the 1996 Nunn, Lugar, Domenici Act mandated the enhancement of domestic preparedness for weapons of mass destruction and terrorism, as of 2001 only 5% of federal WMD training courses included mental health-related topics. In addition, Hall and Norwood (2002) found that none of the 18 surveyed state mental health departments had developed response plans for psychological and behavioral consequence management for chemical and biological terrorism.

PSYCHOLOGICAL REACTIONS TO BE ANTICIPATED

Immediate reactions in the general public may include the following: shock, numbness, disbelief; fear, anxiety, and uncertainty; vulnerability and help-lessness; intrusive thoughts and flashbacks; grief; guilt; anger and resent-ment; suspicion of others; need for information; need to find loved ones; and the need to help. Severity of reactions may range from the adequately functioning but worried individuals to severe, incapacitating psychological distress and physical symptoms (Myers, 2003a).

Immediate reactions in responders may include the following: shock and disbelief; fear, grief, anger; an immediate action response; inability to "let down" or rest; physical stress symptoms (increased pulse, respiration, blood pressure, etc.); cognitive symptoms (memory, concentration, problem solving, making calculations, communication); identification with victims; role conflict regarding the needs of the public versus the needs of one's own family and regarding rescue work versus ongoing work responsibilities; and intense loyalty to fellow responders who died (Myers, 2003a).

Long-term reactions in both the public and responders may include grief and bereavement; fatigue and exhaustion; stress-induced physical illness; a search for meaning; spiritual crisis or strengthening of faith; posttraumatic stress dis-order; anxiety disorders; panic disorders; phobias; obsessive–compulsive disor-der; substance abuse; family and relationship problems; domestic violence; divorce; work and school problems; work disability and Workers' Compensation cases; early retirement; major depression; and suicide (Myers, 2003a).

Research from Oklahoma City suggests it may take months for indi-viduals to pass through the shock and denial stages and to begin to cope with the reality of their losses ("Behavioral Health Community," 2001), so reactions may, in some cases, be delayed.

Predictors for long-term problems include being close to the attacks, being injured, knowing someone who was killed or injured, or watching a great deal of media coverage. Also included are rescue workers who have to cope with their own feelings about the attacks, as well as the demands of the rescue mission ("What are the," 2001). In addition to these trauma exposure factors, other risk factors include prior exposure to traumatic events, presence of acute stress disorder in the month following exposure to the trauma, and peritraumatic dissociative symptoms (Litz, Gray, Bryant, & Adler, 2002; Bremner et al., 1992; Marmar, Weiss, Shchlenger, & Fairbank, 1994). Absence or disruption of the use of social supports (Litz et al.) and high degrees of psychophysiological arousal in the acute aftermath of trauma are also known to be associated with increased risk for chronic PTSD (Yehuda, McFarlane, & Shalev, 1998). Significant loss of resources (e.g., home, job, health, loved ones, financial security, sense of safety) is also considered a risk factor for enduring posttraumatic difficulties, and addressing these issues may be a necessary precondition to an individual's ability to benefit from psychological interventions (Litz et al.).

Reactions of children. Children's reactions may include fear and anxiety; fears about safety; fear of separation; clinging, crying, whining; sleep problems and nightmares; intrusive and fearful memories; irritability; confusion; depression; not wanting to go to school; decline in school performance; fighting and aggression; regression; physical symptoms (headache, stomachache); withdrawal; acting out and risk-taking (teens); seeking to understand what happened and why; and desire to participate in community recovery activities (DeWolfe, 2000; Myers, 2003b).

UNIQUE CHALLENGES TO MENTAL HEALTH PROFESSIONALS IN WEAPONS OF MASS DESTRUCTION AND TERRORIST EVENTS

With nuclear, biological, and chemical events, the *fear* of exposure to these agents can cause huge numbers of people to seek medical care. For example, as a result of the release of the deadly nerve agent sarin in the Tokyo subway in March, 1995, 11 people died, 1,000 people received medical treatment, and between 4,000–9,000 people who had no signs of exposure sought emergency care, believing they had been poisoned (Ohbu et al., 1997; State of California, Governor's Office of Emergency Services, 1999). This presents a ratio of nine psychological victims to every one physical victim, and a ratio as high as 750 psychological victims for every one death. One can also extrapolate from war experience to potential human behavior in terrorist attacks. Karsenty et al. (1991) studied Israeli casualties from Iraqi scud missile attacks between January and February 1991. Whereas more than 1,000 people sought emergency medical care, only 22% were actually injured in the missile explosions. The overwhelming majority, 78%, were behavioral and psychiatric casualties. Most presented with acute anxiety, with others suffering side effects of self-injection of atropine (the antidote for nerve agents), injuries acquired while running to safety, suffocation from incorrect use of gas masks, or acute myocardial infarction (heart attack) from physical or psychological stress.

Some unique and serious clinical challenges present themselves to mental health professionals in terrorist events involving chemical or biological agents. First, in addition to the typical posttraumatic stress reactions, there may likely be organic mental disorders caused by the exposure. Psychiatrists and psychiatric RNs will be key in assisting emergency medical staff in the mental status evaluations of persons who have been exposed to certain chemical or biological agents. Large-scale triage will be needed to differentiate those with psychiatric symptoms that are the result of anxiety from those with agent-induced psychiatric symptoms. Exposed or not, patients may present at emergency rooms with symptoms of tension, rapid heartbeat, increased respiration, nausea, muscle and joint aches, tremors, and headache—all of which could be caused by either exposure or fear of exposure. Medical facilities can easily be overwhelmed by the needs of people who have not actually been exposed (Hall et al., 2002). Patients run the risk of either delay in important therapy or administration of unnecessary medications, with potential serious side effects (DiGiovanni, 1999) unless triage of the physically ill from the psychologically distressed is addressed in the critical first steps of emergency care.

There may be geographic challenges to providing mental health services to victims of biological terrorism. For example, an infectious agent introduced into the ventilation system of an airport would involve large numbers of people who would not immediately know they were exposed and who would then disperse to geographically distant locations. This may result in the disease being spread to locations far afield, where healthcare settings may not have the expertise or resources to diagnose and treat the condition. This scenario psychologically robs the patient of various resources available in more typical disasters where the sense of shared adversity provides the important element of social support (Flynn, 1998).

With biological agents, there is the unique situation where the victim, now contagious, becomes a continuation of the weapon through his ability to pass on the disease. The social and peer support so vital to coping with trauma and loss will inevitably be undermined, if not destroyed, out of fear of contagion. We need only look at the historical treatment of plague victims, those with Hanson's disease, and people with HIV/AIDS to see the psychological and sociological devastation of people who are isolated and ostracized by their support systems, including the medical system (Flynn, 1998).

As with natural and technological disasters, but perhaps with greater magnitude, terrorism presents the challenge of providing mental health services over an extended span of time, as symptoms emerge in the first days and weeks, over ensuing months, years, and decades, and perhaps into future generations (Flynn, 1998). Planning for response to weapons of mass destruction must take these long-term needs into account.

Flynn (1998) also points out the administrative and fiscal challenges of responding to terrorism disasters. In the United States, there is a growing number of disaster mental health resources, including county mental health agencies, the American Red Cross, the Green Cross, the military, the Department of Veterans' Affairs, the National Disaster Medical System, and the FEMA-funded Crisis Counseling Program, administered through the Center for Mental Health Services in the Department of Health and Human Services. Each program has a slightly different focus, process for activation, operational guidelines, etc. It should be noted that there is a void in terms of well-planned and funded *long-term* disaster mental health services. The FEMA–CMHS Crisis Counseling Program has historically limited the use of FEMA funds to individuals with short-term needs. Local and state resources do not have the capacity to handle the long-term mental health needs of victims of catastrophic, mass-casualty disasters. Additional resources are needed in this area. Six years following the Oklahoma City bombing, the American Red Cross was still funding counseling services for over 50 clients (D.V. Hampton, personal communication, August 16, 2001). Careful planning needs to take place to anticipate how these services would be made available, financed, integrated, and coordinated in a variety of possible terrorist scenarios (Flynn, 1998). The mental health response to Oklahoma City and to the events of September 11, 2001, when evaluated in retrospect, will give mental health professionals valuable "lessons learned" regarding effective collaboration among resources.

Especially important in the event of WMD terrorist events is the accurate dissemination of information, which holds the potential for mitigation of mental health and health problems. A coordinated media strategy needs to be a top priority of all groups with policy, planning, and response responsibilities (Flynn, 1998). Risk communication, a scientific system of communication used in time of fear and anxiety, is a necessary skill for mental health and community leaders. Skillful risk communication can dispel rumor and misinformation, mitigate panic and anxiety, ensure appropriate individual and public self-protective behavior, and build trust and confidence (U.S. Department of Health and Human Services, 2002).

In summary, terrorism incidents will require that we think differently from other disasters about how, when, and where psychological sequelae will present themselves. It is essential that mental health be seamlessly integrated into other terrorism preparedness, response, and recovery efforts (Flynn, 1998).

PSYCHOLOGICAL IMPACT: OKLAHOMA CITY FEDERAL BUILDING BOMBING

On April 19, 1995, a terrorist bomb destroyed the Alfred P. Murrah Federal Building in Oklahoma City, killing 168 and wounding 853. The bomb detonation was felt 55 miles away and registered 6.0 on the Richter Scale (U.S. Department of Justice, 2000). It was the first mass-fatality incident of terrorism on U.S. soil. With it, the potential of modern terrorism struck home. In the words of former Senator Sam Nunn, "We are in a new era. The unthinkable is now a reality" (State of California, Governor's Office of Emergency Services, 1999). Preparing for acts of mass violence became an important priority for federal, state, and local officials, and ongoing efforts to develop comprehensive response plans among agencies began at all levels of government (U.S. Department of Justice, 2000). The terrorist attacks of September 11, 2001, proved that U.S. concerns were well grounded. As the United States moves forward with recovery efforts from the 2001 attacks and the subsequent bioterrorist anthrax attacks, the long-term mental health impact of the events is still unfolding. This section of the chapter will describe some of the mental health findings in the aftermath of the Oklahoma City bombing, and suggest some possible projected outcomes in the wake of September 11, 2001.

The following statistics define the physical impacts of the Oklahoma City bombing:

- 168 died, including 19 children.
- 853 were injured.
- 30 children were orphaned.
- 219 children lost one parent.
- 1,500 people were present within the injury perimeter.
- Over 16,744 people worked or resided in the area impacted by the bomb.
- 7,000 people were without a workplace.
- 800 buildings received damage ranging from major structural damage to broken windows.
- Nine structures, including the Federal Building, suffered partial collapse (FEMA, 1995, and Oklahoma City Public Works Department, 1995).

- Following the bombing, the Federal Building and 29 other damaged structures were demolished (Oklahoma City Fire Department, 1995).
- 80% of the schools within the Oklahoma City School District had children who had immediate family members injured or killed in the bombing.
- An estimated 387,000 people knew someone who was killed or injured.
- An estimated 190,000 people went to funerals.

As the statistics indicate, the number of deaths and extent of devastation from the bombing were extensive. Project Heartland was the FEMA Crisis Counseling Program that provided mental health services to survivors and disaster responders. Funded at $4,092,909, the program was allotted an unprecedented three-time extension. By the conclusion of the project, 8,898 individuals had been provided with counseling, support group, or crisis intervention services. This was a ratio of 53 mental health counseling contacts per death. Additional services were provided to 186,000 people (a ratio of approximately 1,000 mental health contacts per death). These services included contacts by outreach workers offering educational materials and information on services; debriefing sessions as part of workplace groups; education seminars on topics such as grief or traumatic stress; and trial-related supportive services (Oklahoma Department of Mental Health and Substance Abuse Services, 1998).

Despite the extensive array of free counseling services, a 1999 study by researchers at Washington University in St. Louis and the University of Oklahoma (North et al., 1999) of 182 survivors 6 months after the bombing found that almost half had a postdisaster psychiatric disorder. One third of the 182 (34%) had full-blown posttraumatic stress disorder, placing them at greater risk of suicide, substance abuse, depression, and other problems. They found that 45% of the subjects had a postdisaster psychiatric disorder, including 22% with major depression.

At 18 to 36 months after the bombing, Shariat, Mallonee, Kruger, Farmer, and North (1999) studied a larger group ($n = 494$) about a broader variety of outcomes. They found anxiety in 28% of the sample and depression in 27%. PTSD symptoms were highly prevalent, with 70% exhibiting startle responses, 60% with event-related distress, 56% with difficulty concentrating, and 49% with difficulty sleeping. Additionally, 31% had worsening of a preexisting medical condition, and 24% disclosed a worsening in their ability to carry out activities of daily living. Other researchers found additional, less severe effects that appeared to be disproportionately prevalent among adults (Smith, Christiansen, Vincent, & Hann, 1999) and children (Pfefferbaum et al., 2000) throughout the Oklahoma City metropolitan area.

The following statistics indicate the impact of the event on responders:

- 1 nurse responder died in rescue attempts.
- 1 reserve deputy sheriff died (a federal employee who escaped the building after the bombing, he reentered the building to assist with rescue and died in his efforts) (J. L. Norman, FBI case agent, personal communication, February 7, 2002).
- 85 responders were injured.
- 12,984 rescue workers and volunteers assisted.
- 115 law enforcement agencies (not including federal agencies) were involved.
- 57 fire departments were in service.
- 75 ambulance services assisted.
- 11 Urban Search and Rescue teams participated.
- Two thirds of responders reported handling bodies or body parts.
- One third of responders felt they were in much or extreme danger.
- Half of responders spent close to the majority of their time at the bomb site for 10 days.

It is clear from these numbers that the Oklahoma City bombing evoked a large-scale response involving multiple agencies from the local, state, and federal levels. Extensive research and experience with emergency personnel indicate that these helpers are exposed to stressors that can produce an array of psychological, social, and physical reactions and difficulties. This was particularly true in the painstaking, dangerous, and heartbreaking job of the rescue and recover workers in the Oklahoma City bombing (American Psychological Association [APA], 1997).

In response to the stress-related needs of rescue and recovery personnel, the Critical Incident Stress Management Network of Oklahoma (CISMNO) put in place a critical incident stress management (CISM) response that had access, cooperation, and endorsement from Incident Command. A CISM center was open 24 hr a day for the entire 17 days of the rescue and recovery effort. The Oklahoma City Fire Department and Police Department required postincident debriefing for all of their personnel. Over 6,500 individuals were defused, and approximately 250 debriefings for over 2,800 personnel were provided in the 5 months after the bombing (APA, 1997).

Despite CISM services from CISMNO and counseling and support services from Project Heartland, stress took a toll on both police and fire personnel. Family violence increased in both the police and fire departments. The police department experienced a 25–30% increase in divorce rate. The fire department experienced an astonishing 300% increase in divorce rate. Five suicides were documented among responders (Oklahoma Department of Mental Health and Substance Abuse Services, 1998).

In addition to emergency responders, mental health staff who counsel victims of disaster are at high risk for "compassion fatigue," or secondary traumatization. A study by Wee and Myers (2002) found that 65% of Project Heartland Crisis Counseling staff tested positive for PTSD while working in the mental health project. Additionally, 77% of Project Heartland Crisis Counseling staff tested at moderate to extremely high risk for burnout while working on the project. Clearly, prevention of secondary traumatization and burnout must be a high priority for mental health agencies and professionals responding to events of terrorism. Chapter 4 of this book discusses at length the prevention of compassion fatigue and burnout for disaster mental health professionals.

IMPACT OF THE SEPTEMBER 11, 2001, TERRORIST ATTACKS

The following statistics summarize some of the physical damages of the September 11, 2001, terrorist attacks:

- 23 NYPD officers killed at WTC.
- 343 FDNY personnel killed at WTC.
- 38 Port Authority Police of New York and New Jersey killed.
- Estimated 2,749 people killed at WTC, as of January 23, 2004 (Report: Final WTC death toll, 2004).
- As many as 10,000 children may have lost parents at WTC (Sealey, 2001).
- 92 people killed on American Airlines Flight 11 that struck WTC.
- 65 people killed on United Airlines Flight 175 that struck WTC.
- 64 people killed on American Airlines Flight 77 that struck Pentagon.
- 125 people killed in Pentagon.
- 44 people killed on United Airlines Flight 93 that crashed in Pennsylvania.
- 5 deaths due to anthrax attacks.
- 18 confirmed incidents of anthrax contamination.

Public officials and mental health leaders realized early on that mental health services would be needed not only for months but for years following the September 11 attacks. Nancy Anthony, executive director of the Oklahoma City Community Foundation, which operated a $40 million recovery fund for victims and rescue workers, said that 6 years after the bombing, the organization still had dozens of open cases, individuals who were still emotionally or physically disabled by the bombing. The Foundation and the Red Cross reported that the rescue workers were among the hardest hit but among the last to seek help (Salmon & Sun, 2001).

Using formulas derived by the federal government following the Oklahoma City bombing, the New York State Office of Mental Health estimated that as many as 1.5 million New Yorkers could need some kind of mental health help in the aftermath of September 11 (Sealey, 2001). Warned by the pattern that emerged after the Oklahoma City bombing, public officials and mental health leaders took a proactive approach to providing mental health services after the September 11 terrorist attacks (Salmon & Sun, 2001). FEMA awarded a Crisis Counseling Program grant of $132 million to New York State Office of Mental Health to provide immediate and intermediate-range services (up to 1 year) (FEMA, 2002). The resulting Crisis Counseling Program was named Project Liberty. The New York State Crime Victims Board provided nearly $6.5 million for the reimbursement of medical bills, personal property, or mental health counseling for injury victims of the WTC attack (FEMA, 2002). In Washington, DC, anyone who worked at the Pentagon was eligible for free counseling through Operation Solace. In New Jersey, Project Phoenix, funded by FEMA at $4.5 million, and Virginia's FEMA Crisis Counseling Project ($4.5 million) also provided free services. At the 1-year anniversary after the attacks, American Red Cross Disaster Mental Health Services had provided free mental health sessions to 238,280 victims of the attacks (American Red Cross, 2003). The American Red Cross in Greater New York trained approximately 1,000 mental health professionals in the private and nonprofit sectors on addressing the long-term mental health effects of the terrorism disaster (American Red Cross, 2001). In New York, the Red Cross also provided teams of disaster mental health workers 24 hr a day to help firefighters, police, emergency medical service (EMS), and other recovery workers at respite centers set up by the city near Ground Zero (Salmon & Sun, 2001).

In the first 5 months after the September 11 attacks, the toll of stress on emergency personnel in New York was clearly evident. The NYPD ordered all of their 40,000+ employees to attend half-day stress management educational sessions about the psychological distress they might experience. The FDNY required mandatory physical examinations for firefighters that included psychological assessments (Salmon & Sun, 2001). Nearly 2,000 firefighters, fire officers, and workers in the FDNY's EMS unit saw a counselor through the department's counseling services unit in the first 5 months after the attacks, tripling the number usually seen in one year. Of those in counseling, 100% were diagnosed with posttraumatic stress disorder or acute stress disorder, according to the counseling unit's director. The Department's counseling unit, which had 22 counselors and clinicians before the attacks, grew to five times that size in the months immediately following the attacks (Weissenstein, 2002), ultimately expanding its staff of licensed clinicians to more than 300 (Jerome et al., 2003). The 14,000-member FDNY said it had put about 350 people with stress-related problems on light duty or medical leave in the 5 months after September 11, more than the number lost in the twin towers' collapse. Additionally, 650 fire personnel were still on light duty or medical leave at the 5-month anniversary due to physical injuries—from respiratory ailments to broken bones. Some of those personnel also had symptoms of extreme stress (Weissenstein, 2002). The Department's counseling unit, with help from academic and government experts, developed an extensive survey to assess and track the psychological needs of the Department. Every member will be asked every 3 to 6 months to fill out a pages-long survey. The survey, which will continue for years, will be the largest-ever research survey on an emergency department's responses to trauma (Weissenstein, 2002). This methodical tracking of personnel will allow for assessment and treatment of ongoing or delayed reactions to the terrorist attacks. The findings will also contribute significantly to the knowledge and understanding of the long-term effects of large-scale terrorist events on responders. Meanwhile, the *New York Times* (Baker, 2002) reported that the FDNY continued to experience losses from the September 11 attacks in the form of early retirements. At the time of publication of the article, the retirement rate had doubled for both officers and firefighters, with 450 retirements, at the rate of 5.5 per day since the attacks, resulting in the loss of over 4,000 years of experience.

While there are, as yet, no long-term studies of the psychological effects of the September 11, 2001, attacks, a few studies have begun to emerge. An early study was conducted 3 to 5 days postattack by Schuster et al. (2001), interviewing 560 adults nationwide to assess reactions of people who were not present at the traumatic event. Using random-digit dialing, they interviewed a nationally representative sample of adults about their reactions, and their perceptions of their children's reactions, to the terrorist attacks. They found that 44% of the adults reported at least one substantial symptom of stress. Nearly 90% had one or more symptoms to at least some degree. The symptoms were found nationwide. In reporting how they coped, 98% said they talked to others, 90% turned to their religion, 60% participated in group activities, and 36% reported making donations.

Regarding children, 84% of parents said they or another adult in the household had talked for at least 1 hr to their children about the attacks. Nearly 34% said they limited their children's viewing of the attacks on television. Adults reported that 35% of children had one or more stress symptoms, and 47% of children were worried about safety issues. The study was important in validating for mental health service providers that the terrorist-related stress needs of citizens were, indeed, not limited to the directly attacked areas but were nationwide.

In another study, Galea et al. (2002) assessed the prevalence and correlates of acute PTSD and depression among residents of Manhattan 5 to 8 weeks after the attacks, using random-digit dialing to contact a sample of adults living south of 110th Street. Of the 1,008 adults sampled, 7.5% had symptoms consistent with a PTSD diagnosis and 9.7% had symptoms consistent with current depression (within the previous 30 days). South of Canal Street, near the World Trade Center, PTSD prevalence was 20%. The study found that predictors of PTSD were Hispanic ethnicity, two or more prior stressors, a panic attack during or shortly after the events, residence south of Canal Street, and loss of possessions due to the events. Predictors of depression were Hispanic ethnicity, two or more prior stressors, a panic attack, a low level of social support, the death of a friend or relative during the attacks, and loss of a job due to the attacks (Hall et al., 2002).

Schlenger et al. (2002) used a Web-based epidemiological survey of a nationally representative cross-sectional sample using a PTSD instrument to measure symptoms 1–2 months following the attacks. They sampled 2,273 adults in New York and Washington, DC metropolitan areas. They found they prevalence of PTSD to be significantly higher in New York (11.2%) than in Washington, DC (2.7%), other metropolitan areas (3.6%), and the rest of the country (4.0%). Over 60% of adults in New York City with children reported that one or more children were upset by the attacks. They concluded that the overall distress levels in the country were within normal ranges but that further research was necessary to document the course of symptoms and recovery among adults and to further specify the types and severity of distress in children.

In a longitudinal study conducted at 3 weeks, 2 months, and 6 months, Silver, Holman, McIntosh, Poulin, and Gil-Rivas (2002) found that 17% of the U.S. population outside New York City reported symptoms of post-traumatic stress at 2 months, with the level of symptomatology diminishing to 5.8% at 6 months.

In examining the impact of the attacks on substance use and abuse, the National Center on Addiction and Substance Abuse at Columbia University

(2002) found that 3 months postattack, there was a 10–12% increase in admissions to substance abuse treatment programs. The percentages were higher in New York City and Washington, DC. The *New York Times* ("More Drinking," 2002) reported that at 2 months postattack, there was a 25% increase in alcohol use, a 10% increase in tobacco use, and a 3% increase in marijuana use in New York City.

The long-term mental health effects of September 11, 2001, will not be known for some time. Likewise, the effectiveness of mental health services developed and provided in the aftermath will not be known for many years. However, based upon what is currently known about disaster mental health services, the "CODE-C" model of mental health response to disaster, discussed at length in chapter 3 of this book, can be used as a model for the range of services that will undoubtedly be needed.

CODE-C: A MODEL FOR MENTAL HEALTH RESPONSE TO TERRORISM

Mental health and behavioral science professionals have major roles to play in all aspects of planning and response to terrorism events. Before planning and implementing service delivery, a needs assessment must take into consideration the mental health issues and needs at the individual, group, family, organizational, situational, and community levels. Factors to be evaluated include disaster damages and losses, demographics, socioeconomic and cultural factors, and the needs of special populations, including disaster responders. Once needs are assessed, services can be delivered in the following categories, symbolized by the acronym CODE-C.

Consultation: Advice and collaboration with decision makers, managers, supervisors, community leaders, providers of recovery services, and survivors regarding mental health needs and issues, oriented toward reducing stress and enhancing the coping of individuals, families, organizations, and the community. Services might include:

- Pre-event consultation, collaboration, and planning among all mental health resources whose skills and services would be needed in the event of a WMD/T event (local, state, federal, government, private, and nonprofit) to ensure adequate and appropriate mental health response.
- Consultation to WMD/T response planners about the nature and number of psychological casualties to be expected. Experience indicates that we must be prepared for *large* numbers of psychological casualties and *long-term* (several years) need for services.

Example:

- 186,000 people were served by Project Heartland outreach services following the Oklahoma City bombing, receiving outreach contacts, debriefing sessions, educational seminars, and trial-related support services in Oklahoma. The ratio of people served to people who died is about 1,000 served per death.
- Using that ratio, we could estimate 3 million mental health contacts of an outreach, educational, debriefing, or supportive nature following the September 11 attacks.
- Advice to planners, managers, administrators, incident commanders, and others in position of power and decision-making regarding psychological impacts of WMD/T events and response activities (e.g., body recovery, identification, death notification, quarantine, decontamination, etc.).
- Consultation and collaboration with public health and medical authorities on issues of differential diagnosis of physical and psychological symptoms, and appropriate treatment of both.
- Consultation and collaboration with spiritual care professionals to ensure that both psychological and spiritual needs of citizens and responders are addressed.
- Situation evaluation and advice to decision-makers, managers, supervisors, and line workers regarding psychological stress and stress management for responders in the course of incident response and recovery.
- Consultation with leaders and the media regarding public information and risk communication in order to prevent widespread anxiety and fear.

Examples of mental health consultation in the September 11 terrorism disaster:

- Consultation with NYPD regarding procedures for dealing with families coming to Family Assistance Center to obtain death certificates.
- Consultation with NYPD regarding process and procedures for family site visits to ground zero.
- Consultation and planning with City of New York officials regarding memorial activities for families.

Outreach and On-Scene Interventions: Taking services to survivors in the environments in which they live, work, and spend time.

Services might include:

- Providing an appropriate array of mental health resources and services to victims and their families, responders, disaster managers, and community leaders at all stages of the terrorist event and its aftermath.
- Providing services that are sensitive and appropriate to the needs and beliefs of various cultural groups affected by the disaster.
- Using flexibility and adaptability in planning and delivering services in order to respond to changing needs that may evolve over time following a terrorist attack.
- Providing services in community-based settings.

Examples of mental health outreach in the aftermath of the September 11 terrorism disaster:

- In Arlington County, Virginia, door-to-door canvassing was done to check on people and to make them aware of resources. They also sent out mailing to all of the county's 86,000 households ("Behavioral Health Community," 2001).
- In Connecticut, where some 30,000 residents commute into New York City for work, and where an estimated 92 residents were dead or missing, teams of mental health workers met train commuters, handing them resource pamphlets as they stepped off the commuter trains ("Behavioral Health Community," 2001).
- In New York City, Red Cross mental health workers accompanied family service workers on home visits and accompanied Mass Care workers feeding rescue and recovery workers at ground zero. They accompanied families on site visits to ground zero. Mental health workers also provided outreach and on-scene services in Red Cross shelters, service centers, the Family Assistance Center, and respite centers for rescue workers.
- Starting in December, 3 months after the terrorist attacks, the City of New York began blanketing subway cars, telephone booths, bus shelters, bars, restaurants, and drugstores with public service posters featuring various messages—such as "Even Heroes Need to Talk" and "Feeling Anxious after 9/11 is Normal"—and advertising a toll-free mental health hot line available for any city resident. With the message "New York Needs Us Strong," officials spread the word about available, free counseling. About 20 radio stations also aired spots describing how listeners were coping (Salmon & Sun, 2001).

Debriefing and Defusing: Structured, time-limited, therapeutic group interactions to help survivors and workers cope with crisis-related stress.

- Providing a comprehensive array of critical incident stress management (CISM) interventions to assist citizens and responders to cope with stress and the psychological impact of the terrorist event, aimed at providing support and linking those in need with available resources.
- After the September 11 attacks, CISM teams from numerous locations on the East Coast provided services to responders. Likewise, Red Cross Disaster Mental Health Services, mental health staff from the City and State of New York, Disaster Psychiatry Outreach, the Green Cross, and private mental health groups provided CISM services to workers and citizens.

Education: Information and/or training for survivors, responders, disaster workers, service providers, and community leaders on common reactions to terrorism, terrorism stress management strategies, disaster mental health issues and interventions, and resources.

- Ensuring that psychological aspects of terrorism and stress management strategies are included in terrorism courses for all responders. A review was recently conducted of a Compendium of Weapons of Mass Destruction courses on WMD/T sponsored by a wide variety of federal departments, posted on the FEMA Website. Sponsoring agencies included DOD, DOE, DOJ, FBI, DHHS, FEMA, EMI, NFA, EPA, and DOT. Of the course agendas and course objectives reviewed for 90 courses, only 4 courses, or 4.4%, included psychological, critical incident stress, or stress management topics (FEMA, 2000).
- Providing training to responders and to community agencies, institutions, and caregivers on the psychological aspects of the terrorist events and mental health resources.
- Developing public information and education strategies and materials (using the print and electronic media, public speaking, etc.) on psychological aspects of recovery, coping with stress, and mental health resources.
- Providing education and training to all levels of responders on effective stress management strategies and mental health resources.
- Following the September 11 attacks, a plethora of mental health brochures and articles on coping tips and resources were distributed to workers and survivors across the country. Likewise, the Internet

provided enormous amounts of mental health educational material. Mental health experts also provided information on TV, radio, and at community meetings.

- Project Liberty, the FEMA Crisis Counseling Program for the Greater New York area, sponsored the "Feel Free to Feel Better" campaign in response to the September 11 attacks. One of their educational resources is *Helping America Cope* (Project Liberty, 2001), a guide book to help parents and children cope with the aftermath of the attacks. It includes sections on talking about feelings with children, normal stress reactions, things that can help children cope, and coping with special situations such as fears and worries, intrusive thoughts, dreams, anger, loss, sadness. It provides numerous interactive exercises for parents and children to do together, and includes a wealth of resources.

Crisis Counseling and Psychotherapy: Therapeutic intervention with survivors for the purpose of stress management, crisis intervention, problem-solving, stabilization, and treatment.

- Providing crisis intervention, individual, family, and group counseling and psychotherapy services to the community to assess and treat the immediate and long-term psychological effects of the event.
- Providing specially tailored stress management and treatment interventions for first responders, disaster workers, and mental health counselors involved in recovery services.
- Because our limited experience indicates that psychological needs continue *long term* following terrorist events, sufficient funding from a variety of resources must ensure that long-term care is available to survivors.

NATIONAL RECOMMENDATIONS FOR EARLY PSYCHOLOGICAL INTERVENTION FOR VICTIMS AND SURVIVORS OF MASS VIOLENCE

The long-term effects of terrorist events such as Oklahoma City and the attacks of September 11 will be learned over time through empirical research and clinical experience. In the interim, mental health practitioners can be well guided in their work by the National Institute of Mental Health (2002) report, *Mental Health and Mass Violence: Evidence-Based*

Early Psychological Intervention for Victims/Survivors of Mass Violence. In the workshop held to reach consensus on best practices following mass violence, the working group that produced the report recommended numerous approaches to early mental health interventions.

First, the report lists the key components of early intervention, including preparation, planning, education, training, service provision, and evaluation of services. Based upon knowledge from the research on disaster recovery, the group recommended that a sensible working principle in the immediate postdisaster period is to expect normal recovery. Presuming a large number of clinically significant disorders immediately after the impact is inappropriate, except for people with already existing conditions. Nonetheless, there is a strong rationale for providing early psychological interventions to those in need (Mitchell & Everly, 2003).

The report emphasizes that mental health professionals have an important role in helping to coordinate service provision so that mental health is an integrated element of comprehensive disaster management plans. This approach is emphasized in the consultation component of the CODE-C model described above.

The document stresses the importance of early mental health needs assessment and intervention being conducted within a hierarchy of needs, basic needs being met first (e.g., survival; safety; security; food; shelter; physical and mental health; triage for mental health emergencies; orientation of survivors to immediate local services; communication with family, friends, and community; and other forms of psychological first aid). In addition, emphasis is placed on the importance of early intervention, taking into account the special needs of individuals and of high-risk groups. The interventions will be most successful when tailored to cultural needs and characteristics of the community.

"Adverse outcomes" to be targeted for early intervention include acute stress disorder, posttraumatic stress disorder, depression, complicated bereavement, substance abuse, poor physical health, fear, anxiety, physiological arousal, somatization, anger control, functional disability, and arrest or regression of childhood developmental progression.

The report suggests that early interventions should be timed to the phase of the event and that a multicomponent, well-integrated model of services be used. Although precise time tables for intervention are not known, the report provides general suggestions. Most survivors of trauma who do not manifest symptoms after about 2 months generally will not require follow-up but should receive services if they request them. The report emphasizes that follow-up services should be offered to individuals and groups at high risk of developing adjustment difficulties following exposure to mass violence.

In addition, it recommends that participation of victims or survivors of mass violence in early interventions, whether individual or group, should be voluntary. It is recommended that services be offered to those:

- Who have clinically significant symptoms
- Who are bereaved
- Who have a preexisting psychiatric disorder
- Who have required medical or surgical intervention
- Whose exposure was especially intense or of long duration

Key aspects of early intervention include the following:

- Psychological first aid
- Needs assessment
- Monitoring the recovery environment
- Outreach and information dissemination
- Technical assistance, consultation, and training
- Fostering resilience, coping, and recovery (i.e., offer family, group, and support group intervention, facilitate networking, etc.)
- Triage (assess and provide emergency psychological treatment)
- Treatment of clinical conditions

The report noted that the use of the term "debriefing" for a variety of mental health interventions is misleading, and recommended that this stand-alone term not be used to describe early mental health interventions. Rather, debriefing should be used only to describe operational debriefing (factual review of an event), and should not be used to describe psychological debriefing or Critical Incident Stress Debriefing (CISD).

Providers of early intervention services should be sanctioned by, and operate within, a structured, sanctioned system of disaster response. They should have proper training and credentials for their scope of practice, and specialized training that confers competence in specific interventions and strategies for responding to mass violence and disasters. Early intervention providers include mental health professionals, paraprofessionals, community volunteers, medical professionals, disaster responders, clergy, school personnel, and staff of paraprofessional helping organizations such as Alcoholics Anonymous.

The report concludes that the scientific community has an obligation to continue to study the effectiveness of early interventions through systematic data collection, evaluation, and research carried out before, during, and after mass violence and disasters.

SUMMARY

In summary, even conservative estimates indicate a staggering need for public outreach, education, and acute mental health care following a CBRNE event (Hall et al., 2002). The behavioral health and psychological consequences of a terrorist event may well be the most widespread, long-lasting, and expensive consequences (Warwick, 2001). Susser, Herman, and Aaron (2002) emphasize that the psychological damage caused by the attacks of September 11 mirrored the physical destruction, and illustrated that protecting the public mental health must be a component of the national defense. Comprehensive planning for terrorist events must include the psychological impacts of these events on the survivors and on the responders; otherwise, planning efforts are incomplete and do not recognize the most fundamental of damages inflicted by terrorism.

REFERENCES

American Psychological Association. (1997). *Final report: Task force on the mental health response to the Oklahoma City bombing.*

American Red Cross. (2001). *The ripple effect from ground zero: Coping with mental health needs in time of tragedy and terror.* New York: Author.

American Red Cross. (2003). September 11 recovery program. In Corpweb: Virtual disaster operations center. Retrieved May 18, 2003, from http://corpweb.redcross.org/ds/terrorism/111401.html

Baker, A. (2002, August 7). City's fire department facing an exodus of its supervisors. *New York Times.* Retrieved September 10, 2002, from: http://query.nytimes.cm/search/restricted/article?res=F50F1EFE3A5F0C7A8EDDAC0894DA404482

Behavioral health community prepares for long-term effects of terrorist attacks. (2001, October). *Mental Health Weekly, 11(37),* 1–4. Retrieved October 17, 2001, from http://www.psychiatry.medscape.com/Manisses/MHW/2001/2001/10.01/mhw1137.01/mhw1137.01.html

Bremner, J. D., Southwick, S., Brett, E., Fontana, A., Rosenheck, R., & Charney, D. S. (1992). Dissociation and posttraumatic stress disorder in Vietnam combat veterans. *American Journal of Psychiatry, 149,* 328–332.

DeWolfe, D. (2000). *Training manual for mental health and human service workers in major disasters* (2nd ed.). (DHHS Publication No. ADM 90-538). Available at http://www.mentalhealth.org/publications/allpubs/ADM90-538/index.htm

DiGiovanni, C. (1999). Domestic terrorism with chemical or biological agents: Psychiatric aspects. *American Journal of Psychiatry, 156,* 1500–1505.

Everly, G. S., Jr., Mitchell, D. J., Myers, D., & Mitchell, J. T. (2002). *National Guard Critical Incident Stress Management (CISM): Terrorism and disaster response. Trainer's guide.* Ellicott City, MD: International Critical Incident Stress Foundation.

Federal Emergency Management Agency. (2000, January). *Compendium of weapons of mass destruction courses sponsored by the federal government.* Retrieved August 3, 2001, from http://www.usfa.fema.gov/pdf/cwmdc.pdf.htm

Federal Emergency Management Agency. (2002, January). *Federal/state disaster assistance for New York World Trade Center attack tops $894.1 million.* Retrieved February 1, 2002, from http://www.fema.gov/diz01/d1391n56.htm

Flynn, B. W. (1996, April). *Psychological aspects of terrorism.* Paper presented at the 1st Harvard Symposium on the Medical Consequences of Terrorism, Boston. Retrieved August 2, 2001, from http://www.mentalhealth.org/newsroom/speeches/terrispeech.htm

Flynn, B. W. (1998, April 6–7). *Terrorist events using weapons of mass destruction: Confronting the mental health consequences.* Paper presented at the 3rd Harvard Symposium on Complex Humanitarian Disasters, Disaster Medical Response: Current Challenges and Strategies, Boston.

Galea, S., Ahern, J., Resnick, H., Kilpatrick, D., Bucuvalas, M., Gold, J., et al. (2002). Psychological sequelae of the September 11 terrorist attacks in New York City. *New England Journal of Medicine, 346,* 982–987.

Goode, E. (2001, October 23). Anthrax offers lessons in how to handle bad news. *New York Times.* Retrieved October 28, 2001, from http://www.nytimes.com/2001/10/23/health/psychology.htm

Hall, M. J., & Norwood, A. E. (2002). Preparing for bioterrorism at the state level: Report of an informal survey. *American Journal of Orthopsychiatry, 72,* 486–490.

Hall, M. J., Norwood, A. E., Ursano, R. J., Fullerton, C. S., & Levinson, C. J. (2002). Psychological and behavioral impacts of bioterrorism. *National Center for Post-Traumatic Stress Disorder (PTSD) Research Quarterly, 13(4),* 1–8.

Hartsough, D. M., & Myers, D. (1985). *Disaster work and mental health: Prevention and control of stress among workers.* (DHHS Publication No. ADM 87-1422). Washington, DC: U.S. Government Printing Office.

Holloway, H. C., Norwood, A. E., Fullerton, C. S., Engel, C. C., & Ursano, R. J. (1997). The threat of biological weapons: Prophylaxis and mitigation of psychological and social consequences. *Journal of the American Medical Association, 278,* 425–427.

Institute of Medicine and National Research Council. (1999). *Chemical and biological terrorism: Research and development to improve civilian medical response.* Washington, DC: National Academy Press. Retrieved January 26, 2003, from http://www.nap.edu/html/terrorism/notice.html

Jerome, R., Fowler, J., Cotliar, S., Herbst, D., & Haederle, M. (2003, December). New victims of 9/11: FDNY marriages. *People,* 81–82.

Karsenty, E., Shemer, J., Alshech, I., Cojocaru, B., Moscovitz, M., Shapiro, Y., et al. (1991). Medical aspects of the Iraqi missile attacks on Israel. *Israel Journal of Medical Sciences, 27,* 603–607.

Litz, B., Gray, M., Bryant, R., & Adler, A. (2002). Early interventions for trauma: Current status and future directions. *Clinical Psychology: Science and Practice, 9,* 112–134.

Marmar, C., Weiss, D., Shchlenger, W., & Fairbank, J. (1994). Peritraumatic dissociation and posttraumatic stress in male Vietnam theater veterans. *American Journal of Psychiatry, 151,* 902–907.

Mitchell, J. T., & Everly, G. S., Jr. (2003). *Critical Incident Stress Management (CISM): Basic group crisis intervention* (3rd ed., rev.). Ellicott City, MD: International Critical Incident Stress Foundation.

More drinking and smoking in 9/11 study. (2002, May 29). *New York Times.* Retrieved August 12, 2002, from http://query.nytimes.cm/search/restricted/article?res=F50F1EFE3A5F0C7A8EDDAC0894DA404482

Myers, D. (2001). Weapons of mass destruction and terrorism: Mental health consequences and implications for planning and training. In *The ripple effect from ground zero: Coping with mental health needs in time of tragedy and terror.* New York: American Red Cross.

Myers, D. (2003a, May). *Mental health consequences of terrorism.* Unpublished training manual. City and County of San Francisco: Division of Mental Health and Substance Abuse.

Myers, D. (2003b, March). *Psychological concepts of emergency response to disaster.* Un-published training manual. Placer County, CA: Department of Health and Human Services.

National Center on Addiction and Substance Abuse, Columbia University. (2002). Survey of admissions to substance abuse treatment centers.

National Institute of Mental Health. (2002). *Mental health and mass violence: Evidence-based early psychological intervention for victims/survivors of mass violence: A workshop to reach consensus on best practices.* (NIH Publication No. 02-5138). Washington, DC: U.S. Government Printing Office.

Norris, F. J., Friedman, M. J., Watson, P. J., Byrne, C. M., Diaz, E., & Kaniasty, K. (2002). 60,000 disaster victims speak: Part I. An empirical review of the empirical literature, 1981–2001. *Psychiatry, 65,* 207–239.

North, C. S., Nixon, S. J., Shariat, S., Mallonee, S., McMillen, J. C., Spitznagel, E. L., et al. (1999). Psychiatric disorders among survivors of the Oklahoma City bombing. *Journal of the American Medical Association, 282,* 755–762.

Obhu, S., Yamashina, A., Takasu, N., Yamaguchi, T., Murai, T., Nakano, K., Matsui, Y., Mikami, R., Sakurai, K., & Hinohara, S. (1997). Sarin poisoning on the Tokyo subway. *Southern Medical Journal, 90,* 587–593.

Oklahoma City Fire Department. (1996). Alfred P. Murrah Federal Building Bombing, April 19, 1995: Final Report. Oklahoma City, Oklahoma: Fire Protection Publications and the Oklahoma City Fire Department.

Oklahoma Department of Mental Health and Substance Abuse Services. (1998). *Project Heartland: Final report.* Oklahoma City, OK: Author.

Pfefferbaum, B., Seale, T., McDonald, N., Brandt, E., Rainwater, S., Maynard, B., et al. (2000). Posttraumatic stress two years after the Oklahoma City bombing in youths geographically distant from the explosion. *Psychiatry, 63,* 358–370.

Project Liberty. (2001). *Helping America cope: A guide to help parents and children cope with the September 11th terrorist attacks.* Coral Gables, FL: 7-Dippity.

Report: Final WTC death toll drops by three; could stand at 2,749. (2004, January). *USA Today.com.* Retrieved June 21, 2004 from: http://www.usatoday.com/news/sept11/2004-01-23-wtc-toll_x.htm

Sack, K. (2001, October 22). With firetruck, Carolinians to return an old favor to N.Y. *San Jose Mercury News,* p. 6A.

Salmon, J. L., & Sun, L. H. (2001, December 19). Victims at risk again: Counselors scramble to avert depression, suicides after September 11. *Washington Post,* p. A01. Retrieved February 25, 2002, from http://www.washingtonpost.com/ac2/wp-dyn/A62699-2001Dec18?language=printer

Schlenger, W. E., Caddell, J. M., Ebert, L., Jordan, B. K., Bourke, K. M., Wilson, D., et al. (2002). Psychological reactions to terrorist attacks: Findings from the National Study of Americans' reactions to September 11. *Journal of the American Medical Association, 288,* 581–588.

Schuster, M. A., Stein, B. D., Jaycox, L. H., Collins, R. L., Marshall, G. N., Elliott, M. N., et al. (2001). A national survey of stress reactions after the September 11, 2001, terrorist attacks. *New England Journal of Medicine, 345,* 1507–12.

Sealey, G. (2001, November 5). Fragile psyches: Mental health counselors gear up for potential crisis in New York. *ABC News.com.* Retrieved February 25, 2002, from http://abcnews.go.com/sections/us/DailyNews/STRIKE_nypsyche011005.html

Shariat, S., Mallonee, S., Kruger, E., Farmer, K., & North, C. (1999). A prospective study of long-term health outcomes among Oklahoma City bombing survivors. *Journal of the Oklahoma State Medical Association, 92,* 178–186.

Silver, R. C., Holman, E. A., McIntosh, D. N., Poulin, M., & Gil-Rivas, V. (2002). National longitudinal study of psychological responses to September 11. *Journal of the American Medical Association, 288*, 1235–1244.

Smith, D., Christiansen, E., Vincent, R., & Hann, N. (1999). Population effects of the bombing of Oklahoma City. *Journal of the Oklahoma State Medical Association, 92*, 193–198.

State of California, Governor's Office of Emergency Services. (1999). *Weapons of mass destruction (WMD) Pilot Course: Training manual.* San Luis Obispo, CA: California Specialized Training Institute.

State of California, Governor's Office of Emergency Services. (2003). *Terrorism: Training manual.* San Luis Obispo, CA: California Specialized Training Institute.

Susser E. S., Herman, D. B., & Aaron, B. (2002, August). Combating the terror of terrorism. *Scientific American, 287*, 72–77.

Union, WTC Workers Suffering. (2001, December 21). *Newsherald.* Retrieved January 21, 2002, from http://www.newsherald.com/articles/2001/12/21/us122101g.htm

U.S. Department of Health and Human Services, Substance Abuse and Mental Health Services Administration. (2002). *Communicating in a crisis: Risk communication guidelines for public officials.* Washington, DC: Department of Health and Human Services. Order free from www.samhsa.gov

U.S. Department of Justice. (2000, October). *Responding to terrorism victims: Oklahoma City and beyond.* Washington, DC: Author. Retrieved March 7, 2001, from http://www.ojp.usdoj.gov/ovc/infores/respterrorism/welcome.html

Warwick, M. C. (2001, April). Psychological effects of weapons of mass destruction. *The Beacon: National Domestic Preparedness Office Newsletter, 3*, 1–4.

Wee, D. (2001). *Disaster mental health.* Unpublished lecture notes, Berkeley, CA.

Wee, D., & Myers, D. (2002). Stress response of mental health workers following disaster: The Oklahoma City bombing. In C. R. Figley (Ed.), *Treating compassion fatigue.* New York: Brunner/Mazel.

Weissenstein, M. (2002, February 27). FDNY personnel have stress ailments. Retrieved February 28, 2002, from http://www.firehouse.com/news/2002/2/27_Apstress.html

What are the traumatic stress effects of terrorism? (2001, September). National Center for PTSD Fact Sheet. Retrieved October 16, 2001, from http://www.ncptsd.org/facts/disasters/fs_terrorism.html

Whitney, W. (2003, November 14). Heart attacks increase after 9/11. *Psychology Today.* Retrieved December 6, 2003, from http://www.psychologytoday.com/htdocs/prod/PTOArticle/pto-20031114-000001.asp

Wright, D. (2001, October 22). Editorial cartoon. *San Jose Mercury News*, p. 7B.

Yehuda, R., McFarlane, A. C., & Shalev, A. Y. (1998). Predicting the development of post traumatic stress disorder from the acute response to a traumatic event. *Biological Psychiatry, 44*, 1305–1313.

INDEX